Ex Libris

THE PRIDE OF THE
CONFEDERATE ARTILLERY

THE PRIDE
OF THE
CONFEDERATE
ARTILLERY

THE WASHINGTON
ARTILLERY
IN THE
ARMY OF TENNESSEE

Nathaniel Cheairs Hughes, Jr.

LOUISIANA STATE UNIVERSITY PRESS
BATON ROUGE AND LONDON

Designer: Amanda McDonald Key
Typeface: Sabon
Typesetter: Impressions Book and Journal Services, Inc.
Printer and binder: Thomson-Shore, Inc.

Library of Congress Cataloging-in-Publication Data

Hughes, Nathaniel Cheairs.
    The pride of the Confederate artillery : the Washington Artillery
in the Army of Tennessee / Nathaniel Cheairs Hughes, Jr.
      p. cm.
    Includes bibliographical references (p.   ) and index.
    ISBN 0-8071-2187-8 (cloth : alk. paper)
    1. Confederate States of America. Army. Washington Artillery
Battalion (New Orleans, La.). Company, 5th—History. 2. New
Orleans (La.)—History—Civil War, 1861–1865. 3. United States—
History —Civil War, 1861–1865—Regimental histories.
4. Confederate States of America. Army of Tennessee—Artillery.
5. United States—History—Civil War, 1861–1865—Artillery
operations, Confederate.   I. Title.
E565.7.W2H84 1997
973.7′468—dc21
                                                          97-16236
                                                          CIP

The paper in this book meets the guidelines for permanence and durability of the Committee on Production Guidelines for Book Longevity of the Council on Library Resources. ⊗

For Frank and David and Sam

Contents

ILLUSTRATIONS

PREFACE

I was introduced to the Fifth Company of New Orleans, Washington Artillery, by a sixteen-year-old, an impressionable St. Louis boy. He had left home in August, 1861, trailing after an older brother he adored. They had gone south to become Confederates. Through young Phil Stephenson's eyes I first saw the battery in bivouac at Corinth, Mississippi, on the eve of Shiloh. The men of the Fifth Company had just arrived after a long, hard march and were sitting around their campfires laughing and singing, drawing attention to themselves by their gaiety. Colorful in speech and dress, they represented sophisticated New Orleans come to backwoods Mississippi.

Rich boys. Some even had bodyservants along, to cook, to pack their haversacks. Could they fight, would they fight, the older Stephenson wondered. Or were they here posturing, like pretty songbirds poised to take flight when rain storms drenched their campfires and blew down their tents, when mud encased the wheels of their cannon and angry Yankee bullets ripped through the bright red facings of their uniforms?

I wondered too. How did they fare? Who were they really?

I had never heard of them, frankly, that is, the Fifth Company, Washington Artillery of New Orleans. I knew of Slocomb's battery with the Army of Tennessee, certainly, and I was familiar with the Washington Artillery, the toast of Robert E. Lee's artillery units, the heroes of Fredericksburg, Longstreet's darlings. But there were just four companies, batteries, in the Washington Artillery, were there not?

There were five. This is the story of the Fifth, the company that never fought with Lee or Longstreet, the battery that never went to Virginia.

This was the battery that fought from Perryville to Mobile, from Atlanta to Jackson.

It would prove a different journey for me. In the past I had done biography and battle study, but never pulled together the story of a military unit. For that matter, I had paid little attention to Civil War artillery. Oh, I knew how cannon functioned, I thought. After all, I had done the work myself with 75 mm howitzers mounted in turrets and 105 mm field pieces. I had run a fire direction control center. My oldest son, Frank, had been a Desert Storm battery executive officer and shared his experiences with me.

I discovered I had much to learn. I did not know a limber from a caisson and had never heard the term *pendulum-hausse*. But that is why one does a book such as this. The search satisfies curiosity and almost invariably chips away—if not reshapes totally—preconceptions. Ignorance surfaces. One ought to finish such an adventure in historical digging with a fresh view, and usually a surprise or two. Such I found to be true in sharing the life of the Fifth Company.

Please bear in mind that this was a "silk stocking" unit, much like the cocky easterners from the Army of the Potomac brought west by Joe Hooker in the fall of 1863 to join Grant's army at Chattanooga. One had "equal men" for associates—educated, refined comrades.

Besides, the artillery was thought to be "by far the easiest branch of the service."[1] But perhaps the most dangerous. What happened when enemy riflemen closed to within two hundred yards of a piece standing in the open, its gunners frantically loading a round of canister? What happened when the battery's supporting infantry melted away to the rear, leaving them isolated and exposed? What happened when enemy sharpshooters disabled so many horses that the gun could be withdrawn only by hand?

As the war wore on, the employment of artillery by the Army of Tennessee tended to become more and more concentrated. Rather than independent batteries working with individual infantry brigades, as in 1862, they were utilized and controlled more and more in battalion organization, at least until John B. Hood came on the scene and artillery doctrine and employment degenerated. Concentration of firepower can

---

1. S. B. Newman to M. Greenwood, April 17, 1864, Moses Greenwood Papers, HNOC.

be seen as early as Murfreesboro. Certainly this was true by the time Joseph E. Johnston overhauled artillery organization and usage in early 1864. Cuthbert H. Slocomb himself, although reputedly refusing promotion time and time again, would fight his last battle as an artillery battalion commander.

For most of the war the Fifth Company would be over-matched and outgunned by the Federal batteries it opposed ("dueled" in Civil War artillery parlance). Not when there was close-in fighting, however. Few artillery outfits could equal the company at such. The shock power of their canister at Murfreesboro, for instance, "could break enemy units and disperse attacks even when it did not hit enemy soldiers."[2] On the other hand, when range was extended, as was often the case in the Atlanta campaign, the heavy-rifled guns of the enemy kept the Washington Artillery pinned down and knocked their beloved Napoleons to pieces.[3]

There were a number of Washington Artillery units in the Confederate army, at least three of which fought with the Army of Tennessee. This, of course, confused contemporaries of the Fifth Company (Confederate and Union), not to speak of latter-day historians. I, for instance, never thought to distinguish between Capt. Isadore P. Girardey's Washington Artillery of Augusta, Georgia, and the Washington Artillery of New Orleans. Perhaps that is the reason the Fifth Company is usually referred to in the annals of the Army of Tennessee as "Slocomb's battery."

In preparing this study I came to appreciate another aspect of unit history. It can reorder the familiar in a refreshing way. The war in the West, when viewed from the perspective of the Fifth Company, appears different. Terrain does too, for that matter.

Finally, I felt I came to know the men of the Fifth Company. I respect them. Of course no one can really know individuals separated by a gulf of 150 years, but nevertheless I grew fond of them collectively and individually. Slocomb is the stuff of which legend is made. The hero basher and gossip within me tried hard to find deficiencies, contradictions, and shortcomings of character. I found none. Adolphe Chalaron, Billy Vaught, and W. Irving Hodgson, on the other hand, are infinitely human and understandable. So are the other members of the company.

I envy Phil Stephenson. He heard them laugh and sing.

2. David Coe, ed., *Mine Eyes Have Seen the Glory: Combat Diaries of Union Sergeant Hamlin Alexander Coe* (Cranbury, N.J., 1975), 152.
3. See Paddy Griffith, *Battle Tactics of the Civil War* (New Haven, 1987), 165–76.

*

Helping me put together this story were many individuals who must be recognized. Their contributions vary. Some gave advice, some gave encouragement, some gave companionship, some swabbed out the bores of cannon, some gave up a Saturday afternoon or a Sunday morning just to help, some kept searching after I gave up, some provided gold nuggets.

Jim Ogden, a historian at Chickamauga and Chattanooga National Military Park, read and criticized several sections of the manuscript, found material for me, and spent hours chauffeuring me down roads I never would have found by myself. He pulled a limber out of a shed and attached it to a Napoleon, just so I could see how it was done. He was my sounding board for all manner of theories and speculations.

Stacy D. Allen, Shiloh National Military Park historian, read and reread the Shiloh chapter with a thoroughness that went far beyond the call of duty or friendship. He generously provided me with indispensable material. David R. Deatrick, Jr., of Louisville, Kentucky, who knows and loves every square yard of the Murfreesboro battlefields, read those three chapters and offered insight and helpful suggestions.

Catherine Landry served as project manager and guided the manuscript through its several stages. Suzanne Maberry, my copy editor, worked with me closely, displaying bushel-loads of patience and encouragement. Blake Magner created the maps promptly and expertly. I wish to thank all three for their graciousness and interest.

Among the other individuals to whom I wish to express my appreciation for their many kindnesses are Bruce S. Allardice, Des Plaines, Illinois; Beverly B. Allen, Woodruff Library, Emory University; Chuck Barber, University of Georgia Manuscript Library, Athens; Arthur W. Bergeron, Jr., Petersburg, Virginia; Tito Brin, New Orleans Public Library; Tim L. Burgess, White House, Tennessee; Mark Cave, Historic New Orleans Collection; Margaret Cleveland, Alabama Department of Archives; George Connor, Baytown, Texas; George Denègre, New Orleans; Pat Eymard, Confederate Memorial Hall, New Orleans; Kevin S. Fontenot, Tulane University; Carole Hampshire, Howard-Tilton Memorial Library, Tulane University; Robert K. Krick, Fredericksburg, Virginia; Jose Lacambra, Clear Water, Florida; W. B. Meneray, Howard-Tilton Memorial Library, Tulane University; Michael P. Musick, National Archives, Washington, D.C.; John M. Poythress, Louisville; Sherrie Pugh, Jackson Barracks Military Library, New Orleans; Guy R. Swanson, Museum of the Confederacy, Richmond; William Turner, La Plata, Maryland; Michael L. Upshaw, Metairie Cemetery, New Orleans; Lt. Jacques D. Walker, Jackson Barracks Military Library, New Orleans; and Dewitt Yingling, Beebe, Arkansas.

I also must express my gratitude to the librarians and archivists at the Howard-Tilton Memorial Library, Tulane University; the Louisiana Department, New Orleans Public Library; the Louisiana Room, and the Louisiana and Lower Mississippi Valley Collections, LSU Libraries, Baton Rouge; and the staffs of the University of Tennessee at Chattanooga and the Chattanooga-Hamilton County Bicentennial Library.

Last, I must mention my wife, Bucky, without whom this, or any of my books for that matter, would have been impossible. As evidence of her sacrifice, she spent ten days in New Orleans without a fancy meal and got to spend her only day off, a promising bright Sunday, transcribing tombstones in a graveyard.

Abbreviations Used in Notes

General

BWA	Battalion Washington Artillery
CHS	Cuthbert H. Slocomb
CSR	Compiled Service Record
5WA	Fifth Company, Washington Artillery
JAC	J. Adolphe Chalaron
PDS	Philip D. Stephenson
WA	Washington Artillery
WCDV	William C. D. Vaught
WIH	W. Irving Hodgson

Repositories

AHC	Arkansas History Commission, Little Rock, Ark.
CCNMP	Chickamauga and Chattanooga National Military Park
DU	Duke University, William R. Perkins Library, Durham, N.C.
HNOC	Historic New Orleans Collection
HTT	Howard-Tilton Memorial Library, Tulane University
KMNS	Kennesaw Mountain National Park, Marietta, Ga.

LC	Library of Congress, Washington, D.C.
LSU	Louisiana State University Libraries, Baton Rouge
NA	National Archives, Washington, D.C.
NCA	North Carolina State Archives, Raleigh, N.C.
NYHS	New-York Historical Society
SHC	Southern Historical Collection, University of North Carolina, Chapel Hill, N.C.
TSLA	Tennessee State Library and Archives, Nashville, Tenn.
UGA	University of Georgia Library, Athens, Ga.
UTA	Center for American History, University of Texas at Austin
UVA	University of Virginia Library, Charlottesville, Va.

BOOKS, PERIODICALS, AND DOCUMENTS

CV	*Confederate Veteran*
CWTI	*Civil War Times Illustrated*
GHQ	*Georgia Historical Quarterly*
MOLLUS	*Military Order of the Loyal Legion of the United States*
OR	*The War of the Rebellion: A Compilation of the Official Records of the Union and Confederate Armies.* Unless otherwise indicated, all volumes cited throughout the notes are from Series 1.
SHSP	*Southern Historical Society Papers*

THE PRIDE OF THE
CONFEDERATE ARTILLERY

1

TRY US

NEW ORLEANS loved its military organizations. As in most nineteenth-century American communities, the militia helped give focus to social and political life. The best people belonged. It was the thing to do. Elitist? Of course. Among the militia companies (one did not think in terms of battalions or regiments), membership in the Washington Artillery was prized, "regarded in much the same light as admission to an equally exclusive club today."[1] Indeed, the Washington Artillery was a club. It regarded itself as a club. One was elected to membership. There were dues (and these would continue during the darkest days of the war) and assessments, a constitution and bylaws, and committees. Officers held their exalted positions at the pleasure of privates.

The militia existed to protect the community, of course, and they had done so—witness their role in repelling the British invasion of 1815—but they also existed to entertain. The reviews were splendid affairs, and young women turned out eagerly to cheer and admire their young men. The music was enthusiastic and exhilarating; one wanted to sing along.

1. Ella Lonn, *Foreigners in the Confederacy* (Chapel Hill, N.C., 1940), 92.

It was all great fun. Things were carefully kept in perspective. That was understood. Privates (or "members"—the terms were interchangeable) merited respect; they had direct access to the captain's tent, and they might resign or "call out" a bully with stripes on his sleeve. No one took drill too seriously for that matter. There would be some shouting, of course, and commands to obey, procedures to follow, but abuse and tyrants were not tolerated (the election process corrected that). So the reins of authority rested lightly in commissioned hands. The militia represented the new American democracy harnessed for action, Jacksonian style. Granted, once in a while a defective cannon might explode and carry away the life of a gunner, or a man might faint from heat exhaustion, or some poor soul might burst an eardrum because of a comrade's careless musket technique, but all in all, being a militiaman was enjoyable and safe, though somewhat expensive.

Certainly the most celebrated militia organization in New Orleans in 1861 was the Washington Artillery. Its lineage was somewhat vague, arguably descended from the militia of the French period and continued under the Spanish and Americans. One is on firmer ground to set the beginnings of this particular unit about 1838, at the time when Elisha L. Tracy went about organizing the company, with the new members, in turn, electing him captain. No one knows for sure who was the treasurer or the names of the committee heads. In 1841 the members of Tracy's battery decided to change their name from the Washington Artillery to the Native American Artillery. It seems they felt a need to distinguish themselves from other New Orleans batteries composed of young men from the French and Spanish elements of the city. In 1844, as war with Mexico neared, the company began to train feverishly, then set out proudly for Texas the following spring under Capt. Henry Forno as part of Maj. Louis Gally's Battalion of Louisiana Volunteer Artillery. They would serve three months in Texas and come back home.

In 1846 the company departed for the Rio Grande again, this time under Capt. Isaac F. Stockton. The Native Americans, however, having offered themselves to the service of the United States army, would be given the inglorious title of Company A, 1st Louisiana Volunteers, or Louisiana's Washington regiment. Fortunately, they would have an extremely able soldier as their regimental commander—Col. Persifor F. Smith. Smith was seconded by the enthusiastic and competent Lt. Col. James B. Walton. Company A and the Washington regiment would serve with Gen. Zachary Taylor only ninety days, yet manage to cross the Rio Grande before returning to Louisiana. Colonel Smith would go back to Mexico, however.

As an able brigade commander, he was destined to be admired by the professional military establishment.

While Persifor Smith was winning honors in the valley of Mexico, the Washington regiment was being disbanded and many of the companies dissolved. Not Company A, however. These volunteers did not scatter. Instead, the members took advantage of the situation, boldly stepped forward, and assumed or regained the name of the parent unit. Henceforward, these New Orleans militiamen would be known as the Washington Artillery.

Nevertheless, enthusiasm began to wane after the Mexican War. The men wearied of the drills, and things military tended to become too professional. Individuals truly interested in adventure, in fighting, could enlist in one of the clandestine filibuster bands forming almost monthly on the streets of New Orleans. So, numbers during the 1850s dwindled badly year after year. By 1857, when Walton became battery commander, the Washington Artillery had dropped to less than company strength.

James B. Walton, however, brought energy and resolve. Moreover, he gave the diminished unit a symbol around which the members could rally—the irate Tiger Head. Their new emblem, like their name, had been appropriated. Once the insignia of the defunct Crescent Hussars, Walton (formerly the Hussars' commander) felt that it would be fitting for the Washington Artillery. The members agreed. They embellished their symbol, of course, mounting or centering the head on crossed cannon. Then just beneath the jaw of the tiger they placed their magnificent slogan: "Try Us." Cocky, patriotic, and catchy, the motto, which may have come from Psalm 26:2, suited the members just fine.

By the close of the 1850s, the Washington Artillery again had become an organization that men wanted to join. Its numbers increased and its character began to change somewhat. Although still confined to the upper class, the corps made an effort, as implied in its name, Washington Artillery, to straddle the Creole/American division of New Orleans, drawing officers and members from both populations.[2] Of course, a military purist might point out that of the battalion's fourteen guns, two were useless

2. The Washington Artillery roster discloses not only a number of Creole names, but, also a significant percentage of foreign born. "It may come as a shock," observed Ella Lonn, the acknowledged authority on foreign born in the Confederate service, "to some readers accustomed to think of the Washington Artillery as composed of the elite of Louisiana to be informed that there were many foreigners in the five companies of that famous organization, amounting to 167 in a total of 1,039." Lonn, *Foreigners in the Confederacy,* 208–209. There was a quite obvious reason for this, as will be revealed, that does not refute the assumption to which Lonn referred.

and four caissons were unserviceable, and that their "ammunition included neither canister nor grape." Nevertheless, no one could deny that Walton and his men had made great strides.[3] For proof, one could point to their new arsenal on Girod Street, now under construction and designed by a brilliant young architect and member, William A. Freret, son of the mayor.[4]

When America went crazy with war fever in the winter of 1860–1861, the Washington Artillery was in place and ready, at least emotionally. They responded enthusiastically with over one hundred men participating in the expedition to seize the Federal arsenal at Baton Rouge in January, 1861. The ease of their astonishing exploit helped send New Orleans wild with excitement and southern patriotism. By May of that year, Walton had so many men on his hands that he divided them into four companies, and the membership, eager to go to Virginia and fight Yankees, voted to offer themselves for Confederate service. So, on May 13, the government in Richmond accepted them as a battalion (with Major Walton commanding) for the duration of the war. Thus, on May 27, the Battalion Washington Artillery loaded their pieces and caissons and themselves aboard trains and rolled off for Virginia.[5]

The last order recorded for the old militia organization was issued by Walton just prior to being mustered into Confederate service. He designated 1st Lt. Washington Irving Hodgson of the Fourth Company to remain behind in New Orleans, specifically charging him to recruit men whom he "will forward from time to time, to the seat of the war . . . and hold himself subject to any further orders from these headquarters." Actually Walton left behind not only Lieutenant Hodgson but eighty-one men, a reserve unit, almost as large as a battery, including four noncom-

3. New Orleans *Commercial Bulletin,* September 27, 1854; Robert C. Reinders, "Militia in New Orleans, 1853–1861," *Louisiana History,* III (1962), 38–39.

4. New Orleans *Daily Delta,* March 15, 1858. See also Powell A. Casey, "The Early History of the Washington Artillery of New Orleans" *Louisiana Historical Quarterly,* XXIII (1940), 471–84; Reinders, "Militia in New Orleans"; David G. McIntosh, "The Confederate Artillery—Its Organization and Development," in *Photographic History of the Civil War,* ed. Francis T. Miller (New York, 1911–12), V, 58; Powell A. Casey, *An Outline of the Civil War Campaigns and Engagements of the Washington Artillery of New Orleans* (Baton Rouge, 1986), i; Allison Owen, "Record of an Old Artillery Organization," *Field Artillery Journal,* IV (1914), 5–8; New Orleans *Daily Picayune,* April 26, 1887. For an appreciation of Persifor Smith, see Justin H. Smith's classic history of the Mexican War, *The War with Mexico* (2 vols.; New York, 1919), or Nathaniel C. Hughes, Jr., and Roy P. Stonesifer, Jr., *The Life and Wars of Gideon J. Pillow* (Chapel Hill, 1993), 83–89, 355.

5. William M. Owen, *In Camp and Battle with the Washington Artillery* (Boston, 1885), 399; 5WA Muster Roll, WA Papers, HTT; Casey, "Early History of the Washington Artillery," 483–84.

missioned officers to assist Hodgson: "ex-sergeants" Jerry G. Pierson and Edson L. Hews and "ex-corporals" Abram I. Leverich and E. H. Wingate.[6]

Hodgson wasted no time in organizing his reserve corps into a Fifth Company. An initial meeting of forty-two members was held on June 6, 1861, at which Hodgson was elected lieutenant and treasurer. Hodgson then proceeded to establish, as was the custom, a group of committees (finance, investigating, etc.) to manage the affairs of the new company and to help him fulfill the responsibilities assigned by Walton.[7]

The lieutenant quickly put the Fifth Company before the public eye. A week after their informal organization, with Hodgson at their head, the men paraded through town with Company B, Confederate Guards, to attend services at Dr. Benjamin M. Palmer's First Presbyterian Church. Then, on June 27, a month after the Washington Artillery departed for Virginia, a formal organization of the Fifth Company was held. The members elected Hodgson captain; Thomas A. James, senior first lieutenant; Pierson, junior first lieutenant; Rinaldo J. Bannister, second lieutenant; and J. H. H. Hedges, secretary.[8]

Since Walton and the battalion had left New Orleans taking with them "everything in the way of Camp and garrison equipage, artillery and ordnance stores," the twenty-seven-year-old Hodgson had much work to do. How would he equip the Fifth Company? It appeared an intimidating task. The demand for weapons and money was overwhelming. In the late summer of 1861, Louisiana felt she must outfit an army, her own army. The war was becoming serious. First Manassas (July 21) had shown that. If the Fifth Company were to retain its identity, then, it seemed Hodgson must put the company on a readiness basis immediately. Otherwise he and the members would constitute merely a manpower pool for the four companies in Virginia or would be swallowed up, cannibalized perhaps, by the Crescent Regiment or the Orleans Guard Battery or some other appealing local military organization recruiting furiously to fill its ranks.[9]

W. Irving Hodgson seemed eager for the challenge. Certainly his heritage appears to have equipped him for such a leadership opportunity. His

6. WA Minute Book #3, WA Papers, HTT; Owen, *In Camp and Battle,* 399; W. I. Hodgson, "History of the 5th Company Battalion Washington Artillery from April, 1861 to June 6, 1862," Confederate Personnel Documents, HTT.

7. WA Minute Book #3, HTT; Hodgson, "History of the 5th," HTT.

8. Also elected: 1st Sgt. Hews; 2nd Sgt. William C. D. Vaught; 3rd Sgt. William B. Giffen; 2nd Cpl. B. H. Green, Jr.; 3rd Cpl. William B. Demerritt; 4th Cpl. John Wood; and Charles H. Waldon, Artificer. WA Minute Book #3, HTT.

9. Hodgson, "History of the 5th," HTT.

father had been an adventurous sea captain, his maternal grandfather had been a hero at Bladensburg during the War of 1812, and one of his mother's ancestors had won a British title for his notable defense of Gibraltar. Hodgson himself had come to New Orleans at age fourteen to work as a clerk with a hardware company. From there this affable and highly ambitious young man moved on, switching companies and jobs frequently, with each new assignment carrying more and more responsibility and requiring greater skill. In 1857 he associated himself with J. B. Walton's firm and under Walton's tutelage began to learn the auctioneer's trade. Very quickly, it seems, he won the confidence of his superior, who encouraged him to seek membership in the Washington Artillery. About town Hodgson was becoming known as charming and energetic, articulate and persuasive, and an extraordinary promoter.[10]

The Fifth Company needed Hodgson. Money had to be raised quickly, not only to outfit the battery but to complete construction of the arsenal (it had no roof). Using his committee structure adroitly, Hodgson dispatched a delegation of members and citizens to the legislature at Baton Rouge; he sent another to the New Orleans city council. Both missions succeeded in obtaining funds. In addition Hodgson organized a group to call upon "merchants and capitalists," not only in the city but throughout Louisiana. From his friend Governor Thomas O. Moore, Hodgson obtained a piece of artillery and caisson complete. From local merchant John Adams he secured another cannon and caisson. In fact, by early fall, 1861, Hodgson and his fund-raising comrades had been able "to complete the arsenal and pay for it." And, more to the point, housed within their new home were six handsome brass field pieces "with limbers, caissons and harness complete." With enormous pride Hodgson would report these accomplishments to J. B. Walton, adding the welcome news (he knew this would please his mentor) that the Washington Artillery "did not owe a dollar."

Quite an achievement by young Captain Hodgson, who had been entrusted to guard and promote his proprietor's, his commander's, interests. But this was not all. Twice Hodgson had sent Lt. Jerry G. Pierson north to Virginia with replacement details. Some thirty men had gone up to Walton's encampment in this manner to fill holes in the ranks of the four advance companies. Hodgson made sure to send off these recruits to Virginia with full equipment, "free of expense to the Battalion." Equally

10. JAC pulled together from many sources a master roster with detailed information about every individual. It is the basis of the roster included in this work as Appendix A and will be referred to hereinafter as 5WA Roster.

important to old members in distant Virginia was Hodgson's practice of dispatching twice a week cases containing mail, "clothing, edibles and family packages." No comparable unit in Joseph E. Johnston's Army of Northern Virginia could surpass the logistical support of the Battalion Washington Artillery.[11]

Meanwhile, back in New Orleans, the Fifth Company continued to grow in size. Indeed, "their aggregate strength was more than that of any two of the batteries of the Battalion in Virginia." Although Hodgson understood their mission more as a reserve component of the battalion, he did see that most of the Fifth Company took part in two weeks of field training at Camp Lewis, "near Carrollton, several miles from the city." It seems to have been a leisurely October encampment, however, and a critical report went back to the Confederate adjutant general's office about that time, stating that although the men of the battery had their field pieces for drill purposes, none of the privates had "haversacks, knapsacks, canteens, sabres, etc."[12]

Clara Solomon, a friend of Jo Pierson Hews (Ed Hews's wife), ventured out with some others to Camp Lewis on October 16. Jo Hews failed to meet her at the appointed station, however, so Solomon had to view the camp from the trolley. "Oh! how indignant, how mad, how disappointed, were we. It was a base, mean action. The Camp looked so inviting. The pretty white tents, wide spreading trees and bright sun gave a picturesque appearance. We thought of the pleasant time that we anticipated, and tears arose in our eyes." Clara Solomon rode on to Carrollton, got off the trolley, and waited in mortification for the "down train," which arrived presently and took them past the camp and the attractive young soldiers back to Tivoli Circle.[13]

Of course, unlike their comrades in Virginia, the Fifth Company did not belong to the Confederate army. As militia they looked to the state of Louisiana and Governor Moore. In the best tradition of their predecessors, however, they observed the proprieties of the Washington Artillery faithfully. In early December, for instance, the Fifth Company, "pre-

11. Hodgson, "History of the 5th," HTT; Owen, *In Camp and Battle,* 400; Napier Bartlett, *A Soldier's Story of the War: Including the Marches and Battles of the Washington Artillery, and of Other Louisiana Troops* (New Orleans, 1874), 147n; New Orleans *Crescent,* May 26, 1861.

12. Casey, *Outline of Civil War Campaigns,* iii–iv; 5WA Order Book, WA Papers, HTT; John D. Winters, *The Civil War in Louisiana* (Baton Rouge, 1963), 22; September 23, 1861, field report, Inspection Records and Related Reports Received, Adjutant General's Office, NA, RG 109.

13. Elliott Ashkenazi, ed., *The Civil War Diary of Clara Solomon: Growing Up in New Orleans, 1861–1862* (Baton Rouge, 1995), 201–202.

ceded by a splendid band of music," paraded to the home of J. B. Walton to serenade his wife and children, as had been the annual custom. Then they marched on, to find Maj. Gen. Mansfield Lovell and the visiting governor of Missouri, Claiborne F. Jackson. They serenaded them as well.[14]

More parades followed. On January 10, 1862, the company participated in the grand review of Louisiana's First Division. It was a demoralizing affair evidently, demonstrating lack of numbers, training, and equipment among Gen. Elisha L. Tracy's First Brigade (many of the Second Brigade did not show up that day). This disaster led the New Orleans *Daily Delta* to comment acidly, "It is high time that there was less parade and more work." And work did intensify throughout the remainder of January and early February, 1862, with drills, inspections, and reviews. Attitudes changed. Stung by criticism from fellow members in Virginia that the reserve company should be at the front, prompted by Federal impetuosity at Paducah and Belmont, and alarmed at the concentration of Yankees at Cairo, Illinois, members of the Fifth Company, according to Hodgson, began to "exhibit much ardor." No longer did they feel willing to remain at home "while their comrades, friends and brothers were sharing the dangers and toil of camp life." Not all agreed, of course. Active duty far away from the city would impose a hardship. Some felt physically unfit. Many had business and family obligations that compelled them to remain behind. Thus a number of members, including officers, dropped out or asked to stay at Girod Street performing a back-up function similar to that rendered by the Fifth Company in 1861. These "reserves" would form the Sixth Company, an inert organization that would never see field service.[15]

It had become apparent that the Fifth Company, by serving as a separate entity for almost a year, "wanted to go into service as a complete battery and not as individual fillers" for the four batteries in Virginia. Thus the Washington Artillery's Fifth Company reshuffled its membership and made ready to fight. Those willing to leave the city implored Captain Hodgson to write General Tracy "asking for a new election of officers intended for active service in the field."

Tracy agreed with the company's request and on February 14, 1862, under the supervision of Maj. Ignatius Caulfield and Maj. John B. Prados

14. New Orleans *Commercial Bulletin,* December 2, 1861.

15. New Orleans *Daily Delta,* January 10, 1862; New Orleans *Daily Crescent,* January 6, 1862; New Orleans *Daily Picayune,* January 15, 1862; New Orleans *Commercial Bulletin,* January 17, 1862; Casey, *Outline of Civil War Campaigns,* iii; Hodgson, "History of the 5th," HTT.

of his staff, an election was held with 185 members voting. They retained Hodgson as captain. The senior first lieutenant, however, was a thirty-year-old veteran from the Second Company, Cuthbert Harrison Slocomb, a wealthy hardware dealer Walton had selected initially as an assistant quartermaster. When the businessman demonstrated unusual leadership qualities, however, Walton shifted him to section commander in the Second Company. Slocomb had fought in half a dozen engagements in Virginia and had been complimented personally by Gen. James Longstreet, who had observed him at two fights at Lewinsville in September, 1861. Slocomb suddenly resigned in November, however, for reasons that are not known, and returned to New Orleans, where he affiliated with the Fifth Company as a private.

The battery's junior first lieutenant was another member of the prewar company, a younger man, a Tennessean with a quick mind who had come to New Orleans, married, and become a clerk. Billy (William Crumm Darrah) Vaught was well liked and commanded respect. The senior second lieutenant was Hodgson's good friend Ed Hews, while the junior second lieutenant was relatively new to the company, having joined the previous August. A fiery, colorful Creole, Adolphe Chalaron was twenty-five years old and a clerk by trade. For the senior battery sergeant (orderly sergeant was the title in those days), the members elected A. Gordon Bakewell. He was old—thirty-nine, a highly questionable age for field service—but this native Kentuckian was beautifully educated (Elizabeth College, England)[16] and a prominent New Orleans businessman, heading an English commission house. Gordon Bakewell was regarded by all as eminently respectable—fair and decent and religious. He would serve as the battery's lay chaplain as well as orderly sergeant.[17]

Battery drills at the arsenal became a regular weekly event beginning February 18, 1862. The company, about 150 strong, would form at 1 P.M. on the levee at the foot of Girod Street and conduct gun drills. Hodgson seems to have left this function primarily in the hands of Slocomb and Vaught while he concerned himself with administrative matters. Hodgson wanted every billet filled, despising the thought of going off to war dependent on a reserve corps having to forward replacements. This is reflected by an ad he placed in the New Orleans *Daily Crescent* a week

16. Founded in 1563, this public school in the Channel Islands (Guernsey) recently had been overhauled and restored.

17. New Orleans *Daily Picayune,* February 18, 1862; Hodgson, "History of the 5th," HTT; Owen, *In Camp and Battle,* 401; Casey, *Outline of Civil War Campaigns,* v, 32.

later: "Gentlemen desirous of joining this command, to be enlisted for the term of the war, may make application in writing." And to ensure that the privates continued to be "drawn from the select young men of New Orleans and vicinity," Hodgson required references.[18]

What about men to manage the animals? That was not gentlemen's work, surely, and a sound grounding in mathematics, so useful to gunners, would be useless for drayman drudgery. As mobile, quick-hitting field artillery, each gun required a team of six strong horses, and each pair of animals required a driver, not to speak of additional men needed to drive the battery's wagons. This meant a minimum of twenty-five drivers for the battery, men capable of handling heavy-duty draft animals, not Sunday afternoon carriage prancers. So Hodgson placed another ad: "Able-bodied men, accustomed to the care of horses, are required immediately" for state service in the Fifth Company. They would be uniformed and equipped right away, according to the ad, with pay to commence when ordered to field duty. They would "rank and be treated as privates in the corps." Drill would be required "once a week, while in city. They must be sober and come well recommended, as to character, Etc."[19]

The promise to be treated as privates seems somewhat disingenuous on Hodgson's part, although the implications may have been clearly understood in 1862 New Orleans. Drivers might be privates in the Fifth Company, but they would not be considered members, and were "not expected to be gentlemen." Thus a distinct social division, even a gulf, existed in the company. Drivers and gunners would not belong to the same messes (eat and sleep and tent together). Granted, they would live and work within sight of each other, but they would remain sharply separated by function and station. There would be many exceptions, certainly, during the course of the war. In an emergency a driver might fill in and help a gun crew, and gunners would, from time to time, relieve a tired driver, or even on occasion offer to help the drivers manage and care for the horses. Nevertheless, they lived in worlds apart, perhaps more distinct than those separating officers and enlisted. The Fifth Company's drivers, as revealed by an examination of the roster, tended to be uneducated, recent immigrants (mostly Irish and German), and somewhat older. Most had been laborers before the war; some had held jobs as policemen, gardeners, and painters. It is also worth noting that a number of Jews served

18. New Orleans *Daily Crescent,* February 26, 1862; Barnes F. Lathrop, "A Confederate Artilleryman at Shiloh," *Civil War History,* VIII (1962), 373.

19. New Orleans *Daily Delta,* February 19, 1862.

in the battery, probably a dozen with 2nd Lt. James M. Seixas holding the highest rank. The composition of the corps—officers, members, and drivers—of course, reflects prewar New Orleans' society and power structure.[20]

During this frantic month of February, 1862, Col. J. B. Walton returned home. He admired Hodgson's accomplishments and encouraged him in preparing the Fifth Company for the field. Indeed, when he inspected his old reserve company, Walton complimented them and presented them with a flag, telling them "that it was one of the pattern flags made for Genl. Beauregard" in Virginia.[21] Colonel Walton, however, needed gunners and drivers for his four thinly manned Virginia companies. So, in direct competition with Hodgson, he began placing recruiting ads himself, taking care to mention the fifty-dollar Confederate enlistment bounty.[22]

Disaster struck the Confederacy in February when the western front collapsed: Forts Henry and Donelson fell; Kentucky was abandoned; Nashville was lost; Tennessee was slipping away. The season of crisis had arrived. On February 28, General P. G. T. Beauregard in Jackson, Tennessee, wired Governor Moore (Beauregard also contacted the governors of Alabama and Mississippi) that he would "accept all good equipped troops" for ninety days. "Let the people understand," Beauregard emphasized, "that here is the proper place to defend Louisiana."[23]

This urgent appeal was published in all the local newspapers and had the expected reaction. Hodgson called the Fifth Company together on March 2. The men voted unanimously "to offer their services for 90 days or the war." A crucial question, it seems, was whether they would be the first to respond to Beauregard's appeal. "*No*," responded the Orleans

---

20. Chester Hearn, in his study of the fall of New Orleans, noted that "men accustomed to working in the warehouses along the levees or crewing steamboats had nothing to do and out of desperation joined the army." Some of these men found their way into the Washington Artillery. Chester G. Hearn, *The Capture of New Orleans, 1862* (Baton Rouge, 1995), 137–38. See Lathrop, "A Confederate Artilleryman," 373; Owen, *In Camp and Battle*, 405.

21. Colonel Walton had received it from Beauregard as a gift. JAC to the editor, New Orleans *Daily Picayune*, n.d., WA Papers, HTT.

22. New Orleans *Daily Delta*, February 26, 1862.

23. Richmond disapproved of Beauregard's call upon the governors and mentioning ninety-day enlistments. It had no basis in law, the War Department argued; furthermore, it interfered with regular recruiting operations. Alfred Roman, *The Military Operations of General Beauregard* (2 vols.; New York, 1884), I, 243–44.

Guard Battery. "We are told," reported the New Orleans *Bee*, "that Capt. Henry Ducatel insists on being sent in preference to the Washingtonians." The *Bee* reminded the feuding Ducatel and Hodgson that the real question "is whether those brave volunteers will arrive in time. . . . They must make the greatest haste." They did. Hodgson warned his men, reinforcing his statements with newspaper ads, that they were to appear on Thursday, March 6, "fully equipped, with knapsacks packed. . . . Those failing to appear, will not be allowed to leave with the command."[24]

Having gathered at the arsenal, the Fifth Company set out for Lafayette Square to be sworn into Confederate service by a member of General Lovell's staff, Lt. F. C. Zacharie. The following morning at 11 A.M. they sat as a body in the First Presbyterian Church, where they and their families heard Dr. Benjamin Palmer, a strong antislavery spokesman but a passionate secessionist, remind them of their obligation. We must repay our debt to Tennessee, he told them. This debt was "incurred nearly a half century ago. When New Orleans was endangered in the last war by a formidable British Army, the men of Tennessee did not hesitate to come to the rescue, and the invader was driven from our soil. Now Tennesseans call upon our people." Palmer emphasized that it was a just war, "purely defensive." He assured the Fifth Company that New Orleans and Louisiana as a whole stood behind them, and he bade them, "Go forth in the trust of God."[25]

The company reassembled at Jackson Depot the next day. One hundred and fifty-six men, "the picked young men of our city, members of our oldest families," observed the *Daily Picayune*, boarded the afternoon train along with the left wing (four companies) of the Crescent Regiment. "The departure of these splendid corps drew an immense crowd of citizens to the depot. Nearly every family in the city was represented in this assemblage." With the battery went "complete camp and garrison equipment," their six shining cannon and full ammunition chests.[26]

Mansfield Lovell watched them depart with great pride. He wrote

24. New Orleans *Daily Picayune*, March 3, 1862; Hodgson, "History of the 5th," HTT; New Orleans *Bee*, March 4, 1862; Roman, *Beauregard*, I, 240–41; Owen, *In Camp and Battle*, 402.

25. New Orleans *Daily Picayune*, March 7, 1862; Hodgson, "History of the 5th," HTT; New Orleans *Daily Delta*, March 8, 1862.

26. New Orleans *Daily Picayune*, March 9, 1862; 5WA Order Book, WA Papers, HTT; WIH to P. G. T. Beauregard, June 2, 1862, WIH CSR, Record Group 109, NA; Lathrop, "A Confederate Artilleryman," 374; Battalion Washington Artillery, *Washington Artillery Souvenir* (New Orleans, 1894), 32; Casey, *Outline of Civil War Campaigns*, iii.

Beauregard that he had taken care to provide them with good powder, supervising some of the testing himself, and had "it made up into ammunition for field guns." He and Governor Moore had answered Beauregard's urgent appeal by dispatching within a week ten infantry regiments and four batteries, "all nominally for ninety days; but there is every reason to believe that once in the field they will remain." By forwarding these troops Lovell had weakened the defense force of New Orleans seriously. That was obvious especially to Lovell, who informed Beauregard that "persons are found here who assert that I am sending away all troops so that the city may fall an easy prey to the enemy."[27]

Among those waving good-bye were a number of older members of the company and some others who, for one reason or another, could not leave New Orleans at this time. They would form a new reserve corps under command of Sgt. William H. Henning. Indeed, already there were almost enough men to form another company.[28] Another who watched, but who did not wave, was Abby Slocomb. She held two-month-old Cora, her only child. A year earlier she had sent her husband Cuthbert off to war in Virginia; now the whole scene was being replayed before her eyes—the same station, the same jaunty music. This young wife with her deep Connecticut attachments watched and wondered and shuddered.[29]

27. *OR,* Vol. LII, Pt. 1, p. 292; Vol. VI, pp. 647–48, 847.

28. From these men Company G, or the Sixth Company, Battalion Washington Artillery, would be organized. Harmon Doane would become its battery commander and lead his men to Camp Moore when New Orleans was evacuated the following month. At Camp Moore, however, the Sixth Company seems to have been disbanded, its members drifting back into the city or heading off to enlist in other units. New Orleans *Daily Crescent,* March 12, 1862; 5WA Order Book, WA Papers, HTT; Powell A. Casey, "Washington Artillery Streamer Study," Jackson Barracks Military History Library, New Orleans; Casey, *Outline of Civil War Campaign,* 92–93.

29. Abby Hannah Day Slocomb, always ready to speak her mind (Chalaron would be astonished by a whiplash letter he would receive from Abby Slocomb after the war when he had rescued the Columbiad cannon the Fifth Company had named "Lady Slocomb" from its muddy grave at Spanish Fort), refugeed in South Carolina and returned to New Orleans after the war, only to abandon the city for good immediately after her husband's death. She sold their magnificent home (four city lots at Esplanade and St. Claude) and settled in Connecticut. Mrs. Slocomb died at age seventy-nine in Zurich, Switzerland, and was buried there. New Orleans *Times Picayune,* December 13, 1917; Stuart O. Landry, *History of the Boston Club* (New Orleans, 1938), 327.

FOR GOD'S SAKE, BOYS, HURRY UP

THE GLORIOUS send-off faded as the fifteen-car train roared into the night through southern Mississippi. It had been a good beginning for the Fifth Company. A quibbler or a fatalist might have pointed out there had been a deserter, a man who had not shown up at the depot, a man who would never show up. But, one might answer, he was a driver, this John Haynes. They did not need him anyway. He was no bad omen; he was simply good riddance.[1]

Nevertheless, March 9, 1862, opened inauspiciously as the engineer arrived too late in Canton (some twenty miles above Jackson) to make connection with the Mississippi Central. The men got off the cars tired and hungry. They had missed supper the night before, the food inexplicably being sent on ahead. So, there they were, in Canton, well into the morning, eating supper for breakfast and entertaining themselves by watching a boxcar catch fire and burn. Sgt. Hildreth Green took the opportunity to write his father and report that they had put out the fire

---

1. See 5WA Roster (Appendix A).

quickly enough, then sat back patiently and waited alongside the tracks, together with many other troops, for transportation to Jackson, Tennessee.[2]

It proved only a short delay, and the Fifth Company once again boarded and headed north toward Jackson, being "treated with great kindness" and cheered all along the route. The next day they stopped at Grand Junction, a little town just over the Tennessee border, about fifty miles below Jackson, yet an important town where the Memphis and Charleston Railroad met the Mississippi Central. There to his surprise Captain Hodgson discovered the Crescent Regiment (24th Louisiana) preparing to encamp. Hodgson believed a mistake must have been made. He ordered the engineer to stop. The Fifth Company would off-load here in Grand Junction with their guns and equipment. Hodgson would straighten matters out himself—he would go to Jackson and see General Beauregard. Surely the general intended for the Washington Artillery to remain with the Crescents, not continue on to Jackson. The idea, the hope, from the beginning had been to keep the Louisianians together.

So, while their commander sped on to Jackson, the Fifth Company prepared to spend their second night away from New Orleans sprawled about on pews inside two churches protected from the cold March air and from ice forming outside, which Hildreth Green reported to be an inch thick. The following day, however, turned out wonderfully warm and the "scenery beautiful." They found Grand Junction to be a town of three hundred inhabitants, with "a couple of hotels," a bookstore, and two government warehouses. Hodgson returned presently, full of good cheer—they had permission to remain. So the company marched out "almost a quarter of a mile from the town" and quickly established Camp Walton on a hill, naming their first camp, of course, for their beloved battalion commander. They pitched tents, taking care to put down wooden floors. Soldiers with a little more experience, like Hildreth Green, dug out "a cellar under our tent, about the size of our champagne basket." Rabbits abounded, "so plentiful they run through camp." Life was good. For supper on Wednesday, March 12, they enjoyed "soup, pork, beans, rice and molasses, in as great quantities as we could eat besides one big

2. Canton was an important junction where the New Orleans, Jackson and Great Northern Railroad met the Mississippi Central. B. H. Green, Jr., to B. H. Green, Sr., March 9, 1862, B. Hildreth Green Letters, HTT; WCDV to Albert Vaught, March 9, 1862, William C. D. Vaught Letters, HNOC.

pilot biscuit a piece. . . . We joke [with] each other and laugh to our heart's content."[3]

The Fifth Company would remain in Grand Junction two weeks. It rapidly became apparent, however, that there must be greater system. Hodgson therefore set about issuing orders and procedures for daily routine: police tents, streets, and parade ground; surgeon's call; morning reports.

It is enjoined upon the chiefs of sections and chiefs of messes that the utmost attention shall be paid to the cleanliness of their men and messmates as to persons, clothing, arms, accoutrements, and equipment and also to their quarters and tents.

During the confusion caused by the removal [from New Orleans], many articles belonging to members of the Corps have been misplaced. Members having in their possession property belonging to others, are requested to hand them to the Orderly Sgt. [so] that the owners may obtain them.[4]

Women from nearby La Grange came to call within a few days. "They cannot compare to our New Orleans girls," observed Green, "as to looks." Company bugler John Fletcher brought out his violin nevertheless and there was dancing, then singing. It appears, however, the company's first real party away from home was a failure. Perhaps it was the La Grange girls, perhaps Fletcher's uninspired playing, or the storm that came up suddenly that night and drenched everything, hurling down "hail stones as large as your thumb." Fortunately for morale's sake, music, so integral to the life and name of the Fifth Company, would improve drastically three days later. On that day (March 21) Andrew Gardner Swain walked into camp and took over as bugler. A free spirit from Ohio, Andy Swain was thirty-four-years old and a veteran river pilot who had graced the old, prewar company with his presence and his enthusiastic renditions whenever he was in town. He would serve the company throughout the war. Fletcher, on the other hand, who was "unenlisted," would be gone by June.[5]

Not that the battery needed more free spirits, at least to Hodgson's mind. He wanted his men to settle down. For instance, for security's sake

---

3. B. H. Green, Jr., to B. H. Green, Sr., March 9, 12, 1862, Green Letters, HTT; WCDV to Albert Vaught, March 11, 1862, Vaught Letters, HNOC; Hodgson, "History of the 5th," HTT.

4. 5WA Order Book, March 11, 1862, WA Papers, HTT.

5. B. H. Green, Jr., to B. H. Green, Sr., March 19, 1862, Green Letters, HTT. Carl Valconi is listed as bugler at the time of departure but does not appear on any muster roll. Chalaron ignores him. John Fletcher was not enlisted but evidently is the individual Green refers to.

the countersign "Beauregard" had to be used. The post commander at Grand Junction, Brig. Gen. John K. Jackson, demanded it. After two days, to foil any enemy or Unionists lurking about, the password was changed to "Davis." Some members, it seems, had already begun to tire of Grand Junction: "This village is the meanest place it has ever been my lot to be stuck." The members, Hodgson knew, must be reminded sharply how serious matters were. There was a war going on.[6]

The company order book quickly began filling with Hodgson's directives designed to curb the men's civilian impulses. The "desire *'to go to town'* is so manifest" that it was becoming disruptive, and visits had to be apportioned. There also could be no more firing of muskets and pistols around camp without permission. On March 20, the captain, evincing "some surprise," resorted to more pointed language regarding the lack of military courtesy: "This corps composed of gentlemen, as it is, having accepted service in the C.S. provisional army voluntarily for ninety days, it was to be hoped . . . [a member would] cheerfully conform to orders . . . [not] disobey & insult his superior officer." Hodgson next took the drastic step of writing post commander J. K. Jackson to request that Pvt. Middleton Eastman be either court-martialed or discharged "for disobedience, dissipation and insubordination." Hodgson cautioned the general that Eastman must be dealt with carefully "on account of his being [from] one of the oldest and most respectable families in our Crescent City." Eastman was discharged.[7]

It hardly helped matters that the nearest unit was another New Orleans battery, Ducatel's rival Orleans Guard. "We do not have anything to do with each other," Hildreth Green told his father, "as they are jealous of us, and think themselves far superior, in fact imagine that they are heroes, but cannot get over the idea that we left the city before them."[8]

The members soon came to disregard the peevish Guards, however, when General Jackson presented the Fifth Company with horses. On March 20, Hodgson receipted for eighty-one battery horses of assorted colors, ten wagon mules, and six officer's horses. This meant the company now could drill realistically as mobile field artillery. Lieutenant Slocomb

---

6. Jackson was a Georgia lawyer who had worked with Braxton Bragg at Pensacola and had been sent to Grand Junction to set up camps of instruction and to forward units to Corinth in an orderly fashion.

7. Special Orders 5–11, WIH to J. K. Jackson, March 20, 1862, 5WA Order Book, WA Papers, HTT; WCDV to Albert Vaught, March 22, 1862, Vaught Letters, HNOC.

8. B. H. Green, Jr., to B. H. Green, Sr., March 19, 1862, Green Letters, HTT.

was in charge of drill, and he worked both men and animals hard. The gunner of the piece and his seven privates would practice over and over the procedures they had to use. When the order "load" was given, for instance, Number One (each individual in the gun crew was given a number in accordance with his functions) would sponge the tube to extinguish any embers from prior discharge (powder was in a cloth bag that sparks or embers could ignite). Number Five would then hand a round (a "fixed round" or projectile with powder bag attached) to Number Two, who would insert it in the muzzle of the cannon. Number One would then ram home the round. All the while, Number Three, his hand protected by a leather pad called a thumb-stall, would hold his thumb over the vent to prevent air from entering through it and causing a premature discharge. Once the gun was loaded, Number Three would move to the trail of the piece and, using a handspike, shift the gun left or right as designated by the gunner who was sighting the piece, which was now ready to fire.[9]

Over and over Slocomb would have the men repeat the drill. The number of shots they could get off in a minute was crucial, but haste could lead to carelessness. Inattention by one man could result in disaster. They must be careful, they must be precise. To relieve the monotony, Slocomb would interchange men and have them learn the functions of one or two other individuals. Endlessly, it seemed, they practiced. It became less tedious, however, when the new horses joined in the drills. Although things appeared hopeless at first, by the evening of March 21, Hildreth Green could report that "our horses are very well drilled now, as also are our drivers, and we get along finely."[10]

The horses presented a serious problem, nevertheless. According to Pvt. Thomas L. Bayne, "many of them were fine young horses entirely unaccustomed to harness." The drivers, moreover, "were Irishmen who had been employed in paving the streets & in other vocations in the city & they had no experience in the management of horses." Slocomb saved

9. 5WA Order Book, March 20, 1862, WA Papers, HTT; "History of the 5th," HTT; B. H. Green, Jr., to B. H. Green, Sr., March 19, 1862, Green Letters, HTT. For information about Civil War artillery, projectiles, and employment, see Thomas S. Dickey and Peter C. George, *Field Artillery Projectiles of the American Civil War*, ed. Floyd W. McRae (Atlanta, 1980) and their *Field Manual for the Use of Officers on Ordnance Duty* (Richmond, 1862); George Patten, *Artillery Drill* (New York, 1861); James C. Hazlett, Edwin Olmstead, and M. Hume Parks, *Field Artillery Weapons of the Civil War* (Newark, Del., 1983). For a compact, readable account, well suited for the layman, see Dean S. Thomas, *Cannons: An Introduction to Civil War Artillery* (Gettysburg, Pa., 1985).

10. B. H. Green, Jr., to B. H. Green, Sr., March 21, 1862, Green Letters, HTT.

the problem by assigning good horsemen such as Robert and Dick Pugh of Lafourche Parish to act as drivers. Slocomb, himself "a fine rider," assisted in breaking in the horses. "This work gave us fine exercise & great sport."[11]

The test would come on March 22. The day turned off cold and it began to rain, but Slocomb nevertheless had them come into battery, fire several blank rounds, then limber up and move to the rear or to another position, then go into battery again. Over and over. Everything seemed so slow at first, but they were getting faster and surer and the members began to feel proud of themselves. Most of the horses stood the firing well and were up very close to the pieces (six yards, by 1861 artillery regulations, separated the butt of the handspike from the nose of the lead horse).[12]

Billy Vaught was ecstatic. "We drilled all day in the sleet, but I enjoyed it. We drill 8 hours a day, rain or shine. I enjoy it all. Aint I a queer fish." To his mother Vaught boasted, "We fired about twenty-five rounds of blank cartridges today [March 22]. Our horses generally behaved well. Our battery is becoming splendidly drilled and is already highly praised & I think will become the *pride* of Bragg's Army."[13]

Not that Lieutenant Vaught and his section had any special affection for Gen. Braxton Bragg. Vaught explained that in the hierarchy revealed to this point, General Jackson was under Bragg, and Bragg was subordinate to Beauregard. It was well that Beauregard was in command, for Bragg "is a *bully*." Vaught could be judgmental, but essentially he was a kind, friendly, religious man who not only attended church when possible but prayed regularly.[14]

11. T. L. Bayne Autobiography, Bayne-Gale Papers, SHC.

12. A piece with its supporting animals, limber, and caisson was about fifty yards in depth. The gun with its handspike occupied about five yards; six yards from handspike to lead horse; the team for the piece and limber occupied eleven yards; eleven yards from limber to the caisson's lead horse; fourteen yards occupied by the caisson and its team. Shiloh National Military Park historian Stacy D. Allen to author, May 14, 1995.

13. B. H. Green, Jr., to B. H. Green, Sr., March 21, 1862, Green Letters, HTT; WCDV to Albert Vaught, March 22, 1862, Vaught Letters, HNOC.

14. WCDV to mother, March 22, 1862, Vaught Letters, HNOC. Despite Vaught's misgivings, the battery would benefit from a special relationship with General Bragg. Cuthbert Slocomb's brother-in-law, commission merchant David Urquhart, had joined Bragg as a volunteer aide-de-camp and won his confidence. Urquhart would ultimately be commissioned lieutenant colonel and serve as Bragg's assistant adjutant general. Following the war, Urquhart wrote a balanced account of Bragg's invasion of Kentucky and the subsequent battle of Murfreesboro. See David Urquhart, "Bragg's

The Fifth Company remained at Grand Junction five more days and practiced. Hodgson and Slocomb learned much about their men, their temperaments and capabilities. It had been an invaluable two-week school of instruction.[15] On March 27, they struck their tents and began the march east to Corinth, some forty-two miles away. The company voted to march rather than ride "the very filthy" railroad cars. This overland journey was a new experience and an excellent shakedown for the company. Pieces became "fastened" (caught in mud or cuts in the road) and required eight horses and seven men to haul them out. Most of the gunners rode part of the time. They would sit on the limbers (as many as three could squeeze together atop the chest)[16] or would talk drivers into trading off with them, but "some of the men did not ride any part of the way [to Corinth], desiring to test themselves." The company bivouacked three nights on the trek, camping beside creeks where the water was good and plentiful. One of these bivouacs they playfully named "Camp Vaught" in honor of the popular Billy Vaught.

Hodgson also had learned from Sgt. David W. Smith, sergeant of drivers (another elected position), that a number of the horses provided by General Jackson would not do. The march to Corinth had demonstrated that clearly. Some were beautiful animals but were saddle horses—fine mounts, indeed, but not animals that would work in harness. Hodgson asked the general to exchange the animals for strong draft horses as soon as possible. The ones on hand "are no use to me."[17]

The battery was fortunate to have Smith. This native of New Jersey could lead men, and he seemed to handle drivers with a special efficiency. Smith, however, longed to be in charge of a gun; if not in the role as chief of the piece, then as gunner on one of the six cannon. It was not the glamor of the firing, necessarily, that appealed to Smith. He had supreme self-confidence and he knew he would make a fine gunner. He had to wait, however. In the Fifth Company, a corporal among the gunners carried greater prestige than sergeant of drivers, and in the eyes of the members, required greater skill. Smith must prove himself.

Advance and Retreat," in *Battles and Leaders of the Civil War,* ed. Robert Underwood Johnson and Clarence C. Buel (4 vols.; New York, 1887), III, 300–309.

15. Regrettably, thirty of the company were detailed to guard a bridge between Memphis and Grand Junction, depriving these gunners of badly needed drill.

16. By regulations all crew members walked. Only drivers and officers rode.

17. Bayne Autobiography, SHC; WIH to W. G. Barth, April 1, 1862, 5WA Order Book, WA Papers, HTT; Casey, *Outline of Civil War Campaigns,* 53.

The men arrived in Corinth on March 31 dead tired. There they joined thousands of other Confederates rushing in from all over the South to become part of Sidney Johnston's great army. Hodgson learned that the Fifth Company was assigned to Brig. Gen. J. Patton Anderson's brigade (following the standard practice of distributing batteries among infantry brigades), Brig. Gen. Daniel Ruggles' division, and Maj. Gen. Braxton Bragg's II Corps. The Fifth Company was to make camp immediately, "notwithstanding our great fatigue," complained the wealthy Lafourche Parish planter Pvt. Richard L. Pugh, who also grumbled that "[we] had to work hard to arrange our tents." The company established their new home close to Ruggles' headquarters, on a hill "with a good spring not fifty yards off." Hodgson and the members decided to call this camp "Camp Moore" in honor of their benefactor, the governor of Louisiana.[18]

Hildreth Green saw General Beauregard the next day. The sight of Louisiana's hero pleased him, as it did most of the men, even though they noted that "his hair was nearly white; but as to his general appearance, looked the same as usual, being in a plain navy-blue uniform, and gray cape." The occasion was brigade review. It was a "beautiful sight . . . [with] several thousand soldiers going through various evolutions, forming and reforming, countermarching, charging, and in fact—doing everything that could be required of them."[19]

Two days later (April 3) the Fifth Company "filed out through the fortifications" of Corinth, heading for Pittsburg Landing, Tennessee, to find Maj. Gen. Ulysses S. Grant's Yankee army. Ingloriously, they were "in the train of the army," which meant they had to start late in the day and travel roads practically destroyed by preceding troops. Start and stop; wait and wait; start and stop. Taking nothing but blankets and three days' rations, Hodgson and his men made six miles before dark, estimated Richard L. Pugh, most of the afternoon being spent "lifting the cannon out of the mud and over hills." That night they "stopped (I can scarcely say slept) in a swamp" because the road was blocked ahead. The men found fence rails and "each man rolled himself in his blanket & laid upon two or three

18. R. L. Pugh to Mary Pugh, March 31, 1862, Richard L. Pugh Letters, LSU; B. H. Green, Jr., to B. H. Green, Sr., April 1, 1862, Green Letters, HTT; Hodgson, "History of the 5th," HTT; Bartlett, *A Soldier's Story,* 152.

19. Ed Hews's wife, Jo, had a special relationship with the Beauregards and during March, 1862, was staying with Mrs. Beauregard, probably in a home at or near Corinth. See Ashkenazi, *Civil War Diary of Clara Solomon,* 304; B. H. Green, Jr., to B. H. Green, Sr., April 1, 1862, Green Letters, HTT.

rails." The second day (April 4) they did better. Leaving early in the morning they progressed about ten miles, reaching Monterey about 11 A.M.[20]

Hodgson and his 156 men hauled six brass (often called bronze) guns: two six-pounder smoothbores, two six-pounder rifled guns, and two twelve-pounder howitzers. The relatively small, inadequate six-pounder howitzers would quickly be rendered obsolete by battle experience.[21] The infantry brigade they labored behind (Anderson's) and were expected to support in the coming battle was a conglomerate of three regiments and two battalions, mixing Texas, Florida, and Louisiana troops—no Louisiana brigade, certainly, and no Crescent Regiment, for that matter. Instead, the company would support and be supported by the Confederate Guards Response Battalion (169 men), commanded by Maj. Franklin H. Clack; the 17th Louisiana Infantry (326 men), drawn primarily from northern Louisiana and commanded by Lt. Col. Charles Jones (Jones would be "dropped" six weeks after Shiloh);[22] the 20th Louisiana (507 men), the strong point of the brigade and a New Orleans regiment commanded by Col. Augustus Reichard; Patton Anderson's old unit, the 1st Florida Battalion (about 250 men), commanded by Maj. Thaddeus A. McDonell; and the 9th Texas Infantry (226 men), commanded by Col. Wright A. Stanley. Anderson's total brigade, including the Fifth Company, totaled 1,636 troops.[23]

James Patton Anderson was a native Tennessean, educated in Penn-

---

20. Hodgson, "History of the 5th," HTT; R. L. Pugh to Mary Pugh, April 13, 1862, Pugh Letters, LSU; E. L. Hews to W. G. Barth, May 23, 1862, Miscellaneous Papers Filed with 5WA Muster Rolls, RG 109, NA; Bayne Autobiography, SHC; Wiley Sword, *Shiloh: Bloody April* (Dayton, Ohio, 1983), 101. Lt. Donelson Caffery Jenkins, 4th Louisiana Infantry, noted in his diary, April 4: "Roads very bad. Met 5th co. Washington Artillery. Roads blocked with trains stopped. . . . Continued our march until 12 P.M. Camped in an old field. Raining hard, no tents or protection of any kind." Liz Waters, "Turning 21 in 1862: The Account of D.C. Jenkins," *United Daughters of the Confederacy Magazine,* LIX (August, 1996), 38–39.

21. *OR,* Vol. X, Pt. 1, p. 513; E. L. Hews to W. G. Barth, May 23, 1862, Miscellaneous Papers, RG 109, NA; Casey, *Outline of Civil War Campaigns,* 54. A round of solid shot, reputed to have been fired by the Fifth Company, was recovered at Shiloh. The projectile weighed eleven pounds, fifteen ounces, and was of the "Archer pattern." Jack W. Melton, Jr., and Lawrence E. Pawl, *Introduction to Field Artillery Ordnance* (Kennesaw, Ga., 1994), 73.

22. Jones was the arch enemy of St. John R. Liddell, Confederate brigadier general from Louisiana, with whom the Fifth Company would serve off and on throughout the war. Jones and his two sons would murder Liddell on Valentine's Day, 1870.

23. *OR,* Vol X, Pt. 1, p. 495; Vol. LII, Pt. 2, p. 27.

sylvania and Kentucky, and a one-time physician who had settled in Mississippi to practice law. He had led a battalion in the Mexican War and returned home to become a Mississippi state legislator, then United States marshal in the Washington Territory. More recently he had operated a plantation in Florida, participated in the state's secession convention, and early on become commander of the 1st Florida Battalion. He had won favor with Braxton Bragg at Pensacola during the winter of 1861–1862.[24]

Friday night, April 4, Anderson and the other general officers of the II Corps met in the commander's tent near the Mickey farmhouse.[25] There they learned from Bragg the plan of attack against the enemy encamped about Shiloh meetinghouse. Bragg's II Corps would form the second line following Gen. William Joseph Hardee's corps. Ruggles' division would constitute the left of Bragg's line. Ruggles' own left should touch Owl Creek, its right "on or near Bark road." Anderson's brigade would be used as division reserve positioned several hundred yards behind Ruggles' other two brigades, commanded by Col. Randall L. Gibson and Col. Preston Pond, Jr.[26]

Confederate plans, however, were doused and shaken by a furious storm in the early morning hours of April 5, and the day would prove to be one of confusion, delay, and frustration. Finally at 3 P.M., finding the road blocked ahead, Anderson took his brigade off the road and cut through the woods north in the direction of Owl Creek, arriving about 4 P.M. at a position close (270 yards) behind the center of Ruggles' line. There he and his men bivouacked. This movement off the road by the infantry would have proved extremely difficult for the Fifth Company, however. It is doubtful that some, if any, of the guns and wagons left the road at all.[27] They would have had to chop their way through a portion of the woods, making a path in the twilight for the guns and caissons. In

24. See Ezra J. Warner, *Generals in Gray: Lives of the Confederate Commanders* (Baton Rouge, 1959), 7–8; Buckner L. Hughes and Nathaniel C. Hughes, *Quiet Places: The Burial Sites of Civil War Generals in Tennessee* (Knoxville, 1992), 5–6.

25. Located at the key crossroads of the Ridge and Monterey-Savannah roads.

26. *OR*, Vol. X, Pt. 1, pp. 494–95.

27. They were in action so quickly the next morning near the road that one is led to believe at least one section encamped on the roadside. There was another road just off Anderson's left flank that led to where the battery would have their initial action. This slight road is labeled "Beauregard Road" on National Park Service maps of battlefield. It is not known which road Hodgson utilized.

any event, once they arrived in their designated position, whether in the woods or close to the road, they tried to make themselves comfortable in their blankets and get some sleep. The night "was calm & beautiful and every one seemed impressed with the solemn thought, that this might be his last night."[28]

Hodgson and Slocomb must have wondered about how Anderson might employ them the next morning. Beauregard's plan of battle called for decentralized action with batteries dispersed in support of infantry brigades, which meant they would be working in close support of Anderson's infantry. Yet, in apparent self-contradiction, the order directed division chiefs of artillery to "mass their batteries in action and fight them twelve guns on a point," whatever that meant.[29]

Soon after daybreak the Confederate first line (Hardee's corps) struck and rolled back the surprised enemy. The Fifth Company went into battery on a "hill" (slight rise of ground) just west of the Pittsburg-Corinth road, south of Shiloh Branch and about one-half mile southwest of Shiloh meetinghouse.[30] Opening at 7:10 A.M., the sections of Slocomb, Vaught, and Chalaron fired some forty rounds of shell and spherical case into one of Sherman's camps, "silencing an enemy battery" (actually an advanced section of Capt. Allen C. Waterhouse's Illinois battery, which had been ordered to fall back and assume a position east-southeast of Shiloh meetinghouse). Ruggles, who appears to have been directing the company's fire at this time, then shifted the target left to another Federal camp. Firing from that point was another Yankee battery "from which shot and shell were thrown on all sides of us."

It was not long before Union resistance stiffened and Hardee's infantry, assaulting over a ridiculously wide front, began to stall and fragment. Disorganized troops of the first line began sifting through the woods to the rear. These were Hardee's men, repulsed by Federal musketry and artillery. From their position just west of the Corinth road, the three sections of the Fifth Company continued to fire, not in support of Anderson's

28. *OR,* Vol. X, Pt. 1, p. 495; R. L. Pugh to Mary Pugh, April 13, 1862, Pugh Letters, LSU.

29. The order was too open ended. The theory of battery/brigade operations apparently did not permit harmony of action between brigade or battery commanders, unless a division or corps commander assumed responsibility and ordered concerted action. L. D. Sandidge, "Battle of Shiloh," *SHSP,* VIII (1880), 173; Larry J. Daniel, *Cannoneers in Gray: The Field Artillery of the Army of Tennessee, 1861–1865* (University, Ala., 1984), 31.

30. Shiloh Branch sometimes was called Owl Creek in Confederate reports.

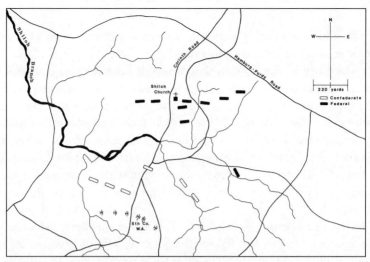

8 A.M. to 10 A.M.
Shiloh, April 6, 1862
Map by Blake A. Magner

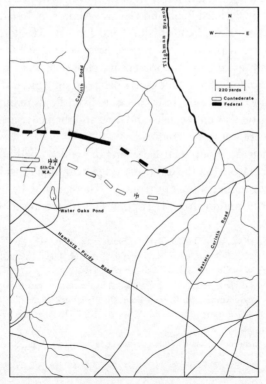

12 noon to 2 P.M.
Shiloh, April 6, 1862
Map by Blake A. Magner

brigade, which was not yet engaged, but to oppose "the enemy's batteries, then sweeping our lines at short range."[31]

It was early in the fighting that Slocomb became worried about the blue jackets worn by the Washington Artillery. They dangerously confused their fellow Confederates. So there on the field, while the battery was in action, he had his men "turn their jackets inside out so that the gray lining would be on the outside." As he reversed his jacket, Pvt. Thomas L. Bayne, who had been offered a staff position by Randall Gibson but refused because he preferred to remain with his comrades, openly admired 1st Lieutenant Slocomb, "who impressed us all with his coolness & bravery."[32]

During this opening fight of the Washington Artillery, below Shiloh meetinghouse, Orderly Sgt. Bakewell would recall that W. Irving Hodgson "was indisposed in the rear." The Fifth Company "went into battle without a Captain." This terrible accusation is odd testimony from Bakewell, a man of irreproachable reputation and word in the battery. Bakewell appears to have been wrong, nevertheless. Hodgson was present at different times during the morning's fighting, perhaps not seen by Bakewell, but observed by Richard Pugh and General Anderson. In fact, later in the day, during the furious fight at Maj. Gen. John A. McClernand's camp, Hodgson's horse was killed. Therefore, Bakewell's April 6 account must be treated with great caution. Something, however, went wrong—badly wrong—regarding Captain Hodgson's behavior on April 6–7. Subsequent attitudes and events would bear this out. Even Pugh maintains that although Hodgson was on the field, and now and then gave an order, "those he did give were not to his credit."[33]

Maj. Francis A. Shoup, Hardee's chief of artillery, had positioned Slocomb and Chalaron "on the crest of a ridge near an almost impenetrable boggy thicket ranging along our front."[34] There, massed with the Arkansas batteries of Captains John T. Trigg, J. H. Calvert, and George T. Hub-

31. *OR,* Vol. X, Pt. 1, pp. 471, 513; Daniel, *Cannoneers in Gray,* 34.

32. Charles Bayne, "Tom Bayne is Wounded at the Battle of Shiloh," Manuscript in possession of George Denègre, New Orleans; Bayne Autobiography, SHC.

33. Lieutenant Ed Hews appears to have remained in the rear, at least part of the time. He is not mentioned in any document. A. Gordon Bakewell, "The Luck of the War Game Sometimes Makes Heroes . . ." *Illinois Central Magazine,* IV (1915), 18; R. L. Pugh to Mary Pugh, April 11, 1862, Pugh Letters, LSU.

34. This was Cleburne's "morass," Shiloh Branch. *OR,* Vol. X, Pt. 1, p. 581.

bard (which constituted Shoup's battalion) and Capt. Smith P. Bankhead's Tennessee battery, they "opened a destructive fire" against Sherman's artillery, which along with his infantry had been effectively checking Hardee's advance.[35]

Sherman's position was strong, primarily because of the "narrow combat frontage (under 1000 yards) utilized by the Confederates directly astride the Corinth Road."[36] It was in this fight that the company suffered its first casualties—several gunners being "slightly wounded by the bursting of shells."[37] Anderson's infantry had come up by now (8:30 A.M.) and pushed enemy skirmishers back through heavy timber and thick undergrowth to a line astride the Corinth road. There the Federals had three batteries stationed on a "domineering hill" that "commanded his camp and the approaches to it."[38] "Federal artillery deployed on this front, was able to enfilade the important Confederate artillery position (which the 5th Company formed an integral part of) located 800 yards beyond Shiloh Branch to the south."[39] The natural approach for infantry was across Rea Field,[40] but enemy pieces controlled the open ground and helped throw back attempts by Anderson and two Tennessee brigades from Leonidas Polk's corps.[41] Anderson now attempted a flank attack. Between the brigade and the enemy camp, however, was "a boggy ravine," so thickly overgrown "as to sometimes require the use of the knife to enable the footman to pass." Moreover, the enemy pieces had a good field of fire as the infantry descended into the ravine.

35. Confederate versions of the final phase of Sherman's defense at the church give the impression that their artillery "silenced" that of the enemy. Actually, Federal artillery dominated the action prior to 9:30 A.M. "Sherman's position was severely weakened by the defeat of Prentiss on his left flank. . . . The artillery fire appears to have had more effect on [Sherman's] infantry than his artillery." *OR*, Vol. X, Pt. 1, pp. 471, 496, 513; Casey, *Outline of Civil War Campaigns*, 54; Stacy D. Allen to author, October 25, 1995.

36. Dumping more and more troops into this confined area, which was suitable for the deployment of only one brigade, led to units being comingled and "brigade (even regimental) command/control was lost." Stacy D. Allen to author, October 25, 1995.

37. R. L. Pugh to Mary Pugh, April 8, 1862, Pugh Letters, LSU.

38. The three batteries were Waterhouse's, Maj. Ezra Taylor's (commanded by Capt. Samuel E. Barrett), and Capt. Adolphus Schwartz's (commanded by Lt. George L. Nispel).

39. Stacy D. Allen to author, October 25, 1996.

40. John C. Rea's name has been misspelled down through the years as "Rhea." Stacy D. Allen to author, May 15, 1995.

41. The two Tennessee brigades were Col. Robert M. Russell's and Brig. Gen. Bushrod R. Johnson's.

When the Fifth Company opened against these batteries, they used solid shot and shrapnel (case shot), according to Patton Anderson, and canister on enemy infantry when possible. It seems that throughout this interval between 8:00 A.M. and 9:30 A.M. Slocomb, Vaught, and Chalaron were receiving commands from Shoup, Anderson, and Ruggles. Anderson's report credits the Fifth Company and Trigg's battery with having suppressed the enemy artillery fire, enabling Anderson's infantry, after suffering several repulses, to cross the ravine successfully and drive the enemy from his camp, with Anderson's men pouring several volleys into the retreating Federal cannoneers.

Patton Anderson attributes too much of the success to the prowess of the Fifth Company (and his own brigade for that matter). It seems the decisive attack that broke the position of the beleaguered Federal artillery concentration and its Ohio supporting infantry came from Alfred Vaughan's 13th Tennessee Infantry, which had completely enveloped their position, attacking from the Confederate right.[42] The Federals, especially Nispel's Illinois battery, had suffered some accurate counter battery fire from the Confederate guns deployed one-half mile south, but it was the infantry musketry that was decisive. Waterhouse withdrew first, then Nispel's battery, then Barrett's, the latter shortly after 10 A.M. They did so, it appears, not from Confederate artillery fire, but because of insufficient infantry support to confront the pressure from a mass of five Confederate brigades pushing northwest from Brig. Gen. Benjamin M. Prentiss' captured camps. This heavy infantry movement turned Sherman's left, placed enfilade artillery fire down his line, and forced him to abandon his excellent position on the commanding meetinghouse ridge.[43]

Although several reports mention the Fifth Company fighting as a battery, and other accounts imply they did, Bakewell states emphatically that each section on April 6 "fought independently, and in the confusion and smoke of battle soon got separated, and lost all knowledge of each other."

42. Hodgson, "History of the 5th," HTT; Sword, *Shiloh*, 185–86, 195–97; *OR*, Vol. X, Pt. 1, pp. 496–97, 509, 513; Roman, *Beauregard*, I, 289; Sandidge, "Battle of Shiloh," 175; D. W. Reed, *The Battle of Shiloh and the Organizations Engaged* (Washington, D.C., 1902), 77. The 13th Tennessee "was able to accomplish their flanking movement due to the previous withdrawal of the Federal infantry (Jesse Hildebrand's brigade in particular) supporting Waterhouse." Stacy D. Allen to author, October 25, 1996.

43. *OR*, Vol. X, Pt. 1, pp. 129–50, 272–77; Sword, *Shiloh*, 195–202; Stacy D. Allen to author, May 15, 1995.

This seems plausible, at least after the initial action that morning, despite the reports of Hodgson and Anderson (the latter often echoing the former's observations).[44]

By mid-morning Sherman's left had been broken and thrown to the rear. Remaining resistance centered about the guns of Capt. Samuel E. Barrett's battery, which remained at Shiloh meetinghouse to fight the Confederates "virtually unsupported." Anderson, supported by a section of the Fifth Company, attacked and a stubborn contest developed in which several attempts to advance by Anderson were tossed back. Finally, in an assault supported by troops of the brigades of Patrick R. Cleburne, Robert M. Russell, and Bushrod R. Johnson, Patton Anderson was able to dislodge the Federal battery. "Even after having been driven back from this position," Ruggles reported, "the enemy rallied and disputed the ground with remarkable tenacity for some two or three hours against our forces in front and his right flank."[45]

Billy Vaught had had quite a morning. Puffing away on his "little mearshaum," he was in action with his smoothbores, "at first engaged on the left not far from Shiloh meetinghouse, and then being utilized toward the center," depending on which general officer seized control of his section. Early on, Vaught got "a powder stain across my face & it staid there all day. . . . The boys say it made my features look *devilish,* indeed. I suppose my face looked savage enough anyhow." One of Vaught's men (unidentified) found a Yankee as they passed through an abandoned camp and "coolly drew his bowie knife & cut the yankee's throat from ear to ear as he passed him & went on as if he had only snapped a twig." Men straggled and pillaged. The "whole Country was covered with their encampments, beautiful tents, Sibley tents shaped like cones." They stopped and picked up loot of every sort. Richard Pugh saw "every luxury that

---

44. It would have been extremely troublesome for the six-gun battery to have moved about the field given the manifold difficulties of terrain and lack of roads, not to speak of control problems, nor the temptation offered to a general officer to utilize a two-gun section. Perhaps some of the confusion in the Confederate reports stems from the presence of Capt. Isadore P. Girardey's Washington Artillery of Augusta, Georgia, the "pride of old time Augusta," which may have been mistaken for the Fifth Company, although Girardey operated on the extreme right of the Confederate line throughout most of the day. Bakewell, "Luck of the War," 18; Sword, *Shiloh,* 226–74.

45. *OR,* Vol. X, Pt. 1, pp. 471, 496–97, 517; Sword, *Shiloh,* 205–207, 509; Roman, *Beauregard,* I, 296–97; Clement A. Evans, ed., *Confederate Military History* (12 vols.; Atlanta, 1899), XIII, 166.

you could imagine. . . . We nearly killed ourselves eating apples and I found a fine lot of paper and envelopes . . . splendid knapsacks and splendid blue overcoats. . . . In truth there never was an army more beautifully equipped and furnished in the world. And there never was one so perfectly surprised."[46]

The positions and movements of the Fifth Company from mid-morning until mid-afternoon on April 6 are extremely difficult to pinpoint. They lost contact with Anderson because of "a ravine" and were pulled this way and that by other general officers, although Anderson's report makes it appear that they operated as a battery in close support of his infantry throughout most of the day. The terrain confused everyone. "To describe this battle," wrote Richard Pugh, "I feel my utter incompetency, for at the time our position with regard to the rest of the army was almost unknown to me. I could see nothing, but trees, and men and hear nothing but cheers & guns."[47] Moreover, the ground, being "broken and thickly wooded," gave the Fifth Company little opportunity "to see the effects of the artillery shots or to know what battery you were fighting." Chalaron, in later years when disputing a claim by the Chicago Light Artillery that they "bested" the Fifth Company in several "duels" on April 6, described their role as having "fought most of the day on the Confederate left centre, opposite to, or on the right flank of [W. H. L.] Wallace and Prentiss. The battery was moved to different-points between the center and the left, as the battle shifted."[48]

At the command of Beauregard, the Fifth Company moved up the Corinth road some time before noon, slanted somewhat to the right toward the exact center of the Confederate line, and "passed through three or near three Federal camps." There in Woolf Field (four-tenths of a mile north of Shiloh meetinghouse) they were joined in the attack by an assorted group of Confederate units against Sherman's left (which had taken a new position two-tenths of a mile north on line with McClernand) and

46. Lathrop, "A Confederate Artilleryman," 376; WCDV to Albert Vaught, April n.d., 1862, Vaught Letters, HNOC; R. L. Pugh to Mary Pugh, April 13, 1862, Pugh Letters, LSU.

47. R. L. Pugh to Mary Pugh, April 8, 1862, Pugh Letters, LSU.

48. Chalaron is inaccurate. Not until after 3 P.M. did the battery attack the "right flank of Wallace and Prentiss." Casey, *Outline of Civil War Campaigns*, 54; *OR*, Vol. X, Pt. 1, p. 497; J. Adolphe Chalaron, "Battle Echoes from Shiloh," *SHSP*, XXI (1898), 215, 218, 220; New Orleans *Picayune*, October 1, 1893; Lathrop, "A Confederate Artilleryman," 376; R. L. Pugh to Mary Pugh, April 8, 1862, Pugh Letters, LSU.

McClernand's battle line, composed of eight organized brigades and some unassigned units.[49] It was at these camps of McClernand's 1st and 2nd brigades that the "enemy fought well generally," their infantry screened by heavy undergrowth. "Here we suffered terribly," reported Richard Pugh. "Here for the first time we were placed face to face with them, and for the first time found out the danger of sharpshooters, who were not more than two hundred yards off behind trees, aiming deliberately at us. The balls hissed around our heads and struck at our feet, striking men and horses."[50]

The battery moved in extremely close and blasted the tents with canister.[51] "The skirmishers of the enemy, lying in their tents only a stone's throw from us," Hodgson wrote, "cut holes through their tents near the ground, and with 'white powder,' or some preparation which discharged their arms without report, played a deadly fire in among my cannoneers."[52] A gunner (Sgt. John W. Demerritt, probably) went down, "just as he was about to fire the gun." He was "struck in front of the ear, and he fell backwards." Another gunner and a driver died here, and a half-dozen men were wounded, including Richard Pugh's cousin, the Scotsman John M. Davidson. When one of the gunners (probably "Caz" Hartnett) dropped beside the piece, Pugh took his place "and had so much to do that [he] had no time to think." Two guns from an unidentified battery, probably Robert Cobb's Kentucky battery, fought beside the Fifth Company at this time and also endured the deadly musket fire. They "stood by us manfully, and we had the glory of being told by Gen[.] Hardee that we had carried the point, and afterwards, when I visited the spot, I saw where our canister had mown down the enemy and but for the artillery the place could never have been taken."[53]

Following this fight at the Federal tent camp (about 1:45–2:00 P.M.), the section (probably Vaught's) limbered up on the command of Beau-

49. "Half of their effective forces on the field will fight on this front for the day." Stacy D. Allen to author, October 25, 1995.

50. Sword, *Shiloh*, 310–23; R. L. Pugh to Mary Pugh, April 8, 1862, Pugh Letters, LSU.

51. This was the camp of Col. C. Carroll Marsh's Illinois brigade.

52. WIH to J. P. Anderson, April 9, 1862, Confederate States of America Papers, DU.

53. Other casualties of this fight were "some of my most valuable horses," reported Hodgson, "mine among the rest." R. L. Pugh to Mary Pugh, April 8, 1862, Pugh Letters, LSU; WIH to W. G. Barth, April 9, 1862, CSA Papers, DU; Casey, *Outline of Civil War Campaigns*, 54; Sword, *Shiloh*, 324–28; *OR*, Vol. X, Pt. 1, p. 513; WA Record Roster, Chalaron Papers, HTT.

regard's staff officer Brig. Gen. James Trudeau, and moved through the camp and across a "beautiful parade ground" to another abandoned camp, about a quarter of a mile northeast. There they went into battery, shelled a fifth camp,[54] and fought a duel with a Federal battery,[55] "silencing" it and enabling Confederate infantry to charge and take the position.[56]

Vaught's section at this point came under orders from Lt. William Kearny of Hardee's staff and Lt. A. R. Chisolm, of Beauregard's staff, "and in fact from other aides whose names I do not know," reported Hodgson. "[I went] to points threatened and exposed and where firing was continued, rendering cheerfully all the assistance I could with my battery, now reduced in men and horses, all fatigued and hungry."[57]

It was sometime after 3 P.M. when General Ruggles sent for the Fifth Company again. He and Beauregard had sent staff officers scurrying to collect guns to attack a stubborn Union position across Joseph Duncan's field and below the main Corinth-Pittsburg road.[58] Batteries, sections, and individual pieces from eleven Confederate artillery units massed there, with the Fifth Company (one or two sections) in position on the extreme left. It took well over an hour to collect these pieces, but once they had been concentrated they unleashed a terrible fire, "enfilading Prentiss' division on his right flank." Most of these Federals, however, belonged to W. H. L. Wallace, not Prentiss, and they hung on with incredible stubbornness. The fight to reduce Wallace's and Prentiss' strong point (the "Hornet's Nest") raged into the late afternoon, almost until dusk, when at last the Federals surrendered.[59] The Fifth Company did good work here, winning compliments in the report of Captain Smith P. Bankhead, a rival battery commander in Polk's corps.[60]

---

54. Tent camps of Col. Abraham H. Hare, commanding McClernand's First Brigade, in Jones's Field.

55. "Probably Dresser's and Taylor's guns in S. Jones Field just before they pulled back east over Tilghman's branch ravine." Stacy D. Allen to author, May 15, 1995.

56. R. L. Pugh to Mary Pugh, April 8, 1862, Pugh Letters, LSU; *OR,* Vol. X, Pt. 1, p. 514.

57. Hodgson identifies Lieutenant Kearny as "Col. Kearney." Kearny was a West Pointer born in New York, an officer in the old army who resigned and became a staff officer under Hardee. WIH to J. P. Anderson, April 9, 1862, CSA Papers, DU.

58. Credit must be given to some independent Confederate battery commanders who brought their guns to this sector on their own initiative.

59. According to Larry Daniel, Ruggles' collection of guns "was the largest concentrated use of field artillery on the North American continent up to that time." Daniel, *Cannoneers in Gray,* 44.

60. Earlier in this fight (between 12 noon and 2:00 P.M.), Gibson's Louisiana brigade had met with a sharp repulse. Gibson sent Pvt. Robert Pugh (his personal friend and neighbor, and a member

When this final Union position collapsed at 5 P.M., a portion of the battery, on orders of General Ruggles, pushed on in support of several thin, intermingled brigades of Polk's and Hardee's corps that were forming into a line of battle to the east, toward Cloud Field, for an attack against the Federals' final line close to the Tennessee River. Although this assault never developed, at least one section doggedly continued on, stopping and going into battery more than once to fire at retreating Federals. As night approached, Chalaron and Hodgson agreed, the battery stood ready "to ascend the last ridge overlooking Pittsburg Landing and the river." It was at this time, however, that Ruggles, in accordance with instructions from Bragg and Beauregard, ordered the battery to halt and pull back. They bivouacked too close to Pittsburg Landing, however, and "being under fire from two ships," had to move again in the night, back to one of the enemy camps, away from the harassing naval shells.[61]

That evening Hodgson went to army headquarters near Shiloh meetinghouse and presented two Union flags to General Beauregard's chief of staff, Col. Thomas Jordan. Hodgson did so in the presence of Brig. Gen. John C. Breckinridge and the miserable but proud captive Brig. Gen. Benjamin M. Prentiss. Two of the Fifth Company privates, Charles A. Adams and Anthony Sambola, had spied the colors in the tent of the colonel of an Illinois regiment as they passed through its camp. The privates seized the flags and tucked them in their haversacks. When the fighting finally ended, they triumphantly handed the captured colors to Hodgson and he led them to Beauregard.[62]

Patton Anderson, immediate superior of Hodgson and the Fifth Company and indirect observer of their conduct, lavished praise on their

of the Fifth Company on loan for the occasion) to request artillery support from Bragg. But Bragg had no artillery to provide. About two-thirds of the Confederate artillery was in action, west of the Hornet's Nest. The remaining one-third was with Sidney Johnston on the far right. So Pugh's request was refused and Gibson was told to charge again, which he did with heavy loss. There was no artillery on this section of the line from noon until about 2:30 P.M. *OR,* Vol. X, Pt. 1, pp. 471, 475–79, 485, 498, 513; Hodgson, "History of the 5th," HTT; Sandidge, "Battle of Shiloh," 176; Casey, *Outline of Civil War Campaigns,* 55; Sword, *Shiloh,* 275–82; Daniel, *Cannoneers in Gray,* 203–204 n. 39; Arthur W. Bergeron, Jr., *Guide to Louisiana Confederate Military Units, 1861–1865* (Baton Rouge, 1989), 24–25; James L. McDonough, *Shiloh: In Hell Before Night* (Knoxville, 1977), 162–67; Stacy D. Allen to author, May 15, 1995.

61. Sword, *Shiloh,* 332–33; Chalaron, "Battle Echoes," 218; *OR,* Vol. X, Pt. 1, pp. 499, 514; Casey, *Outline of Civil War Campaigns,* 55; Bayne Autobiography, SHC.

62. WIH to W. G. Barth, April 16, 1862, 5WA Order Book, WA Papers, HTT; WIH to J. P. Anderson, April 9, 1862, CSA Papers, DU.

achievements of April 6. Few Civil War units would ever bathe in such warm extravagance:

Capt. W. Irving Hodgson, commanding the Fifth Company, Washington Artillery, added fresh luster to the fame of this already renowned corps. It was his fine practice from the brow of the hill overlooking the enemy's first camp that enabled our infantry to rout them in the outset, thus giving confidence to our troops, which was never afterward shaken. Although the nature of the ground over which my infantry fought was such as frequently to preclude the use of artillery, yet Captain Hodgson was not idle. I could hear of his battery wherever artillery was needed. On several occasions I witnessed the effect which his canister and round shot produced among the enemy's masses, and once saw his cannoneers stand to their pieces under a deadly fire when there was no support at hand, and when to have retired would have left that part of the field to the enemy. When a full history of the battles of Shiloh shall have been written[,] the heroic deeds of the Washington Artillery will illustrate one of its brightest pages, and the names of Hodgson and Slocomb will be held in grateful remembrance by a free people long after the sod has grown green upon the bloody hills of Shiloh.[63]

Although the battery won compliments and trophies on the first day of Shiloh, the reputations of several men within the membership had been damaged badly—Hodgson's, probably that of Lieutenant Hews, and certainly that of Hodgson's friend, Corporal of Drivers Fred N. Thayer. Although Hodgson would report officially that Thayer had been wounded, Chalaron would declare Thayer had injured himself "by striking a mule and breaking a finger." Thayer, upon returning to New Orleans with the wounded, told the *Daily Delta* that "though badly injured early in the struggle, he remained at his post, ... indefatigably procuring fresh horses." According to Thayer, "it was mainly due to his efforts that the battery was enabled to continue in action as long as the fight lasted." Thayer also maintained that he spent a great deal of time that night collecting the dead of the company and digging their graves, "reading himself the Episcopal burial service, the few of the Artillerists present making the response."[64]

Three members of the company had been killed on April 6: Sgt. John W. Demerritt, Pvt. "Caz" Hartnett, and the Irish driver John O'Donnell. Wounded were 1st Sgt. William B. Giffen, who was listed as slightly wounded and yet would die of his leg wound a month later; Third Caisson

63. *OR,* Vol. X, Pt. 1, pp. 502–503.
64. 5WA Master Roster, WA Papers, HTT; New Orleans *Daily Delta,* April 18, 1862.

Cpl. Lawrence Macready; the Canadian "Alf" Bellanger, who lost his left hand; the prominent thirty-eight-year-old lawyer Thomas L. Bayne, who was severely wounded in the right arm and thus lost to the company for the war; John M. Davidson, also so badly wounded he could not continue to serve; another Irishman, driver Andy Hopkins; Will Steven; and Bostonian John W. Watson.[65]

That night, once they had encamped, Orderly Sgt. Gordon Bakewell called the members of the company together. This New Orleans cotton factor, this "brave, good man," suggested "that we should all unite in thanks to God for our safety and a prayer for those whom He had taken away. It was probably the most impressive scene of that battle, and one which will never be forgotten by any of us," wrote Richard Pugh. "If daylight had suddenly broke upon us, it would have discovered tears stealing down the cheeks of nearly all present."[66]

It was miserable that dark night in the captured Yankee camp. Noises bothered the men—agonizing battlefield noises that they could not identify or bring themselves to identify. Then, just before midnight, "a terrific rain-storm" crashed down on them and continued almost until dawn on April 7. As it began to subside, infantry firing was heard on the right near Wicker Field, in the direction of Pittsburg Landing. The small-arms racket intensified to the surprise of the Confederates, and then they heard the deeper sounds of cannon fire. Ruggles' division, including Anderson's brigade and the Fifth Company, was dispatched to the scene (to support Gen. James R. Chalmers' brigades, they were told).[67] Hodgson saw that the ammunition chests were replenished, yet, believing this order a false alarm or certainly a temporary move, he directed many of the company to put their luggage, blankets, and trophies "in a log house just there, anticipating an opportunity to return for them in the afternoon."[68] Richard Pugh, echoing the sentiments of his comrades, could hardly believe his ears. They found themselves "called upon after heavy marching and still heavier fighting on the day previous and a drenching rain that night, to fight a battle they had already won." Quickly it became apparent that

65. 5WA Record Roster, Chalaron Papers, HTT; New Orleans *Daily Delta,* April 11, 1862; New Orleans *Commercial Bulletin,* April 15, 1862.

66. R. L. Pugh to Mary Pugh, April 21, 1862, Pugh Letters, LSU.

67. *OR,* Vol. X, Pt. 1, pp. 499, 524.

68. They never returned, unfortunately, and their belongings were lost. 5WA Order Book, WA Papers, HTT; Bakewell, "Luck of the War," 19.

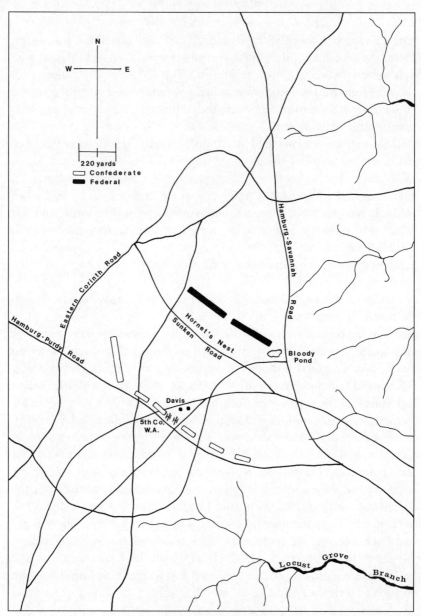

Shiloh, April 7, 1862
Map by Blake A. Magner

something was wrong. Stragglers began to drift to the rear past the Fifth Company, then bits and pieces of disorganized units, the debris of serious fighting.[69]

Chaos reined within the Confederate army during the early daylight hours of April 7. Conflicting orders were issued; units were terribly mixed; thousands of stragglers wandered the fields and woods. On the extreme right of the army, in the vicinity of the junction of the eastern Corinth road and the Hamburg-Purdy road, division commander Brig. Gen. Jones M. Withers was marching to the left when he received an urgent appeal from Brig. Gen. James Chalmers. Chalmers, who formed the right of Withers' division, "had already had one fierce engagement with the enemy and was then in the second." Withers reversed his column immediately, gathering up troops as he marched, and formed a line of battle along the Hamburg-Purdy road, between its junctions with the eastern Corinth road and the Hamburg-Savannah road.[70]

As Withers passed the 19th Louisiana of Randall Gibson's brigade, he ordered the regimental commander, Col. Benjamin L. Hodge, to take command of a demi-brigade composed of the 19th Louisiana, Lt. Col. Marshall J. Smith's Crescents of Col. Preston Pond's brigade, and the Fifth Company, Washington Artillery. Hodge was to place the Fifth Company and the 19th Louisiana in the line of battle forming along the Hamburg-Purdy road while the Crescents remained in reserve.[71]

Hodgson had been ordered by Anderson at 5:30 A.M. to trail the latter's infantry as they prepared to follow Bragg's and Ruggles' directives "to move out and meet the enemy." Hodgson had limbered up by 6:00 A.M. but, as he explained lamely in his official report, "could not ascertain [Anderson's] position, so took position on the extreme right of our army, supported by the Crescent Regiment." Having separated himself from his parent infantry organization, Hodgson went into battery just south or southwest of Daniel Davis' wheat field, apparently being placed in position by either Withers or Hardee. There, about 9 A.M., Hodgson's six pieces fired seventy rounds under the immediate direction of corps commander General Hardee. Most of this firing seems to have been in duels with John Mendenhall's two batteries of the 4th U.S. Artillery and William R. Terrill's Battery H, 5th U.S. Artillery. During the duels, the mount

69. R. L. Pugh to Mary Pugh, April 13, 1862, Pugh Letters, LSU.
70. *OR,* Vol. X, Pt. 1, p. 534.
71. *Ibid.,* 494, 524, 534.

of newly appointed brigade commander Hodge became excited and threw the colonel, injuring him so that he had to leave the field. Marshall J. Smith took command.[72]

About 10 A.M. the Fifth Company moved across the Hamburg-Purdy road into the south edge of Daniel Davis' fenced field.[73] There they went into battery again, on a regulation seventy-five-yard front, facing northeast.[74] To their right was the 19th Louisiana (now commanded by Lt. Col. James M. Hollingsworth); behind them and in support, Marshall J. Smith's Crescents; to their immediate left the battered 13th Arkansas (commanded by the wounded third in command, Maj. James A. McNeely, who would remain in the field); and Col. William B. Bate's 2nd Tennessee Regiment commanded by Lt. Col. D. L. Goodall.[75]

After occupying this position about an hour, the company observed enemy infantry emerging from an oak thicket directly to the north, or front. They were moving toward the guns at the double-quick. This was the brigade of William Sooy Smith.[76] Into the Davis wheat field, to the battery's right front, came the brigade of William B. Hazen, also at the double-quick.[77] The hinge of these enemy assaulting lines of battle was the northeast corner of Davis Field. All six guns of the Washington Artillery opened fire at the approaching enemy, assisted by two pieces of Captain Hugh L. W. McClung's Tennessee battery.

Despite the blasts of case shot and canister from the eight guns, the blue infantry continued their advance to "within some 20 yards of us." Just in time, rushing to the support of the Fifth Company came Marshall J. Smith and the Crescents. The Louisiana infantry abruptly "came face to face with the enemy" as they entered an open field. "We had scarcely taken position when an officer came up at breakneck speed, crying out at the top of his voice: 'For God's sake, boys, hurry up, or our battery is gone!'" It was Adolphe Chalaron.[78]

72. *Ibid.,* 514, 494, 499, 514.

73. Hodgson's position is marked by tablet Number 363. One always should bear in mind that men and units move, and continue to move, in battle. Therefore, the "lines as marked by the commission are approximate—the location best representing the line of action along the Hamburg-Purdy Road." Stacy D. Allen to author, October 25, 1995.

74. It is highly probable that at different times during the confused and very fluid action here, the company may have changed front (completely or by guns or sections) to the east and north.

75. *OR,* Vol. X, Pt. 1, p. 514.

76. 13th Ohio, 11th and 26th Kentucky, supported by 14th Wisconsin ("unassigned troops," Grant's Army of the Tennessee); Reed, *Shiloh,* 64–65.

77. 6th Kentucky, 9th Indiana, and 41st Ohio.

78. *OR,* Vol. X, Pt. 1, pp. 514, 524; *CV,* XII (1904), 343.

There are several versions of what happened next. Hodgson reported that the Fifth Company was rescued by the Crescents, who made a timely counterattack "saving our three extreme right pieces, which would have been captured."[79] Hodgson then pulled back the three pieces on the left, "my men broken down, my horses nearly all slain, ammunition out, and sponges all broken and gone," thereby abandoning the three pieces on the right. He was preparing to make another attack when Beauregard ordered him to retire to Monterey.[80]

Chalaron maintains that the battery took position on the left of Chalmers and fought two "lively artillery engagements" against Mendenhall and Terrill. The company then displaced and took a second, even more advanced position. One hundred yards ahead lay woods full of Federals. The Fifth Company opened on them with canister. As though in retaliation, the woods suddenly came alive and out "sprang" the Yankees, "in a heavy mass, rushing with irresistibility to within 20 yards of the pieces." To compound the company's peril, from their rear poured the fire of the Crescent Regiment, "an unexpected and murderous fire, as deadly to men and horses as that which came from the front."[81] The Fifth Company hurriedly withdrew, leaving three guns "standing unmanned between the contending lines." The retreat was disorderly, however, and the frightened horses "became unmanageable, and in their terror bore guns and caissons straight through Company C of the Crescents, scattering them."[82]

Richard Pugh contends that one of the battery's supporting infantry units "gave way and fell back. . . . Then we were left entirely unprotected."[83] Up came the Crescents, "to meet the advancing enemy now not more than a hundred yards off. . . . We were ordered to get out of the way, but the order was too late by five minutes. The balls were falling about us like hail, and before we could get ready three horses at my piece and the same number at two others were killed, our sergeant [Hildreth

---

79. According to Stacy D. Allen, the Crescents' counter-attack may have been decisive in the minds of the Fifth Company, but actually fire from Breckinridge's line northwest of the Davis wheatfield took the Federals in right flank and rear and was a major reason why the Federals gave way. Allen to author, October 25, 1996.

80. *OR,* Vol. X, Pt. 1, p. 514; Reed, *Shiloh,* 79.

81. As the Crescents advanced, Colonel Smith picked up portions of the 1st Missouri (Bowen's brigade, Breckinridge's reserve corps) and troops from an unidentified Arkansas regiment, perhaps the 13th. *OR,* Vol. X, Pt. 1, p. 524; *CV,* XXII (1915), 343; Chalaron, "Battle Echoes," 218.

82. Chalaron, "Battle Echoes," 217–19; Evans, *Confederate Military History,* XIII, 169.

83. Pugh identified the regiment as the 9th Texas, but is mistaken. That regiment was with Anderson on the Confederate left, nearly a mile away. Probably it was Bate's 2nd Tennessee or the 13th Arkansas.

Green] killed and Lieut[.] Slocomb wounded, and we had to run leaving these three pieces on the field."[84]

Orderly Sgt. Bakewell (who maintained Hodgson was not even present) was with Slocomb when the latter was wounded, and took charge of the guns on the right that had been deployed either as a half-battery or in sections. At least one of the pieces had been disabled, however, some horses had been killed, and a number of gunners wounded. Moreover, they were separated from the three guns on the left, having become divided earlier during the "terrible artillery duel" with Mendenhall and Terrill. It was time to limber up and retire, but the three guns were "so buried in the soil by recoil" that they were immobilized. Short of horses, short of men, Yankees to his front about to charge, Crescents to his rear "coming up in a counter charge," Bakewell was in a desperate situation. Quickly, from front and rear came enemy and friend, many firing "as they advanced." Bakewell yelled to his men, "We can do nothing more; let's get out of this, or we will all be dead men." Bakewell himself had a horse. He mounted and galloped around the right flank of the oncoming Crescents, but, to his dismay, as he reached their flank the beast dropped to the ground exhausted. So Sergeant Bakewell scampered to a dip in the ground where he and others, including Cpl. Joe Denègre, took cover.[85]

After a while the firing on their left subsided. "Peering cautiously over the knoll I espied our cannon," remembered Bakewell, "just where we left them, with no enemy in sight, and only a few stragglers from our army. . . . With the help of these we were enabled to extricate our guns, and from the abandoned Federal artillery (whose carriages were of the same pattern as ours) we replaced our broken wheels and harness."[86]

Bakewell got together eight or ten men (including Richard Pugh's brother-in-law, Pvt. Will Williams) and had them scurry about, catching stray horses wandering the battlefield. They harnessed these animals to the pieces and caissons, then made their way cautiously back west along the Hamburg-Purdy road, searching for friendly forces. After going about a mile, to their delight they spotted the flag of the Fifth Company and heard their comrades raise a mighty shout. Bakewell called a halt and quickly gathered his men about him. "Boys, I want you all to swear that you will never tell how we recovered these guns. If you don't blab, our

86. Bakewell, "Luck of the War," 19; see also Daniel, *Cannoneers in Gray,* 44; Edwin C. Bearss, "Artillery at Shiloh," unpublished article, Shiloh National Military Park Library, Shiloh, Tenn.

85. *OR,* Vol. X, Pt. 1, p. 524; Bakewell, "Luck of the War," 19; Reed, *Shiloh,* 63. Denègre would be promoted to sergeant for gallantry at Shiloh.

reputation as heroes is made forever." Solemnly the group of cannoneers took the pledge. The company happily ran out to meet their lost battery mates. They were full of questions, of course, but Bakewell and his men, "every mother's one of us[,] remained as 'dumb as a drum with a hole in it.'" According to Bakewell the secret was maintained until years later (1915), when he finally felt all should be revealed. Upon their return not only were they treated as heroes by their comrades, but General Beauregard rode up with his staff and said to Bakewell, "You have done nobly, Sir."[87]

Beauregard's army, however, was spent. Don Carlos Buell's and Lew Wallace's large, fresh counter-attacking forces had done their job well. Confronted by these troops, which were augmented by Grant's battered but vengeful veterans of Sunday's fight, the battle-weary Confederates were no match. By early afternoon Beauregard knew "many of the troops were beyond further effort." An appalled Hardee watched as one of the "best" Confederate regiments "fled from the field without apparent cause, and were so dismayed that my efforts to rally them were unavailing." Preparations began at once for withdrawal to Corinth.[88]

Hodgson's battery had been bloodied at Shiloh: four killed and seven wounded on April 6. Four more were killed or mortally wounded on April 7 (the Irish drivers John Leary and Pat Long, Pvt. John McDonald and Sgt. B. Hildreth Green, Jr.).[89] Seventeen gunners and drivers (excluding Sergeant Thayer) were wounded on that bloody Monday. The most serious loss, certainly, was Cuthbert Slocomb, the battery's most skilled soldier and their acknowledged leader. Noticeable among the other casualties were six drivers and one of the blacksmiths, William M. Dooley.

In all, the two-day fight at Shiloh had cost the Fifth Company eight killed and twenty-four wounded, the losses being particularly high in sergeants and corporals. In addition, and of special importance to the Fifth Company, almost half of their horses (thirty-nine) were now "dead or disabled."[90] Chalaron and Hodgson maintained that all of these casualties

---

87. R. L. Pugh to Mary Pugh, April 13, 1862, Pugh Letters, LSU; Bakewell, "Luck of the War," 19.

88. *OR,* Vol. X, Pt. 1, p. 570; Sword, *Shiloh,* 402–403.

89. Despite being seriously wounded, Leary was named first chief of caissons on June 4, 1862. He would be sent from Corinth to the hospital at Holly Springs, Mississippi, where he lingered through October, 1863, before dying. The date of Leary's death is unknown.

90. Hodgson reported twenty-eight horses killed, "exclusive of officers' horses," two of which (his own and Slocomb's) are known.

came as a result of "minnie balls." The battery's "carriages and wheel spokes [were] riddled by them only." In every instance during the two-day battle, the company had been "run in close to Federal infantry." Its canister supply had been exhausted twice, replenished the first time from captured ammunition chests, the second time from loans from Capt. Felix H. Robertson's Florida battery. During the two-days, the Fifth Company had expended 723 rounds, most from smoothbores and howitzers, a large proportion of which were canister.[91]

Fortunately, the Federals did not press the pursuit.[92] John C. Breckinridge, commanding the Confederate rear guard at Mickey's farmhouse, watched the last of the Confederates pass. He worried about having to fight again. "My troops are worn out, and I don't think can be relied on after the first volley." Nevertheless he deployed his men in position to defend the road junction and protect the rear of the retreating column. Among these defenders were twenty of the Fifth Company, volunteers who had agreed to man the abandoned guns of a Mississippi battery. Breckinridge placed these guns on high ground "commanding both roads and a ravine, the only possible chance of an advance on the part of the enemy."[93]

"We expected to remain there only about three hours," wrote Richard Pugh, "but were kept there all night, standing in the rain, I without either jacket, overcoat or blanket. . . . As it turned out, there was [no] necessity of leaving a battery there, for the enemy did not dare move from the place to which we had driven them."[94] These worn-out volunteers left their position at Mickey's the morning of April 8 and started their march "of eighteen miles over the worst roads and through the deepest mud you

---

91. Casualty lists and rosters in Chalaron Papers and WA Papers, HTT; New Orleans *Daily Delta,* April 11, 1862; New Orleans *Commercial Bulletin,* April 15, 1862; New Orleans *Picayune,* October 1, 1893; *OR,* Vol. X, Pt. 1, p. 515.

92. A noisy and bloody encounter did occur about dusk, April 8, between Sherman's infantry and Forrest's cavalry on the Bark road to Mickey's farmhouse, but Grant and Buell were content to allow the Confederates to retreat and did not permit this action to escalate. *OR,* Vol. X, Pt. 1, pp. 639–41, 923–24.

93. Pugh (who was there) states they were Mississippi guns. Vaught and Hodgson (who were not there) state they belonged to Capt. Edward P. Byrne's Kentucky battery. Sword, *Shiloh,* 426; Thomas Lawrence Connelly, *Army of the Heartland: The Army of Tennessee, 1861–1862* (Baton Rouge, 1967), 175; R. L. Pugh to Mary Pugh, April 11, 1862, Pugh Letters, LSU; WCDV to Mary Vaught, June, n.d., 1862, Vaught Letters, HNOC; *OR,* Vol. X, Pt. 1, p. 515.

94. R. L. Pugh to Mary Pugh, April 11, 1862, Pugh Letters, LSU.

ever saw."[95] What had been a road turned into "a quagmire in which men and horses floundered and cannon sunk deep, requiring the utmost efforts of man and beast, amidst the cracking of whips and shouts of drivers, to extricate them from the deep and tenacious mire." The road was "lined with wounded men unable to get transportation." What had been an army had turned into a "miserable column," churning along, "blinded by a cold rain, sleet, and hail," with disorganized clumps of troops stretching "eight miles over the muddy roads." They realized they were in retreat, reported Bakewell, and felt "disappointed—but not disheartened." It did not appear so to a discouraged Braxton Bragg. "I am powerless and almost exhausted. Our artillery is being left all along the road by its officers; indeed I find but few officers with their men."[96]

95. Actually fourteen miles.
96. R. L. Pugh to Mary Pugh, April 11, 1862, Pugh Letters, LSU; Bakewell, "Reminiscences of an Orderly Sergeant of the Fifth Company of the Washington Artillery, C. S. Army . . ." *Illinois Central Magazine,* III (1914), 22; J. T. Skillman to sister, April 12, 1862, Confederate Personnel Documents, HTT; Sword, *Shiloh,* 427; Connelly, *Army of the Heartland,* 175.

3

PASSIONATELY FOND OF GUNNERY

THE FIFTH Company mirrored the wreckage of Beauregard's army. All along the road to Corinth lay its caissons, forge, ordnance, tent wagons, and other vehicles. The men, wet and miserable, mourned their dead and hurting comrades. They were angry at their captain and uneasy about the wounding of Slocomb. Pushing ahead on foot, they camped at Monterey on Monday night, April 7, and arrived in Corinth the following day. The volunteers who had remained behind helping the rear guard rejoined the battery late that afternoon.[1]

Hodgson attempted to act decisively, hoping to boost morale and restore confidence. He sent Corporal Thayer back along the Monterey road with a party of men and several teams of horses to recover the valuables abandoned by the roadside. Thayer retrieved the forge and battery wagon without great difficulty and was making his way back to Corinth when he was ambushed by Texas Rangers. They stripped his work detail of all its "tools, implements and extra sponges," warning Thayer that "if he

---

1. R. L. Pugh to Mary Pugh, April 11, 1862, Pugh Letters, LSU; New Orleans *Daily Delta,* April 18, 1862; Casey, *Outline of Civil War Campaigns,* 55.

spoke of it, they would kill him." Thayer, however, did report his misfortune to Hodgson, who in a fury reported the wanton act to Anderson's headquarters. A week later, basking in the warmth of New Orleans comforts and enjoying the full attention of newspaper reporters, Fred Thayer would bend the truth of the embarrassing event. The *Daily Delta* sympathetically reported that the good corporal had "succeeded in securing and carrying back" all the lost equipment to Corinth, apparently without incident.[2]

Hodgson also protested to Patton Anderson about the rumor circulating in the army that the Fifth Company would be armed exclusively with rifled guns and become a long-distance battery. He reminded Anderson that the company excelled at close-in fighting and would not only be deeply disappointed by but outright opposed to such a change. This idea, he supposed, had come at the instigation of Bragg's organizational genius and chief of artillery, Maj. James H. Hallonquist. Hodgson had also learned (incorrectly) that Ducatel's Orleans Guard Battery was being sent home to New Orleans to ward off an "unexpected attack" by the Federals. "Not supposing there will be a battle here for some time to come, and in case these reports be true, may I ask at your [Anderson's] hands the favor of being transferred to that point, where our families, friends, ties and interests are, and where we can possibly be of more service than here."[3]

Meanwhile Hodgson set to work rebuilding the battered Fifth Company. He resisted efforts by the 20th Louisiana to regain Pvt. William Casey, loaned to the battery during Shiloh. The "daring and brave" Casey, protested Hodgson, is "an A 1 Blacksmith, a mechanic, much needed in my battery." Hodgson managed to keep him. Now that the shortage of drivers had become acute through death and injury, Hodgson sent Thayer back to New Orleans on April 14 along with the wounded Slocomb, authorizing the former to offer fifteen dollars per month plus clothing to obtain recruits.[4]

2. WIH to W. G. Barth, April 12, 1862, 5WA Order Book, WA Papers, HTT; New Orleans *Daily Delta*, April 18, 1862.

3. WIH to W. G. Barth, April 12, 1862, 5WA Order Book, WA Papers, HTT.

4. WIH to R. R. Breedlow, April 12, 1862, 5WA Order Book, WA Papers, HTT. Thayer still would be in New Orleans when Benjamin Butler's expeditionary force arrived. It was only then that he left the city and returned to the company. Special Order No. 25, April 14, 1862, 5WA Order Book, WA Papers, HTT; New Orleans *Daily Delta*, April 18, 1862; F. N. Thayer, "Account of Military Service," Confederate Personnel Documents, HTT.

The battery needed men. On April 17, Hodgson could report only 134 present, less eight to ten incapacitated from diarrhea. Many others were sick as well, most from respiratory ailments resulting from exposure and sleeping under damp blankets for two nights. Hodgson needed horses also. Discounting mounts for officers and noncommissioned officers, he had forty animals available. He was turning in fifteen of these as "worthless," leaving only twenty-five (some of which had been captured from Yankee batteries at Shiloh) to haul the guns and wagons. Hodgson felt he required eighty-seven new horses to bring the company up to strength.[5]

The Fifth Company at this time was still armed with 4 six-pounder smoothbore and rifled cannon and two twelve-pounder howitzers. Oddly, Hodgson appears to have split the twelve-pounders, giving Vaught and Chalaron one each along with a rifled piece. Although this enhanced each section's capability for counter battery fire and gave them opportunity for miraculous target shoots, it doubtless presented a logistical nuisance for the section commander. Ammunition chests, nonetheless, were kept packed and ready, Hodgson reporting 400 fixed rounds for the smoothbores, 400 for the rifled guns, and 312 for the howitzers. This represented the battery's full complement of ammunition.[6]

Hodgson submitted his official report of Shiloh to Anderson on April 12, then amended it and resubmitted it. The report was a blunder of the first order, highlighting the actions of the battery commander and those of a few chosen members. "It has caused a great deal of dissatisfaction," wrote Commissary Sgt. Joseph T. Skillman to his sister, "as [Hodgson] has done the company great injustice in it. He has rendered himself Very unpopular. In fact he has not been popular since we left N. O."[7]

While the company licked its wounds from Shiloh and waited for Cuthbert Slocomb, whom they trusted, to recuperate and return from New Orleans, Billy Vaught got his chance for recognition. On April 26, he took a three-gun section out on the Monterey road in support of Patton Anderson's infantry. There, during the late morning of April 29, Confederate

5. WIH to W. G. Barth, April 17, 1862, WIH to J. H. Hallonquist, April 21, 1862, 5WA Order Book, WA Papers, HTT; J. T. Skillman to sister, April 12, 1862, Confederate Personnel Documents, HTT.

6. Special Orders, May 10, 19, 21, 1862, WIH to W. G. Barth, May 12, 1862, 5WA Order Book, WA Papers, HTT; Daniel, *Cannoneers in Gray,* 44.

7. J. T. Skillman to sister, April 12, 1862, Confederate Personnel Documents, HTT.

cavalry stationed in Monterey "came dashing through my lines," wrote Anderson, "reporting the enemy in hot pursuit in largely superior cavalry force and infantry; not known how many." On came the enemy down the Monterey road until they struck Vaught's position. Vaught "opened upon the head of his column with canister and round shot and soon put the whole to flight." As soon as the enemy retreated out of artillery range, Anderson sent a token infantry force in pursuit while he took up an even stronger defensive position.

Anderson highly complimented Lieutenants Vaught and Chalaron and their men "for the coolness, courage, and skill with which they handled their pieces. . . . The infantry did not fire a volley." Vaught proudly wrote his sister a week later, "I have been on outpost in command of 3 guns for a week & have won new laurels for myself & the company. I have made a friend in General Hardee & of Gen. Anderson.[8]

Wary of Gen. Henry Halleck's methodical advance from Pittsburg Landing toward Corinth, the Confederates attempted to strike back twice in May, 1862. Beauregard's scheme was to catch a division of Halleck's exposed and unsupported, and destroy it. Sound, basic military doctrine, indeed, and its implementation would be sought time and time again from Shiloh to the last stand at Bentonville. Both attempts at Corinth failed, however, largely because of coordination problems among Confederate senior officers.[9]

The Fifth Company participated in the May 8–9 effort, a minor affair designated as the "Engagement at Farmington" in military annals, yet proudly sewn alongside "Shiloh" on the banner of the battery. It began the afternoon of May 8 when Ruggles' division, four brigades strong, advanced out of the fortifications of Corinth and took position on the lower road leading to Farmington, a village seized by the Federals on May 3, and located some four and one-half miles northeast of Corinth.[10] The Fifth Company (two sections) advanced to an open field about one-half mile out. There they went into battery on a hill in front of Anderson's infantry and opened fire, the howitzers and smoothbores using spherical

---

8. *OR,* Vol. X, Pt. 1, p. 800; J. A. Chalaron, "Slocomb's Battery in the Tennessee Army, 5th Company, Washington Artillery," Jackson Barracks Library, New Orleans; Muster Roll, 5WA, WA Papers, HTT; WCDV to sister, May 5, 1862, Vaught Letters, HNOC.

9. See Connelly, *Army of the Heartland,* 175–77.

10. The lower road was the Farmington-Danville road.

case. Never did the Fifth Company shoot more accurately. For four hours they acted as "skirmishers and sharpshooters," reported Hodgson, "often firing at a single man with good effect . . . something very unusual in artillery warfare." [11]

Billy Vaught bragged to his sister on his proficiency (probably with his six-pounder rifle rather than his twelve-pounder howitzer): "I fired a cannon, in one instance, at a single enemy, who annoyed us with his apparently unerring rifle. *The shell burst in his face.* I have become passionately fond of gunnery and have attained to great skill. In action I frequently train the guns myself, though it is none of my business. Two generals, with their staffs, witnessed the shot I mentioned." [12]

Vaught outdid himself with another incredible shot. This time he "fired at a wagon galloping across [his] position a mile off. The shot carried off the head of the saddle horse." Remarkable gunnery, to be sure. Realistically, however, one should attribute this instance of Vaught's fine shooting to luck more than skill. The immodest section leader did qualify his euphoria somewhat. "Do not think that I am become hardened," he told his sister, "by looking upon the dead & by narrow escape. I am a better (I hope & believe) & more religious man. My time is in His hands. He only knows when I may be called." [13]

The following morning, May 9, as Ruggles' division prepared to continue on toward Farmington, Vaught's section was temporarily assigned to Brig. Gen. Lucius M. Walker's brigade. Chalaron remained with Anderson, and Ed Hews's section was sent back within the works at Corinth. Ruggles, instead of proceeding directly ahead to Farmington, swung right and south, snapping three roads entering the village from that direction. Then he began an advance north upon the town, moving his brigades in separate columns "in readiness to deploy into line of battle." About 11 A.M., Vaught was sent ahead of Anderson's column, to the "extreme front," where he found a favorable position and opened fire upon Federal cavalry, "with spherical case-shot, scattering them in the wildest confusion." Chalaron joined Vaught about noon and the two sections opened on the retreating enemy; then they dutifully fell in behind Anderson's

11. *OR,* Vol. X, Pt. 1, pp. 812, 823; WIH to W. G. Barth, May 10, 1862, 5WA Order Book, WA Papers, HTT.

12. WCDV to sister, May 17, 1862, Vaught Letters, HNOC.

13. *Ibid.*

infantry and waited to be recalled to the front. As the Federals gave way before Ruggles' advancing brigades, the two sections would be ordered up from time to time. Vaught's and Chalaron's guns would "wheel" into battery and pour "a few rounds into [the enemy] in order to facilitate them in their movement."

Closing to within half a mile of the enemy, Ruggles halted and formed a division line of battle, three brigades up, one in reserve. Then he moved forward again. With some difficulty they drove Federal skirmishers out of a forest, through an open field, back into and through Farmington, to the bridge across Seven Mile Creek. There, about 3 P.M., Ruggles broke off the action, ordered the bridge to be burned, and marched back to Corinth, where he took his place within the fortifications. The Fifth Company fired over eighty rounds in this two-day expedition and had one man, Pvt. George W. Crawford, wounded.[14] One horse died from fatigue the night they returned.[15]

In effect, Ruggles' effort of May 8–9 turned out to be a raid in force. Although James H. Trapier's division assisted in the operation, maneuvering on Ruggles' left, Maj. Gen. Earl Van Dorn's troops, necessary to the operation's success, arrived too late to exploit any opportunities gained.

Once again, the performance of the Fifth Company received notice and praise from Ruggles and Anderson. Anderson's official report read: "Nothing can be said on this occasion in praise of the conduct of the Washington Artillery which would add to its well-earned reputation on a former and bloodier field. Suffice it to say they were ever present in the right place at the right time, displaying that skill in the management of their pieces and the practice of their gunners which always wins fights as well as laurels."[16]

Indeed, among the company's growing number of admirers was a cavalry captain from Missouri. He watched Vaught and Chalaron repulse a Yankee cavalry charge made by some eight hundred troopers. The imaginative captain reported carnage of catastrophic proportions: "only 40 or

14. It appears Hodgson mistakenly identified his gunner. The compiled service record and Chalaron's roster show J. T. Crawford wounded at Farmington.

15. Proudly Hodgson announced the capture of "a number of spades, shovels, pickaxes, etc; also several hundred feet of telegraph wire." *OR*, Vol. X, Pt. 1, pp. 715, 808–10, 811–15, 820, 823; WIH to W. G. Barth, May 10, 1862, 5WA Order Book, WA Papers, HTT.

16. *OR*, Vol. X, Pt. 1, p. 815.

50 regained their saddles, the rest being killed or wounded. He saw this with his own eyes being a support of the battery."[17]

May proved to be a trying month for the Fifth Company. Camp Anderson, as they called their new home in Corinth, was the scene of much illness and discontent, as it was for Beauregard's entire army (20,000 were on the sick list). To relieve the overcrowded and unsanitary conditions, some of the battery's sick (including Orderly Sgt. Bakewell) were sent down to New Orleans.[18] Happier tidings came, however, when the company received new horses, mostly white and sufficient in number to bring the total to 106. Unfortunately, these animals almost immediately began to suffer from want of forage, as recorded in the terse company muster roll commentary: "horses broken down with scarce forage and bad water." Corinth was a miserable, deadly home.[19]

It helped when Dr. Benjamin Palmer reappeared. Although the Washington Artillery claimed him, he belonged to all Louisianans, indeed the whole of Beauregard's army. He was "as full of hope and determination" as ever. "He addressed the whole of Gen. Hardee's division drawn up around a stand in a large open field and his words brought tears in the eyes of many whose hearts were softened by the pictures he drew of our once happy homes now rendered desolate by the Vandal, and for every tear which fell that day a gallon of Yankee blood will be demanded."[20]

The month of May was a time of detached, fractionalized service. Someone, perhaps Braxton Bragg, believed the best use of a light battery with a reputation for high accuracy and steadiness would be on outpost duty. So, following the attack on Farmington, Chalaron's section (like Vaught's in late April) was sent outside the works to take an isolated position (supported by the 25th Louisiana) at Bridge Creek, on the Monterey Road. There they stayed and stayed, not being relieved for almost

17. Edwin H. Fay, *This Infernal War: The Confederate Letters of Sgt. Edwin H. Fay*, ed. Bell I. Wiley (Austin, Tex., 1958), 50.

18. On his return trip to the army, Bakewell aroused the suspicions of fellow travelers and was saved from summary execution and "an ignominious death" by the intervention of Secretary of War Judah P. Benjamin. Bakewell, "Reminiscences of an Orderly Sergeant," 22.

19. Special Order No. 17, May 3, 1862, WIH to W. G. Barth, May 6, 1862, E. L. Hews to W. G. Barth, May 23, 1862, 5WA Order Book, 5WA Muster Roll, May and June, 1862, WA Papers, HTT; Connelly, *Army of the Heartland*, 176–77.

20. R. L. Pugh to Mary Pugh, May 17, 1862, Pugh Family Papers, UTA; Joseph H. Haney Diary, May 25, 1862, AHC.

two weeks. Meanwhile, Hews's section remained within the works and Vaught's was detailed again to the brigade of General Walker.[21]

These days and nights at Corinth, were nervous times, even in camp—subject to alarms and sudden "call-outs." To the men much of this excitement seemed to be unnecessary, exhibitions of another "scare" on the part of "Old Ruggles." An alarm would come and they would have to drop what they were doing (usually cooking), grab their blankets, canteens, and haversacks, rush down to the breastworks, fall in at the guns "when the enemy are nowhere near," remain all night, and return to camp (only five hundred yards away) the next morning. Stupid, futile it all seemed. Even Patton Anderson, the "gallant general commanding our brigade, was intensely disgusted!" Richard Pugh wrote to his wife that "we hardly know now at any time, a half an hour ahead what we are going to do. I have slept so little in my tent for the last three weeks that I hardly feel at home in it." During the six weeks following Shiloh, Pugh and his "second detachment" (piece number two) had been out five times "varying in time from two to seven days."[22]

It was the practice for one brigade with a section of guns to block each of the "several roads leading to Pittsburgh landing." Nothing much seemed to be accomplished, however, except to test the troops physically and emotionally. "It is sometimes dangerous duty and frequently one of a great deal of suspense and anxiety when an attack is expected." Usually nothing would come of it. "Scouts would come in reporting the enemy advancing in force and though we have had one or two skirmishes, we have not as yet been in any real or great danger." The purpose of these brigade-strength outposts, they were told, was to "check the advance [of the enemy] until the whole army can be in readiness."[23]

As far as they could make sense of Confederate strategy, it seemed that "it has been the design of our generals to draw the enemy on. We have been constantly falling back." Yet the Federals seemed "afraid to retire, and still more afraid to advance." They expected a battle—"though when, God only knows. Meantime every body is cheerful and we all are *determined* upon a great victory. . . . We feel that we are fighting for our fire-

21. Special Orders, May 10, 19, 21, 1862, WIH to W. G. Barth, May 12, 1862, 5WA Order Book, WA Papers, HTT.

22. R. L. Pugh to Mary Pugh, May 16, 1862, Pugh Papers, UTA; Haney Diary, May 28, 1862, AHC.

23. R. L. Pugh to Mary Pugh, May 16, 17, 1862, Pugh Papers, UTA.

sides and loved ones, and come when it will, you will hear of a great victory—one which will turn the tide in our favor." [24]

Beauregard, however, saw no hope of holding Corinth. Halleck tightened the noose daily. No longer did the Union commander dangle unsupported elements of his superior army before Beauregard's eyes. Each day Corinth seemed more like a trap. Each day the sick list grew longer. The only answer was to evacuate. This Beauregard and his corps commanders decided on May 25, 1862. On the night of May 29th, beginning about 8 P.M., the army cautiously and quietly began to withdraw. By 3 A.M. the last units had passed through Corinth. The Fifth Company and Patton Anderson's brigade helped cover the evacuation and retreat. They made good time, reaching Clear Creek (some forty miles below Corinth) on the morning of June 1. There they went into camp. The Federals pursued only with cavalry, and only for about ten miles. After a brief stay at Clear Creek, Beauregard retired farther south, to Tupelo, Mississippi, where there was an "abundance of good water and forage." There the Confederate Army of the Mississippi went into regular camp on June 9. [25]

As the company prepared to break camp at Clear Creek and march to Tupelo, a singular event occurred. Army headquarters had issued a directive that "all officers and men who were unable to march twenty miles a day would go on to the hospital at Okolona, Mississippi, on surgeon's certificate." Hodgson, who had been "sick & confined to his bed for some days," therefore went ahead by special train to Okolona, turning over command of the battery to Billy Vaught. Then, from Okolona, on June 2, Hodgson wrote Beauregard resigning his commission, giving as his reason that the ninety days he and the battery had agreed to serve was about to expire. He asked that he might be transferred back to the state rolls. Beauregard, however, was embroiled with President Jefferson Davis in an attempt to explain the "victory" at Shiloh and the subsequent siege of Corinth. Thus Braxton Bragg, who handled administrative matters, undoubtedly astonished Hodgson by immediately accepting his resignation and appointing Slocomb to command the battery. This led Hodgson to reconsider his hasty action. He appealed to the War Department for reinstatement. His application, however, was referred to Bragg, who sub-

---

24. *Ibid.*

25. Hodgson, "History of the 5th," HTT; Company Muster Roll, May and June, 1862, WA Papers, HTT; William C. Davis, ed., *Diary of a Confederate Soldier: John S. Jackman of the Orphan Brigade* (Columbia, S.C., 1990), 39; Casey, *Outline of Civil War Campaigns,* 57.

mitted it to the Fifth Company. With a crushing, humiliating vote, the members unanimously rejected Hodgson's reinstatement on August 13, 1862.[26]

Unfortunately, there are no known accounts that adequately explain what happened to destroy the confidence of the battery in W. Irving Hodgson. One may only surmise that his action or lack of action at Shiloh discredited him. Hodgson was J. B. Walton's chosen one, but the members of the company considered him unqualified to lead them in battle. Certainly Hodgson had been instrumental in organizing the Fifth Company and putting it in serviceable condition. In all fairness, he should be credited largely with staffing the company with three highly competent officers—Slocomb, Vaught, and Chalaron—as well as with a number of capable noncommissioned officers. He attempted to run the company as a sophisticated club, to be sure, but the times and the nature of the Washington Artillery probably dictated that. In any event Hodgson was gone. He would spend the remainder of the war, it seems, drifting about, serving, according to his own account, on the staff of "his good friend" Governor Henry W. Allen, and doing odd jobs in the Trans-Mississippi Department. The *Official Records* and Hodgson's compiled military service record, however, do not verify such a claim.

When Hodgson left, others left. Ed Hews resigned and disappears from Confederate annals. Fred Thayer left too, a doctor's certificate in his pocket. He joined his family in Covington, Louisiana, and took them to Texas. There in the Trans-Mississippi, sometimes in association with his friend Hodgson, Thayer would be connected loosely with the Commissary Department. They would receive their paroles together in Alexandria, Louisiana. Thayer, a man of "questionable reputation" (in Chalaron's eyes), would find his calling ten years later in New Orleans, where he listed himself in the city directory as an "Arranger." (It is known that he wrote and directed at least one play at the Varieties Theater in that year—1875.)

Another man finding a different calling was Sergeant Bakewell. Discharged at Clear Creek as "overage," Bakewell would be influenced by Doctor Palmer and General Polk (who ordained him) to enter the chap-

---

26. Hodgson, "History of the 5th," HTT; WIH to P. G. T. Beauregard, June 2, 1862, and correspondence with War Department, in WIH, CSR, RG 109, NA; Special Order No. 34, June 6, 1862, Army of Mississippi, 5WA Order Book, WA Papers, HTT; Casey, *Outline of Civil War Campaigns,* 32; Owen, *In Camp and Battle,* 412; Evans, *Confederate Military History,* XIII, 166n.

laincy. He became chaplain for the 28th and 8th Mississippi (consolidated), serving the rest of the war in that capacity. At age eighty-five, as an Episcopal priest in New Orleans, the well-liked and well-respected Bakewell was described as "active as a cat, as erect as an Indian, as striking in appearance as Cardinal Richelieu."[27]

In all, over forty-five men left the Fifth Company during the months of May through July, 1862. Combined with the casualties of April 6–7, it meant a loss of about one third of the command. One member, Pvt. W. E. Phillips, had died of disease since Shiloh, but most were discharged as overaged or having disabilities, as Bragg and Hardee set about purging and reorganizing the Army of the Mississippi. About ten members left the company to find different work. Pvt. William Freret transferred to the engineers, where he would render far more valuable service to the Confederacy. Some joined the medical department, some became clerks, others officers. It seems only one, Robert W. Simmons, preferred another line unit in order to serve with his younger brother, a member of Bragg's escort. In compensation, a trooper from the escort was swapped to the Fifth Company.[28]

Some forty-five privates joined the battery during this period. At least a dozen came from the Confederate Guards Response Battalion, while others transferred from Ducatel's Orleans Guard Battery, the Crescents, and miscellaneous outfits. The talented John H. Haney had been a private in the 3rd Arkansas. E. H. Wingate had been a member of the old company but remained at home until New Orleans fell, when he set out to join the battery at Tupelo. Another important addition was Charles Folse, a thirty-four-year-old Assumption Parish sugar planter, doubtless a friend of the Pughs. Immediately he was named "artificer," one who prepares shells, fuses, and and so on—an "in-house" ordnance specialist in effect. Folse would remain in this capacity throughout the war, as would the Welshman Morris Williams, a twenty-four-year-old New Orleans blacksmith.

The nephew of the battery's surgeon, Dr. Cecil Legaré, also showed up—sixteen-year-old Oscar Legaré. This bright lad, a native of Illinois,

27. New Orleans *Times Picayune*, February 23, 1920.

28. The conscript law passed April 16, and had a demoralizing effect. Among other provisions, it allowed men under eighteen and over thirty-five to apply for discharge. Slocomb set up a board of officers to examine the applications of these men. CHS to T. B. Roy (Hardee's new assistant adjutant general and soon to become his chief of staff), July 15, 1862, 5WA Order Book, WA Papers, HTT.

was eager to fight. With him appeared New Yorker Henry Vining Ogden. But Ogden was forty, a substitute, and already had been discharged from the Confederate Guards Response as overaged. Ogden said he wanted to be a driver, and that is where Billy Vaught assigned him. As the months wore on, however, Ogden quickly stood out from the crowd and came to be known, "by common consent of officers and men," according to Chalaron, as "the best soldier in the company & [who] commanded the most respect. Known to all as the *Old Gentleman*." [29]

Two officers were needed to fill spots vacated by Hodgson and Hews. Vaught moved up to senior first lieutenant and Chalaron to junior first lieutenant. As senior second lieutenant the members chose Sgt. Thomas McMillan Blair, twenty-three years old, popular and highly respected, a soldier who had demonstrated exceptional bravery and energy at Shiloh. James Madison Seixas became junior second lieutenant. Unlike Blair's, Seixas' appointment came directly from General Bragg. Deeply saddened, demoralized even, by the death at Shiloh on April 12 of his law partner and mentor, Gen. Adley H. Gladden, Seixas had been discharged on that date so he could accompany the remains to New Orleans. He then re-enlisted.[30] He was regarded as unusually able and, like the Pugh brothers, had direct access to the high command of the army.

To replace Bakewell as orderly sergeant the men chose Abe Leverich, bright and well educated, a man with fierce personal loyalties who had held the position of first sergeant since John Demerritt was killed on the first day at Shiloh. The new first sergeant would be John Bartley, a favorite of everyone. The tone of the battery seemed to change overnight. Of course just being in Tupelo, at "Camp Louisiana" as they called it, helped enormously. "When we left Corinth," wrote Vaught to his sister Mary, "*half* the army was sick in the hospitals about the country. Here there is rest from the eternal hardship & fatigue & excitement of the constant fighting around Corinth. The sick are returning to duty." [31]

---

29. There would be four other significant infusions of personnel during the war: in Mobile during the summer of 1863; at Chattanooga in the early fall of 1863; at Dalton in the spring of 1864; and at Spanish Fort in the spring of 1865. Chalaron's Master Roll, WA Papers, HTT.

30. Seixas had spent the days since Shiloh at Gladden's bedside, sleeping in the room with him and holding out hope that he might recover. J. M. Seixas to the son of A. H. Gladden (first name unknown), April 9, 11, 1862, quoted in Bruce S. Allardice to author, March 4, 1995.

31. 5WA Order Book, WA Papers, HTT; WCDV to Mary Vaught, June 17, 1862, Vaught Letters, HNOC.

THE PRIDE OF THE CONFEDERATE ARTILLERY

There was much to do to reorganize the battery with officers in different roles, new officers, new noncommissioned officers, and many fresh recruits for gunners and drivers, most unfamiliar with battery routine. Although it is not known on what day Slocomb returned to the company, his Special Order Number One, dated June 17, 1862, shows a shift in emphasis.[32] He demanded close attention to drill and care of the pieces and "implements," charging each "Chief of the Piece" with responsibility for the readiness of his crew. He demanded better care of the animals, stipulating that the entire harness was to be washed every Saturday at 11 A.M., collars every Wednesday. Revealing his meticulous interest in equipment, tools, and readiness, Slocomb made certain that the battery had the regulation number of artificers and blacksmiths.[33]

By June 30, the effectiveness of Slocomb's work could be seen clearly, as evidenced by the report of the inspecting officer and veteran artillery captain Walker Anderson:

The six pieces of artillery I found in good order and condition; with implements &c complete. The caissons were also in perfect working condition, with the exception of one which had the tongue broken, it was then being repaired at the Company forge—the requisite implements were in their places. The wheels and running gear of guns and caissons and the harness belonging to them were in very good condition.

Each gun was supplied with the proper amount of ammunition which I found to be in perfect order, and securely kept. The Battery wagon, forge, and tool chest, were all in good order, and well supplied. The horses were not in perfect condition.

32. That June, while her son returned to fight the enemy in Mississippi, Mrs. Cora Ann Slocomb engaged the fearful Union commander of New Orleans, Maj. Gen. Benjamin F. Butler. Butler wanted her splendid home for his headquarters, but the general proved no match for Cora and her daughter Augusta Urquhart. He relented almost apologetically. "I have taken the house of General [David] Twiggs, late of the United States army, for quarters. . . . It is gratifying to be enabled to yield to the appeal for the favor and protection by the United States. Yours shall be the solitary exception to the general rule." Mrs. Slocomb responded with equal graciousness on June 23, 1862. "Knowing that we have no claim for any exception in our favor, this generous act calls loudly upon our grateful hearts. . . . We shall never forget the liberality with which our request has been granted by one whose power here reminds us painfully that our enemies are more magnanimous than our Citizens are brave." See Benjamin F. Butler, *Autobiography and Personal Reminiscences of Major General Benjamin F. Butler* (Boston, 1892), 423–25; Jesse A. Marshall, ed., *Private and Official Correspondence of General Benjamin F. Butler During the Period of the Civil War* (5 vols.; Norwood, Mass., 1917), I, 631; II, 1.

33. 5WA Order Book, WA Papers, HTT; Casey, *Outline of Civil War Campaigns,* 58–59.

Many looked thin and unable to endure hard service. Five were reported to me as unserviceable. The Camp & grounds were clean and well kept. . . . I was greatly pleased throughout the inspection and in according to this company that credit for efficiency &c to which they are so justly entitled.[34]

34. Two days before Anderson's inspection "some incendiary fiend" had set fire to the Washington Artillery armory on Girod Street, destroying much of the upper and rear of the building. W. Anderson to W. G. Barth, July 2, 1862, WA Papers, HTT; New Orleans *Commercial Bulletin,* June 30, 1862.

4

THE WHITE HORSE BATTERY

BRAXTON BRAGG, who had replaced Beauregard as commander of the army on June 20, 1862, faced an emergency a month later. Department commander Edmund Kirby Smith wired that "Buell with his whole force, is opposite Chattanooga, which he is momentarily expected to attack." He called for help. "The successful holding of Chattanooga depends upon your co-operation." Bragg himself had been hoping to launch a counterstrike into middle Tennessee. Indeed, it seemed everyone in the army, in the War Department, wanted an offensive campaign, and the repossession of Tennessee and Kentucky.[1]

Partially as a response to Kirby Smith, partially to fulfill his own dreams and ambitions, Bragg set out on the daring invasion of Kentucky on July 23. It was a formidable task logistically—"to move an army of almost thirty-five thousand men eight hundred miles across four states."[2] The Fifth Company shipped its guns and men by rail via Mobile while

---

1. *OR,* Vol. XIV, Pt. 2, pp. 730–31; Connelly, *Army of the Heartland,* 195–98.
2. Connelly, *Army of the Heartland,* 203.

the drivers took the horses and mules overland through Aberdeen and Talladega.[3] In the latter town, drivers from several batteries "got tight and wanted to fight." Although the particulars are not known, Slocomb's Fifth Company drivers became involved. Before the awful fracas ended, a member of the Jefferson artillery lay dead.[4]

Meanwhile the gunners, under command of Chalaron, arrived in Mobile on August 1, at 2 P.M. There they found Vaught, who had been detailed to the city by army headquarters since July 20. Most pleasant duty for Billy Vaught. He worked directly with General Hardee, even receiving an invitation to dinner from the senior corps commander. Vaught also got to spend the week with his wife, Isadore (who had been refuging with his sister Mary in Canton). The battery did not delay in Mobile, however. They left that very night by steamer (the *Lilly*) for Montgomery, Alabama, arriving in the capital the morning of August 4. Vaught was in command.[5]

The scenery on the Alabama River was "very fine—high rocky bluffs." After a hearty breakfast at the "Exchange" in Montgomery, they loaded the pieces upon railcars and set out once again that afternoon, arriving in Atlanta at noon on August 5. They left "at dark" for Chattanooga.[6] "Through Alabama & Georgia our course was a perfect ovation—greeted everywhere by the ladies and pelted with fruit & flowers, candy & notes, cheering us on," Vaught reported to his sister. He continued:

After leaving Atlanta our engine broke down, & a train behind ran into us, breaking up two or three cars, knocking all our guns out of their places, but hurting no one seriously. I was asleep on a platform in between two guns, but *never awoke*, till I was called up. *That's the way I sleep nowadays.*

We made their [the ladies'] acquaintance without ceremony. They expressed their satisfaction in meeting "the famous Washington Artillery." One of the handsomest women I saw in Georgia asked one of the boys who I was, then asked if I was *married*. The envious fellow was *spiteful* enough to say I was. She said "I

3. The route took them from Tupelo to Columbus, to Tuscaloosa, Talladega, and Jacksonville, Alabama, through Rome, Georgia, to Chattanooga. Chalaron, Marches of the Fifth Company, WA Papers, HTT.

4. Ironically, these Mississippians would fight beside the Washington Artillery at Perryville. They worked together splendidly. John E. Magee Diary, August 14, 1862, DU.

5. WCDV to Mary Vaught, July 31, August 9, 1862, Vaught Letters, HNOC; 5WA Order Book, July 25, 1862, WA Papers, HTT; Haney Diary, August 1, 1862, AHC.

6. Haney Diary, August 5, 1862, AHC.

thought so, he is good looking enough to marry *anybody!*" Wasn't that a *bully* compliment? I wrote Isadore about it & told her she had no idea of how many sweethearts I had made in Alabama & Georgia.[7]

The Fifth Company arrived at Chattanooga on August 7, then moved east to Tyner's Station. There they remained two weeks, naming their temporary encampment "Camp Orleans." This was appropriate since they had received the happy news that they were being brigaded with Louisianans—Dan Adams' brigade (13th, 16th, 20th, and 25th Louisiana and Ned Austin's 14th Battalion of Sharpshooters). This Louisiana organization would last until the eve of the battle of Missionary Ridge in November, 1863.[8]

Daniel Weisiger Adams was a highly popular leader and believed to be a competent, courageous commander by privates and senior officers alike. Forty-one years old, Yale valedictorian, native Kentuckian, a lawyer by profession, and a man marked for having killed a newspaper editor in a duel, Adams had led in the effort to prepare Louisiana for war. Named colonel of the 1st Louisiana, he took command of Gladden's brigade at Shiloh after the latter was killed, only to be seriously wounded himself (losing his right eye). He was promoted to brigadier general in May, 1862, and after recuperating, returned to the army, arriving in Chattanooga to take charge of the brigade that would be called henceforth both Adams' brigade and the Louisiana brigade. Meanwhile Patton Anderson, the battery's old brigadier, had been promoted to division command and was their division commander. Thus he would retain reasonably close contact with the Fifth Company. Their corps (wing) commander would be Hardee.[9]

Second Lt. Abe Leverich was hospitalized on Lookout Mountain. It looked as though he would not be able to go along on the coming campaign. His friend Vaught went up on the mountain to visit him and was dismayed by the poorly managed facility. He helped Leverich dress and led him to the nearby hotel. "Doctor" Vaught had made a good prescrip-

7. WCDV to Mary Vaught, August 9, 1862, Vaught Letters, HNOC.

8. On June 30 the battery is shown as belonging to Anderson's brigade, composed of the 25th Louisiana, the 30th, 37th, and 41st Mississippi, and the consolidated Florida–Confederate Guards Response Battalion. Casey, *Outline of Civil War Campaigns*, 59; *OR,* Vol. X, Pt. 1, p. 787; Vol. XVII, Pt. 2, p. 632.

9. For the army's chief of artillery, Bragg chose his friend James H. Hallonquist, whom he promoted to lieutenant colonel. See Evans, *Confederate Military History,* XIII, 291; Warner, *Generals in Gray,* 1, 7; Daniel, *Cannoneers in Gray,* 49.

tion. Abe Leverich recovered rapidly in his new sick quarters, and he was with the company when the army crossed the Tennessee River on August 25. Once across, however, they found it difficult to procure forage for the horses or food for themselves. "All our supplies," complained Vaught, "except fresh beef, [are] brought from Chattanooga."[10]

The battery crossed Walden's Ridge to Dunlap, Tennessee, then headed slowly up Sequatchie Valley to Pikeville, to Spencer, to Sparta.[11] From Sparta, on September 8, the column turned directly north, moving through Pekin to Carthage and on toward Glascow, Kentucky, a march of fifty-five miles. There, on September 14, they heard that Gen. James Chalmers had attacked the garrison at Munfordville and had been repulsed with heavy loss. "Soon after, we suddenly got orders to move," reported Vaught. The Fifth Company broke camp about 3 P.M. and marched all night. They rested a few hours in the morning, then pushed on to Munfordville. By noon, September 15, the Confederates had surrounded the town with seventy-six pieces of artillery, unlimbered and eager to fire. Negotiations for surrender dragged on, however, for a day and a half before the Federals capitulated on the morning of September 17. Good thing, thought Vaught. If they had dallied much longer, even "with all their fortifications (which were very strong) [they] would have been blown to atoms in half an hour. . . . We had not fired a shot. . . . If Kentucky rises & joins us in this course we may go to Louisville immediately."[12]

The defeated garrison surrendered and stacked arms. As they marched humiliated out of their fortifications past the Fifth Company on their way north, a young Yankee artillery officer (F. A. Mason, 13th Indiana Artillery) saw the Fifth Company's pieces. He called over and asked what battery it was. "When told, he said he had heard of it, and was very anxious that his battery should meet it on the battle-field." According to

10. WCDV to Mary Vaught, August 15, 25, 1862, Vaught Letters, HNOC; James Lee McDonough, *War in Kentucky: From Shiloh to Perryville* (Knoxville, 1994), 154–55.

11. Pvt. Richard Pugh marched with the wagon train and messed each night with officers. He arrived in Pikeville on September 8. Chalaron does not mention Pikeville in his itinerary, so it is possible, though unlikely, the battery went directly from Dunlap to Spencer because of the mountainous nature of that area. R. L. Pugh to Mary Pugh, September 8, 1862, Pugh Letters, LSU; Chalaron, 5WA Itinerary, Chalaron Papers, HTT.

12. WCDV to Mary Vaught, September 27, 1862, Vaught Letters, HNOC; Chalaron, 5WA Itinerary, Chalaron Papers, HTT; Kenneth A. Hafendorfer, *Perryville: Battle for Kentucky* (Louisville, 1981), 15–19; McDonough, *War in Kentucky,* 155, 181–83.

Adolphe Chalaron, "He was told the Fifth Company hoped to have that pleasure some day, and would give his battery their best attention."[13]

Bragg, who was ignorant of Buell's location, wasted precious time inspecting his prize and celebrating, and it was not until the night of September 17 that he realized he had miscalculated the intentions of his opponent, Don Carlos Buell. Bragg thereupon lost his nerve and placed his army temporarily in a defensive posture, allowing the initiative to pass to Buell. His and Kirby Smith's strategy for the invasion of Kentucky fell apart. To compound these miseries, Bragg seemed "unable to commit himself to a defensive position." The Confederates vacillated, floundered. Gone went the dreams of attacking Louisville, of racing to the Ohio River, of chasing down Buell and thrashing him.

Buell's forces came roaring out of Louisville on October 1, fifty thousand strong, searching for Bragg's army in four parallel columns, the primary thrust being aimed at Bardstown. Bragg, confused as to the enemy's intent, confused as to the location of the Federal's heaviest strength, had dispersed his army dangerously. The climax of the Kentucky campaign would come on October 8 at Perryville, where three Union corps concentrated against Hardee's wing, aided by Benjamin Franklin Cheatham's division of Polk's corps, with odds potentially as high as fifty thousand against sixteen thousand. Bragg, nevertheless, decided to attack.[14]

Perryville opened with the Confederates aligned along a ridge behind Chaplin's Fork. Wanting to attack, they first had to cross that stream, then, venture over a beautiful open, rolling meadow, and then ford another stream, Doctor's Fork, which was lined on the opposite side with stone walls and other excellent infantry firing positions.[15] Most of the Federals who had arrived on the field by that time were massed higher, on an uneven ridge behind Doctor's Fork, their lines running roughly north–south. Initially Bragg had one brigade west of Perryville, on the west side of Chaplin's Fork—St. John Liddell's Arkansas infantry—and it was being driven back steadily toward town.

13. New Orleans *Picayune,* October 1, 1893.

14. See Hafendorfer, *Perryville,* 32–46; Connelly, *Army of the Heartland,* 242–61; McDonough, *War in Kentucky,* 218–61; Grady McWhiney, *Braxton Bragg and Confederate Defeat* (New York, 1969), 274–80.

15. Kenneth Hafendorfer, who has spent over ten years researching and writing the story of Perryville, refers to Chaplin's Fork as a "river" and Doctor's Fork as a "creek." In an attempt to keep the narrative consistent with official reports and previous accounts, however, I have employed the more usual term "fork."

Bragg, believing he held numerical superiority, immediately ordered Bushrod Johnson's Tennessee brigade north, across Chaplin's Fork. Intending a crushing *en echelon* flank attack that would first hit the Federal left, Bragg began massing troops north of Perryville. Frank Cheatham's division, which would deliver the initial assault, was moved to that end of the line. As soon as the last of Cheatham's three brigades had passed through town (shortly after 11 A.M.), heading north toward their assault positions, Patton Anderson moved Dan Adams' brigade through Perryville and across Chaplin's Fork on the north bridge. He put the Louisianans into line of battle west of the town between the Springfield and Mackville pikes. Meanwhile Col. Sam Powell's brigade of Anderson's division also crossed the fork, swung to Adams' left, and took position just south of Springfield Pike. To prepare for the infantry advance, Slocomb's battery opened fire on the enemy stationed on the opposite ridge with good effect, the enemy withdrawing over the crest.[16]

Anderson ordered both brigades to oblique north, which would bring them to the left of where Bushrod Johnson was expected to attack with support from Cleburne's brigade. There were no friendly units, however, to the left of Adams and Powell (south of Perryville and along the Lebanon pike) save Gen. Joseph Wheeler's cavalry and Capt. Henry C. Semple's Alabama battery. An enemy advance from this direction (which was unexpected), along the thinly held Lebanon pike, would place Federals in the rear of Adams and Powell and close to the town of Perryville itself, hard against the left flank of Bragg's main line.[17]

Dan Adams was across Chaplin's Fork and preparing to oblique to the right (north) when Anderson ordered him to halt and wait for Powell. The Louisianans waited, then moved forward again slowly, then halted and waited. An impatient Adams sent a courier to Powell urging him to hurry; then he sent another. The advance was maddeningly slow. Adams and his men could see the enemy dead ahead to the west, across Doctor's Creek, on "broken heights." Finally, when he felt comfortable that both brigades had reached their assigned positions, Patton Anderson advanced both farther west, then north, toward Bull Run, a creek about a mile west of Perryville, midway between Chaplin's Fork and Doctor's Creek. He continued to have Dan Adams' Louisianans wheel more to the north,

16. *OR,* Vol. XVI, Pt. 1, p. 1057.

17. Hafendorfer, *Perryville,* 169–79; St. John R. Liddell, *Liddell's Record,* ed. Nathaniel C. Hughes, Jr. (Dayton, Ohio, 1985), 88–89; Connelly, *Army of the Heartland,* 262–63.

however, creating a wide interval between the two brigades. This maneuver placed Adams ever closer to Bushrod Johnson, who was supported by Putnam Darden's Mississippi battery (Jefferson Light Artillery). Johnson, under orders from his division commander Simon B. Buckner, had occupied Chatham Hill, a small, uneven ridge running parallel to, but six hundred yards east of, Doctor's Creek. The 17th and 23rd Tennessee infantry seized this high ground above Mackville Pike without opposition, and there Darden went into battery. By noon all six of Johnson's regiments were poised and ready on Chatham Hill. Darden's guns opened at 12:30 P.M., hoping to soften the Federal position on the ridge for the coming Confederate assault.[18]

At about 1 P.M., according to Hardee, Cheatham's division crossed Doctor's Fork and began to engage the enemy left on the ridge behind that stream. Fighting grew furious as the Confederates attacked, were repulsed, then formed and attacked again. Unit after unit assaulted, the attack rippling from the Confederate right to left. About 2:45 P.M. Anderson's division launched its attack in force against the Union right. Col. Tom Jones's Mississippi infantry brigade crossed Doctor's Fork and was struck with deadly blasts of canister from Capt. Peter Simonson's 5th Indiana Battery stationed on high ground north of the creek.[19] Bushrod Johnson attacked on Jones's left. His infantry came marching down Chatham Hilt through Chatham's orchard toward the creekbank. A section of Simonson's battery, unfortunately, shifted its fire from Jones to Johnson's Tennesseans. Johnson now came under combined artillery and infantry fire. It was deadly.[20]

With Johnson committed to the attack, Buckner ordered Dan Adams to support this effort by advancing on Johnson's left. The Washington Artillery moved forward at 1:15 P.M. and went into battery on high ground called Bottom Hill, a forward position selected by Adams. There the Fifth Company opened fire about 2:30 P.M., at very close range. The enemy skirmishers bolted. Adams told Slocomb to hold his fire while the Louisiana infantry attacked to his front. In effect, however, Buckner and Anderson "had no idea of the Federal strength on Peters Hill. . . . Buckner

18. Hafendorfer, *Perryville*, 172–75, 179–90; *OR*, Vol. XVI, Pt. 1, pp. 1120–24.

19. Thomas Marshall Jones had been named acting brigadier general by Bragg following Shiloh, but he ran afoul of both Patton Anderson and illness and never received formal promotion. Bruce S. Allardice, *More Generals in Gray* (Baton Rouge, 1995), 139–40.

20. *OR*, Vol. XVI, Pt. 1, pp. 1056, 1126–27; Hambleton Tapp, "The Battle of Perryville, 1862," *Filson Club History Quarterly*, IX (1935), 176–77.

was sending a full brigade (Adams) across the front of Gilbert's entire corps which was not more than seven to eight hundred yards away." [21]

The Fifth Company displaced again, going forward in support of Adams about one hundred yards to the front and left. It was another good position, and after a few rounds they found they had enfilade fire on the enemy. Again the enemy fell back before their well-directed rounds. [22]

Meanwhile, after pushing forward to the edge of Doctor's Creek, Bushrod Johnson's brigade "found they could go no further." They became confused and intermingled. Some regiments had made a left oblique wheel prior to the attack. Others had not. Two of Johnson's regiments, the 25th and 44th Tennessee, had swung so far to the left that they had entered the right rear of Adams' lines. Even worse, they appeared to the Fifth Company as enemy advancing on Adams' flank and one section opened fire upon them. The Tennesseans recoiled and General Buckner rushed an aide to tell Slocomb to hold his fire. [23]

Slocomb now ordered the battery to limber up and advance down Bottom Hill even closer in support of Adams' regiments. They crossed Doctor's Fork and went into battery west of the Henry Bottom home and Mackville Pike, choosing a position that gave them an excellent field of fire toward the right flank of the 3rd Ohio, which was stubbornly holding the hill above Bushrod Johnson's men. The Fifth Company fired with destructive effect, and the Federal commander, Col. John Beatty, declared, "For a time, I do not know how long, the air was filled with hissing balls, shells were exploding continuously and the noise of guns deafening." [24]

Slocomb's men worked steadily, carefully. Once a piece had been loaded, the gunner took careful aim, waving his hand at Number Three, who was behind him prepared to shift the trail to attain the exact alignment. The gunner sighted on a barn close to the position of the 3rd Ohio. While he aimed, Number Five already had gotten another round from Number Seven at the limber where Number Six stooped, busy cutting fuses. Satisfied with his aim, the gunner stood clear of the piece and

21. Hafendorfer, *Perryville,* 241; *OR,* Vol. XVI, Pt. 1, pp. 1056, 1126–27; Charles M. Cummings, *Yankee Quaker Confederate General: The Curious Career of Bushrod Rust Johnson* (Rutherford, N.J., 1971), 226–27. Sam Powell's brigade remained between Bull Run and Perryville, inactive and isolated, but providing the valuable function of holding, or occupying, the Confederate left flank.

22. CHS to G. D. Bradford, October 11, 1862, 5WA Order Book, WA Papers, HTT.

23. Hafendorfer, *Perryville,* 251; *OR,* Vol. XVI, Pt. 1, pp. 1030–31, 1133; *CV, XVI* (1908), 225.

24. *OR,* Vol. XVI, Pt. 1, p. 1058; John Beatty, *Memoirs of a Volunteer,* ed. Harvey S. Ford (New York, 1946), 136–38; McDonough, *War in Kentucky,* 262.

shouted, "Ready." Now Number One and Number Two jumped away from the gun while Number Three took the vent pick and punched it down the vent through the powder bag. Number Four (who had secured the lanyard to the friction primer) inserted the primer in the vent. Once again Number Three cautiously covered the vent with his thumb pad. Number Four stepped to the left and rear of the piece with the lanyard securely held in his left hand. "Fire," shouted the gunner. Number Four yanked the lanyard and the gun roared, simultaneously recoiling about six feet (sometimes ten to twelve feet) to the rear. Now the entire crew rushed to the wheels to run the piece back up and reload.[25]

The spherical shell smashed into the side of the barn and exploded. Filled with hay, the barn burst into flame. Soon smoke became so thick it blew into the eyes of the 3rd Ohio riflemen and helped send that beleaguered regiment retreating to the bottom of the reverse slope. Up came Federal reinforcements, "but the fire of the enemy's battery was so deadly that these men were again ordered to retire."[26]

Adams' infantry, led by Ned Austin's sharpshooters deployed as skirmishers, now attacked the hill with a loud cheer. "A perfect storm of bullets was rained upon us," however, and Austin's men fell back and took shelter behind a stone wall. Then they edged left to a sheltered assault position. From this point Austin attacked the hill again, only to be driven back once more to the creek. Adams' other regiments now joined in the attack. Thus the Union force holding the hill confronted half of Bushrod Johnson's brigade and Austin's sharpshooters to their front, while Adams' other regiments maneuvered to the extreme left and opened a devastating enfilade fire on the Federal right. If this were not enough, Cleburne's brigade came up at this time and launched a crushing assault against the Yankee left flank. Resistance quickly collapsed. It was now between 3:00 P.M. and 3:30 P.M.[27]

Adams' Louisianans and Johnson's Tennesseans were aided by the Fifth Company positioned "on an open knob about seven hundred feet from the stone wall." Behind this wall was the regiment defending the hill (15th Kentucky, USA). While this struggle was at its height, one of John-

25. Dean S. Thomas, *Cannons: An Introduction to Civil War Artillery* (Gettysburg, Pa., 1985), 3.

26. *OR*, Vol. XVI, Pt. 1, pp. 1057–58, 1070, 1131; Nathaniel Cheairs Hughes, Jr., *General William J. Hardee: Old Reliable* (Baton Rouge, 1965), 129.

27. John W. Headley, *Confederate Operations in Canada and New York* (New York, 1906), 55–60; Irving A. Buck, *Cleburne and His Command,* ed. Thomas R. Hay (Jackson, Tenn., 1959), 112–13; Hafendorfer, *Perryville,* 257–58, 272, 275.

son's regiments, the 44th Tennessee, reached the scene and saw the battery atop the knob. Assuming them to be Yankees, the 44th fixed bayonets and charged. To their (and the Fifth Company's) astonishment they found Slocomb's men working their guns in support of Adams' attack. Sheepishly they took position in support of the battery. They would remain there temporarily.[28]

After helping drive the enemy from the ridge behind Doctor's Creek, the Fifth Company again advanced, came into battery for the third time, and redirected their fire toward the line of Col. Leonard Harris, holding firm against the attacks of A. P. Stewart's and John C. Brown's brigades of Cheatham's division. Again the battery occupied a good position near Henry Bottom's house. With the battery's "right resting on some haystacks, from which the enemy had been recently driven," their shots struck Harris' regiments in the right flank with "deadly effect." Billy Vaught wrote, "Our battery did terrible execution. . . . We found Kentucky a pretty place to fight in—so open to the view. We could see what we were doing. We could see whole ranks of their men go down before our fire." To stop Adams' advance the remnants of the 3rd Ohio, aided by elements from the shattered 15th Kentucky, tried to establish a line of battle along a fence line. The resulting fight, according to Dan Adams, was "short but spirited." It ended quickly with the Federals "in great disorder, panic and confusion, throwing their arms and equipment away as they fled."[29]

Adams drove on, smashing into the right flank of the Harris line. Maj. Ned Austin rode beside him, waving his hat as a signal for his men to continue the charge. They broke into the rear of Brig. Gen. William H. Lytle's and Col. Leonard Harris' line. Lytle attempted to rally enough troops for a counterattack just below the Mackville road. Lytle fell wounded, however, and Adams' men captured him. Providing covering fire for Adams' dash forward was a mini-concentration of Confederate artillery above the Bottom house—the Fifth Company, Putnam Darden's Jefferson artillery, and Capt. J. H. Calvert's Arkansas battery (one section on each side of the Mackville pike). It was a splendid position selected by Bushrod Johnson. They trained their pieces on the vicinity of the Russell house close to the intersection of the Mackville and Benton roads. The

28. *OR,* Vol. XVI, Pt. 1, pp. 1058, 1131, 1133; Cummings, *Yankee Quaker,* 226–27; McDonough, *War in Kentucky,* 260.

29. *OR,* Vol. XVI, Pt. 1, pp. 1055–56, 1123; WCDV to Mary Vaught, October 24, 1862, Vaught Letters, HNOC; Hafendorfer, *Perryville,* 285–86.

seizure of this position would mean that "the Yankees opposing Cheatham and Buckner would be cut in half." It was now close to 4 P.M.[30]

A furious artillery duel ensued. Replying to the twelve guns concentrated at the Bottom house were the 1st Michigan (Cyrus O. Loomis) and 5th Indiana (Simonson) batteries. For forty-five minutes the cannoneers fought, shells screaming out over the infantry that was crouching below the trajectory of the deadly missiles. It was a cannoneer's idea of a battlefield: the Fifth Company and their opponents were in "full view of each other on hillsides, with open fields and orchards between. . . . Results could be seen." The men witnessed a shell strike a Yankee ammunition chest; they watched their opponents limber up their guns and shift position, limber up and fall back. "Balls and shells continued to fall thick and fast from the enemies' guns," observed Bushrod Johnson, "while our batteries replied with great rapidity." Brig. Gen. Lovell H. Rousseau, the Union commander at the Russell house reported, "the air seemed full of [shells]. . . . Four or five burst at one time."[31]

"Everything in front of us seemed to be routed," remembered one of Adams' soldiers. As the Louisianans closed on the Federals positioned near the Russell house, however, they ran head on into a counterattack led personally by General Rousseau and supported by direct fire from Capt. Cyrus O. Loomis' 1st Battery, Michigan Artillery. Volley after volley hit Adams' men. The Louisiana brigade, isolated except for Cleburne's brigade to their right and rear (but almost out of ammunition), gave way and retreated toward the Washington Artillery and Doctor's Creek. Meanwhile the Fifth Company, with Darden's and Calvert's guns, continued to fire away. Once again Simonson's battery (posted now on a hill about one hundred yards in rear of the Russell house) attempted to engage them, but the contest was unequal and Simonson soon withdrew. "Seldom, if ever, were the guns of Bragg better served."[32]

The men grew weary as the ceaseless firing continued. At first piece,

30. Headley, *Confederate Operations,* 55–60; *OR,* Vol. XVI, Pt. 1, pp. 70, 1127–28, 1131; Vol. LII, Pt. 1, p. 53; Cummings, *Yankee Quaker,* 226–27; Kenneth A. Hafendorfer, ed., "The Kentucky Campaign Revisited: Major General Simon B. Buckner's Unpublished After-Action Report on the Battle of Perryville," *Civil War Regiments,* IV (1995), 58–59; Connelly, *Army of the Heartland,* 265.

31. Chalaron, "Battle Echoes," 221–22; *OR,* Vol. XVI, Pt. 1, pp. 345, 1133, 1041; Daniel, *Cannoneers in Gray,* 51.

32. *OR,* Vol. XVI, Pt. 1, pp. 1124, 1131–33; Headley, *Confederate Operations,* 55–60; Hafendorfer, *Perryville,* 309–10, 321; Ralph A. Wooster, "Confederate Success at Perryville," *Kentucky State Historical Register,* LIX (1961), 318–23.

Number Two yelled back to the Parisian Caisson Corp. Edward Fehren-back, asking him to leave his post of "comparative safety" and take his place at the gun. Fehrenback did. After some time placing rounds in the mouth of the cannon, Fehrenback now heard William Murphy (Number One) say he had "given out." Would Fehrenback relieve him? Again, Fehrenback agreed, grabbed the rammer, and stepped to the right side of the piece as though he were Murphy. While he was "driving a shot home" about dusk, Fehrenback was struck, knocked down and bloodied, and carried to the rear. There he was placed in an ambulance containing two other company members.[33]

But up came more Yankee guns and more blue lines of infantry. As the afternoon closed, the Fifth Company found itself "subjected to the fire of infantry and artillery in front and on [Slocomb's] left." Dan Adams ordered the battery to retire, and as it moved to the rear, it was halted by Hardee in the Doctor's Creek bottom. Hardee repositioned it on a hill "to the right of that just left, where I remained until after dark," Slocomb reported. There, in its fifth position that day, the Washington Artillery would continue firing until about 7:30 P.M.[34]

Not long before dark the Fifth Company's ammunition was running low. Slocomb thought he had a sufficient supply on hand, at least enough to complete the day's firing missions, but Capt. Thomas R. Hotchkiss disagreed. This ordnance officer, acting chief of artillery of Anderson's division on October 8, was a controversial figure and certainly no favorite of the Fifth Company's. Hotchkiss told Slocomb to send a detail, commanded by an officer, to division headquarters and get a fresh stock of ammunition. Slocomb obeyed and so instructed Lt. Tom Blair. It seems he did so reluctantly, however, as his report implies that sending Blair was done against his wishes.[35]

In any event, Blair followed instructions and gathered a detail of eleven men and two caissons and began the trip back toward Anderson's headquarters on the Harrodsburg road. It was growing dark. Accompanying

33. N. E. Fehrenback to Officers and Members of the 5WA, September n.d., 1875, WA Papers, HTT; *OR*, Vol. XVI, Pt. 1, p. 1124.

34. N. E. Fehrenback to Officers and Members of the 5WA, September n.d., 1875, WA Papers, HTT; *OR*, XVI, Pt. 1, p. 1124; CHS to G. D. Bradford, October 11, 1862, 5WA Order Book, WA Papers, HTT.

35. *OR*, Vol. LII, Pt. 2, p. 54; Daniel, *Cannoneers in Gray*, 83–84, 130, 138; Howell Purdue and Elizabeth Purdue, *Pat Cleburne: Confederate General* (Hillsboro, Tex., 1973), 167.

Blair was Surgeon Cecil Legaré and an ambulance containing three wounded. Little did these two officers know that by going to the rear, they were riding directly into two regiments of Yankees.

What had happened was that Sam Powell's brigade, fighting an isolated battle of its own on the army's extreme left, had attacked, head on, Phil Sheridan's and Robert B. Mitchell's entire divisions and met with a bloody repulse. Union commander William P. Carlin had then counterattacked the disorganized Confederates with his brigade, overwhelming Powell and mounting an audacious pursuit, sending two of his regiments to the very edge of Perryville. The town was his. He was in rear of the Confederate batteries. But the aggressive Carlin had no support. He sought instructions, but none came. Union commander Charles C. Gilbert was ignorant of the incredible opportunity presented his corps and allowed it to slip away.[36]

Poor Blair ran afoul of Carlin's victorious troops. As the tiny Confederate train neared the cemetery on the west side of town, Blair saw a large body of troops. Believing them to be Confederates, of course, he continued on, and before he could react, he and his detail were summarily surrounded by several hundred Yankees. Blair surrendered on the spot. Soon another group of Confederates rode up (Lt. Philip Sayne, fifteen men, and Dan Adams' ammunition wagons), also totally unaware of the presence of the Yankee troops. Carlin's men bagged them too.[37]

Union division commander Robert B. Mitchell reported Carlin's two regiments had seized "thirteen wagon loads of ammunition, two ambulances [including Fehrenback's], and two caissons."[38] Mitchell continued, "Had I been supported, I could have taken the Washington Battery. I had made a reconnaissance in person, and there was no infantry supporting the battery except those that were taken prisoners—about 170. Every-

36. See Tapp, "Perryville," 175–76; Hafendorfer, *Perryville*, 325–44; *OR*, Vol. XVI, Pt. 1, pp. 1077–78, 1120, 1122, 1127; CHS to G. D. Bradford, October 11, 1862, 5WA Order Book, WA Papers, HTT.

37. Hafendorfer, *Perryville*, 345; *OR*, Vol. XVI, Pt. 1, pp. 94, 1078, 1123–24; Daniel, *Cannoneers in Gray*, 52; Evans, *Confederate Military History*, XIII, 177. See also William E. Patterson, *Campaigns of the 38th Regiment of Illinois Volunteer Infantry, 1861–1863*, ed. Lowell W. Patterson (Bowie, Md., 1992), 18; William P. Carlin, "Military Memoirs," *National Tribune*, July 5, 1885.

38. Fehrenback was taken to Louisville and imprisoned. After receiving his parole he was transported down river to Vicksburg, then taken to Jackson where he waited a few weeks until "the order of Exchange was finally promulgated." He returned to the battery in late December, 1862, just before the Battle of Murfreesboro. Edw. Fehrenback, CSR, RG 109, NA.

thing I did discover was in advance of the batteries and fighting [Alexander McD.] McCook; the battery was also shelling McCook."[39]

Night brought an end to operations, however. Each army regrouped, rested, and took stock of its situation. Bragg, in consultation with his principal subordinates, decided to withdraw from Perryville that night. His Confederates were battered and had been badly outnumbered (20,000 against 35,000). To remain invited disaster. The army would march immediately for Harrodsburg and unite with Kirby Smith. There the situation could be reassessed. So Bragg issued orders to have the army retire east of Perryville in a few hours. From there they would leave very early in the morning for Harrodsburg. Adams' brigade remained in position until 2:00 A.M., then marched off toward Perryville about 3:30 A.M., preceded by Slocomb's battery. From there the Louisiana brigade, acting as rear guard, took the road to Harrodsburg.[40]

The retreat to Harrodsburg was accomplished without incident, although the junction with Kirby Smith occurred only after Bragg's army had passed through Harrodsburg and begun the tramp toward Bryantsville. Yet it was in Harrodsburg that citizens surprised the Fifth Company by cheering the retreating cannoneers. Appreciating such an enthusiastic welcome, Chalaron exclaimed that "those shouts shall ever ring in the ears of [the battery's] survivors."[41] And it was there in Harrodsburg that they stopped and "the roll was called for the first time." The men dreaded this ritual—the first roll after a battle. "A long silence followed the name of each comrade. Then some would tell where he had seen him last. . . . The roll call after the battle is never forgotten by those that stand in that line."[42]

The Fifth Company had been fortunate. Perryville could have been much worse. Although the battery spent much of the afternoon of October 8 well advanced, within musket range of the enemy (canister range, gunners called it), only a few were hit and no member lost his life. Slocomb reported to General Adams that he had five privates wounded, among them Villeneuve "Fatty" Allain and the Tennessean James Dabney.

39. *OR,* Vol. XVI, Pt. 1, pp. 94, 97, 1077–78.

40. McWhiney, *Braxton Bragg,* 318–19; Hafendorfer, *Perryville,* 383.

41. J. Adolphe Chalaron, "The Washington Artillery in the Army of Tennessee," *SHSP,* XI (1883), 219; Owen, *In Camp and Battle,* 413.

42. It would be in Bryantsville that CHS would write his report on October 11. Frank Liddell Richardson, "War as I Saw It," *Louisiana Historical Quarterly,* VI (1923), 224; *OR,* Vol. LII, Pt. 2, pp. 53–54.

The blundering encounter with Carlin's men at dusk had cost him two officers (Blair and Cecil Legaré) and eleven privates (including the German William Gollmer, as well as John Metsler and Hugh McCormack) captured and three drivers missing. Two of the latter Slocomb had allowed to go for water during the fighting; they never returned. These men (George Nish and the substitute Pat Ryan) henceforward would be carried on the rolls as deserters. Many members of the unit had close calls at Perryville. Billy Vaught wrote his sister that "again the musket & cannon shot hissed from all around me but passed me harmless. A rifled shell passed within a foot of my body," striking two horses nearby.[43]

Although they had suffered losses, the men of the Fifth Company had distinguished themselves. Their immediate commander, Dan Adams, was most pleased with their performance, so much so that he recommended "they be allowed to have Perryville inscribed on their banner." Division commanders Buckner and Anderson and wing commanders Hardee and Polk also had "very high praise" for the company. It was at Perryville that they first earned the name "The White Horse Battery," a name by which the Yankees would sometimes refer to them. It appears that it was the men of Loomis' Michigan battery who fastened them with that sobriquet. It was one that the company always regarded as a badge of honor. The Fifth Company also began to be called more and more often "Slocomb's battery." Sometimes they would be called the Fifth Company, sometimes the Washington Artillery, but certainly after the fall of 1862, they would be most commonly known as Slocomb's battery, as was customary in the designation of batteries in the Army of Tennessee.[44]

Nevertheless, it was all such a disappointment. Everyone, it seems, had misunderstood and overrated the reaction of Kentuckians. Recruiting failed. The Confederates even had guns to create several artillery batteries, but barely managed to scrape together sufficient men for one. Indeed, illustrating Confederate lack of foresight, "the one artillery company that might have attracted prospects, Cobb's Kentucky Battery, was with Breckinridge's division in Mississippi."[45]

43. Chalaron, 5WA Master Roster, CHS to G. D. Bradford, October 11, 1862, 5WA Order Book, WA Papers, HTT; WCDV to Mary Vaught, October 24, 1862, Vaught Letters, HNOC.

44. R. L. Pugh to Mary Pugh, December 16, 1862, Pugh Letters, LSU; WCDV to Mary Vaught, October 24, 1862, Vaught Letters, HNOC; OR, Vol. XVI, Pt. 1, p. 1124; Casey, Outline of Civil War Campaigns, 60; Chalaron, "Battle Echoes," 221.

45. Daniel, Cannoneers in Gray, 53.

So the short stay at Bryantsville ended with the bitter decision by Bragg and Kirby Smith to abandon Kentucky and all dreams of wintering on the Ohio. Fearing they could be cut off by fast-moving Yankee columns, the Confederates braced themselves and began the long, agonizing trek home on October 13, 1862. They withdrew to the east, through the mountains, through Cumberland Gap, back into Tennessee. Billy Vaught summed up the sentiments of many: "Enough of Kentucky." [46]

46. Connelly, *Army of the Heartland,* 277–80; Hughes, *Hardee,* 133; WCDV to Mary Vaught, October 24, 1862, Vaught Letters, HNOC.

5

DOING SOME FANCY PRACTICE

D ISCOURAGED AND suffering, Bragg's soldiers retreated from central Kentucky. Pressed by Yankees, they moved southeast into the high country as fast as they could, leaving "tracks of blood" as marks of passage. Finally they broke free of the inhospitable Cumberland Mountains, with their swollen streams and slippery roads and sullen inhabitants. The head of the column reached Morristown, Tennessee, on October 21, 1862, then continued on to Knoxville. Slocomb's battery reached the latter point on October 24. The army was sick, hungry, and exhausted. They had been humiliated, having to slink out of Kentucky like dogs. The "feeling against Bragg was great." Resentment not only infected the officer corps, it had spread to the ranks.

Braxton Bragg thought the best tonic was boldness. So he had his infantry climb aboard trains, the cars taking the men south through Chattanooga, to Bridgeport, Alabama. There they crossed the Tennessee River and turned north—their second "invasion of Tennessee" within four months. Incredible, considering their having just "marched for 60 days, with about 10 days rest." As historian Thomas Connelly has observed,

"Probably never had a Confederate offensive been so hastily planned and an invading army so unready for a new campaign."[1]

The Fifth Company waited, however, encamped some forty miles west of Knoxville, at Kingston, Tennessee. The artillery, unlike the infantry, would go over land to middle Tennessee. It was there at Kingston that the astonished Louisianans met the "first blasts" of winter. Snow in October! Most had never seen snow. "By November 1, six inches lay on the ground," most unusual weather even for upper east Tennessee. The men, of course, were totally unprepared for the cold and their suffering continued, but now in a different way. Tents offered little protection; light uniforms betrayed them. Sickness, a familiar companion in the Kentucky mountains, now reached enormous proportions.[2]

Adolphe Chalaron nearly froze to death. According to nurse Fannie Beers, Chalaron had been chosen by Patton Anderson to proceed to Savannah, Georgia, and secure blankets, shoes, and clothing for the division. Chalaron dropped out of the column at Knoxville during the last week in October and attempted to board a train for Chattanooga. Every boxcar and cattle car was full, however, with "suffering men helplessly sick." So, with a couple of other hearty souls, he climbed on top of a car and rode twelve hours in the open to Chattanooga, chilled by the cold and whipped by the wind. It is not known whether Chalaron succeeded in his Savannah mission, but it is recorded later that during the three winters he would spend in Tennessee or at Dalton, Georgia, the fiery little Frenchman would remain under his blanket and inside his tent or hut unless stern duty forced him outside into the cold.[3]

Soon, however, it became time for the Washington Artillery to move away from frozen and inhospitable east Tennessee. They harnessed up and set out south from Kingston. They quickly broke into Sequatchie Valley, marched down through Pikeville and Dunlap to Jasper. From Jasper they turned sharply north and climbed over Monteagle Mountain at

---

1. WCDV to Mary Vaught, October 24, 1862, Vaught Letters, HNOC; Daniel, *Cannoneers in Gray*, 54–55; Owen, *In Camp and Battle*, 413; Thomas L. Connelly, *Autumn of Glory: The Army of Tennessee, 1861–1862* (Baton Rouge, 1971), 13–16.

2. Chalaron, "Washington Artillery in the Army of Tennessee," 219; Connelly, *Autumn of Glory*, 16.

3. Fannie A. Beers, *Memories: A Record of Personal Experience and Adventure During Four Years of War* (Philadelphia, 1888), 72–74; Phillip D. Stephenson, "War Memoirs," Phillip D. Stephenson Papers, LSU.

University Place.[4] Finally, on November 18, they descended the mountain and camped at Allisonia, Tennessee, a hamlet on the Nashville and Chattanooga Railroad a few miles north of Winchester. There, at the edge of middle Tennessee, they were greeted with disheartening news. Adam Giffen, the father of Cpl. James F. Giffen and the young Bob Giffen, had arrived from New Orleans, like one of Leo Tolstoy's "living letters," full of messages and stories from home.[5]

The elder Giffen had been forced to leave the city, being declared "an enemy" by Gen. Benjamin Butler, which of course he was. What Giffen wanted most was to be with his surviving sons. His oldest, Sgt. William Butler Giffen, had been wounded at Shiloh and been taken to New Orleans where he lingered more than a month, kept alive by the ministrations of his family. Despite all they could do, he had died in July. The Giffens stayed on, nevertheless, determined to hold on to their home, determined to outwait Butler. Adam Giffen told of the atrocities by the occupying Yankees, the hardships endured by the citizens, and of course succeeded in upsetting the men who worried helplessly about the fate of their families and friends. The Washington Artillery named its Allisonia camp "Camp Giffen," a gesture, no doubt, in honor of their dead sergeant; a gesture, perhaps, to boost the spirits of this brokenhearted father who had traveled so far.[6]

It was at the time of Giffen's visit that the battery lost a good officer, Lt. James M. Seixas. He gave up his commission in the Washington Artillery and went to Richmond at the request of former private Thomas L. Bayne, the Fifth Company's badly wounded lawyer-cannoneer who had sought less rigorous duty in the Ordnance Department assisting his brother-in-law, Gen. Josiah Gorgas. Bayne had risen rapidly in rank and responsibility, and now it appeared he (as a lieutenant colonel) would be heading the Bureau of Foreign Supplies within the War Department. Bayne needed dependable, well-connected men of ability to help him, so he called for his friend Seixas (Judah P. Benjamin's brother-in-law). Seixas,

4. The site of Leonidas Polk's dream—the University of the South at Sewanee.

5. Chalaron, 5WA Itinerary, Chalaron Papers, HTT; R. L. Pugh to Mary Pugh, December 16, 1862, Pugh Letters, LSU; WCDV to Mary Vaught, November n.d., 1862, Vaught Letters, HNOC; 5WA Order Book, November, 1862, WA Papers, HTT.

6. R. L. Pugh to Mary Pugh, December 16, 1862, Pugh Letters, LSU; Casey, *Outline of Civil War Campaigns*, 61.

within a short time, would become the commercial agent representing the War Department at Wilmington, North Carolina.[7]

To replace Seixas, Slocomb recommended Sgt. Abe Leverich be promoted to second lieutenant and section commander. Leverich had served with distinction both as crew chief and orderly sergeant. In his stead, John Bartley was promoted to orderly sergeant at Allisonia and would remain in that capacity throughout the war. In the meantime Lt. Tom Blair returned from Yankee captivity to the delight of everyone. He had been exchanged on November 1 and rejoined the company at Allisonia.[8]

In early December, 1862, Slocomb's battery left the Allisonia-Winchester area and moved north to Shelbyville. Then, as Bragg deployed his corps over a forty-mile front, the company marched north and west twenty-seven miles to Eagleville, Tennessee, where they and Adams' brigade remained through Christmas on "outpost duty."[9] It was from Eagleville that Richard Pugh wrote his wife Mary that he had attempted to see their old family friend Braxton Bragg about securing leave to return home so he could check on his family and plantation in Assumption Parish. He found Bragg, a changed man, however. "Gen. Bragg here and at home are two different beings, besides he is so much embittered by his failure in Ky and the evident loss of confidence, on the part of the troops, and the loss of his own property that I have no confidence in being able to get anything from him." Billy Vaught echoed these sentiments, although he maintained that the army (which officially had been named the Army of Tennessee that November) would "fight with enthusiasm [against] any odds & whip them."[10]

Another change confronted the Fifth Company. Patton Anderson's di-

7. The likeable and extremely able Sgt. Joe Denègre also would join Bayne in the War Department after the Battle of Murfreesboro, as would Adolphe Chalaron's brother Stephen, the former as a captain, the latter as a major. J. Gorgas to B. W. Saunders, June 17, 1863, John F. H. Claiborne Papers, SHC; D. W. Adams to S. Cooper, November 22, 1862, Special Order No. 21, November 16, 1862, 5WA Order Book, WA Papers, HTT; George G. Shackelford, *George Wythe Randolph and the Confederate Elite* (Athens, Ga., 1988), 127.

8. 5WA Order Book, WA Papers, HTT; T. M. Blair, CSR, RG 109, NA.

9. Chalaron maintains they were somewhat farther north at Triune. Probably the battery, or sections of it, were positioned there as "outposts." J. Adolphe Chalaron, "Memories of Major Rice E. Graves, C.S.A.," *Daviess County* [Ky.] *Historical Quarterly,* III (1985), 3.

10. R. L. Pugh to Mary Pugh, December 16, 1862, Pugh Letters, LSU; WCDV to Mary Vaught, November n.d., 1862, Vaught Letters, HNOC.

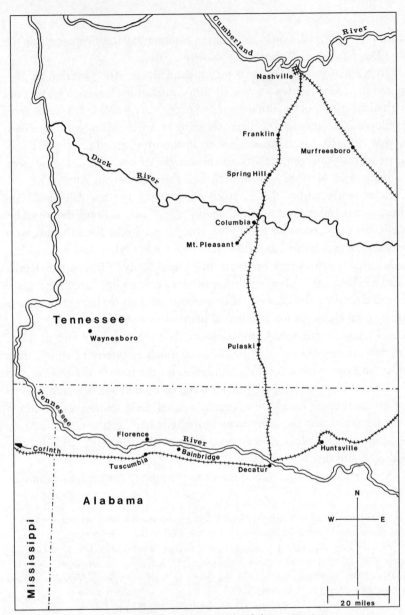

The Middle Tennesse–North Alabama Region
Map by Blake A. Magner

vision had been broken up.[11] Some units went to Polk's corps, some to Hardee. Dan Adams' Louisiana brigade now became part of Maj. Gen. John C. Breckinridge's division of Hardee's corps, joining the brigades of John C. Brown, Roger Hanson, and William Preston, and making it "the most diversified division in the army, with men from eight different states." Breckinridge suited the Fifth Company fine. They were "delighted with the assignment."[12]

By Christmas, 1862, the bulk of the Army of Tennessee had gathered near Murfreesboro, supremely confident despite having lost by transfer almost one-sixth of its infantry (Carter L. Stevenson's division had been dispatched to Mississippi on December 15) and an even higher proportion of its cavalry (John H. Morgan, on December 22, had begun his raid into central Kentucky). Thirty miles away in Nashville, the Federal army, now commanded by Maj. Gen. William S. Rosecrans, had grown in strength until it had become twice the size of Bragg's force. Bragg oddly had "made few preparations for a possible advance" south by the Federals from Nashville although intelligence reports suggested such a development as likely.

The day after Christmas Rosecrans began his offensive, pushing heavy columns down three pikes. Murfreesboro, it appeared, was his objective although one Union column pointed toward Columbia. On December 27, Bragg ordered Hardee's corps, scattered in encampments near Eagleville, to come to Murfreesboro. Hardee's corps (including the Fifth Company) marched to Murfreesboro via Triune, displaying not the slightest nervousness about the approaching Yankee column on their left flank.[13]

Riding out to meet the Fifth Company came their new battalion commander—Maj. Rice Evan Graves, Jr., Breckinridge's chief of artillery. This distinguished and popular young professional soldier was known to the battery and promised competent leadership and cordial support in the days to come. Twenty-four years old, Graves had resigned from West Point when war broke out, then served as a Kentucky infantry officer before being appointed commander of a Tennessee field battery. It was while acting in this capacity that he was captured at Fort Donelson. Fol-

---

11. Anderson himself would command a brigade after having led a division at Perryville.

12. This command reorganization occurred between November 22 and December 15, 1863. Special Order No. 22, Army of Tennessee, RG 109, NA; *OR*, Vol. XX, Pt. 2, pp. 447–48, 456, Pt. 1, p. 659; Don Carlos Seitz, *Braxton Bragg: General of the Confederacy* (Columbia, S.C., 1924), 79; William C. Davis, *Breckinridge: Statesman, Soldier, Symbol* (Baton Rouge, 1974), 334; Chalaron, "Memories of Rice Graves," 3.

13. Chalaron, 5WA Itinerary, Chalaron Papers, HTT.

lowing his exchange in the early fall of 1862, Graves's friend Breckinridge named him chief of artillery of his division with the rank of major.[14]

When he met his new charges as the Fifth Company approached Murfreesboro, Rice Graves was disappointed to find that Cuthbert Slocomb was not with them. He was on leave. Graves rode past Billy Vaught's section, then Abe Leverich's. The Louisianans were "covered with mud and mire," which was not unexpected, but the gun carriages of the Washington Artillery "were loaded with all sorts of plunder, in which figured extensively the denizens of barnyards and henroosts . . . [in anticipation of] an elaborate preparation for Christmas enjoyment." Although Graves did not know it, encumbering gun carriages with provisions was most unusual for Slocomb's battery, but a "special exception" had been made because of the Christmas transfer to Murfreesboro.

Graves rode by each section solemnly until he reached Chalaron's. Then, "with disgust depicted on his countenance, in answer to my salute, he said to me: 'Is this the way the Washington artillery travels?' " This degrading episode, according to Chalaron, made the members "all determined to win him over to us in the coming battle." Interesting looking man, this stern-faced Graves with his piercing command voice; he appeared to lean forward as he walked, probably because of the angle at which he wore his kepi.[15]

When Hardee's corps arrived in Murfreesboro on December 28, Bragg positioned him and Polk along Stone's River blocking the Nashville-Murfreesboro Pike and astride the Nashville and Chattanooga Railroad. An obvious disadvantage of the army's position, however, was that Stone's River separated Bragg's two corps—Hardee on the east bank, Polk on the west.[16]

On Monday afternoon, December 29, Breckinridge's division, Hardee's corps, deployed in line of battle between Stone's River on its left and Lebanon Pike to its right. Six hundred yards north of Breckinridge's position lay a commanding terrain feature—Wayne's Hill—from which "ar-

14. Rice E. Graves, CSR, RG 109, NA; Owensboro (Ky.) *Messenger,* November 29, 1877; Glenn Hodges, "An Officer and a Gentleman," Owensboro (Ky.) *Messenger-Inquirer,* May 14, 1996; Edwin P. Thompson, *History of the First Kentucky Brigade* (Cincinnati, 1868), 462, 860.

15. Chalaron, "Memories of Rice Graves," 4; Owensboro (Ky.) *Messenger,* November 29, 1877.

16. See Peter Cozzens, *No Better Place to Die: The Battle of Stone's River* (Chicago, 1990), 40–61; Connelly, *Autumn of Glory,* 25–29; Daniel, *Cannoneers in Gray,* 55–57.

tillery batteries could enfilade Polk's right on the west bank of Stone's River." Although its importance was "obvious," somehow it had not been occupied by the Confederates. Adams' brigade and the Fifth Company deployed just left or west of Lebanon Pike. To their right, on high ground across the pike lay John K. Jackson's brigade, the extreme right infantry brigade of the army. To Adams' left, although separated by three hundred yards of open field, lay Brig. Gen. William Preston's brigade. To Preston's left was Joseph B. Palmer's brigade, then came Roger Hanson's brigade with its left touching Stone's River. Just across that stream rested James R. Chalmers' brigade, the right brigade of Polk's corps.[17]

Breckinridge on December 29 commanded five brigades and five batteries: Robert Cobb's (four guns), Charles Lumsden's (four guns), Eldridge Wright's (four guns), S. A. Moses' (four guns), and Slocomb's (six guns). In addition, Henry C. Semple's battery of six Napoleons came up, giving the division an artillery battalion under Maj. Rice Graves consisting of twenty-eight guns and howitzers. The Fifth Company itself was armed with two six-pounder rifled guns, two twelve-pounder howitzers, and two James rifled guns.[18]

It was late afternoon, December 29, before the Confederates awoke to the importance of Wayne's Hill. About 4 P.M. Breckinridge ordered three regiments of Hanson's brigade forward to secure it. With them went Cobb's Kentucky battery. By placing these guns on this critical terrain with infantry "directly in rear with a strong line of skirmishers in front," Wayne's Hill in effect became a strong outpost. Although advancing this wing of Hanson's brigade placed these troops in an exposed position well forward and left of Breckinridge's line, it proved fortunate. At 7 P.M. Union skirmishers from Col. Charles Harker's brigade forded Stone's River, brushed back Confederate pickets along the river bank, and pursued them through a corn field to the base of Wayne's Hill. Up the slope they charged and began firing on Cobb's vulnerable cannoneers. When all appeared lost, two of Hanson's supporting regiments appeared, counterattacked, and drove the Yankees off the hillside back to the bank of the river (they would recross the river shortly before midnight). The hill itself was too exposed, and vulnerable to an enemy rush to occupy during the night, however, so Cobb's battery was withdrawn under cover of dark-

17. Cozzens, *No Better Place to Die*, 60–61; Davis, *Breckinridge*, 334–35.
18. R. E. Graves to J. C. Breckinridge, January 25, 1863, John C. Breckinridge Papers, NYHS, New York; *OR*, Vol. XX, Pt. 1, pp. 908–909.

ness. Just before daylight the next morning, the cannoneers returned to the crest where they were posted in positions selected by Major Graves.[19]

Robert Cobb found himself beleaguered. Although he managed to repulse another Federal column that closed to within seven hundred yards of Wayne's Hill, Federal guns, of "much longer range," opened on his position. Soon he was again forced to abandon the hill. Wayne's Hill was too important to be lost, however, so Rice Graves ordered Lieutenant Vaught, who acted as commander of the Fifth Company at Murfreesboro while Slocomb was on leave, to send two rifled pieces in support. Vaught detached a section under Adolphe Chalaron who reported to Graves on the night of December 30 and initially was placed "near the river in front of Hanson's position." Graves also brought up a rifled section of Lumsden's Alabama battery.[20]

Who would command these two sections? Chalaron was eager for the responsibility, but Graves designated one of Breckinridge's staff officers, Lt. A. C. Gibson. The lieutenant placed the two sections "directly in rear of Cobb's guns that were on the crest of the hill, and when the enemy batteries opened on [Cobb] at about 7 in the morning, we found ourselves the recipients of the shots intended for him." Asked by Gibson to inform Graves of the dangerous situation, Chalaron rode off across a field swept by artillery and rifle fire. He found Graves atop Wayne's Hill "moving about erect among the belching guns" of Cobb's battery. Graves told Chalaron that he wanted Gibson to take his battery out of the line of fire and to wait for further orders. After the fire slackened at Cobb's position, Graves sent additional orders. Gibson was to come up on the crest and place his guns on Cobb's right. Gibson, upon receipt of Graves's directive, seems to have crumpled under the responsibility. He asked Chalaron to take command, and Chalaron complied eagerly, having the two sections limber up and bringing the four guns to Wayne's Hill. Lumsden's section went into Cobb's works, but the two guns of the Fifth Company did not. They went into battery unprotected by earthworks, "on the very highest point of the crest, and . . . here they stood and fought most of the day, until their ammunition was completely exhausted."[21]

19. *OR,* Vol. XX, Pt. 1, pp. 825, 836; Cozzens, *No Better Place to Die,* 66–67; R. E. Graves to J. C. Breckinridge, January 25, 1863, Breckinridge Papers, NYHS.

20. Graves to Breckinridge, January 25, 1863, Breckinridge Papers, NYHS. Capt. Charles Lumsden's battery was commanded throughout this action by Lt. Edward Tarrant.

21. Chalaron, "Memories of Rice Graves," 5; *OR,* Vol. XX, Pt. 1, pp. 782, 829.

At one point "when it was all important to check an advancing line of the foe," the Fifth Company's friction primers failed repeatedly. Exasperated, Chalaron ran to Graves. "'See, Major, what d——d stuff is given us to fight with.' Elevating his hand as in rebuke, [Graves] said to me, 'Lieutenant, don't swear.'" At the height of this fighting, Cpl. David W. Smith ("Hawkeye" when comrades wished to compliment, "Cockeye" when they wished to deride) sighted his piece carefully and made one of his best shots of the war. "A remarkable shot," Chalaron declared. With Rice Graves as his spotter, Smith had fired a round of spherical case shot at the color-bearer of a charging line of Federals. The ball exploded in the midst of the color guard and succeeded in "stopping a whole line of battle."[22]

Chalaron and Graves worked together closely during the day. Once a cannon ball whistled by in the space between them. Graves ducked. "It happened that [Chalaron] did not. Rice Graves 'straightened up' and explained to Chalaron, 'Lieutenant, it is stronger than me.'" The modesty of the admission reminded Chalaron of Slocomb, whom he adored. Chalaron noticed Graves's professionalism, his bearing. "How cool his courage! How intense his energy! How alive his senses were to the fray around!"[23]

Chalaron and his section remained here in support of Cobb and Hanson and helped hold Wayne's Hill throughout December 30 and 31 all the while "subjected to a heavy fire from enemy batteries and skirmishers." Graves proudly reported, "line after line of the enemy would come upon the plateau [directly in front of their position] to be driven back a mass of broken and disorganized fugitives. Also as the retreating masses of the enemy, flying before our advancing lines [Hardee's envelopment of the Union right] crowded upon this point, every gun upon the hill was brought to bear upon them with murderous effect."[24]

---

22. 5WA Master Roster, WA Papers, HTT; *OR*, Vol. XX, Pt. 1, p. 804; Chalaron, "Memories of Rice Graves," 6. Rice Graves reported the incident differently: "I cannot omit to mention an admirable feat of skill performed by Corporal Smith. Observing one of the enemy's ammunition wagons crossing the plateau in front of our batteries, I ordered the Corporal to explode it. He did it handsomely at the second shot." Graves to Breckinridge, January 25, 1863, Breckinridge Papers, NYHS.

23. Chalaron, "Memories of Rice Graves," 5–6.

24. *OR*, Vol. XX, Pt. 1, pp. 803, 825, 836; Graves to Breckinridge, January 25, 1863, Breckinridge Papers, NYHS; Thompson, *First Kentucky Brigade*, 183, 194; Evans, *Confederate Military History*, VIII, 182–83.

Chalaron had tried to leave his position on Wayne's Hill on December 31. With his ammunition gone and with both pieces "stripped of implements and splintered by shot and shell," Chalaron asked Graves's permission to ride to the left, where Hardee's corps had been driving the enemy and capturing batteries. There he would secure replacements for his "nearly useless" guns. Graves agreed and sent the young lieutenant off on a long circuit to the left of the army, but on the way, Chalaron ran afoul of General Bragg who denied him permission to swap weapons.[25]

Bragg became increasingly nervous as Tuesday, December 30, wore on. There was pressure against the Wayne's Hill outpost, certainly, but more important, heavy columns of Federals had appeared on the west side of the Nashville pike, stretching in that direction as far as the Franklin road. This convinced the Confederate commander that his left flank was about to be turned. In response, he directed Hardee to move with Cleburne's division to the left, across Stone's River, leap-frogging Polk's corps, and to take command in that sector (the army's left flank). As he was leaving, Hardee cautioned Breckinridge. The latter's division was now separated from the army by the river and his position, "to which Wayne's Hill was the key," must be held "at all hazards." Breckinridge acknowledged Hardee's advice by placing all of Hanson's brigade on and about Wayne's Hill. He also directed Dan Adams to move laterally to Palmer's left, occupying the ground originally held by Hanson's brigade.[26]

Breckinridge believed his situation was precarious on the morning of the 31st. He alone held the right and he did not have sufficient troops to occupy and defend the interval between Stone's River and Lebanon Pike. He and Bragg both remained anxious about an enemy advance down that road into the flank and rear of the Confederates. They also worried about Federals crossing Stone's River or its tributary, Sinking Creek, which bisected Breckinridge's line. Then there was Wayne's Hill. "Exposed to a constant and galling fire both from the enemy's artillery and sharpshooters," it continued to hold firm, although Hanson (and Breckinridge) expected an infantry attack in strength momentarily.[27]

When Hardee launched his assault against Rosecrans' right at 6:00 on the morning of December 31, his brigades from Patrick R. Cleburne's and

25. Chalaron, "Memories of Rice Graves," 6.
26. *OR*, Vol. XX, Pt. 1, p. 782; Thompson, *First Kentucky Brigade*, 183, 194; Cozzens, *No Better Place to Die*, 72; Connelly, *Autumn of Glory*, 51–52.
27. *OR*, Vol. XX, Pt. 1, pp. 826, 829–30; Davis, *Breckinridge*, 335.

John P. McCown's divisions succeeded in surprising the enemy and routing them (capturing the guns that Chalaron coveted). Hardee, although handicapped by insufficient numbers, pressed the attack and managed to roll up the Federal right, ultimately pinning it against the Nashville pike. To win victory, however, to cross the Nashville pike and snap the spine of Rosecrans' army, Hardee needed more men and he pleaded with Bragg for reinforcements. Bragg, however, seemed transfixed by the Union strong point at the Round Forest, opposite the Confederate center, and hammered away at this salient throughout the afternoon with poorly coordinated attacks by Polk's troops.[28]

Bragg also squandered Breckinridge's ten thousand troops on the east side of Stone's River with a series of contradictory orders that kept the Kentuckian and his troops marching and countermarching until early afternoon. At 1 P.M., however, definite orders came from Bragg to Breckinridge: send help to Polk in his attack against the Round Forest. Breckinridge was to come with three brigades, leaving Hanson behind to hold Wayne's Hill.[29]

John K. Jackson's brigade crashed into the Union line near the Round Forest and was tossed back with heavy loss. Dan Adams came up next and attacked up the Nashville and Chattanooga railroad, to the west of the Cowan house, against what he believed to be a four-gun battery. In the process he was pummeled mercilessly by massed artillery fire, not from four guns, but from at least four batteries. "Huge gaps were torn into the Confederate line at every discharge." Adams broke off the attack, his brigade disorganized and confused, having lost "a third of his men," being struck by artillery and musket fire "front, right, and left." Adams himself was wounded and replaced in command by Randall Gibson. Palmer and Preston, arriving somewhat later, also attacked and met similar fates.[30]

While Adolphe Chalaron was having his adventures with Graves and Cobb on Wayne's Hill, Billy Vaught and the remaining two sections of the Fifth Company had been held in reserve until Wednesday morning, December 31. After two false starts on contradictory missions, Vaught crossed Stone's River not long after noon, taking with him Tom Blair and

28. Connelly, *Autumn of Glory,* 57–58; Cozzens, *No Better Place to Die,* 159–60; Hughes, *Hardee,* 142–43.

29. *OR,* Vol. XX, Pt. 1, p. 783; Connelly, *Autumn of Glory,* 59–60; Davis, *Breckinridge,* 336–37.

30. *OR,* Vol. XX, Pt. 1, pp. 783–84, 793–94; Connelly, *Autumn of Glory,* 61; Hughes, *Hardee,* 144; Daniel, *Cannoneers in Gray,* 61–62; Cozzens, *No Better Place to Die,* 163–66.

Abe Leverich as section commanders. Graves also gave him a section of Semple's battery (two Napoleons) under command of 2nd Lt. Joseph Pollard.[31] Dan Adams directed Vaught and his six pieces to remain near the river while the brigade charged. When Adams was repulsed, Vaught, with the assistance of Breckinridge's staff officer, Col. Theodore O'Hara, positioned all of his guns on the hill to the left of the Nashville pike and railroad. When Adams' battered infantry had retreated past his guns, Vaught opened fire on a Federal battery attempting to advance down the pike in pursuit of the Louisiana infantry, hoping to secure a firing position between the Nashville pike and the river. This artillery duel did not last long, the Washington Artillery "silencing their battery and checking their pursuit." While Adams regrouped, using the Fifth Company as cover, Vaught gave splendid, highly accurate fire support to Brig. Gen. Daniel S. Donelson (Cheatham's division, Polk's corps) in another abortive assault against the Round Forest just before dark. One of Vaught's sections, perhaps two, also obtained enfilade fire on the batteries attempting to engage Cobb and Chalaron atop Wayne's Hill. This forced the Federals to cease their attack on Wayne's Hill and withdraw. When night fell, Vaught limbered up and took the battery back across Stone's River to Breckinridge's sector, reporting once again to Major Graves.[32]

Meanwhile, Confederate fire from Wayne's Hill was blind and ineffectual. Although Cobb, Tarrant, Semple, and Chalaron tried to assist Breckinridge's infantry as they plunged into the mindless assaults against the Round Forest, they did little more than harass the determined Federals concealed in the cedar thickets. One round, however, became the most celebrated of all those fired at Murfreesboro. A solid shot, probably from a rifled piece, "flew past Rosecrans" as he rode toward the Round Forest, "sparing the general but decapitating his closest friend in the army, [the Cuban] Julius P. Garesché." The Confederates on Wayne's Hill also inflicted hits in their duels with Federal batteries across the river. Their rifled guns "succeeded several times in forcing the enemy to retire with their batteries behind the shelter of the ridges and heavy timber in our front."

31. Capt. Henry C. Semple's Alabama battery (S. A. M. Woods's brigade, Cleburne's division) had been assigned to support Breckinridge on the east side of Stone's River and thus came under Graves's control.

32. OR, Vol. XX, Pt. 1, pp. 803, 909, 721, 783–84; Graves to Breckinridge, January 25, 1863, Breckinridge Papers, NYHS; Haney Diary, December 31, 1862, AHC; Thompson, *First Kentucky Brigade*, 186.

Capt. Robert Cobb complimented section commanders Chalaron and Tarrant particularly. They "handled their guns with consummate skill and coolness."[33]

On New Year's Day the two armies made minor adjustments in their lines and shook themselves in disbelief as they realized the appalling losses they had suffered the day before. Polk's corps advanced without opposition and occupied the Round Forest which Rosecrans, after defending so ferociously, had decided to vacate. Vaught was sent back to the east side of Stone's River. Perhaps through the prompting of his friend, General Hardee, Vaught was once again assigned a section from another battery to supplement his four guns. Rice Graves (at the command of Breckinridge) positioned Vaught's reenforced Washington Artillery first on Hanson's right, then later in the day, ordered the battery split, three guns remaining beside Hanson while three others limbered up and went into position on the right of Brig. Gen. Joseph B. Palmer and his Tennesseans. Chalaron and his two rifled guns remained at Wayne's Hill under command of Captain Cobb and General Hanson himself until about 3 P.M. on Friday, January 2, 1863.[34]

Sometime in the late morning on Friday, January 2, Billy Vaught and his two sections were ordered forward through a driving sleet, up with Palmer's skirmish line, almost a mile north of Wayne's Hill. They were to replace Capt. Edward P. Byrne's reserve battery, which lacked "proper ammunition," and drove in enemy pickets which had advanced "perhaps 1,000 yards from the river." They were also to engage Yankee sharpshooters occupying some houses off to Palmer's right. It was to be an "artillery attack," and as a precaution Vaught asked Rice Graves that Chalaron be permitted to come along and take command of one section of the Napoleons while he directed the other. So, Adolphe Chalaron left his two rifled guns on Wayne's Hall and galloped over to the battery, which already had limbered up. Major Graves, as always, wanted a piece of the fight, so he came, too, and actually took charge.

As the Fifth Company passed through Roger Hanson's brigade to engage the enemy skirmishers, a regimental commander shouted to his fellow Kentuckian, Rice Graves: "Why are you taking that battery so far in

33. Cozzens, *No Better Place to Die*, 166; *OR*, Vol. XX, Pt. 1, pp. 837, 908.
34. *OR*, Vol. XX, Pt. 1, pp. 803, 826; Haney Diary, January 1, 1863, AHC.

front?" Graves called back, "These boys will go anywhere." When he heard this exchange, Chalaron smiled to himself, reflecting the sentiments of the entire company—"We all felt secure of his [Graves's] admiration after these words."[35]

While their superiors were arguing tactics, Vaught, Chalaron, and Graves kept advancing in their mini-battle against the Yankee picket line. Limber up, go forward, go into battery; limber up again, and advance. Although modest and limited in scale and objective, it was truly an "artillery charge," the kind of fighting the Fifth Company liked. Aggressive assault work. The thin enemy skirmish lines fell back in the direction of the high ground that Breckinridge's division would attempt to seize five hours later.

"Here we remained a couple of hours," reported Vaught, "doing some fancy practice." The Federal infantry counterattacked once, but the Washington Artillery repulsed them handily. Chalaron and Vaught then turned their attention to the houses and by noon had set them afire and scattered the Yankee sharpshooters. Breckinridge sent a courier forward to Graves bringing congratulations and a directive to withdraw the Fifth Company. This was all well and good, of course, to be complimented by the division commander himself. But in the process of stampeding Yankee skirmishers and artillery sharpshooting, Vaught and Chalaron had consumed valuable ammunition that would be needed to support Breckinridge's main attack.[36]

This dash and roar of the Fifth Company had a second and grander purpose—to help disguise preparations being made by Breckinridge's infantry for its assault against a high ridge, a terrain feature Bragg believed pivotal. With these heights in Federal hands, "Polk's line [in the Round Forest] was open to enfilading artillery fire" which "involved consequences not to be entertained." Breckinridge, using his entire division, must take the crest. Breckinridge protested that even if he succeeded in seizing this high ground, he would only be occupying a position lower than, and subject to fire from, higher terrain across Stone's River at McFadden's Ford. Fire from that high ground would command the position he would be attacking, a tactical absurdity. Breckinridge would be

35. Graves to Breckinridge, January 25, 1863, Breckinridge Papers, NYHS; Chalaron, "Memories of Rice Graves," 7.

36. *OR*, XX, Pt. 1, pp. 785, 803, 805; Graves to Breckinridge, January 25, 1863, Breckinridge Papers, NYHS; Haney Diary, January 2, 1863, AHC; Thompson, *First Kentucky Brigade*, 187; Chalaron, "Memories of Rice Graves," 6–7.

leading his men into a trap. But Bragg was adamant. The time of attack was set at 4 P.M.[37]

Meanwhile, Vaught had withdrawn the battery shortly after noon to a great open field "a battle north of east of where the skirmish had taken place." There they were joined by Wright's and Moses' batteries and, in mid-afternoon, by the infantry, which formed in two lines in front of the artillery. The Fifth Company's position now was fifty yards behind the second line of Breckinridge's division (Gibson's and Preston's brigades), ready to support their charge. Gibson's Louisiana brigade, however, had been split by Breckinridge just as the units were deploying, the division commander holding back the 32nd Alabama and the Washington Artillery's old friends, the 14th Louisiana Battalion (Ned Austin's sharpshooters) as a reserve. So Vaught prepared to follow the 13th-20th Louisiana (consolidated), on the right, and the 16th-25th Louisiana (consolidated), on the left. The two regiments now constituted all of Gibson's attacking force. The infantry stepped off precisely at 4 P.M. Hanson's Orphan Brigade, positioned 150 yards in front of Gibson's Louisiana line, led the way. They moved steadily forward and encountered only slight resistance for the first nine hundred yards. When they approached the crest that Breckinridge sought, they were met with one, then two, musket volleys, but they closed ranks, fixed bayonets, and charged with a cheer. It was splendid. Hanson's Kentuckians drove the two lines of bluecoats from the high ground and found themselves looking down at Stone's River. Yet, at the moment of jubilation, came a sudden, terrible fire from the higher ground on other side of the river—massed Yankee batteries.

Gibson's men had reached the river bank by this time. He ordered them to lie down for protection from the bursting shells and whistling canister balls while he rode up the bank to ask Hanson for instructions about where he should position the Louisiana brigade. Before he could speak to Hanson, however, the general was hit. Gibson, now on his own, advanced one regiment to the right and the other down the riverbank. Vaught and the Fifth Company went into battery in the position vacated by Gibson's infantry, "on the bank of the river, in the open field near some houses that had been destroyed by fire." Under cover of this fire from the Washington Artillery's two six-pounders and two twelve-pounders, the

---

37. Graves to Breckinridge, January 25, 1863, Breckinridge Papers, NYHS; *OR,* Vol. XX, Pt. 1, pp. 803, 826, 830; Connelly, *Autumn of Glory,* 62–63; Cozzens, *No Better Place to Die,* 177–79; Davis, *Breckinridge,* 339–41; Daniel, *Cannoneers in Gray,* 64.

16th-25th Louisiana, masked from the concentrated artillery on the high ground, fought their way across Stone's River and secured a lodgment. The Federal skirmishers on the far side of the river fell back.

Vaught's four guns continued firing. The blasts from the two sections took their toll on the Federal infantry and, perhaps more importantly, suppressed the fire of at least one enemy battery. It was at this time, however, at the height of Breckinridge's attack, at the moment when every Confederate piece needed to be in action, that the ammunition of the Fifth Company "gave out." Billy Vaught "sent for a supply and waited there for it."[38] Rather than stand idly by, though, the crew of Piece Five, Cpl. Charles A. Adams commanding, saw an unmanned piece from Moses' Georgia battery, its gunners prone, seeking cover.[39] Adams and his men ran over to the gun, loaded it and opened on the enemy.[40] More guns were needed, however, desperately needed, to answer the Federal pieces on the high ground across the river. Breckinridge and Graves looked about for the reserve artillery (Felix H. Robertson's and Byrne's batteries), but these cannoneers, despite Breckinridge's specific instructions, never came forward in support of the infantry attack.[41]

It was useless. The Federal infantry had regrouped and was heavily reinforced. Then, supported by the deadly, plunging artillery fire (over fifty guns) from the west side of Stone's River, the Yankees counter-attacked. The Confederate line collapsed and Gibson's two Louisiana regiments were in danger of being surrounded. Only the gunners manning Moses' piece could help—the ammunition still had not arrived. Rice

---

38. According to Chalaron, the battery's caissons had been ordered "away from where we had placed them, and they could not be found. . . . More pressing became our calls for ammunition, and messenger after messenger was dispatched in search of our caissons." Chalaron, "Memories of Rice Graves," 8.

39. This battery was commanded by Lt. R. W. Anderson and was part of Georgia's 14th Artillery Battalion. At Murfreesboro it formed the support for Brig. Gen. Gideon Pillow's Tennessee brigade.

40. Vaught specifically commended not only Adams, but Privates Charles G. Johnsen and John A. Walsh for their initiative and "remarkable gallantry." Johnsen and Adams had been commended previously for their meritorious service at Shiloh. Walsh had been wounded there. *OR*, Vol. XX, Pt. 1, p. 804.

41. Two sections of Semple's battery sent over from Wayne's Hill and under command of Robertson were found by Graves and immediately ordered forward. There is also question whether all of Semple's guns came forward. Graves to Breckinridge, January 25, 1863, Breckinridge Papers, NYHS; *OR*, Vol. XX, Pt. 1, pp. 796–99, 803, 825; Cozzens, *No Better Place to Die*, 187–88, 192–95; Connelly, *Autumn of Glory*, 64–66; Davis, *Breckinridge*, 345; James L. McDonough, *Stone's River: Bloody Winter in Tennessee* (Knoxville, 1980), 179; Daniel, *Cannoneers in Gray*, 64–67.

Graves commanded the artillery to stand, however, "feeling that this was one of the cases it being necessary to sacrifice one arm of the service for the safety of another." Graves himself was wounded twice, musket balls striking him in the head and the knee—"his kepi shot off, his horse wounded in the head and neck."[42] Capt. Eldridge Wright, commander of a Tennessee battery, busy firing double charges of canister, was mortally wounded. Their supporting infantry gone, the artillery watched the Federal infantry close in, hungry to seize their guns. "I remained until the last regiment and the last battery were from the field," reported Vaught, "the enemy swarming upon my front and flank and within 50 yards, pouring volley after volley into us." His two sections then limbered up and raced for their lives, back across the open field to the strip of woods from where the attack had begun. There Vaught, his guns intact, went into battery alongside Capt. Robertson's guns.[43] This concentrated Confederate artillery opened fire, halting the Federal pursuit.[44]

That night, as the gunners stood vigilant beside their pieces, it turned cold. Again sleet began to fall. While the troops shivered, back at army headquarters division and corps commanders gathered to meet with Bragg. The Confederate leaders decided to remain on the field.

The Battle of Murfreesboro, as the Confederates would call the fighting of December 31–January 2, cost the Fifth Company the lives of two members. Pvt. John W. Reid, a driver, was killed by a minié ball that struck him in the back of the head on January 2. Pvt. John W. Anthony, a gunner who had enlisted in May at Corinth, was struck in the foot by a cannonball on December 31. His foot was amputated, but Anthony died of shock and loss of blood on January 4. For his "conspicuous con-

42. Graves summoned Chalaron to him and said, "Lieutenant, I appoint you chief of artillery of the division. Save Wright's guns." Chalaron rushed to Wright's battery, but it was too late. Enemy infantry swarmed over the pieces. Chalaron rejoined Vaught and instructed his superior, his acting battery commander, "to plant our battery, that had now replenished its limbers in the skirt of woods from which we had entered the field." Chalaron also attempted to rally the retreating infantry in the same woods. That evening General Breckinridge thanked Chalaron and informed him that Capt. Felix Robertson had been appointed chief of artillery. This singular transformation of a lieutenant to chief of artillery is substantiated in the official report of Vaught. Chalaron, "Memories of Rice Graves," 8–9; *OR*, Vol. XX, Pt. 1, p. 804.

43. At least four Federal units claimed to have captured one to four pieces of the Washington Artillery at Murfreesboro. They did not. The guns to which they referred in their reports undoubtedly were those of Wright's battery. *OR*, Vol. XX, Pt. 1, pp. 588, 593, 595, 615.

44. *OR*, XX, Pt. 1, pp. 587, 761, 796–97, 803; Connelly, *Autumn of Glory*, 62–63; Cozzens, *No Better Place to Die*, 177–79, 195; Daniel, *Cannoneers in Gray*, 66–67.

duct" at Murfreesboro, Anthony was named by his comrades to the Roll of Honor. Pvt. Hudson J. Boatner, an Assumption Parish planter, had two fingers shot off. Two drivers, the Irishman Andy Hopkins and New Yorker Thomas McDonald, were wounded and captured on January 2. Hopkins was seriously injured and hospitalized for so long that he could not be exchanged. McDonald rejoined the battery that spring. In typical Fifth Company fashion, official chroniclers noted that two horses had been killed and two disabled. The company's losses at Murfreesboro had been light, though, at least when compared with Shiloh.[45]

The Federals, including a brigade commander (Col. James P. Fyffe) as well as the commanders of the 11th Kentucky and 51st Ohio, mistakenly believed they had inflicted even more damage on the battery. They proudly reported that they had overrun the company, "capturing four pieces of the celebrated Washington Artillery."[46]

The battery performed well at Murfreesboro under Vaught's leadership. Breckinridge, Adams, and Gibson thought so, as did Robert Cobb, who went out of his way to commend Chalaron. Vaught mentioned that Maj. Rice Graves, when he had been wounded, appointed Chalaron "upon the field" to act as "temporary chief of artillery."[47] Vaught had very good days on December 31 and on January 2, but it seems only fair to fault him for the battery running out of ammunition during Breckinridge's charge. As battery commander, he was responsible for replenishing the limbers of the four pieces before advancing in support of Gibson's infantry. Perhaps it was not available, or perhaps there was not time. But Vaught was responsible.

On the morning of January 3, 1863, only a few hours after their council of war, the senior officers held another meeting at Bragg's headquarters. Intelligence reports revealed the true strength of the enemy they faced across Stone's River. The army must abandon Murfreesboro, all agreed. They would withdraw that night.[48] The Army of Tennessee retreated south across Duck River and took up a broad defensive line deep in

45. CHS to Maj. Victor von Shelihu, March 17, 1862, WIH, CSR, RG 109, NA; New Orleans *Daily Picayune*, January 18, 1863; 5WA Muster Roll, March–April, 1863, RG 109, NA; *OR*, Vol. XX, Pt. 1, p. 804.

46. Actually three guns belonging to Semple's and Wright's batteries had been lost. *OR*, Vol. XX, Pt. 1, pp. 593, 599, 615, 909, 785.

47. *OR*, Vol. XX, Pt. 1, p. 804.

48. Stanley F. Horn, *The Army of Tennessee: A Military History* (Indianapolis, 1940), 210; Connelly, *Autumn of Glory*, 67–68.

Middle Tennessee with concentration points at Shelbyville (Polk) and Tullahoma (Hardee).

The Fifth Company, once again under the direct command of Cuthbert Slocomb, went into winter quarters at Allisonia, about seven miles southeast of Tullahoma. The morning report of January 8, 1863, showed five officers present for duty and 132 men, with an aggregate (present and absent) of 161 (the batteries in Hardee's corps averaged 96 men present for duty).[49] The men first built stables for the horses at Allisonia; then they took wagon tarpaulins and made tents for themselves. "It was in this camp that we first began to understand how to make our-selves comfortable by building fire-places and chimneys to our tents," wrote Pvt. Edwin Mussina. When the temperature dropped that January and February, the Louisianans would stay in their beds, "not coming from under their blankets unless absolutely compelled." It was cold or it was raining—every day it seemed. So the men spent their time sleeping and reading. Other amusements consisted of "bumping some of the boys against trees, tossing them up in blankets." Sometimes they would smoke out a mess. Even more fun was to load another mess's firewood with powder. Then there would come those awful days when Gibson's brigade, sometimes the entire division, would be called out to witness an execution. It is "said to be a good preventative for the home-sick," observed Private Mussina bitterly.[50]

Discipline was vital, especially now. Men realized this, but subordinating precious individualism came at a high price for most. Slocomb, acknowledged without exception as a fine disciplinarian yet a considerate officer, handled a delicate insubordination matter in a manner that might have been considered unusual in other units. The popular and capable Virginian Sgt. Thomas C. Allen, crew chief of Piece Four, was tried by "company court-martial." With battery officer Chalaron and trial lawyer Pvt. Anthony Sambola pleading his case as counsels for the defense, the charge (unspecified) "was not proven," but Slocomb nevertheless believed it in the interest of good discipline to have Allen "reduced to the ranks for 60 days." Once this period had expired, however, Slocomb immediately reappointed Allen sergeant.[51]

49. Daniel, *Cannoneers in Gray,* 71.

50. *OR,* Vol. XX, Pt. 1, pp. 799, 803; 5WA Muster Rolls, January–April, 1863, WA Papers, HTT; Edwin Mussina Diary, January 7, 1863, January–March, 1863, Robert W. Woodruff Library, Emory University, Atlanta; Richardson, "War as I Saw It," 235–36; Bromfield L. Ridley, *Battles and Sketches of the Army of Tennessee* (Mexico, Mo., 1906), 285–86.

51. Mussina Diary, n.d., 1863, Emory.

The stay at Allisonia was not pleasant. Rations were short. "The Bill of Fare of all the Army could be written in two words Bacon and Meal. Corn Bread and bacon for breakfast. Bacon and Corn Bread for dinner and as for supper a very small cup of mush and corn coffee without sweetening." Rice Graves and Cuthbert Slocomb got along famously, and Graves encouraged the latter in his insistence on drill. "Gun crews rehearsed at their pieces two and a half hours daily. Drivers practiced harnessing and unharnessing an hour and a half and were then put through three hours of battery drill." Officers had to undergo daily classes as well. This was beneficial for all, but especially for Tom Blair and Abe Leverich, who had been in their roles less than six months.[52]

Drill was long. Major Graves "was a most unmerciful drill-master," complained Mussina, "and would keep us continually on the go for two or three hours at a time." It paid off, nevertheless. By late spring an entry in the Fifth Company order book read: "By recent tests our Battery can be gotten ready to move to any point in 15 minutes. Yesterday Batt. hitched up in 14 min; piece #6 hitched up in 4 min. Today batt. hitched up in 9 min (piece #6 in 7 min.) Allowing from 5–6 minutes for storing of personal effects of cannoneers [took] 6 min; hitching up 9 min [for a total of] 15 min."[53]

Other than increased proficiency and discipline, intensive training was important because armament was changing. The six-pounder was, at last, being phased out. Replacing it, indeed becoming the standard artillery piece of the Army of Tennessee and the Fifth Company, was the twelve-pounder Napoleon, a bronze smoothbore gun. Historian Larry J. Daniel describes the effectiveness of the new weapon. "Designed as a hybrid weapon, it had a range of a gun (1,680 yards for solid shot) and could also fire the explosive shell or spherical case shot of the howitzer. At distances of 300 yards or less, it could spew out canister balls like a giant, sawed-off shotgun. Also, the reliability of smoothbore ammunition stood in stark contrast to that of the unsure rifle projectiles." The transition from six-pounders to Napoleons proceeded with excruciating slowness, however. Priority, as always, went to the Army of Northern Virginia. They, for instance, "received forty-nine new light 12-pounders, the Army

52. Mussina Diary, March 31, 1863, Emory; Daniel, *Cannoneers in Gray,* 56; *OR,* Vol. XX, Pt. 2, pp. 399–400; Chalaron, "Memories of Rice Graves," 9.

53. Mussina Diary, April 7, 1863, Emory; 5WA Order Book, quoting Mussina's diary, WA Papers, HTT.

of Tennessee, only five!" Rosecrans' army meanwhile received new weapons, particularly the deadly twelve-pounders with "lightning speed." [54]

For greater uniformity, batteries were reduced to four guns (even Henry Semple's five-gun Alabama battery and Cobb's six-gun Kentucky battery). The only exceptions in the Army of Tennessee were Felix H. Robertson's battery in Polk's corps and Slocomb's battery in Hardee's corps, which were allowed to retain their six-gun configurations. Each brigade continued to be assigned one four-gun battery. [55] "When on outpost duty," the battery "will be exclusively under the control of the brigadier general to whose command it is attached, except all returns will be made through the division chiefs of artillery." The chief of artillery for Breckinridge's division was the able Graves, respected and popular with the company. The corps chief was the West Pointer and former ordnance officer Maj. Llewellyn G. Hoxton, an unspectacular but dependable officer. Lt. Col. James H. Hallonquist, Bragg's protégé and a South Carolinian "preoccupied with housekeeping details," was chief of artillery for the Army of Tennessee. [56]

Almost any perceptive artilleryman could see that the employment of artillery was undergoing transition. The rush to Napoleons signaled this. Furthermore, the one battery–one brigade arrangement was outdated. Bragg himself, by training and experience an artillery officer, still seemed unable to appreciate the change. "His old army mentality prevented him from fully grasping the concept of centralized control, the tactical massing of guns, and the changing supportive role of the artillery. His approaches were tried and tested, but by the time of the Civil War they were obsolete." [57]

The company had to adopt new battle tactics the last day of March, 1863. It had turned cold, very cold, and the ground was covered with snow. Someone instigated a fight between friends, and at 8:30 that morning a battle began between Slocomb's battery and Ned Austin's battalion of sharpshooters. The "enemy" (Austin's men), "after making two or three feints on our right and left—charged in a fine style our centre, and it was not until after a very desperate and hard fought struggle that we succeeded

54. Daniel, *Cannoneers in Gray,* 75–77.

55. *OR,* Vol. XX, Pt. 2, p. 499; "Artillery Strength, February 1 and March 1, 1863, and Statement of Guns on Hand, April 30, 1863," Braxton Bragg Papers, Western Reserve Historical Society, Cleveland.

56. *OR,* Vol. XXIII, Pt. 2, p. 831; Daniel, *Cannoneers in Gray,* 78–81.

57. Daniel, *Cannoneers in Gray,* 85.

in driving them back and not until we had rallied every man in our Camp black and white." The battery, however, had not the manpower "to follow up our success." So they negotiated and succeeded in obtaining a peace convention by which all prisoners were returned as well as all captured property. The cannoneers and their reliable sharpshooter friends then formed an alliance and "assumed the offensive against a Georgia regiment." They crept up, concealed themselves behind logs and stumps, and attacked. The Georgians, however, fought with determination, taking their stand behind a creek. The "air was filled with snowballs and pieces of Ice." Finally the Louisianans, just as on January 2 at Murfreesboro, made a lodgment across the creek—only this time they had the strength to exploit their advantage. They charged the enemy camp, "winning a complete victory." Among their trophies of war were almost a dozen caps, one frying pan, four or five pones of cornbread and the Georgians' flag. The victory proved costly, however. Slocomb lost two front teeth and Chalaron received a black eye. Among the privates appeared five bloody noses and black eyes.[58]

Fortunately the late snow was an aberration, and April arrived with all its promise. On the fifth the battery moved north to Wartrace, Tennessee, and camped about two miles from town. The weather was "pleasant and warm, the woods filled with the most beautiful flowers."[59] Soon after their arrival, on April 7, Hardee's corps held a "grand sham fight," to celebrate the anniversary of Shiloh. As usual Hardee knew how to make these occasions festive spectacles and delight participants and observers alike. Carriages full of young women from the nearby towns and "the fairest from the surrounding country" appeared to watch and applaud.[60] Thus Slocomb's battery passed a leisurely month near Wartrace. Private Mussina recorded in his diary that the men "haven't much else to do but lay back under some large tree and drink sweet and butter milk to our heart's content. This is a splendid foraging country: Turkeys, Chickens, eggs, honey, butter Milk and *Whiskey*."[61]

58. Mussina Diary, March 31, 1863, Emory; Larry J. Daniel, *Soldiering in the Army of Tennessee* (Chapel Hill, 1991), 94.

59. 5WA Company Muster Roll, March and April, 1863, WA Papers, HTT; Mussina Diary, April 24, 1863, Emory; Diary, Bell I. Wiley Papers, Robert W. Woodruff Library, Emory University, Atlanta.

60. Corps level reviews were held March 19 and 23, as well as drill contests between regiments chosen from Breckinridge's and Cleburne's divisions. Mussina Diary, April 7, 1863, Emory; Haney Diary, March 19, 23, 1863, AHC.

61. Mussina Diary, May 5, 1863, Emory.

Sudden as a thunderbolt, however, came orders ruining this idyllic respite. The Washington Artillery was to proceed on May 20 and report to Gen. Bushrod Johnson at Liberty Gap. Aroused at 2 A.M. that morning, they marched some twenty-five miles "for the purpose of cutting off some foraging parties of Yanks but the 'birds had flown.'" They advanced northeast through the range of hills near Bell Buckle, on north to Ready-ville, about twenty miles east of Murfreesboro. Then they turned about and retraced their path to Hoover's Gap, a march of fifty miles. Between that point and Wartrace the company bivouacked and the next morning began building stables for the horses. It proved "very hard work" because the timber was cut "some distance off and was carried across a creek and up a steep hill on the shoulders of the men." Then they had to "cut down large trees, saw them up in logs and split them into clapboards to cover the stables." [62]

What made the labor all the more frustrating was the knowledge that Adams' brigade and Breckinridge's division were loading aboard trains for Mississippi. The Fifth Company expected to go themselves, so they knew well that these elaborate stables would prove ones "from which we were to derive but little benefit." [63] According to Chalaron, it may not have been meant for them to make the Mississippi trip, although they considered themselves organic to Adams' brigade. Hardee wanted them to remain; Bragg did also. Slocomb had to negotiate hard for their release. He and Chalaron rode all night to see the commanding general and se-cured their transfer only at the sacrifice of their guns and of their "horses of which we were very proud." [64]

Breckinridge had received orders on May 23 to be ready to move im-mediately. Federals under Ulysses S. Grant had invested Vicksburg and the fortress as well. John C. Pemberton's army would be lost unless a relief column could smash through. Joseph E. Johnston attempted to or-ganize such a force, writing Pemberton on May 19, "I am trying to gather a force which may attempt to relieve you. Hold out." Thus Breckinridge

62. Mussina Diary, May 23, 1863, Emory; Chalaron, 5WA Itinerary, Chalaron Papers, HTT; Journal of unidentified member of Fifth Company, WA Papers, HTT; Haney Diary, May 25, 26, 1863, AHC.

63. Mussina Diary, May 23, 1863, Emory.

64. His vision dimmed by forty years and by anti-Bragg bias, Chalaron would recall for his surviving comrades: "What pang they felt at being left behind, at being separated from *our* Brigade. What abandonment they made of guns, equipments and splendid well drilled horses, to obtain from Genl. Bragg the privilege of being sent to fight the foe nearer their home." J. A. Chalaron, Speech upon Acceptance of Piano for Memorial Hall, May 31, 1902, Chalaron Papers, HTT.

with the brigades of Adams, Benjamin H. Helm (Hanson's Orphan Brigade), and Preston (commanded by Brig. Gen. Marcellus A. Stovall) set out for Jackson, Mississippi, aboard three trains.[65]

Most welcome orders came for the Fifth Company during the night of May 27. They were to report to the depot at Wartrace at 6 A.M. They arrived as directed, and at 10 A.M. loaded themselves and the precious little equipment Bragg had left them aboard a train bound for Chattanooga, arriving there about 8 P.M.[66] The next morning they rode through Atlanta, arriving at West Point, Georgia, at 3 A.M. on the thirtieth. From there they continued on to Montgomery, Alabama, where they boarded the steamer *Le Grand* which took them down the Alabama River to Mobile.

The train ride to Montgomery had been a replay of the delightful journey the previous September. Citizens greeted them warmly and fed them at every stop. The men got off the cars whenever they could, the breaks giving "us an opportunity of replenishing our little stock of odds & ends but which are as indispensable even to the comfort of a soldier. Then getting in or rather in the neighborhood of civilized society we have all been replenishing our wardrobe to a considerable extent." Eventually, to their great joy, they arrived in Mobile on June 1. As they sought to take "full advantage of all the comforts & pleasures," Captain Slocomb beckoned them to the train. It was off to war again.[67]

---

65. Horn, *Army of Tennessee,* 217; Connelly, *Autumn of Glory,* 90; Davis, *Breckinridge,* 364–65.

66. In fairness it should be mentioned that Breckinridge had promised the Fifth Company that if they could break loose from the Army of Tennessee and accompany his division, they would be reoutfitted in fine style. Chalaron, "Memories of Rice Graves," 10.

67. Journal of unidentified member of Fifth Company, WA Papers, HTT; Haney Diary, May 29, 30, 31, June 1, 1863, AHC.

Alexander Pierre Allain
Courtesy Howard-Tilton Memorial Library, Tulane University

Thomas C. Allen
From Even More Confederate Faces *(Orange, Va., 1983),*
courtesy William Turner, LaPlata, Md.

Felix Arroyo
Courtesy Howard-Tilton Memorial Library, Tulane University

Charles William Fox
Courtesy Howard-Tilton Memorial Library, Tulane University

James Fortescue Giffen
Courtesy Howard-Tilton Memorial Library, Tulane University

Lawrence Macready
Courtesy Howard-Tilton Memorial Library, Tulane University

John Miller
Courtesy Howard-Tilton Memorial Library, Tulane University

Philip Daingerfield Stephenson
Courtesy Louisiana and Lower Mississippi Valley Collections, LSU Libraries

William F. Tutt
From Even More Confederate Faces *(Orange, Va., 1983),*
courtesy William Turner, LaPlata, Md.

Thomas E. Williams
Courtesy Howard-Tilton Memorial Library, Tulane University

6

YOU SHAN'T HAVE ANY OF MY PEANUTS

PASSING THROUGH Mobile, "the neighborhood of civilized society," produced a happy dividend—the enlistment of about forty men. Most were former New Orleans residents who had been expelled from the city "for disloyalty" and were "refuging" in Mobile.[1] They made eager recruits.[2] Now some two-hundred strong, rich with privates and drivers, the Fifth Company moved on by rail to Jackson, Mississippi. They decided to announce their arrival dramatically. So on June 3, they held a parade in a most strategic location—the grove of Mrs. Oakly,[3] a woman of sixty-three years, "who will

1. The sharp-eyed English observer Lt. Col. James A. L. Fremantle carefully noted the presence and condition of these New Orleans refugees in Mobile at almost the exact time the Fifth Company passed through. James A. L. Fremantle, *Fremantle Diary,* ed. Walter Lord (Boston, 1954), 105.

2. This was the second needed infusion of personnel, the first having come at Corinth and Tupelo a year earlier. Most of these Mobile recruits would prove good soldiers and serve throughout the war. Dates of their enlistments may be found in the 5WA roster (Appendix A). See also Account Book, Louisiana Relief Association of Mobile, Chicago.

3. Mrs. S. S. Oakly (fifty-nine), wife of Englishman Thomas Oakly (fifty-two), with twenty-one-year-old daughter, "F," as shown in 1860, U.S. Census, Hinds County, Miss., pp. 37–38. The Oakly place and school were located just "back of the Penitentiary." New Orleans *States,* July 1, 1894.

ever be remembered by the 5th Co. for her kindness & attention to us." It so happened that Mrs. Oakly operated a "young ladies institute," and it so happened that she afterward invited Captain Slocomb to use her grove as the encampment for the young gentlemen of his command.[4]

June 3 also proved of significance in that the Washington Artillery was issued four new twelve-pounder Napoleons and two James Rifles to replace their 6-pounders and howitzers. This vastly improved the firepower of the battery. Moreover, true to their word, Breckinridge and Graves presented the Washington Artillery with fine harness and "fresh and splendid horses, impressed from the rich planters."[5]

Thus the Fifth Company would pass a month under the most pleasant circumstances. They, and indeed Breckinridge's entire division, were virtually inactive during June, 1863, engaged passively in "picketing and fortifying" activities, despite the plight of Pemberton and his beleaguered Confederates only a two-day march away at Vicksburg. Army commander Gen. Joseph E. Johnston, meanwhile, waited at Jackson with excruciating patience. He had to gather as many troops as possible, he thought, and obtain "field transport and other supplies" before making an advance against the enemy. Capt. Cuthbert Slocomb did make positive use of the time, nonetheless, securing new issues of clothing, wagons, "camp equipage, artificers tools, etc.," and by July 1, it appears from inspection reports, the company had replenished its needs and become better equipped than it had been for over a year.[6] While Slocomb procured necessities of war, the men relaxed, enjoying themselves thoroughly. A private recorded that it was "the first time that our battery had ever been stationed near a City of any size. . . . The boys have seemed to forget that they are soldiers—and are spending their time morning & evening with some of Jackson's fair belles."[7]

---

4. Journal of unidentified member of Fifth Company, May 28–June 30, 1863, WA Papers, HTT; New Orleans *States,* July 1, 1894.

5. Haney Diary, June 3, 1863, AHC. According to Chalaron, Breckinridge and Graves had promised Slocomb that "they would see that we were fully fitted out upon reaching Jackson." They made good on their promise with "brand new" Napoleons and rifles. Chalaron, "Memories of Rice Graves," 10.

6. *OR,* Vol. XXIV, Pt. 1, pp. 244–45; Chalaron, 5WA Itinerary, Chalaron Papers, HTT; 5WA Muster Roll, May–June, 1863, WA Papers, HTT; Journal of unidentified member of Fifth Company, June 30–July 5, 1863, WA Papers, HTT; Thompson, *First Kentucky Brigade,* 206; CHS Report, July 1, 1863, Inspection Records and Related Reports Received, Adjutant General's Office, RG 109, NA.

7. Journal of unidentified member of Fifth Company, June 30–July 5, 1863, WA Papers, HTT.

The close proximity of the Yankees' huge army seemed to make no difference. There were alarms and rumors of all sorts, inevitably, but it was not until June 30 that the company at last received "positive orders." They would march the next morning to the relief of Vicksburg. This presented the company with a terrible "clashing of duty." They had been working and planning for days for a "Grand Fete . . . in appreciation of the many kindnesses & favors of the ladies of Jackson." Already they had foraged the "surrounding country" gathering delectables, so they rushed ahead with their party plans, "determined to have their fun while they can."

At some of our friends houses we are having supper prepared for our guests. [Mrs. Oakly's lawn suits our purposes] most admirably, [being] as smooth as a floor. . . . We have taken our tarpaulins & having fastened them securely to the ground, it makes a most excellent place for those who intend doing it [dancing] on the light fantastic toe. Our pieces or guns having been thoroughly cleaned & burnished up & also decorated with miniature flags, wreaths, ribbons & flowers [and] are posted at one side of the lawn in the shape of a Crescent. . . . [Between their bronze guns were] stacks of muskets & stands of regimental flags; [on the opposite side—benches and tables]. In front has been erected a Stand (for the brass band of the 13th-20th Louisiana Infantry) which has been handsomely decorated. The grounds have been most beautifully arranged & brilliantly *illuminated,* colored transparencies hanging from the trees & rows of them strung across the dancing ground. [Early in the afternoon of the 30th] our fair guests began to arrive & as carriage after carriage rolled up to the gate with its fair load it reminded one of similar occasions in happier days in our own city.[8]

The Grand Fete, of course, "passed off delightfully."[9] No group of soldiers could entertain like the Fifth Company.

On the other hand, no one slept much that night. And early the next morning when the battery marched out of Mrs. Oakly's grove en route for Clinton, Mississippi, some ten miles west toward Vicksburg, the procession moved wearily. "After a long march, over a dusty road, with little or no water & unprotected from a hot July sun, we arrived at that place [Clinton] at about 9 o'clock & bivouacked for the night near a muddy creek, completely worn out." The following day, July 2, they moved on to Bolton, then on the third reached the battlefield of "Champion Hills."

8. Daily journal of unidentified member of 5th Company, June 30–July 5, 1863, WA Papers, HTT; see also New Orleans *States,* July 1, 1894.
9. Haney Diary, June 29, 30, 1863, AHC.

Johnston ordered reconnaissances in force against the Federal lines, checking particularly the area north of the railroad, and found the enemy in heavy strength everywhere. Johnston's grand strategy, at least as it appeared to privates in the company, seemed pointless. "The 4th and 5th [of July] was occupied in marching around the country, with seemingly no object in view but to keep moving." [10]

They never reached Vicksburg; never breached the enemy lines. On the morning of the sixth, "dispensing with the usual bugle calls," the Fifth Company found themselves marching east to Jackson. So back they went, back the way they had come. Rumors raced up and down the plodding column: the enemy was across the Big Black in force and a fight might come any hour. Vicksburg had surrendered. "But that is not believed."

The battery learned the awful truth that night—Vicksburg had fallen. "We had seen some of the paroled prisoners." By midnight they resumed their dusty tramp, arriving at Clinton at 6 A.M. on the seventh. On they went that awful Tuesday, "a March of 24 miles on one of the warmest days I ever remember. . . . So great was the suffering of the Army that hundreds sank on the road side completely exhausted & every few hundred yards we would come across some poor fellow—lying dead on the road from sun-stroke." Time and time again the company had to stop, swing about, and go into battery, setting itself to protect the rear of the column. Then would come the shout to move on. They would limber up and start out again. Finally they arrived back in the city "in the midst of a heavy rain & storm about 10 o'clock" that night. [11]

Johnston had used this first week in July, 1863, probing for a soft spot in the Union line, trying to find an opening, a way to break through to Pemberton with his four infantry divisions. But Johnston was too weak and the enemy seemed to anticipate every move, blocking him effectively with seven infantry divisions on a line extending from Big Black Bridge to Snyder's Bluff.

After the fall of Vicksburg on July 4, Sherman, with Grant's blessing, determined to maintain the initiative. [12] He immediately set out with 46,000 men to snap the railroad north of Jackson, his seven divisions

10. Journal of unidentified member of Fifth Company, July 2, 4, 5, 1863, WA Papers, HTT; Haney Diary, July 1, 1863, AHC; *OR*, Vol. XXIV, Pt. 1, p. 244.

11. Journal of unidentified member of Fifth Company, July 1–10, 1863, WA Papers, HTT; New Orleans *States*, July 1, 1894.

12. The name of the Washington Artillery is inscribed on the Louisiana monument in the Vicksburg National Military Park, although the battery never reached the siege lines.

now reinforced by six additional divisions from the XII and XV Corps. Johnston had fallen back before this overwhelming force and on July 8 occupied fortified positions on the western edge of Jackson. The Fifth Company originally was posted "opposite the Lynch house," then moved into a position straddling the New Orleans and Jackson Railroad on the morning of the ninth.[13]

Breckinridge's division, about 3,600 strong, held the southern portion of Johnston's line, immediately left of the division of Maj. Gen. Samuel G. French. Breckinridge's sector extended from the New Orleans and Jackson Railroad east to the banks of the Pearl River, a relatively short line, but one of critical importance. Close behind Breckinridge's left flank lay the pontoon bridges across the Pearl (the escape route of Johnston's army) and the tracks of the Southern Railroad of Mississippi. Breckinridge's veteran division was Johnston's most reliable, consisting of the infantry brigades of Adams, Helm, and Stovall, Austin's battalion of Louisiana sharpshooters, and the batteries of Capt. John W. Mebane, Cobb, and Slocomb.[14]

Slocomb's battery (and Adams' Louisiana brigade) held the "extreme right of Breckinridge's line, planted across the railroad, its four 12-pounder Napoleons to the right [of the railroad], facing south between the railroad and a dirt road and its two rifled guns to the left of the railroad." Cobb's guns (four Napoleons) and Stovall's Florida brigade came next, then Mebane's Tennessee battery and Helm's Orphan Brigade. It was an excellent defensive position, remembered Chalaron, giving "a full view of any approaching foe, and offered them little or no protection against our fire."[15]

Sherman knew Johnston's lines were strong, probably too strong to gamble an assault. But that was not his style anyway, nor was it the most

13. See Edwin C. Bearss, *The Siege of Jackson, July 10–17, 1863* (Baltimore, 1981), 55–67; *OR,* Vol. XXIV, Pt. 3, p. 462; Craig L. Symonds, *Joseph E. Johnston: A Civil War Biography* (New York, 1992), 211–16; New Orleans *Times-Democrat,* June 17, 1884; CHS to Capt. Emile P. Guillet, July 19, 1863, 5WA Order Book, WA Papers, HTT; Casey, *Outline of Civil War Campaigns,* 63.

14. Mebane's battery was the battery of Eldridge E. Wright who had been killed at Murfreesboro. Mebane took command at Wright's death and continued until he himself was killed June 18, 1864, just after the fighting at Pine Mountain. The battery at that time would become known as J. W. Phillips' battery. It retained that name and remained in Cobb's artillery battalion cooperating with the Fifth Company until the end of the war. This west Tennessee battery was also known as the "Johnston Light Artillery" and J. Wesley Eldridge's battery.

15. New Orleans *Times-Democrat,* June 17, 1884.

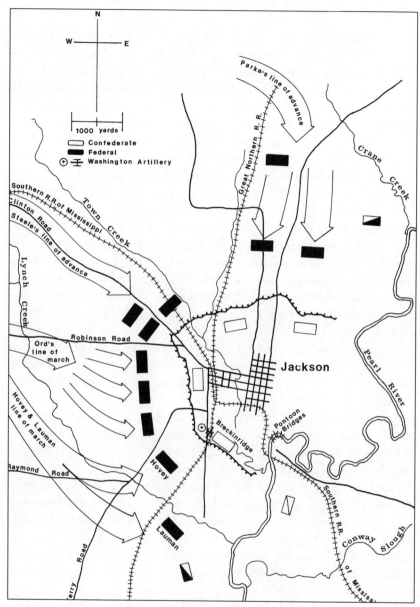

Jackson, Mississippi, July 11–12, 1863
Map by Blake A. Magner

feasible manner of seizing the Mississippi capital. Sherman knew Johnston had problems with his line of communications, and he also knew he could bring up sufficient artillery to reduce the city to a shell not worth defending. So, in that deliberate manner of his, Sherman set about establishing lines some 1,500 yards from Confederate strong points, "with skirmishers close up, and their supports within 500 yards," thus maintaining great pressure with minimum risk. Protecting the right flank of Sherman's army as it deployed was the division of Brig. Gen. Jacob Lauman, a fighter and a veteran of Belmont, Donelson, and Shiloh.[16]

By July 12 Sherman had sufficient guns and ammunition to begin the bombardment of Jackson, and early that morning his batteries opened up, quickly firing some three thousand rounds into the city. Following this terrible barrage, Lauman swung his division out to the right, prolonging the Union line toward the Pearl River. He acted under orders from corps commander Edward O. C. Ord. "If it is necessary to form a line and to drive the force in front, do so," directed Ord, "so as to keep your connection with General [Alvin P.] Hovey, who is the connection with the main corps."[17]

Lauman dutifully moved his division east of the railroad, Col. Isaac C. Pugh's brigade in advance, and Col. George E. Bryant's in reserve. A mile from Breckinridge's line, Lauman threw out a heavy line of skirmishers with Pugh's troops in close support. After wading across Lynch's Creek, Pugh halted and brought up the six guns of the 5th Ohio Light Artillery which proceeded to pound the Confederate lines. Two rebel guns responded with accurate fire, but Pugh felt confident enough to continue his advance. He passed through woods and presently found himself on the edge of a broad cornfield. There Pugh halted his brigade. He had come abreast of Hovey's division and made a connection, fulfilling the essential part of his mission. Besides, the wide cornfield, with the hint of rebel works in the distance, looked like a trap, so Pugh called for his superior, Lauman. The situation presented no problem for Lauman, however. Without further reconnaissance, the impetuous Lauman ordered Pugh to press forward once again.[18]

Pugh advanced across the cornfield, driving rebel skirmishers before him. It all seemed so easy. The Yankee line of battle quickened its step.

16. Bearss, *Siege of Jackson*, 73, 75, 80.
17. *OR*, Vol. XXIV, Pt. 3, p. 503; Bearss, *Siege of Jackson*, 84–85.
18. *OR*, Vol. XXIV, Pt. 2, pp. 575, 603–607; Bearss, *Siege of Jackson*, 85.

Then, about three hundred yards from the works, the brigade encountered a makeshift abatis of "slashed brush and stumps." It was at this point, almost within reach of the rebel line, that Pugh's assault slowed and regimental formations began to fragment. Then the Confederates opened fire.[19]

The gun emplacements of the Fifth Company had been built under protest. It was not manly, crouching behind embankments, barricades. It was not their way. The company "grumbled exceedingly . . . and asked to be allowed to fight without protection, as they had done on so many fields before. But nothing availed." So the battery dug—"their first initiation handling picks and shovels." Most, according to Chalaron, "had never handled anything heavier than a pen." Their first "works," as can be imagined, "were of the flimsiest and poorest nature. The ditch was on the outside, and shrubs and brush were cut and thrown up against the outer slope, hiding such low works very effectively." Indeed, that whole right section of Breckinridge's line was largely concealed. Yet it was but "a mere show of entrenchments." Johnston himself considered them "but slight obstacle to a vigorous assault."[20]

To the right of Fifth Company the Confederate works ran about 150 yards then turned sharply to the right, thus exposing the flank of battery. On July 10, the Federals had fired down this line greatly "annoying" the company, so Slocomb had "erected a strong traverse of cotton bales" on that flank, placing additional bales (also for traverses) between the pieces.[21] "Thus we formed quite a comfortable redoubt for ourselves," protected, if not secure from the "severe crossfire" of the Federals. To the left of Slocomb's battery were the 32nd Alabama and the 16th-25th Louisiana; to the company's right, the 13th-20th Louisiana and the 19th Louisiana.[22]

On Saturday, July 11, they observed the Federals crossing the railroad some 1,700 yards out. Billy Vaught was sent some five hundred yards

19. Bearss, *Siege of Jackson,* 85–86.

20. New Orleans *Times-Democrat,* June 17, 1884; New Orleans *States,* July 1, 1894; *OR,* Vol. XXIV, Pt. 1, p. 244.

21. A traverse was a parapet or wall, usually of earth, placed crosswise and designed to stop enfilading fire.

22. New Orleans *Times-Democrat,* June 17, 1884; Journal of unidentified member of Fifth Company, July 9, 1863, WA Papers, HTT; New Orleans *States,* July 1, 1894.

beyond the works with one rifled piece to annoy their advance. Enemy artillery responded and, after firing nine rounds, Vaught withdrew, but not before David "Hawkeye" Smith had made another of his spectacular shots. The second round "struck one of their guns on the muzzle, ruining it entirely."[23] Both of Slocomb's rifled pieces also engaged Federal artillery on Bailey Hill, some 1,700 yards out. "I had some sharp practice then," wrote Vaught, and "made a great many fine shots," at least one striking the Federal parapet.[24]

Nevertheless, Pugh's infantry continued to advance. "Austin and his sharpshooters," serving as the skirmish line, screening at least Adams' sector of the line, "had their hands full," and had to be reinforced by details from each regiment. Pioneers from the 16th-25th Louisiana had the special assignment of draining a pond (a large cistern) of "good water" about halfway between the two armies "to prevent the enemy from using it." On July 11 and early on the next day, it appeared that the Federals' objective, at least their intermediate objective, was this water supply.

Pressure against the skirmish line was constant, but not severe. Ned Austin's men were outstanding in this type of work, enabling the pioneers to clear fields of fire and to erect a makeshift abatis. There was a problem, however. To the right front of Slocomb's battery was "a splendid mansion . . . which had been deserted by the family, leaving most of the household effects behind."[25] Breckinridge ordered the home occupied and protected until such time as his skirmishers must retire past it. Then General Adams was to have it burned. "Our position would be untenable [from enemy sharpshooters] if the enemy made a lodgment there." Knowing their home was in jeopardy, the Cooper family who owned it requested that Adams' men attempt to save as many possessions as possible. Col. R. H. Lindsay, commander of the 16th-25th Louisiana, and all men (including Austin's sharpshooters) functioning as Dan Adams' skirmishers on July 11–12

23. WCDV to Mary Vaught, July 25, 1863, Vaught Letters, HNOC.

24. The accuracy of the Washington Artillery long-range fire was acknowledged by the enemy. WCDV to Mary Vaught, July 25, 1863, Vaught Letters, HNOC; Bearss, *Siege of Jackson*, 85.

25. The house belonged to William A. Cooper, although it is sometimes referred to as the Scott home or the Lynch home. Cooper's daughter, Mrs. J. E. Barnes, a friend of the Fifth Company and of battery member Pvt. Frank Hull, was responsible for seeing that her family's piano got to Confederate Memorial Hall in New Orleans. Mrs. A. Q. May to B. N. Duff, February 26, 1905, Chalaron Papers, HTT; Douglas Cater, *As It Was: Reminiscences of a Soldier of the Third Texas Cavalry and the Nineteenth Louisiana* (Austin, Tex., 1990), 154–55; *CV,* XI (1903), 23; Casey, *Outline of Civil War Campaigns,* 63.

went through the house and admired the elegant appointments, noting especially "the library, costly carpets, and furniture." Some items Lindsay directed to be removed inside the Confederate works. Among the pieces Lindsay and his men managed to salvage was a handsome piano. They carried it back, lifted it over the parapet, and placed it in the Fifth Company redoubt, against the traverse close to the right gun.[26]

Sunday morning, July 12, about 11 A.M., the Yankees moved forward in force, closing on Breckinridge's lines. Bullets began flying into the works. Lt. Col. Henry Maury, commanding the 32nd Alabama (Adams' brigade), was struck in the chest and dangerously wounded. It seemed as though the front of the advancing enemy line was aimed directly down the railroad tracks at the Fifth Company redoubt. In anticipation of an assault at that point, Gen. Dan Adams moved his headquarters behind Slocomb's guns. As the Federals drew nearer, they suddenly "moved by the right flank through a hollow, which concealed their further movements." Their maneuvering was studiously ignored, however. Instead, Slocomb's cannoneers had turned their attention to their new toy—the piano. Lawrence Pugh rushed to play first, then Andy Swain pushed him aside, pulled up an ammunition box, adjusted its height, fingered the keys gently, then took "hold with song and play." The gunners immediately crowded around Andy and began to join in the choruses. "The music has drawn officers and men of other commands, who hang outside the group. Gen. Adams lends his ear from his headquarters." A hundred voices sang lustily, as though for the benefit of the approaching Yankees: "Auld Lang Syne, Lorena, Dixie, The Mocking Bird and the 'jolly' You Shan't Have Any of My Peanuts." All the while "Our Major Graves is on the parapet, like some grand orchestral leader."[27]

Despite their show of imperviousness, the singers could hear behind them the "ceaseless crack on the skirmish line." Over their shoulders, the familiar noise of sharp musketry came closer and closer. Soon, out across the cornfields to their front, attentive gunners could see enemy skirmishers advancing directly upon their works. Behind these Yankees appeared a

26. B. N. Duff to Adjutant General Fidge, February 1, 1905, Chalaron Papers, HTT; Journal of unidentified member of Fifth Company, July 11, 1863, WA Papers, HTT; *CV,* XI (1903), 23; New Orleans *States,* July 1, 1894; Evans, *Confederate Military History,* VIII, 597; New Orleans *Times-Democrat,* June 17, 1884.

27. Journal of unidentified member of Fifth Company, July 11–13, 1863, WA Papers, HTT; New Orleans *States,* July 1, 1894; *OR,* Vol. XXIV, Pt. 2, pp. 656–57; New Orleans *Times-Democrat,* June 17, 1884; Davis, *Breckinridge,* 367.

line of battle, another behind that. Ned Austin and his sharpshooters had begun to retreat rapidly now, past the mansion, dashing from the cornfields through holes in the abatis. Soon they were tumbling into the works. Austin then reformed his men, placing them in the railroad cut and in the battery's rear as supporting infantry. Once the skirmishers were safely inside the lines, Slocomb shouted, "Man the guns!" The singers scattered, abandoning the piano, transforming themselves once again into gun crews.

Rice Graves waited, "conspicuous by his white coat and red kepi," allowing Pugh's troops to approach even nearer. Then, when the Yankee line of battle encountered the abatis and their formations became clotted, he gave the command to fire. The Napoleons opened with canister, but the determined Federals continued to advance, fighting their way through the obstructions, then attempting to restore company and regimental formations. "Still they came in brilliant style," wrote an admiring Vaught, "steadily & slowly, to within 125 yards of my guns." The Confederate abatis, according to Isaac Pugh, "broke our line and threw the men into groups, thus giving the enemy's artillery an opportunity to work with the most deadly effect." Billy Vaught was wild with excitement.

When I saw those blue coated devils pressing steadily upon us, not withstanding the storm of canister from my two guns & Cobbs from the front & Slocombs from almost on their flank, my head grew *very slightly* warm and my anger began to rise. My body seemed too small for my pent up evil, and I felt like a demon of destruction. . . . I tore down part of my breastwork in the midst of the fire & ordered double charges of canister to be fired. At that moment too a battery which had appeared unobserved, opened upon my devoted section. I heeded it not though every shot from [it] screamed past my ears.

My double charges of canister still tore wide gaps in their still advancing line of infantry. They bore a splendid banner right toward me—three times that banner went down & as often sprang up. "Aim at that flag!" was my order—down it went, never to rise again except as a trophy.[28]

"Fire low, boys," Rice Graves ordered, but the gun crews were rushing to get off each shot. Graves, "standing on the parapet," had to repeat the order, "FIRE LOW!" Slocomb ordered a bag of gunshot rammed down for one load. Still the persistent Yankees came on, charging "through the

28. The flag-bearer of the 53rd Illinois "had his head shot off by one of our shells," Chalaron added, in confirmation of Vaught's comments. WCDV to Mary Vaught, July 25, 1863, Vaught Letters, HNOC; New Orleans *Times-Democrat*, June 17, 1884.

dust our shrieking canister has raised as it tears its way in ricochets across the field . . . to strike the foe about the waist." Adams' infantry now began firing away with their muskets on both sides of the gunners. Dan Adams himself joined in the fun. He grabbed the rifle of a private, "mounted the breastworks and fired two rounds." Slocomb now had the charges double-shotted. At each blast, it seemed, a wide hole would appear in the blue ranks. At last the Yankees halted. Their line of battle had been destroyed. The men in blue began to mill about, confused, frightened, looking to their officers. Those in advance were only fifty to eighty yards from the Confederate parapet.

The Federal colonel, Pugh, attempted to veer away from the direct fire of Slocomb's pieces, trying to angle his regiments to the left toward rifle pits held by Stovall's men. This maneuver, however, resulted in exposing them to the fire of Cobb's guns. Raked front and flank, the Yankees began dropping to the ground to hide from the merciless canister. Meanwhile, to support Pugh's floundering infantry, a section of the 5th Ohio Light Artillery came up and went into battery on the railroad, about eight hundred yards from Vaught's section (Pieces one and six) on the left of the company. "I turned my fire then upon that saucy battery," said Vaught, and "drove it away in such a hurry that it left its dead men & horses in the [woods]." The Ohio battery was put out of action and "limbered to the rear," Slocomb reported, "leaving their implements, trail, handspike, and four rounds of ammunition, which are now in my possession." Federal division commander Jacob Lauman sent up additional fire support—the 15th Ohio and 53rd Indiana batteries, but it was too late. The attack had failed.[29]

"Cease Firing!" commanded Graves. Then he himself joined Ned Austin's sharpshooters and Stovall's Florida brigade as they leapt over the parapet with a shout "to finish them." The enemy was done—up went white handkerchiefs while officers raised the hilts of their swords as a sign of surrender. Ignoring the mopping up action to their immediate front, the Fifth Company abandoned their pieces and gathered once again around the piano. Andy Swain, "the musical spirit" of the battery, again

29. WCDV to Mary Vaught, July 25, 1863, Vaught Letters, HNOC; Thompson, *First Kentucky Brigade*, 207; *OR*, Vol. XXIV, Pt. 2, pp. 575, 603–607, 655; Davis, *Breckinridge*, 367; Journal of unidentified member of Fifth Company, July 12, 1863, WA Papers, HTT; New Orleans *States*, July 1, 1894; Chalaron, "Memories of Rice Graves," 10; Cater, *As It Was*, 156–57; New Orleans *Times-Democrat*, June 17, 1884; Bearss, *Siege of Jackson*, 87.

took charge of the keyboard. "Not twenty minutes have sped since its last notes have died away. A thousand men have lost life or limbs, or, writhing have been made to lie around four stand of colors." The Fifth Company began to sing, "'Oh, Let us be joyful,' and every heart and every throat joins in the chorus." A smiling Cuthbert Slocomb shook his head in disbelief. He confessed to an infantryman over the singing "that he was afraid when he got to his guns that he had let them get too close to stop them."[30]

It was a costly repulse for the two brigades of Jacob Lauman's division. Advancing rashly "up square" in front of Slocomb's guns, Lauman lost 533 men (441 from Pugh's brigade), more than half of the one thousand troops who attacked.[31] Almost all wounds inflicted by the Confederates appeared to have been made by canister according to Dr. D. W. Yandell, Johnston's medical director. Two hundred Yankee infantry surrendered to Adams' infantry. Lost also were three regimental flags.[32] Confederate losses were minimal—a few wounded in Breckinridge's division. In the battery itself, only three horses (including Vaught's) and a mule were killed.[33]

It should be underscored that this sharp repulse of an infantry division was accomplished almost completely by the guns of Cobb and Slocomb. For their work they received resounding praise, beaded with heady expressions such as "most excellent and efficient service," from Breckin-

30. *OR,* Vol. XXIV, Pt. 2, p. 656; *CV,* X (1902), 315–16, 439, 532; Cater, *As It Was,* 154–55; New Orleans *Times-Democrat,* June 17, 1884; CHS to Capt. Emile P. Guillet, July 19, 1863, 5WA Order Book, WA Papers, HTT; New Orleans *States,* July 1, 1894; Evans, *Confederate Military History,* VIII, 597.

31. When Union XIII Corps commander Edward O. C. Ord was informed, he relieved Lauman on the spot for having acted "without orders, and directly in violation of the instructions." *OR,* Vol. XXIV, Pt. 4, pp. 654–57, Pt. 1, p. 245, Pt. 2, pp. 547–48, 597, 599, 604, 656; William C. Davis, ed., *Diary of a Confederate Soldier: John S. Jackman of the Orphan Brigade* (Columbia, S.C., 1990), 80; Bearss, *Siege of Jackson,* 87; New Orleans *Times-Democrat,* June 17, 1884; Thompson, *First Kentucky Brigade,* 207.

32. Chalaron maintained there were four flags captured. Adams believed either three or four. Three (those of the 28th, 41st, and 53rd Illinois) seems correct. New Orleans *Times-Democrat,* June 17, 1884; New Orleans *States,* July 1, 1994; *OR,* Vol. XXIV, Pt. 2, p. 655; Bearss, *Siege of Jackson,* 87.

33. There was a report of a man slightly wounded, but this is questionable. Chalaron or Slocomb, with their meticulous record keeping, would have mentioned the individual. *OR,* Vol. LII, Pt. 2, p. 75, Vol. XXIV, Pt. 2, p. 655.

ridge, Adams, and other observers who made official reports or diary entries. A delighted Breckinridge ordered that Jackson be inscribed on the Fifth Company flag.[34] In his report Adams (as well as Chalaron and many other Confederate participants) added a back-handed note of admiration for the gallant Union assault. The enemy, admitted the Confederates, had displayed "a courage and determination . . . worthy of a better cause."[35]

July 13 and 14 proved hard, indeed ghastly, days for the company. The enemy kept up a steady artillery fire. "So far we have been extremely fortunate in our battery. No body hurt. The city of Jackson has been on fire in different places a dozen times." The Yankee rounds seemed "principally directed against the State House." Lauman's dead lay before their works for two or three days, "literally festering in the scorching sun. The stench is so great that it is almost impossible to stay in our works." According to a member of Charles Fenner's battery who came over to the Washington Artillery's redoubt, "It was the most sickening sight I ever beheld." At last Johnston and Sherman agreed to a two-hour truce, but it was Confederate burial details that did the awful work of "pulling or pushing the swollen and discolored corpses into the trenches with the aid of long hooked poles."[36]

Meanwhile Sherman had brought up his ordnance train and prepared to resume bombarding the city. He also extended his lines until both flanks rested on the Pearl River. Another Union force, Johnston learned, was en route to Yazoo City, thus threatening to cross the Pearl and turn his right flank. Johnston knew he must abandon Jackson. He began by quietly withdrawing his artillery from the lines; following them would be the infantry. At 9 P.M. on July 16, the Fifth Company pulled their pieces out of the redoubt, limbered up, and made their way to the rear, crossing the Pearl on a pontoon bridge before midnight.[37]

The company sadly bade farewell to their piano. Sherman's men found it when they occupied the Confederate works but did not destroy it. Al-

34. Special Order No. 21, Breckinridge's Corps, November 15, 1863, reproduced in New Orleans *Times-Democrat,* June 17, 1884.

35. *OR,* Vol. XXIV, Pt. 2, p. 656; Davis, *Breckinridge,* 367; New Orleans *States,* July 1, 1894.

36. Journal of unidentified member of Fifth Company, July 13, 14, 1863, WA Papers, HTT; Lionel C. Levy, "Memoirs of Army Life in Fenner's Louisiana Battery," American Jewish Archives, Cincinnati; Davis, ed., *Diary of a Confederate Soldier,* 80.

37. Slocomb noted that during their stay at Jackson the company had fired 211 rounds. *OR,* Vol. XXIV, Pt. 1, p. 246, Vol. LII, Pt. 2, p. 75; Bearss, *Siege of Jackson,* 88–89; Milo W. Scott Diary, July 16, 1863, Chattanooga–Hamilton County Bicentennial Library, Chattanooga.

though Fifth Company members would tell recruits about the piano and the Yankee charge, the instrument itself seems to have been forgotten until Pvt. Frank Hull, long after the war, secured it from its owner and had it transported to New Orleans. There in 1902, Hull presented it to his surviving comrades "as a war relic, to be placed in Memorial Hall." [38]

Using the old Brandon road, Johnston's army retreated by easy marches to Morton, Mississippi, about thirty-five miles east. The weather was very hot and made for dusty, disagreeable marching. If that were not enough, heavy rain conspired to make them miserable. On the night of July 18, "rain poured in torrents," some water "rising so high as to endanger the safety of the ammunition in our 'limber chests.'" It seemed there would be no respite. "The moment the soldier gets a small chance to rest," complained a member, "orders are given to clear the camp ground—make troughs—erect shelter for the harness—Guns—horses. After all this is attended to the soldiers may then provide for his own comfort." On they went toward Morton, arriving there on July 21. They were greeted by still more rain. [39]

Much more depressing than the rain, however, were the desertions on the march from Jackson to Morton. They were "frequent," lamented Johnston. [40] There appear to have been eight in the Washington Artillery, an exceptionally large number for this unit known for its high morale and selectivity. Those who deserted on the retreat were the Irish artificer John G. White; a forty-five-year-old substitute for Richard Pugh named Pat Keyes; the English plasterer Mike Hayes; Irishman Richard Farrell and his Canadian-born brother Mike, both drivers; Irish drivers Joe and Jim Byrnes; and Kentuckian Joe Banfil, who had been captured just prior to Perryville and exchanged. [41]

The Fifth Company did not linger in Morton. They moved on to Forest, Mississippi, some twelve miles farther east. An idle month in the

38. Mrs. Albert Q. May to B. N. Duff, February 26, 1905, Chalaron Papers, HTT; Evans, *Confederate Military History,* VIII, 597, X, 315; Cater, *As It Was,* 154–55; Casey, *Outline of Civil War Campaigns,* 63.

39. Journal of unidentified member of Fifth Company, July 16–21, 1863, WA Papers, HTT; *OR,* Vol. XXIV, Pt. 1, p. 246; Cater, *As It Was,* 157; Davis, ed. *Diary of a Confederate Soldier,* 80; WCDV to Mary Vaught, July 25, 1863, Vaught Letters, HNOC.

40. *OR,* Vol. XXIV, Pt. 1, p. 246; Joseph E. Johnston, *Narrative of Military Operations Directed During the Late War Between the States by Joseph E. Johnston, General, C.S.A.* (New York, 1874), 210.

41. See 5WA roster, Appendix A.

Department of Mississippi and East Louisiana followed. As always, there were rumors of all sorts, false starts and stops, angry disappointments, raised and lowered expectations. Then, suddenly on August 25, came orders for Breckinridge's division to load aboard the cars once again. They were to hasten back to Tennessee and Bragg's army. A fight was brewing, it seemed, a big one.[42]

42. It appears that Adams' brigade moved to Morton, Mississippi, on the evening of August 25. From there they boarded trains for Meridian. Davis, *Breckinridge,* 368; Samuel Pasco Diary, August 25, 26, 1863, CCNMP, Fort Oglethorpe, Georgia.

7

WICKEDEST ARTILLERY DUEL I EVER SAW

BRECKINRIDGE'S DIVISION (forty-five hundred strong) arrived at Tyner's Station, eight miles east of Chattanooga, on September 1, 1863.[1] There they rejoined old comrades in the Army of Tennessee and found themselves assigned to the corps of Daniel Harvey Hill, the choleric outcast from the Army of Northern Virginia who was brand new to the western army. Hill and Breckinridge, however, seemed to get along famously from the start which pleased soldiers in the division and boded well for the hard days that lay ahead. Less than a week after their arrival, Breckinridge's division as part of Hill's corps headed south to La Fayette, Georgia, as Bragg abandoned Chattanooga to protect his line of communications. The Confederate commander, nevertheless, hoped through this deception to lure

1. The division consisted of Stovall's, Helm's, and Adams' brigades; the latter was composed of the 13th-20th Louisiana, the 16th-25th Louisiana, the 19th Louisiana, and John E. "Ned" Austin's 14th Battalion Sharpshooters. The four batteries of the division (Slocomb's, Cobb's, Spencer's, and Mebane's), as at Jackson, constituted a battalion commanded by Maj. Rice E. Graves. *OR,* Vol. XXX, Pt. 2, p. 13; They had traveled via Meridian, Mobile, Montgomery, West Point, and Atlanta; Pasco Diary, August 25–September 1, 1863, CCNMP.

Rosecrans' army across Lookout Mountain then attack him "whenever he should emerge from the mountain gorges."

One can trace the movements of the gunners of the Fifth Company from Chalaron's meticulous itinerary. The battery traveled by rail and water from Morton, Mississippi, to "Chickamauga" (apparently Chickamauga Station, just to the east of Chattanooga and on the east side of Chickamauga Creek), a trip of some 620 miles, then moved to La Fayette, then farther south to Cartersville, then west to Rome. In Rome they picked up their horses which had traveled overland. Only the horses of Graves's battalion had marched across Alabama, the others having been transported by railroad. The Fifth Company took pride in this display of the good treatment their animals had received. Once the battery had reassembled they made their way back north to La Fayette to rejoin their infantry supporting unit (Adams' brigade). This short journey proved an adventure when "a column of federal cavalry almost ran into our battery." Graves wanted to engage them with "artillery alone," Chalaron remembered, noting that "nothing to him seemed impossible of accomplishment with artillery." Such thoughts worried their infantry comrades, though. On September 14, a private in Stovall's brigade, Breckinridge's division, entered in his diary, "our Batteries all arrived this evening much to our relief for it has been feared that the Yankee Cavalry had cut them off."[2]

These early September peregrinations by the Fifth Company mirror the vacillations of their commander-in-chief. Bragg did not know the location of Rosecrans' army, and from the afternoon of September 7 until the evening of the ninth, he worked under the assumption that the enemy's objective was Rome. Bragg planned to confront him there.[3] On the night of September 9, however, Bragg changed his plans and attempted to entrap or at least attack an isolated portion of Rosecrans' army on the east side of Lookout Mountain. Every effort failed in deplorable fashion, however, and September 13–16 found the Army of Tennessee in a state of "seeming paralysis." All the while Breckinridge's division, now rejoined by the Fifth Company, stood by, waiting impatiently at La Fayette.

Bragg's blind thrashing about in northwest Georgia had succeeded cer-

---

2. Unfortunately JAC does not provide dates, only mileage between points. Chalaron, 5WA Itinerary, WA Papers, HTT; *OR,* Vol. XXX, Pt. 4, p. 595; Chalaron, "Memories of Rice Graves," 11; Pasco Diary, September 14, 1863, CCNMP.

3. Connelly, *Autumn of Glory,* 173–75.

tainly in one aspect. He had alerted Gen. William S. Rosecrans to danger. The Federal commander set about at once concentrating his badly scattered and vulnerable army. Bragg, still incredibly ignorant of Rosecrans' intent and location during these crucial early days of September, decided to assume the offensive once again on the fifteenth. He directed that "strong demonstrations" be made in the vicinity of Lee and Gordon's Mill, while "the rest of the army should move quickly by the right flank as far as Reed's Bridge and the nearby fords over Chickamauga Creek." The army would then march "west to interpose the Army of Tennessee between Chattanooga and the Federals."[4]

Hill's corps (consisting of the divisions of Cleburne and Breckinridge), according to Bragg's field order of September 16 and subsequent directives, would form the rear of the army as it moved north, paralleling Pigeon Mountain (an eastern spur of Lookout Mountain), then Chickamauga Creek. Hill would "occupy the gaps across Pigeon Mountain and observe the roads to the south," in effect protecting the left and rear of the army.[5]

Breckinridge was at Catlett's Gap, one of the three main passes across Pigeon Mountain, on the evening of September 17, "about twenty miles south of the coming battle." Cleburne was at Dug Gap. The following day Breckinridge moved north, carefully watching "a succession of mountain passes and fords." By late afternoon he had passed the nose of Pigeon Mountain and arrived at an important ford near Glass's Mill. There he took position alone high ground on the east bank of Chickamauga Creek where his division "composed the extreme left [and rear] of the infantry of [Bragg's] army."[6]

While Breckinridge prepared to encamp at Glass's Mill the night of September 18, Harvey Hill received word that cavalry pickets had been driven away from Owens' Ford on Chickamauga Creek, about two miles south. Hill rushed to the scene, taking with him Adams' Louisiana brigade and the Fifth Company. The Federal threat evaporated, however, so, after passing the night at that point, Adams' brigade retraced their steps the

4. Peter Cozzens, *This Terrible Sound: The Battle of Chickamauga* (Urbana, Ill., 1992), 55–59, 89. See also Davis, *Breckinridge,* 368–69; Horn, *Army of Tennessee,* 239;2–54; Connelly, *Autumn of Glory,* 173–97; Ed Porter Thompson, *History of the Orphan Brigade* (Louisville, Ky., 1898), 209.

5. *OR,* Vol. XXX, Pt. 4, p. 657.

6. Pasco Diary, September 18, 1863, CCNMP; Davis, *Breckinridge,* 369; *OR,* Vol. XXX, Pt. 2, p. 197; Felix Arroyo Journal, WA Papers, HTT.

following morning.[7] It is probable that the Washington Artillery accompanied Hill and Adams, and probably it was while they rode north from Owens' ford that twenty-four-year-old Lt. Tom Blair gloomily told his companion Adolphe Chalaron that he had had a premonition. He did not expect to survive the next fight.[8]

Apparently, as the Fifth Company returned from Owens' Ford to the cutoff leading west to Glass's Mill, sometime before 11 A.M., Cuthbert Slocomb was hailed by Breckinridge or one of his staff and sent down to the ford.

In accordance with Bragg's orders of September 18, Harvey Hill had set about on the morning of the nineteenth to "ascertain if the enemy is reenforcing at Lee and Gordon's Mills [where the La Fayette road crossed Chickamauga Creek], in which event [Hill] will attack them in flank." Hill intended this effort to be a "diversion," however, not an all-out attack by his corps. Breckinridge's division would be his instrument (Cleburne's division had been sent north to join in the concentration at Lee and Gordon's Mills). One of Gen. Ben Hardin Helm's regiments, the 2nd Kentucky, had crossed Chickamauga Creek on the evening of the eighteenth and created a lodgement on the west bank. At 9 A.M. on the nineteenth Helm ordered the 2nd Kentucky, supported by the 6th Kentucky, forward "to feel the enemy's position." To support this effort, Capt. Robert Cobb took two guns across the creek and moved them out to the skirmish line in front of the 2nd and 6th Kentucky. Helm ordered Cobb to open fire on a house "in an open field, distant 500 yards," which served as cover for Union skirmishers. Cobb's fire was answered immediately by an enemy battery, "posted to the right and rear of the house, and distant about 900 yards." After firing five rounds, Cobb, outgunned, withdrew to a sheltered position.[9]

Having found the enemy in strength (Brig. Gen. John Beatty's brigade, Maj. Gen. James S. Negley's division) and to give the impression of an attack in force, Breckinridge sent over the balance of Helm's Orphan

7. Union cavalry in small numbers, perhaps only a patrol or scouting party, crossed to the east bank of Chickamauga Creek during the afternoon of the eighteenth and were seen by Wheeler's cavalry who reported to Hill. Hill, either in a precautionary move, or an overreaction, or a reaction to an exaggerated report, dispatched Adams. Interview with J. H. Ogden III, CCNMP historian, May 30, 1995.

8. *OR,* Vol. XXX, Pt. 2, pp. 140, 197; Chalaron, "Slocomb's Battery in the Tennessee Army," Jackson Barracks Library, New Orleans.

9. *OR,* Vol. XXX, Pt. 2, pp. 31, 140, 215, 197, 208–11.

Brigade. Apparently these Yankees west of the creek were a covering force guarding the ford and protecting a larger column moving up the road from McLemore's Cove to Crawfish Springs. To insure he had ample firepower, Breckinridge sent with Helm's infantry Slocomb's two Napoleon sections under Blair and Chalaron, plus the remainder of Cobb's battery (three guns). Rice Graves would command. As support for the crossing itself, Breckinridge stationed Billy Vaught and his section of two "brass James' rifles" on a "bluff" on the east side.[10] It was about 11 A.M. Cobb's fight had occurred between 9 A.M. and 10 A.M.

Disaster almost struck as these reinforcements crossed Chickamauga Creek. The Federal field pieces that had silenced Cobb reopened their fire with deadly accuracy. An initial round struck the team of horses pulling one of Blair's guns, killing at least one horse. The dead animal "blocked the way and halted the column under a most accurate and intense fire." Slocomb, despite the chaos, succeeded in clearing the ford and getting his guns across. Once he had reached the west bank, General Helm directed Slocomb to take position to the left of Cobb in the open field "to the left and front of Glass's Mill."[11] Cobb's other guns went into battery "in the woods on its [Cobb's section] right."[12]

Slocomb unlimbered and went into battery rapidly. The enemy was posted on higher ground, however, alert, ready to fire. A brisk, furious, but short artillery duel ensued. In Pvt. Felix Arroyo's words: "un déluge de boulets, de bombes et de mitraille [case-shot]."[13] After the exchange of only a few rounds the Federals' guns were silenced, the enemy battery having sustained losses in men and horses, as well as at least one caisson.[14]

10. Bronze six-pounder James rifles weighed 886 pounds and had a range of about 1,700 yards. The relatively soft rifling in their tubes, however, tended to break down after repeated use. This, of course, would lead to inaccuracy. Nevertheless, Vaught had had great success with them up until this time.

11. The map of the Chickamauga battlefield prepared in 1896 by Edward E. Betts, park engineer, shows the Confederate artillery position to the front and *right* of Glass's Mill. On Betts's map, however, is a broad open field to the south side of Glass's Mill road. It was in this field, presumably, that the house to which Cobb referred was located.

12. Slocomb went into the fight at Glass's Mill with a strength of six officers and 120 men. *OR,* Vol. XXX, Pt. 2, pp. 197, 229, 215, 202; Cozzens, *This Terrible Sound,* 258; Chalaron, "Slocomb's Battery in the Tennessee Army"; Evans, *Confederate Military History,* XIII, 185.

13. Arroyo Journal, WA Papers, HTT; Arroyo file, Confederate Personnel Documents, HTT.

14. Bridges reported two killed, nine wounded, and twelve horses killed or disabled. "Schultz's loss, if any, is not known." *OR,* Vol. XXX, Pt. 2, pp. 215, 229, Pt. 1, pp. 367, 374; Chalaron, "Slocomb's Battery in the Tennessee Army."

The Federals' pieces pulled back. Slocomb paid dearly for this victory, however. Just as Tom Blair's section unlimbered, before a shot had been fired by the Washington Artillery, an enemy round struck. It apparently hit one of Blair's pieces, killing Blair and two men on the gun served by Arroyo: Pvt. C. P. Bailey (Number Three) and Pvt. Emile Reichart (Number Two). A shell passed through Bailey's body and it was the same round, in all probability, that blew off part of Reichart's face and an arm. Arroyo himself was struck on the head by a shell fragment and knocked unconscious. As he lay unconscious, the horses attached to a limber ran away, a driver having been killed, and one of the wheels of the limber rolled over Private Arroyo's back, "injuring his spine." [15]

When they observed the enemy withdrawing, Slocomb and Cobb ceased firing. Despite the disaster to Blair and his gun crew, they prepared to advance. John Beatty's Federal brigade, which opposed them, appeared to have been staggered by the rebel artillery fire and the advancing Kentucky skirmishers. Beatty had requested reinforcements and division commander Maj. Gen. James S. Negley sent Col. Timothy R. Stanley's infantry brigade and its battery to help contain the rebel crossing. [16]

Chalaron observed "the movement of horses at the enemy's position" and rode up to Graves to inform him. "I see it," said Graves and he ordered Slocomb to move his four pieces forward about one hundred yards, laboriously hauling them by hand because of the lack of horses. Before they could come into battery, however, they were hit again. This time when the Yankees reopened, their fire came from two directions, "having brought up another battery of rifled guns," positioned "farther to the right" of the first battery and protected by hasty works. The engagement developed into a "furious artillery fight . . . lasting some thirty or forty minutes." Pvt. John S. Jackman of the 9th Kentucky, a veteran infantryman, called it "the wickedest artillery duel . . . I ever saw." Helm's regiments (2nd, 4th, 6th, 9th Kentucky and 41st Alabama) retired behind the batteries, closer to the creek. They suffered from this artillery fight, nevertheless, with four of the regiments losing men killed and wounded. Why the infantry fell back is unknown. Probably they did so in response

15. Pvt. John A. Walsh, who would be wounded himself the following day, cared for helpless Arroyo and saw that he was carried back across Chickamauga Creek and out to the La Fayette road. Arroyo Journal, WA Papers, HTT; Arroyo file, Confederate Personnel Documents, HTT.

16. Although Timothy R. Stanley's brigade, James S. Negley's division, was dispatched, only the 18th Ohio Infantry seems to have become engaged.

to an order to withdraw to the east bank, or Helm himself may have ordered them back in anticipation of a Union infantry attack in force.[17]

It turned out to be a most unequal contest. The two sections of Capt. Lyman Bridges' battery that Slocomb and Cobb had fought initially had returned to the high ground west of Glass's Ford, but this time reinforced by Bridges' third section. Chalaron and Slocomb thought there were eleven enemy pieces opposing them, "most of them rifles." It certainly seemed like that many. Actually they and Cobb had engaged nine Federal pieces firing from three different positions: Bridges' First Illinois Light (three sections armed with two twelve-pounder Napoleons and four three-inch rifles) and a section of Battery M, First Ohio Light Artillery (three guns—either three inch rifles or James rifles) commanded by Lt. Eben P. Sturges. The Federal pieces opened with deadly effect, concentrating primarily upon the two sections of the Fifth Company.[18]

A factor equally as important as firepower appears to have been the Federal advantage of position, as they blasted away at a range of about seven hundred yards. "Their caissons and limbers [were] sheltered from our fire by the brow of the hill." "Their fire was very accurate, and plunging upon us . . . sloping through fields down to the fords, in front of which the Fifth Company stood in an open space, just wide enough for its battery front [50 yards, or 54 paces by 1861 artillery regulations] of four guns. . . . Encased in this open space by woods on three sides, the battery formed a splendid target," and Yankee fire "told severely. . . . One solid shot of the enemy killed three of the Fifth Company's drivers, passing clear through each of them as they sat on their horses."[19]

While the duel raged, sounds of heavy fighting could be heard to the north as advance forces of Bragg and Rosecrans collided in the vicinity of Jay's Mill, some three miles above Lee and Gordon's Mill. Indeed, in the midst of his "diversionary" attack, Breckinridge received orders from Hill to break off the action, withdraw to the east bank and move up the La Fayette-Chattanooga road to a point (Snow Hill) south of Lee and Gordon's Mill. Breckinridge accordingly sent word to Helm to disengage and recross Chickamauga Creek. The infantry, hapless onlookers at

17. Chalaron, "Memories of Rice Graves," 11; Davis, ed., *Diary of a Confederate Soldier*, 87; *OR,* Vol. XXX, Pt. 2, pp. 203, 207–209, 211, 213, 215, 229.

18. "The powerful Federal artillery comprised thirty-four batteries, almost all six-gun outfits, which counted 204 pieces, half of which were rifles and half smoothbores." Daniel, *Cannoneers in Gray,* 93.

19. *OR,* Vol. XXX, Pt. 1, pp. 337, 339, 367, 373–74, 382–83, Pt. 2, p. 229; Chalaron, "Slocomb's Battery in the Tennessee Army"; Beatty, *Memoirs of a Volunteer,* 245.

Glass's Mill, welcomed the order.[20] The Fifth Company, angered at having to abandon the field soaked with their comrades' blood, complied reluctantly, and limbered up only after receiving "repeated orders of General Breckinridge to retire the guns and join his column."[21]

They withdrew shortly after noon "in a crippled condition."[22] Six horses had been killed and one disabled. Blair was dead. In addition six privates had been killed, four wounded.[23] It is presumed that most of these casualties occurred during the fight in the field on the west side, not during the crossing of the creek. The company's dead included the teenage Missourian, John Robert Anderson; Louisianans Louis D. Daigle of Assumption Parish and Joseph Belsom, Jr., of St. Charles Parish; Martin F. Duggan, a "molder" in New Orleans and a driver in the battery; thirty-year-old C. P. Bailey, a native of Worcester County, Massachusetts, and a law clerk in New Orleans; and Emile F. Reichart, a German-born bookbinder. All the dead and wounded, according to Billy Vaught, who detailed their wounds in a letter to his mother, had been victims of shells or solid shot, not rifle fire.[24] "We buried our dead," Chalaron recalled, "in one common pit, rolling each in his blanket, leaving a detail to cover them up, and marched off as Wheeler's cavalry crossed over to continue the fighting at the ford."[25]

The Fifth Company recrossed Chickamauga Creek and limped out to the Chattanooga-La Fayette road, not quite a mile east of the ford. Vaught rejoined on the way, apparently having taken little if any part in the fighting.[26] Probably the position in which he was placed on the east bank was

20. Sam Pasco of the 3rd Florida commented about the artillery duel: "The shells fell all about our lines but none of the Infantry was struck." Pasco Diary, September 19, 1863, CCNMP.

21. *OR,* Vol. XXX, Pt. 2. p. 197; Chalaron, "Slocomb's Battery in the Tennessee Army."

22. This is an estimate. Reports of Helm's regimental commanders are contradictory regarding this timing sequence. They report being withdrawn "after . . . a very short period," or "about 10 o'clock [A.M.]," or the "middle of the day," or "until 2 or 3 p.m." *OR,* Vol. XXX, Pt. 2, pp. 208, 210–11.

23. The names of three of the four are known: Arroyo, Henry Férand, and the New Yorker John R. Murray, who would transfer to the Confederate navy two months later. The two latter members were slightly wounded by shells.

24. Cobb's battery suffered far less: one killed, one wounded. *OR,* Vol. XXX, Pt. 2, pp. 201, 215, 229; 5WA Order Book, WA Papers, HTT; WCDV to mother, October 10, 1863, Vaught Letters, HNOC; New Orleans *Daily Picayune,* October 6, 1863.

25. Chalaron, "Memories of Rice Graves," 11–12. One of the company's dead (unidentified), according to Sam Pasco, was left behind and found by the Floridians. "Our boys brought him across the creek and buried him about sundown." Pasco Diary, September 19, 1863, CCNMP.

26. Vaught's sharpshooting chief of the piece, Sgt. David "Hawkeye" Smith, was missing during September, 1863. He lay sick in Mobile.

poorly chosen, not affording the observation necessary to assist Slocomb. On the other hand, Vaught may have been placed there as a precaution: to provide covering fire for the crossing or for withdrawal from the west bank. His two James rifles certainly would have been a welcome addition to the beleaguered sections on the west side.[27]

The result of this failed foray, referred to as the Battle of Glass's Mill in Fifth Company annals, was that the battery not only got bloodied, it got whipped. On the other hand, in a larger sense, Glass's Mill succeeded in being diversionary in that it drew the attention of Federal division commander Negley for several hours and delayed to some extent his march north. Breckinridge believed he and his men had achieved positive results. With becoming restraint, he summed up the importance of the engagement as revealing that the enemy force west of the creek "was a covering force to columns passing down the valley to unite with the center and left of [Rosecrans'] army."[28]

The short march from Chickamauga Creek back east to the La Fayette and Chattanooga road (less than one thousand yards according to the map of the Chickamauga battlefield prepared in 1896 by Edward E. Betts) was slow and annoying to the infantry, who chafed at the delay "occasioned by the blocking of the road by the artillery, the movements of which were impeded by the loss of horses." Just as they reached the La Fayette road, Slocomb happened to see Felix Arroyo seated on a log by the side, head in his hands. The captain pulled up his horse, realizing the man needed help. He called to Sgt. Jim Browning and told him to stay with Arroyo and see that he was placed in one of the ambulances trailing along behind the battery.[29]

The column turned north and proceeded a short distance to a road junction below Lee and Gordon's Mill held by Zachariah C. Deas's brigade, Thomas C. Hindman's division. They remained there a short time then marched north again "to relieve Brig. Gen. Patton Anderson's divi-

27. The placement and role of Vaught is confusing. The heavily wooded high ground ("bluff") on the east side of the creek (Betts's map shows him just to the south of the mill itself, which seems logical) is somewhat elevated but appears not more than twenty feet above the west bank. From there Vaught could have reached Union batteries on the high ground to the west if he had had time to move the battery off the Glass's Mill road to that position and to cut down sufficient trees and brush to give him adequate fields of fire. No mention of Vaught's firing is made by participants, however. Breckinridge probably chose a poor position for him or placed him there too late of be of assistance to Slocomb.

28. *OR,* Vol. XXX, Pt. 2, p. 198.

29. *Ibid.,* 211; Arroyo Journal, WA Papers, HTT; Arroyo file, Confederate Personnel Documents, HTT.

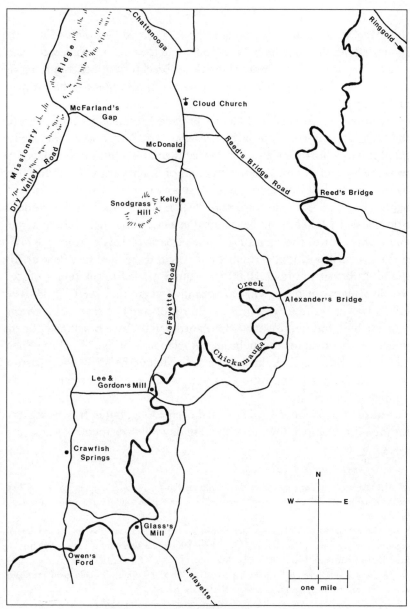

Chickamauga, September 19–20, 1863
Map by Blake A. Magner

sion, which was facing the enemy opposite Lee and Gordon's Mill.[30] Arriving "late in the afternoon," no sooner had they taken position than an order came from General Bragg himself for Breckinridge's division to continue its march north, "cross the Chickamauga at a point farther down, and occupy a position to be indicated."[31]

The division (Adams' and Helm's brigades) resumed its tramp, north then east, then north, approaching Alexander's Bridge well after nightfall.[32] It was a horrible sight that greeted them. On both sides of the road were the hospitals of most of the divisions of Bragg's army. Wounded men by the hundreds lay close to the road, surgeons busy at work by lantern light. The Fifth Company crossed Chickamauga Creek at Alexander's Bridge about 10:30 P.M. and encamped in a great open field "about a mile and half in rear of the right of our line of battle." This was not the division's assigned position, certainly, but Breckinridge had met Polk at Alexander's Bridge at about 10:00 P.M. and appealed to the senior officer to allow his worn out troops to encamp "where they were."[33] Harvey Hill, however, wanted Breckinridge in position and had sent a staff officer to guide him, but Polk set aside Hill's order and "gave Breckinridge permission to bivouac for the night near Alexander's Bridge."[34] Thus in one day Breckinridge had fought on the extreme left of the Army of Tennessee, then marched north to position his command to fight again the next day on the extreme right.[35]

Saturday, September 19, 1863, had been a long, bitter, frustrating day for the Fifth Company. What would Sunday hold for them?

30. *OR,* Vol. XXX, Pt. 2, pp. 211, 198.

31. The reader may be confused by the column marching north, which seems "up," yet crossing the creek "farther down." Chickamauga Creek (or river) flows north, thus north is "down" and south is "up." *Ibid.,* 198.

32. Stovall and Mebane's battery would remain at Glass's Mill to guard the crossing and did not begin their march north until 10 P.M. They did not join the division until 8 A.M., September 20. Pasco Diary, September 19, 20, 1863, CCNMP.

33. Lieutenant General Polk's headquarters (where Breckinridge himself would spend the night) were on the east bank, close to the road and close to the creek.

34. Col. Joseph H. Lewis, 6th Kentucky, reported they bivouacked "about two hours after nightfall" at "a point 1½ miles beyond Alexander's Bridge." *OR,* Vol. XXX, Pt. 2, pp. 203, 198, 211; Casey, *Outline of Civil War Campaigns,* 66; Connelly, *Autumn of Glory,* 215.

35. It is interesting to contemplate the Fifth Company, Breckinridge's division, and Bridges' battery, Beatty's brigade, who had just met at Glass's Ford, moving parallel down opposite sides of Chickamauga Creek, from one extreme of their respective armies to the other, as though fated to meet one another again in an even bloodier fight on the Sabbath.

8

ANOTHER BLOODY SUNDAY

BRAGG'S PLAN of battle for Sunday, September 20, 1863, was a continuation of his attempt to turn Rosecrans' left. Hill's corps would attack first, then assaults *en echelon* from the Confederate right, intending ultimately to drive the Federals back into McLemore's Cove, a large cul-de-sac between Lookout Mountain and Pigeon Mountain. There Bragg would destroy what remained of Rosecrans' army. The plan had merit, but, as pointed out by Army of Tennessee historian Tom Connelly, Bragg lacked sufficient strength on his right, his crucial strike force—a replay of Murfreesboro.[1] Bragg's right at Chickamauga consisted of Hill's corps (Patrick Cleburne on the left, Breckinridge on the right), unsupported by a reserve. Beyond Breckinridge was Bedford Forrest's cavalry, which was burdened with the responsibility of guarding the army's right flank and interdicting the battlefield from any Federal force that might advance south from Rossville into the rear of the Confederate turning force.

Breckinridge was to have opened the attack at dawn. Apparently, he never received orders to do so. Indeed, the Confederate chain of command

---

1. Connelly, *Autumn of Glory,* 209–10.

had changed overnight. Bragg, as was his practice, had proceeded to reorganize his army in the immediate presence of the enemy. He had divided his troops into two wings, placing Lieutenant General Hill and his corps under former corps commander and now right wing commander Lieutenant General Polk. Polk's own corps was divided between both wings. The new command structure, with a number of unfamiliar relationships, thus would be initiated, and tested, on the battlefield.[2]

During this chilly, restless night of September 19–20, Breckinridge did learn from Polk that he was to form the extreme right of the army. So the Kentuckian had his troops aroused at 3:00 A.M. and guided to their assigned position at 5:30, seventeen minutes before dawn. There, in an old field, behind a protective screen of skirmishers, Breckinridge formed a three-brigade front facing west. Helm held the left, Stovall the center, and Adams the right. Dan Adams' line centered on the Reed's Bridge road,[3] which ran almost due west intersecting at a ninety-degree angle the La Fayette-Chattanooga road at the farm of John McDonald.[4]

While they waited for further orders, the Fifth Company and Adams' brigade leisurely ate their rations and rested. The sun, meanwhile, rose higher and started burning off the frost that covered the grass and the fog clinging to Chickamauga Creek. It was not until shortly after 9:00 A.M. that Hill sent word for Adams to advance at 9:30 directly down the Reed's Bridge road.[5] Stovall would guide right on Adams, Helm on Stovall. At 9:20 Adams told Slocomb to follow behind the brigade's line of battle, allowing a sixty-yard interval.[6] Some three hundred yards to the front of the main body of the Louisiana brigade were Ned Austin and his sharp-

2. Cozzens, *This Terrible Sound,* 299–310; Davis, *Breckinridge,* 370–71; Connelly, *Autumn of Glory,* 208–11.

3. CCNMP historian James H. Ogden III believes Adams had his right on Reed's Bridge road. Since it would have been expedient for the Confederates to hold the road and since using the road would have facilitated the movement of at least some artillery, it is felt that Adams, who had responsibility for the right flank, would have placed a portion of his force above the road, although doing so would have extended Breckinridge's front to the north.

4. Cozzens, *This Terrible Sound,* 305; *OR,* Vol. XXX, Pt. 2, pp. 226, 237, 203, 197.

5. Randall Gibson gives 10 A.M. as the time he was ordered to advance, but this is half an hour later than indicated in the balance of the reports. Polk had ordered Breckinridge to advance "soon after sunrise," but Hill delayed the movement in order for "the troops to get their rations, and on other accounts." *OR,* Vol. XXX, Pt. 2, pp. 198, 220–21; Connelly, *Autumn of Glory,* 221.

6. Slocomb would take five officers and 107 men into action on September 20. *OR,* Vol. XXX, Pt. 2, p. 202.

shooters. For about seven hundred yards Adams and his men advanced in this formation meeting no resistance except from "thickly wooded" terrain that slowed movement and played havoc with regimental alignments. It was worse for artillery. The division's four batteries were virtually road-bound.[7]

After proceeding through the woods for about half an hour, Adams' brigade was "greeted, on approaching a dense thicket, by cheers and volleys from the enemy." Fortunately for Breckinridge's Confederates, however, they had caught John Beatty's Federal brigade in the flank. That morning Beatty, most reluctantly, had detached his four regiments from the main Union line, which fanned out in a semicircle just east of Kelly Field. Staff officers of corps commander George H. Thomas, in an effort to secure his left and thus the left of the Federal army, had ordered Beatty to move up the La Fayette road and position his brigade on high ground near the McDonald house. From that point Beatty could command the junction of Reed's Bridge road and the La Fayette road, anticipating any enemy turning movement or any effort to lodge a Confederate force between the main army and Chattanooga. So Beatty marched off to the north, separating himself and his brigade from Thomas' line. How was he to cover more than a division front with only one brigade?

Just as Beatty's lead regiment, the 88th Indiana, reached its assigned position, his other three regiments, trailing in a rough column through the woods east of the La Fayette road, were hit in the flank by Stovall and Col. Joseph Lewis' right wing of Helm's brigade (soon to be commanded by Lewis himself). To provide fire support for Lewis' three regiments attacking the 15th Kentucky (USA) or, more probably, for Stovall's Florida brigade fighting its way through Beatty's 104th Illinois to reach the La Fayette road, division artillery chief Maj. Rice E. Graves had detached a section of the Fifth Company under Lt. Abe Leverich.[8] This unfortunate Union commander, John Beatty, his brigade strung out, surprised and assaulted by Breckinridge's division, was the same officer who had faced the attack of Ben Hardin Helm, Cobb, and Slocomb at Glass's Mill only twenty-four hours before.[9]

7. Cobb's battery (at least one section) seems to have followed through the woods behind Helm, but their advance must have been agonizingly slow. *OR,* Vol. XXX, Pt. 2, pp. 198–99, 203, 229, 219, 221; Davis, *Breckinridge,* 373; Cozzens, *This Terrible Sound,* 320.

8. *OR,* Vol. XXX, Pt. 2, p. 229.

9. *Ibid.,* 221; Cozzens, *This Terrible Sound,* 317–18; Beatty, *Memoirs of a Volunteer,* 246–47.

Accompanying Beatty's two Indiana regiments on the extreme Union left was a section of Bridges' battery, the same men who had fought against the Fifth Company on Saturday. These three guns escaped, at least for the moment. Upon order of General Beatty, Lyman Bridges had pulled back this section ("half-battery" of three guns) as soon as Breckinridge's Confederates "came pouring out of the woods into the field 400 yards in our front and right." Bridges united his six guns in a position to the south—at the junction of the Alexander's Bridge road and the La Fayette road, but about five hundred yards northwest of, and apart from, Thomas' fortified position. Apparently expecting support from Beatty's two battered rear regiments—the 104th Illinois and the 15th Kentucky— Captain Bridges went into battery at the junction, a three-gun, half-battery above the road, and a three-gun, half-battery below. When the Confederate "battle-flags emerged from the woods," to the northeast of his position, Bridges opened with case-shot, then canister, having to exercise great caution not to fire into the rear of the 42nd and 88th Indiana and the 104th Illinois.[10]

Meanwhile, Dan Adams' brigade, to the north, assaulted Beatty's Hoosiers who had not had time to erect even hasty field fortifications. The 88th Indiana held the high ground just east of the La Fayette road; the 42nd just west, probably very near or at the McDonald home. Adams hit with "such impetuosity" that these two isolated regiments at the McDonald house were overwhelmed, and fled west to avoid being surrounded and captured.[11] "For the rest of the day," according to Peter Cozzens,

10. *OR*, Vol. XXX, Pt. 1, pp. 351, 353, 368, 374.

11. The sequence of events during this initial attack by Adams' brigade is quite contradictory in the *Official Records*. Gibson maintained that his 13th-20th Louisiana smashed into the enemy ahead of the rest of the brigade and captured eighty troops as well as one gun and several caissons; "the balance . . . were taken possession of by the troops of our brigade." This occurred, according to Gibson, before the time Adams and Stovall turned by the left flank perpendicular to the La Fayette road. Austin also reported his Company A captured two brass six-pounders, three rear chests of caissons filled with ammunition, five officers, and eighty-one enlisted men. Company B captured thirty-three of the enemy. Capt. H. A. Kennedy reported that skirmishers of the 19th Louisiana (Adams' brigade) had captured a section "in rear of the houses" across the ravine and thus in the vicinity of the McDonald house. For that matter, Breckinridge himself attributes the capture of "a battery" to Adams before the latter changed his direction of attack from west to south.

The balance of the evidence, on the other hand, indicates that the two guns of Bridges' battery (located east of the La Fayette road) were captured by the right wing of Helm's brigade (the left wing of that brigade having crashed into Thomas' breastworks and thus becoming separated) as they drove

"they drifted over the foothills of Missionary Ridge, lost and confused."
A sizeable number of these troops, according to Chalaron, made their
way northwest toward the Cloud house, a large white structure standing
on "an eminence some 700 yards off beyond open fields." [12]

In textbook fashion Adams continued on, crossing the La Fayette road,
passing through and beyond the enemy position, before halting in an open
field west of the McDonald house.[13] Stovall, advancing somewhat slower
than Adams, halted just east of the road. Up came Slocomb and Graves.
At once they saw the advantages of the position at the McDonald house.
Graves recalled Leverich and united the Washington Artillery on high
ground (a "low ridge"), just west of the McDonald house, "200 yards
from the road in front of the orchard." Slocomb with all six pieces now
opened on Beatty's fleeing troops, then receiving fire from his right,
changed front and fired "shrapnel" on Federals concentrated to the north
near "a white house to our front and right."[14] We "dispersed them in
double quick time." As they rejoiced over this quick victory, the battery
began to receive "a heavy fire in our backs," probably from the guns
Thomas had positioned on Snodgrass Hill (Bridges' battery had been subdued and forced to withdraw by this time by Joseph Lewis' surge.)[15]

Breckinridge joined Adams about this time, informing him that Helm's
brigade, at least the left wing, had met with disaster—a bloody repulse
against breastworks. The Orphan Brigade was smashed, Helm mortally

---

the battered 15th Kentucky, USA, before them. James H. Ogden, CCNMP historian, believes the
guns and caisson bodies referred to as being captured by Adams' command actually were those of
Absalom Baird's and John M. Brannan's divisions which had been either lost or damaged on September
19. The limbers belonging to these artillery commands seem to have been removed successfully and
were not mentioned by the Confederates as having been captured. Besides, Bridges had no six-
pounders. Cozzens, *This Terrible Sound*, 325–26; *OR*, Vol. XXX, Pt. 1, pp. 197–232, Pt. 2, pp. 199,
204, 210, 212, 221, 226–27.

12. Cozzens, *This Terrible Sound*, 325–26; J. Adolphe Chalaron, "Vivid Experiences at Chickamauga," *CV*, III (1895), 278.

13. Although Gibson states he had to halt to realign, Adams' movement to and through the
enemy's position was doctrinally sound. *OR*, Vol. XXX, Pt. 2, pp. 221, 225.

14. This was the Cloud house located to the north, in present-day Ft. Oglethorpe. To Slocomb
"the enemy seemed to be in force." Actually the area was a large Federal field hospital, a beehive of
activity that morning. The men Slocomb saw were the wounded themselves and their attendants and
undoubtedly the remnants of Beatty's two Indiana regiments. *OR*, Vol. XXX, Pt. 2, p. 229; Chalaron,
"Memories of Rice Graves," 12; James H. Ogden III to author, May 23, 30, 1995.

15. Chalaron, "Vivid Experiences at Chickamauga," 278; Chalaron, "Memories of Rice Graves,"
12; Casey, *Outline of Civil War Campaigns*, 66.

wounded.[16] In a dramatic display of personal initiative, Breckinridge now ordered his two remaining brigades to change front ninety degrees so that they faced south down the La Fayette road. Adams deployed west of the road, Stovall east, both in single line. They were to advance down the road supported by the Fifth Company. Breckinridge realized that he had turned the left of Rosecrans' army and this advance south on both sides of the La Fayette road should crash into the flank and rear of the enemy. Without securing permission from corps commander Hill, Breckinridge ordered the attack to resume.[17]

Slocomb raced to get into position. He turned the battery about ("changed front") and "limbered to rear," angling through the McDonald orchard to the La Fayette road, and then turned south. In this latter movement Slocomb gambled. He exposed the battery to direct fire down the length of his column as his teams hauled guns and caissons at a gallop down La Fayette road, across the single bridge over the ravine.[18] The daring and speed of his movement succeeded, nevertheless. The company crossed the bridge safely, exited La Fayette road to the right, and took position "on favorable ground on the west of the road," a slight rise just beyond the ravine that ran perpendicular to the road. The position provided the company with an excellent field of fire commanding the south portion of the McDonald farm.[19] From there they could easily support the Adams-Stovall attack down the La Fayette road, at least until the infantry reached the woods some two to three hundred yards immediately south.[20]

16. *OR,* Vol. XXX, Pt. 2, pp. 199, 221; Cozzens, *This Terrible Sound,* 317–18; Davis, *Breckinridge,* 374.

17. Breckinridge, however, had sent a staff officer to inform corps commander Hill. Cozzens, *This Terrible Sound,* 326.

18. This fire could have come from any one of several Federal batteries racing down the La Fayette road themselves, attempting to get into position to support Thomas' left. Bridges' battery, by this time, was presumably gone, forced from its position by Lewis' assault.

19. Four Napoleons mark the site of the Fifth Company's subsequent position. Since Chalaron participated in erecting these tablets and establishing battle positions on the field thirty years later, their presence (as well as customary battle tactics) strongly suggests Slocomb positioned his Napoleons there.

20. Slocomb probably left his caissons behind, several hundred yards to the rear, close to the McDonald house (present CCNMP headquarters). Horses for the limbers and guns (and the limbers themselves) probably were hidden in the ravine just behind the battery position. *OR,* Vol. XXX, Pt. 2, p. 229; Chalaron, "Slocomb's Battery in the Tennessee Army"; Daniel, *Cannoneers in Gray,* 98; artillery firing demonstration, CCNMP, fall, 1994.

Everything seemed to be in order. But was it? Could Breckinridge be committing his division in a reckless tactical absurdity? Truly he faced a terrible dilemma. His was to be the crucial attack, the one that ultimately would come the closest to winning the battle as Bragg had envisioned. This consideration argued that Breckinridge mass all available power on the cutting edge of his division. To this end he sent staff officer after staff officer back to D. H. Hill and Polk requesting, pleading for, additional manpower with which to make the flank attack.[21] On the other hand, Breckinridge and/or Rice Graves seemed unusually sensitive, almost preoccupied, about the safety of the rear of the division. After all, they did form the right of the army except for Forrest's cavalry, and Breckinridge must have questioned the latter's effectiveness as he saw Yankee cavalry to the north in a threatening posture.[22] Consequently, Graves had ordered Slocomb to split the Fifth Company, having him post a section (probably Vaught and his rifled guns) on the high ground at McDonald farm, facing north, to fire across a "large open field" upon the Federal cavalry "harassing our extreme right." To provide infantry support for these guns and to secure the rear of the division, Breckinridge, in yet another move that would diminish the strength of his attack force, had Adams leave behind Austin's fine sharpshooter battalion and the 32nd Alabama.[23]

The Kentuckian was alone, with only two organized brigades and a weakened battery, about to confront an enemy of undetermined strength. Not only was he blocking the road north, but he was about to assault the flank and rear of the enemy, an enemy who surely would lash back with a fury born of desperation. It is understandable yet appalling that Breckinridge weakened his small attack force—removing one section from Slocomb and the two infantry units from Adams—thereby jeopardizing any hope for success of this risky solo effort down the La Fayette road.[24]

21. Interview with J. H. Ogden III, July 12, 1995; Davis, *Breckinridge*, 374.

22. His flank, according to William C. Davis (*Breckinridge*, 373), could hardly have been protected by Forrest's dismounted cavalry.

23. *OR*, Vol. XXX, Pt. 2, pp. 219, 228; Chalaron, "Vivid Experiences at Chickamauga," 278; Daniel, *Cannoneers in Gray*, 101.

24. An interesting question arises. What was the role of Lewis' wing of Helm's brigade while Adams and Stovall attacked? Col. Joseph H. Lewis reports that they, under the command of Lt. Col. Martin H. Cofer, recrossed La Fayette road and were heading east through the heavy woods to rejoin the regrouping and shattered half of their brigade. Their role thereafter on the twentieth until about 4 P.M. is veiled in the ambiguities of Lewis' and Cofer's reports. *OR*, Vol. XXX, Pt. 2, pp. 204–205, 212.

This meant that Slocomb's four guns south of McDonald field would provide the entire fire support for Breckinridge's infantry—only four pieces of the twenty in Rice Graves's artillery battalion.[25] The division had brought four batteries to Chickamauga, but neither Cobb's nor Mebane's battery, according to Breckinridge, was available to assist at this crucial time, both having been handicapped in their movements "by the nature of the ground" and by their attempting, albeit unsuccessfully, to fill by fire the gap between Breckinridge and Cleburne.[26]

Breckinridge opened his attack about 10:30 A.M., and the brigades of Adams and Stovall moved "in fine order over a field and entered the woods beyond." Stovall, by guiding right on the La Fayette road, actually passed the extreme left of Thomas' breastworks and stopped at the edge of Kelly field. He saw to his front two batteries of Union artillery and determined to take them.[27] His men entered Kelly field and launched their attack. It was short-lived. When they emerged from the wood line, Ferdinand Van Derveer's brigade, which had been lying prone, arose and delivered a volley with great shocking power. The Floridians hesitated when hit by this heavy frontal fire. Within an instant, it seemed, Van Derveer's fusillade was compounded by enfilade fire down Stovall's left flank, not to speak of canister blasts from the Federal batteries directly ahead.[28] Beset by artillery and musket fire, Stovall's Florida brigade, "by far the smallest brigade [818 men] in the Army of Tennessee," came apart and fled Kelly field.[29]

25. As infantry support for these two sections, Major Graves ordered the 4th Florida of Stovall's brigade to remain behind. This regiment, however, left soon after and rejoined its parent brigade in time for the fight at Kelly field. *OR,* Vol. XXX, Pt. 2, p. 235.

26. In the mid-morning fighting, as Breckinridge's division moved west toward La Fayette road, Cobb had tried to support Helm's desperate attempts against Thomas' breastworks, but was ineffective because of the "density of the timber." One of Cobb's sections, later in the afternoon, would play a detached support role in the unsuccessful attack by Forrest north of the Reed's Bridge road and La Fayette Road junction. Otherwise Cobb's battery would remain quiet throughout the twentieth. Mebane's and Graves's own batteries (commanded by Lt. S. M. Spencer) do not appear in the Chickamauga reports, and it is assumed they also took no direct role in the fighting. *OR,* Vol. XXX, Pt. 2, pp. 199–200, 217, 221, 220, 224, 227, 229, 235.

27. Actually there were four batteries.

28. This devastating cannon fire came primarily from Capt. Wilbur Goodspeed's Battery A, First Ohio Light Artillery.

29. *OR,* Vol. XXX, Pt. 2, p. 232; Cozzens, *This Terrible Sound,* 331–32; Pasco Diary, September 20, 1863, CCNMP.

Adams had advanced as far as the ravine behind Slocomb's guns. There he halted till Slocomb could suppress (aided by the musket fire of Stovall's charging regiments, east of La Fayette road) the guns firing from south of the junction of the La Fayette road and the McFarland Bridge road.[30] Once the Federal guns had been silenced, Adams' three Louisiana regiments emerged from the ravine, charged across the south McDonald field and pushed on into the woods. As the infantry advanced past them, the Fifth Company ceased firing. "During this time the Company was exposed to an artillery fire which it could not return owing to our troops in the woods." The enemy's "shrapnel was continually bursting over us."[31]

It was then, as the Louisianans drove into the woodline, some three hundred yards south, that shrapnel struck Rice Graves as he sat on his horse beside Slocum observing Dan Adams' attack.[32] Graves fell mortally wounded into Slocomb's arms. He was borne away and placed in the hollow behind the battery. Chalaron opened Graves's coat and discovered he "had been pierced by a shrapnel bullet from side to side through the bowels." Breckinridge rushed over at a gallop from the left, where he had been busy reorganizing Helm's smashed brigade. He knelt beside his young artillery chief, saw his desperate condition, then ordered him carried off the field.[33] As members of the company crowded around grasping Graves's hand and saying goodbye, the mortally wounded chief of artillery turned his head and said, "Boys . . . I know you think that I prefer my old battery to yours. It is not so. There is none that I admire and love more than yours. I wish a detail of your boys to carry me off and to remain with me until I die."[34]

30. Probably Goodspeed's guns since Bridges' battery by now had withdrawn from the area as a result of Lewis' attack.

31. Although Slocomb suppressed the enemy artillery fire directly ahead, he had little luck with the Federal guns on Snodgrass Hill, which kept firing from the right front into the south McDonald field. These guns, virtually unseen, bit into Breckinridge's infantry as they advanced and retired across the field. They also would harass and hurt Slocomb as long as his guns remained south of the ravine. Chalaron, Notes on Chickamauga, Chalaron Papers, HTT (notes were the basis for two articles Chalaron wrote, one appearing in the New Orleans *Times-Democrat,* May 29, 1883, and the other in the *Confederate Veteran* in 1895); Chalaron, "Memories of Rice Graves," 12.

32. Slocomb's horse was wounded by the shell that struck Graves. New Orleans *Times-Democrat,* May 29, 1883.

33. It was evident that Adams had been repulsed by the time Breckinridge arrived, as "the tide of battle seems to be driving back against us." New Orleans *Times-Democrat,* May 29, 1883; Davis, *Breckinridge,* 376–77.

34. Breckinridge wrote of Graves in his official report: "Although a young man, he had won eminence in arms, and he gave promise of the highest distinction. A truer friend, a purer patriot, a

Meanwhile, Adams' diminished brigade, "not exceeding 800 men," had smashed through one line of Federals at the junction of the Alexander's Bridge road and the La Fayette Road—in effect a line of skirmishers—most from the remnants of Beatty's 104th Illinois and 15th Kentucky.[35] The Louisianans continued on through the woods west of the La Fayette road (generally on a line with the Glen-Kelly country road, paralleling the La Fayette road). Dan Adams next drove through a second skirmish line (from Timothy Stanley's brigade), penetrating to a point west of La Fayette road nearly opposite the center of Kelly field and in rear of Thomas' corps. There suddenly the Louisianans encountered a devastating volley from three concealed regiments commanded by Stanley.[36] Down went General Adams, down went "nearly 150" of the 19th Louisiana and their colonel. As the Louisianans recoiled from this deadly fire from their front, a Union brigade (Van Derveer's), supported by artillery, threatened to cross the La Fayette road and strike Adams' beleaguered brigade in the rear.[37]

At this point Col. Randall Gibson (13th-20th Louisiana) took charge. He ordered a retreat back to the McDonald farm. There he intended to rally the brigade "on the rear slope of the hill upon which [Slocomb's Battery] was posted." The demoralized Louisianans streamed back through the woods, their ranks broken, leaving the wounded Dan Adams

---

better soldier never lived." Graves lingered until the next day in the division field hospital, a log house not far to the east of Reed's Bridge. Helm would die in the same room. Chalaron paid his friend a visit that morning but Graves was "in a dying condition, apparently unconscious, and did not recognize me." New Orleans *Times-Democrat*, May 29, 1883; *OR*, Vol. XXX, Pt. 2, pp. 201, 218, 229; Chalaron, "Vivid Experiences at Chickamauga," 279; Davis, *Breckinridge*, 377; Chalaron, "Memories of Rice Graves," 13; Glenn Hodges, "An Officer and a Gentleman," Owensboro (Ky.) *Messenger-Inquirer*, May 14, 1996.

35. Breckinridge's initial attack threw these two regiments back upon the La Fayette road. Captain Bridges expected these units to stop and support him at the junction of the La Fayette and Alexander's Bridge roads. They failed to do so, and the pursuing Confederates, probably Lewis' right wing of Helm's brigade, disabled the half-battery west of the road: "Every man and horse was hit." Its commander, Lt. William Bishop, was killed and two pieces captured. After he realized he had no infantry support, Bridges managed to extricate his four remaining guns. Cozzens, *This Terrible Sound*, 324; *OR*, XXX, Pt. 1, pp. 351–53, 368, 374–75; Glenn Tucker, *Chickamauga: Bloody Battle in the West* (Indianapolis, 1961), 233.

36. 11th Michigan, 19th Illinois, and 18th Ohio.

37. Playing an important role in the repulse of Stovall and Adams was Capt. Wilbur Goodspeed's Ohio battery. *OR*, XXX, Pt. 2, pp. 141, 199–200, 224–25; Beatty, *Memoirs of a Volunteer*, 248; Cozzens, *This Terrible Sound*, 326–29, 334–35; Evans, *Confederate Military History*, XIII, 185.

behind to be plundered (several times) and captured. They fled across McDonald field, past Slocomb, and over the ravine, pursued by Beatty's and Stanley's troops.[38]

Adolphe Chalaron watched the distant woodline. Dan Adams' "horse and his adjutant's dash riderless and madly out and past our guns. They've fallen both." Slocomb knew what he must do. He immediately ordered the battery to limber up, retire across the ravine, and take position on the high ground just to the north.[39] Once he had reached that point and gone into battery (undoubtedly Vaught's section rejoined him or at least changed front), Slocomb again had to hold his fire and wait impatiently until Adams' men (now Gibson's) reached the ravine to his "immediate front," so that the ravine's "shelter may be used by our retreating infantry and let us sooner sweep the field in front." Once Gibson's troops had taken cover, the Washington Artillery opened on the pursuing enemy "and drove them back in fine style," keeping the McDonald field "clear with canister while numerous opposing guns cut us up with shot and shell." The battery succeeded in throwing back "repeatedly the attempts of the foe to emerge from the woods." Breckinridge, who was observing, reported the Fifth Company "repulsed the enemy by a rapid and well-directed fire, rendering on this occasion important and distinguished service."[40]

Gibson, using the cover of Slocomb's fire, set about establishing a new line for Adams' brigade. The ravine was unsuitable because the men were "under too much fire," so Gibson chose a spot farther to the rear—north of the position on the McDonald farm from which the charge down the La Fayette road had originated. Using Austin's sharpshooters and the 32nd Alabama as a nucleus, Gibson restored a brigade line of battle. Forrest assisted him in re-forming the Louisiana infantry. Chalaron saw Forrest at work—a "splendid appearing" officer. "I heard him say to them, 'Rally here, Louisianians, or I'll have to bring up my bobtail cavalry to show you how to fight!'" To further strengthen his line, in effect turning

---

38. Cozzens, *This Terrible Sound,* 228–31; Beatty, *Memoirs of a Volunteer,* 248; *OR,* Vol. XXX, Pt. 2, p. 225, Pt. 1, p. 301.

39. Here he would either combine once again with Vaught's section on high ground west of the McDonald home or place his guns on high ground close to the intersection of the Reed's Bridge and La Fayette roads.

40. *OR,* Vol. XXX, Pt. 2, pp. 229–30, 200, Pt. 1, p. 301; Chalaron, "Slocomb's Battery in the Tennessee Army"; New Orleans *Times-Democrat,* May 29, 1883.

it into a division line of battle, Gibson (helped by Slocomb) also rallied two of Stovall's regiments, placing them on the left at the new position.[41]

The time required for Gibson's reorganization was bought at a dear price. The enemy focused their attention on the Fifth Company, conspicuous now that they were positioned "far in advance of the whole line." Quickly they became the target of several Federal batteries that had advanced to the south edge of McDonald field and along both sides of the La Fayette road. Fire also came from the vicinity of Snodgrass Hill to the west. In addition, the short distance to the wood line at the south edge of McDonald farm enabled concealed Union infantry to join in the shooting. "I was soon subjected to a terrific fire," reported Slocomb, "from the enemy's batteries in front, right, and left." Despite this enemy artillery and musket fire, the Fifth Company clung to its position and did its best to respond as rapidly and effectively as possible. They remained there exposed, taking casualties, "for half an hour and more."[42]

Randall Gibson, seeing the plight of Slocomb, outgunned and being pounded relentlessly by well-directed enemy fire, withdrew the battery to the brigade line of battle. Upon receipt of that order, recalled Chalaron, "we picked up from around our guns and threw upon our limbers and caissons the bodies of six killed and fourteen wounded of our company, leaving many horses [dead and disabled]." When the company reached the safety of the infantry's position, Slocomb approached Breckinridge and requested that the company be permitted "to retire from the field to refit." Breckinridge told Slocomb to wait until "he could bring up Liddell's division," so the Fifth Company unlimbered once again. Daniel C. Govan's brigade of Liddell's division came up presently, passed through the "intervals of the battery," and took position. This allowed Breckinridge to grant permission to withdraw, so Slocomb had his six guns limber up and pass to the rear through the ranks of Gibson and Stovall. Then Slocomb led his battered command down the Reed's Bridge road close to the point from which they had begun the advance that morning.[43]

The battery was in shambles. Four men had been killed. One was Pvt. Ben Stakeman, who had joined up as the Fifth Company passed through

41. *OR,* Vol. XXX, Pt. 2, pp. 216, 221–22, 224, 226, 229; Chalaron, "Vivid Experiences at Chickamauga," 279; Chalaron, "Slocomb's Battery in the Tennessee Army."

42. *OR,* Vol. XXX, Pt. 2, p. 230; Chalaron, "Vivid Experiences at Chickamauga," 278–79.

43. *OR,* Vol. XXX, Pt. 2, p. 230; Chalaron, "Vivid Experiences at Chickamauga," 279.

Mobile on its way to Jackson. Also dead was driver James Bayle, an Englishman who had been employed as a gardener in New Orleans before the war. His leg had been shot off close to the body. Pvt. Fred Morel, a thirty-two-year-old printer, who had transferred from the Confederate Guards Response at Tupelo, had been shot through the body. Particularly mourned by Slocomb was young Leon Brocard, formerly a member of the First Company, Chasseurs à Pied, Louisiana Militia. Brocard had been captured by the enemy at New Orleans and for months been too sick to be exchanged. Finally, when well enough, he made his way north to the army, and appeared on the field at Chickamauga. He approached Slocomb, insisting "upon serving with the Battery." While helping at one of the guns Brocard had been struck in the mouth and was killed. Although Brocard was not "formally enlisted," Slocomb saw fit to mention him individually (the only private so mentioned) in his report of Chickamauga and Glass's Mill: "Where every man in the company did his duty so nobly it is impossible to discriminate, I cannot refrain from expressing my admiration of the bravery of Leon Brocard, a youth of 16, who volunteered his services as the battery was going into action, and nobly met his death in performance of a self-imposed duty."[44]

Among the sixteen members wounded in the fight at McDonald's farm was Asa Woods, a steamboat crewman born in Ohio. Woods had been refuging in Mobile when the Fifth Company passed through, and he took the opportunity to join up. He had fallen ill at Jackson, however, and had just rejoined the battery. Woods was struck in the leg during the fight at McDonald's field and carried to the rear when the battery withdrew. Surgeons amputated his leg below the knee, but Woods did not recover and died less than two weeks later at the Confederate hospital in Marietta, Georgia.[45]

When they reached the old field from which they had launched their attack five hours earlier, the men laid the dead aside gently, ministered to the wounded as best they could, and began refitting. Fortunately they had the captured guns and caissons of Lyman Bridges to cannibalize. Battery blacksmiths and artificers set to work with a fury restoring the six-pieces

44. *OR*, Vol. XXX, Pt. 2, p. 230; 5WA Report Book, WA Papers, HTT.

45. Account Book, Louisiana Relief Association of Mobile, Chicago Historical Society; Chalaron, Master 5WA Roster, Chalaron Papers, HTT; WCDV to mother, October 4, 1863, Vaught Letters, HNOC; New Orleans *Daily Picayune*, October 6, 1863.

to proper working order, replacing or repairing wheels and sometimes entire carriages.[46] The drivers brought over four artillery horses captured from the enemy and hitched them up. Meanwhile, the limbers were replenished somewhat by the distribution of 120 rounds found in the chests of Bridges' battery.[47]

Having completed repairs, reorganized gun crews, and replenished ammunition, Slocomb reported to Randall Gibson about 3:00 P.M., having been absent two hours. He found Gibson and the Louisiana brigade close by, the division having been withdrawn not long after the Fifth Company retired. Breckinridge had moved Gibson's men east down the Reed's Bridge road to "where we first formed in the morning." There they would remain about two hours, inactive except for one change of position to the left. Finally, almost at sundown, Breckinridge formed in support of W. H. T. Walker's corps (S. R. Gist's and Liddell's divisions). When Liddell attacked to the south and west, the Louisiana brigade followed closely, passed through Liddell's lines, and charged, driving the enemy from the left of Thomas' breastworks and pursuing them across the La Fayette road. Since it was growing quite dark, Gibson halted a short distance east of the road, happy in the knowledge that the "ground fought upon in the morning had been entirely regained." What role the Fifth Company played in this last Confederate assault is unknown, but their participation was probably minimal since the attack angled southwest through difficult terrain.[48]

That Sunday night the company encamped. They broke into their customary messes and gathered around campfires, physically exhausted and emotionally wrung out. So much had been compacted into the previous forty-eight hours. They could take pride, however, in having performed their duty well. They had contributed in helping the Army of Tennessee win its greatest victory at Chickamauga. They had been blasted when they ventured west of the Chickamauga Creek at Glass's Mill on Saturday,

46. Some of these implements and spare parts could have come from the remains of Baird's and Brannan's batteries abandoned on September 19 in that sector of the field.

47. Bridges also had suffered severely during the two-day fight along Chickamauga Creek. He lost six killed, sixteen wounded, four missing, as well as forty-two horses killed and two wounded. *OR*, Vol. XXX, Pt. 2, p. 230, Pt. 1, p. 371; Chalaron, "Vivid Experiences at Chickamauga," 279; Chalaron, "Battle Echoes," 223.

48. *OR*, Vol. XXX, Pt. 2, pp. 143, 200, 205, 217, 220, 222–24, 226, 228, 231–35; Davis, *Breckinridge*, 377–78.

but on Sunday, September 20, they had played a significant role on the Confederate right. They *were* the division artillery on that day, the sole fire support, offensive and defensive, for Breckinridge's attack west toward the La Fayette road and his subsequent two-brigade attack south down that road. This was the all-important flank attack that, at least in Bragg's mind, carried with it hope of Confederate victory.[49]

Following Breckinridge's failed effort, the Fifth Company had stayed in an exposed position covering Adams' (and Stovall's) infantry as they retired. Slocomb's men paid a price for their conspicuous performance— they had suffered more casualties than any other battery in Bragg's army.[50] Indeed, they had fired far more rounds (682) than any other battery in the Army of Tennessee.[51] According to Bragg's ordnance chief, Lt. Col. Hypolite Oladowski, the Washington Artillery fired almost 20 percent of all Confederate rounds expended during the three days' fighting at Chickamauga. Since over twenty-five Confederate batteries were engaged, one can see that the Washington Artillery played a heavy role.[52]

The day after the Battle of Chickamauga, some of Bragg's units, such as Austin's sharpshooters and Forrest's cavalry, moved north to "find and feel" the enemy, but most remained on or near the field, burying the dead, reorganizing, and resting.[53] It is not known when or where the Fifth Company buried their dead from Glass's Mill. The four men killed at Chickamauga, however, were carried just north to the farm of Elijah Miabee (McAbee). There Slocomb read the funeral service and the men placed

49. "It should be noted that neither Colonel Walton nor the four batteries of the Washington Artillery in Virginia came westward with General Longstreet's corps to participate in this battle. Major William Miller Owen [successor to Walton as commander of the battalion following the war] was in the battle but as a member of the staff of [Gen. William] Preston's division in Polk's Corps." Casey, *Outline of Civil War Campaigns,* 67.

50. Of the 196 officers, noncommissioned officers, and privates killed and wounded at Chickamauga, the Washington Artillery lost 33 or about 17 percent.

51. Slocomb reported 562 rounds fired in two days, but Robert Cobb, Breckinridge's acting chief of artillery, maintained the company fired 682 rounds. *OR,* Vol. XXX, Pt. 2, pp. 230, 201; Interviews with James H. Ogden III, September 19, October 19, 1994, May 30, 1995; Casey, *Outline of Civil War Campaigns,* 67.

52. H. Oladowski, "Guns Engaged, Ammunition Expended, &c. in the Army of Tenn. commanded by Genl. B. Bragg. C.S.A., in the Battle of Chickamauga, Sept. 18, 19, 20, 1863," Letters Received, Adjutant and Inspector General's Office, RG 109, NA.

53. Cozzens, *This Terrible Sound,* 517.

their comrades side by side in a single grave out in a field, blazing a tree to mark the location.[54] Billy Vaught wrote home a week later, detailing the losses suffered. Although "my clothes & horses suffered," he was happy to relate to his mother, "I again escaped without a scratch."[55]

54. Notations in 5WA report book indicate the grave was located "in a skirt of woods near road leading to Bridge over Chickamauga Creek," and that the men were "buried in field ½ mile from Anderson's bridge on left side of road going from Anderson's Mill to river and about 200 yards from road. Four bodies. Stakeman is 3rd from tree which is blazed." CCNMP historian Ogden believes the burial at McAbee's suggests that Adams' hospital may have been established there. WCDV to mother, October 4, 1863, Vaught Letters, HNOC; 5WA Report Book, WA Papers, HTT; Interview with J. H. Ogden III, May 30, 1995.

55. WCDV to mother, October 4, 1863, Vaught Letters, HNOC.

9

TIME TO GIT

ON SEPTEMBER 23, 1863, the Army of Tennessee moved on Chattanooga and established itself aggressively atop Missionary Ridge. Realizing it would be unwise to assault Rosecrans in his prepared defenses, Bragg decided to besiege the city. He occupied Lookout Valley (west of Lookout Mountain) with a fragile picket line sufficient only to snap the main Union supply conduits from Stevenson and Bridgeport, Alabama. Longstreet supported these pickets, posting his corps in a flimsy, jagged line that extended from Lookout Creek in that valley eastward across the face of Lookout Mountain into Chattanooga Valley.[1] Polk and Hill placed their men in front of the western slope of Missionary Ridge, stretching their lines until they touched Longstreet's right flank at Chattanooga Creek. In all, Bragg's army manned makeshift defenses extending at least seven miles. After Bragg had posted his army on the commanding terrain,

---

1. The first week in October, 1863, Longstreet had works constructed for his batteries on top of Lookout Mountain. To help haul these guns up the steep mountain road, horses were "removed" from the Fifth Company. John Thompson Brown Diary, October 5, 1863, CCNMP, Fort Oglethorpe, Georgia.

however, he waited, allowing the initiative to pass to the enemy. By October 1 word came of heavy Union troop shifts: two corps coming west from the Army of the Potomac, and Sherman and the Army of the Tennessee coming east from Mississippi. Bragg continued to wait, nevertheless, preoccupied with waging war within the high command of his own army.[2]

That suicidal war would rage for six weeks, drawing the president of the Confederacy to Missionary Ridge, and would result in the wholesale rearrangement of units and serious if not irreparable damage to the morale of the officer corps, not to speak of that of the rank and file. Bragg reorganized his army not with an eye to increasing its effectiveness, but with transparent political design—"eliminate certain cliques and thus 'keep down the anti-Bragg men.'" Breckinridge's division proved no exception. It would be scattered and new elements substituted. Breckinridge himself, though closely tied to the anti-Bragg party, escaped Bragg's vengeance. Indeed, the Kentuckian advanced to corps command (Hill's corps), at least until such time as Lt. Gen. John B. Hood might recover from his most recent wound and return to the army. In the meantime, Breckinridge's division would be led by Brig. Gen. William B. Bate, a fighter.[3]

This genial, popular Tennessean was thirty-seven. Unlike the urbane, well-educated Breckinridge, Bate had enjoyed few advantages of birth. An open man, impossible to dislike personally, Bate was a man one trusted instinctively. Even Unionist Parson William G. Brownlow characterized this former enemy as "absolutely devoid of duplicity." Bate had pushed his way through life, trying his hand at a variety of endeavors: clerking on a steamboat, fighting in Mexico, editing a newspaper, practicing law, representing Sumner County in the Tennessee general assembly. Perhaps most fitting of all, Bate had served as a Breckinridge elector in 1860. He was a leader of men and constantly sought the "post of danger" for himself and his command. Would Bate prove an effective division commander, men wondered. His impetuosity at Chickamauga had caught the attention of Bragg and President Davis, but his men had paid a high price in blood for following "Fighting Billy."[4]

2. See Connelly, *Autumn of Glory,* 232–34; Peter Cozzens, *Shipwreck of Their Hopes: The Battles for Chattanooga* (Urbana, Ill., 1994), 23–33.

3. Wiley Sword, *Mountains Touched with Fire: Chattanooga Besieged, 1863* (New York, 1995), 166.

4. Davis, *Breckinridge,* 382–85; Park Marshall, *A Life of William B. Bate* (Nashville, 1908), 19–64; Cozzens, *This Terrible Sound,* 256–57; Sword, *Mountains Touched with Fire,* 165–66. See

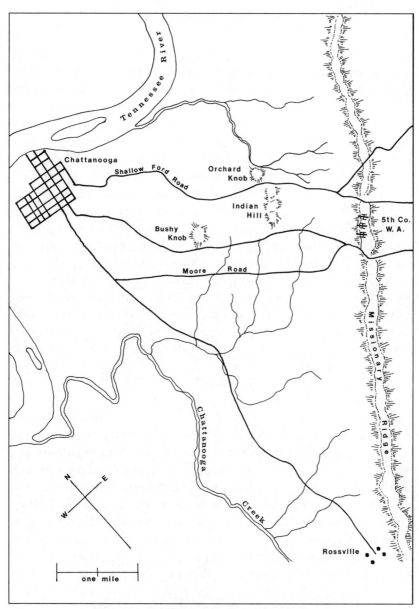

Missionary Ridge, September–November, 1863
Adapted from Randall L. Gibson's 1883 drawing
Map by Blake A. Magner

Helm's Orphan Brigade remained in the division. Now it would be commanded by Brig. Gen. Joseph H. Lewis, who had led the right wing against the Federals strung out along La Fayette Road on September 20. Stovall's Florida brigade had been reconstituted, two regiments being removed (47th Georgia and 60th North Carolina) and three added (6th, 7th Florida, 1st Florida Cavalry [dismounted]). These five Florida regiments would be under Brig. Gen. Jesse J. Finley. Stovall himself was transferred to A. P. Stewart's division, where he would command Georgians. Also to Stewart's division went Adams' Louisiana brigade, the Fifth Company's parent unit. In their stead appeared Bate's brigade, a mix of Tennessee and Georgia troops, led by the brave but reckless Col. Robert C. Tyler. This reorganization, of course, was highly unpopular with the Fifth Company. They were not confident of Bate at all, nor Tyler. More to the point, "it was the first time the battery had been separated from Louisiana infantry units." [5] When the reorganization order came, it created "quite a commotion" in the Louisiana brigade. Gibson's infantry shouted to the Washington Artillery, " 'Boys, you will lose your guns to-day; we will not be there to stand by you.' A petition was drawn up . . . asking that we be left to fight together. Col. [Wesley P.] Winans, 19th Louisiana circulated it around. But orders had to be obeyed and we marched off." [6]

Changes affecting the company also occurred within the artillery organizational structure. The Kentuckian Capt. Robert Cobb, who had replaced Rice Graves as division chief of artillery, moved up with his friend Breckinridge to become corps chief of artillery. To command the division artillery battalion (Cobb's battery under Capt. Frank P. Gracey, Mebane's battery, and the Fifth Company), Breckinridge and Cobb selected Slocomb, thus placing Billy Vaught in command of the Washington Artillery. Vaught may have been pleased with the opportunity, but, according to Chalaron, Slocomb apparently regarded the assignment merely as temporary. He wanted it that way, having repeatedly "refused promotion" because it would remove him from direct association with the men for

also Connelly, *Autumn of Glory,* 250–52; *Senate Documents,* 59th Cong., 2nd Sess., No. 403, pp. 148–52.

5. On the other hand, the Floridians seemed pleased, having their dispersed regiments gathered in one brigade under Brig. Gen. Jesse J. Finley. *OR,* Vol. XXXI, Pt. 2, p. 739; J. Adolphe Chalaron, "Missionary Ridge," Chalaron Papers, HTT; Casey, *Outline of Civil War Campaigns;* 69; Pasco Diary, November 13, 1863, CCNMP.

6. Winans was killed at Missionary Ridge on November 25. Chalaron, "Missionary Ridge," Chalaron Papers, HTT.

whom he felt responsible. Within the battery itself a new officer was needed to replace Tom Blair, who had been killed at Glass's Mill. The company elected Charles G. Johnsen. This thirty-year-old Mississippian of Danish descent had moved to New Orleans before the war and become a cotton merchant. Commended for his brave service at Shiloh and Murfreesboro, Johnsen had been promoted to second lieutenant October 2, 1863.[7]

The spirits and health of the members of the Fifth Company deteriorated as October wore into November, reflecting the plight of the army at large. More than a fourth of the battery had to be furloughed for sickness during November. Encamped at Antipas Moore's farm (vineyard) at the foot of Missionary Ridge, in front of Bragg's headquarters, they passed "tedious days of inaction."[8] They heard rumblings of infighting among their general officers.[9] They shared the widespread "feelings of disgust," of "impaired confidence," regarding Bragg as they pondered their barren victory at Chickamauga and the wasted lives of their comrades. When added to the discontent arising from being isolated from their Louisiana friends, it made their state miserable. Indeed, Charles Johnsen remembered seeing about him an army of "starved and demoralized men." Throughout the army, but not yet from the battery, men began to desert in larger and larger numbers. "They cannot stand the cold nights . . . without overcoats and not half enough to eat." To their front was the enemy; to their rear, between Missionary Ridge and Chickamauga Station, water and mud had rendered the entire area an almost impassable quagmire.[10]

7. *OR*, Vol. XXXI, Pt. 2, p. 662, Pt. 3, p. 642; Vol. LII, Pt. 1, p. 96; J. A. Chalaron, "Notes on C. H. Slocomb," Chalaron Papers, HTT; Robert Cobb, CSR, Charles G. Johnsen, CSR, RG 109, NA; 5WA Master Roster, WA Papers, HTT.

8. Two of Antipas and Rebecca Frazier Moore's sons would be casualties in the fighting on November 25: Lt. Col. Beriah Frazier Moore, 19th Tennessee (killed) and Pvt. Nicholas Gibbs Moore, 19th Tennessee (wounded). John Wilson (Hamilton County, Tennessee, historian) to author, November 4, 1994.

9. See Connelly, *Autumn of Glory*, 233–50.

10. It was at this time, when spirits were low, that Lallande Fevriers arrived from New Orleans to "carry home the remains of poor Lt. Blair." WCDV to mother, October 4, 1863, Vaught Letters, HNOC; 5WA Clothing Book, WA Papers, HTT; Chalaron, "Missionary Ridge," Chalaron Papers, HTT; Philip D. Stephenson, *Civil War Memoir*, ed. Nathaniel C. Hughes, Jr. (Conway, Ark., 1995), 135; Arroyo Journal, October 15, 16, 23, 30, 1863, WA Papers, HTT; Pasco Diary, November 13, 1863, CCNMP; C. G. Johnsen to JAC, September 18, 1894, Chalaron Papers, HTT; Sword, *Mountains Touched with Fire*, 167; Cozzens, *Shipwreck of Their Hopes*, 29–31.

Chalaron recalled how hungry they were that fall of 1863, cut off from their supply depots by the treacherous bottoms of Chickamauga Creek that ran behind Missionary Ridge. Rations could not get through, and to ensure that the horses were fed, guards had to be doubled. "Daily starving soldiers crave of us permission to pick out of the dirt around the horses the soiled and trodden grains of corn that remained after feed time." Furthermore, it seemed to be raining constantly—for almost two months. Then it turned cold and the wind heightened. "Last night we had ice about an inch thick," wrote one of Bate's infantrymen on November 10. Two days later he lamented, "Our brigade has not drawn but one day's ration of beef in eight days." Offers of reassignment tempted one's sense of duty. Felix Arroyo, while at the hospital recovering from head and leg injuries, was approached by Bragg's director of hospitals, Dr. Samuel Stout, and given the chance to become a hospital clerk. Arroyo refused. "If I were to keep away from the [battery], I never would have left my wife and child."[11]

Despite the weakened state of his army, and in the face of an enemy obviously growing daily in strength, Bragg dispatched Longstreet and Wheeler with 17,000 men to Knoxville on November 4. This resulted in stretching hopelessly the thin Confederate siege lines. One division replaced Longstreet's corps guarding Lookout Mountain; another held the space from the middle of Chattanooga Valley to Missionary Ridge.

At last the dreaded time came. It was at noon, November 23. Before the Confederate rifle pits on Orchard Knob, a strong point anchoring the outposts in advance of infantry at the base of Missionary Ridge, appeared unit after unit of Federals. Well over twenty thousand in blue poured out of their Chattanooga entrenchments and formed, as if on review, in front of Orchard Knob. It was George Thomas' Army of the Cumberland. Straight toward Missionary Ridge they came, irresistibly. They swept over the Confederate position at Orchard Knob with ease, then entrenched, barely twelve hundred yards from the base of Missionary Ridge, the center of the Confederate line.[12]

---

11. Two men deserted during this period, both while on furlough: Pennsylvanian W. A. Crawford, who was recovering from his Chickamauga wound, and G. H. Shotwell, former sergeant of drivers. Chalaron, "Missionary Ridge," Chalaron Papers, HTT; Sword, *Mountains Touched with Fire*, 165; Daniel, *Cannoneers in Gray*, 107–108; Arroyo Journal, WA Papers, HTT; 5WA Master Roster, WA Papers, HTT.

12. See Cozzens, *Shipwreck of Their Hopes*, 128–37; Sword, *Mountains Touched with Fire*, 178–86.

Bragg took immediate steps to redeploy his army. He recalled Cleburne's division, which was loading upon cars to join Longstreet; he recalled Joseph H. Lewis' Kentucky brigade from Chickamauga Station; and he shifted W. H. T. Walker's division from the Lookout Mountain defenses back to the ridge. Hardee (newly returned from Mississippi) was given command of the right of Missionary Ridge, Breckinridge the left. The latter ordered A. P. Stewart to rest the right of his attenuated line (four thousand troops manning a line almost two-miles in length across Chattanooga Valley) on Slocomb's battery at the eastern edge of the valley close to the foot of Missionary Ridge, thus making a connection with Bate. In the old Louisiana brigade's sector in Chattanooga Valley, Randall Gibson reported that he had so much ground to cover that it would take half the brigade simply to furnish the required picket detail.[13]

On November 24, the Fifth Company and Bate's division watched helplessly as Federal Gen. Joseph Hooker's soldiers smashed the feeble defenses at the base of Lookout Mountain. With the company at noon that day was corps commander Breckinridge himself, together with his staff, guests of Slocomb, and the other officers of the battery, "to partake of some delicacies received from far off Louisiana." For over an hour the group had been listening to the "deep report of one of our batteries" on the nose of Lookout Mountain as it responded to fire from "Moccasin Point and other positions." Chalaron remembered that "instinct tells us that the mountain is lost."[14]

That afternoon Bragg ordered the mountain abandoned, as well as Chattanooga Valley. This exposed the left flank of Missionary Ridge and required further shifting of troops. Early that night Breckinridge ordered Bate up the ridge to take position on the crest with Tyler's right in front of Bragg's headquarters, with Finley extending to the left. Lewis and his Kentuckians were sent off to help Cleburne and Hardee on the Confederate right, that flank being threatened by Sherman's sudden crossing of the Tennessee River in strength. The Army of Tennessee was facing a double envelopment by a vastly superior foe, all the while to their rear, Chickamauga Creek continued to rise, as though in concert with the enemy.[15]

13. *OR*, Vol. XXXI, Pt. 2, pp. 739, 676; Vol. LII, Pt. 2, p. 96. See Cozzens, *Shipwreck of Their Hopes*, 137–42.

14. Chalaron, "Missionary Ridge," Chalaron Papers, HTT.

15. *OR*, Vol. XXXI, Pt. 2, p. 739; Connelly, *Autumn of Glory*, 272–73; Cozzens, *Shipwreck of Their Hopes*, 196–97.

Bate's infantry left after dark and began their climb to the top of Missionary Ridge. Not the division artillery, however. According to Chalaron, they had been forgotten. So they awaited orders to move out—tents folded, guns hitched up. With fires prohibited, the members lay upon the ground "seeking shelter from the cold wind, from dark until 3:30 o'clock in the morning." Finally the Fifth Company received Bate's order. "Chilled and benumbed, with horses stiff and balky" (they had not been exercised much for two months), they started out. They could not proceed directly up the sharp eastern face of the ridge like infantry, of course.[16] When the time came, they and Mebane's and Gracey's batteries began the long trek south to Rossville, through Rossville Gap, then turned about to the north retracing their steps on the back side of the Missionary Ridge. "Owing to the nature of the country and the terrible condition of the roads, the horses showed great unwillingness to work," reported Slocomb, who commanded the battalion during this movement, "and it was with great difficulty that the point indicated was reached by 9 A.M."[17]

Robert Cobb met Slocomb at Bragg's headquarters the morning of the twenty-fifth. He directed that Gracey be placed there; he wanted the Washington Artillery about three hundred yards south of Gracey. The company went into battery as directed about 10 A.M. and for the remainder of the morning they remained in that position firing at long range "upon the forming masses of the enemy in the valley. The distance was, however, too great for effect," lamented Slocomb. During a pause in the firing, Captain Cobb informed Slocomb that he was relieved of command of the battalion. The veteran Capt. Henry C. Semple of Alabama had just returned to the army and as senior officer had taken charge of the artillery of Breckinridge's corps. This meant that Cobb would resume command of the battalion in Bate's division, and Slocomb would return to the Washington Artillery.[18]

Slocomb and Cobb seemed to work together well. Their two batteries had fought side by side at Shiloh, Murfreesboro, Jackson, and Glass's Mill. They were brother officers and their batteries, for a year and a half,

16. Lt. René Beauregard managed to get his battery up with the assistance of a company of infantry assigned to each gun. "Using ropes and pulleys, they were slowly drawn to the top." Daniel, *Cannoneers in Gray,* 112.

17. *OR,* Vol. XXXI, Pt. 2, p. 739; Vol. LII, Pt. 1, p. 96; Chalaron, "Missionary Ridge," Chalaron Papers, HTT.

18. *OR,* Vol. LII, Pt. 1, p. 96.

had been considered sister artillery companies. Robert Cobb, a former lawyer from Lyon County, Kentucky, and a great favorite of Breckinridge and Simon Bolivar Buckner, had commanded the former's division artillery since the death of Graves. As battalion commander, he suited Slocomb and the Fifth Company fine.[19]

The Confederate position on the ridge looked strong. At least Chalaron thought so—the wrinkled western slope had been cleared, though with no thought of building an abatis. "We had never seen a position so easy to defend." Although open ground lay in front of the entrenchments at the base of the ridge, the infantry just below the guns "was strung out along the ridge in single file, yards and yards apart." There were intervals in the infantry line that "appeared to us as left for other batteries, or for the skirmish lines when forced to retreat from the base of the ridge."[20] Complicating defensive arrangements significantly was the face of the ridge itself, scarred with numerous ravines and declivities, each providing the enemy an avenue of approach. To defend the ridge properly would take care and effort. Wiley Sword with cutting directness points out that Bragg, despite having occupied Missionary Ridge for sixty-two days, only now, "on the eve of a pending battle," directed that works be "constructed along the crest of this crucial ridge." Peter Cozzens dismisses Bragg's defenses as a "horribly improvised, sadly neglected patchwork." The Confederate commander and his chief lieutenants were preoccupied with the flanks of Missionary Ridge.[21]

Bate's division had been further weakened on November 24. Breckinridge wanted more men on the picket line between the base of the ridge and Orchard Knob, so Bate sent Finley's two smallest regiments. He soon became concerned about them, and, on the morning of the twenty-fifth, sent down the 7th Florida as support. Given orders by Bate to "hold the trenches at all hazards," these three units would be lost to the division when the attack on the center came that afternoon.[22] Further confusing things in Bate's sector was an order by Breckinridge moving the division

19. Robert Cobb, CSR, RG 109, NA; *CV,* XXIII (1915), 309; Thompson, *First Kentucky Brigade,* 930.

20. Chalaron, "Missionary Ridge," Chalaron Papers, HTT.

21. *OR,* Vol. XXXI, Pt. 2, pp. 739–40; Sword, *Mountains Touched with Fire,* 188; Cozzens, *Shipwreck of Their Hopes,* 249.

22. In fairness to Bate it should be noted that he changed his mind and ordered his Florida troops up from the trenches, but Breckinridge directed that they remain.

to the right (north). The men dropped their picks and shovels and marched off. Once they arrived at the designated place, however, a countermanding order came, so the men, cursing the outrageous stupidity of their superiors, retraced their steps to their old positions. Then, in a clear example of command befuddlement, Bragg and Breckinridge divided responsibilities. Breckinridge rode off toward the south end of the ridge, leaving army commander Bragg in immediate charge of the center and of Breckinridge's old division (Bate's).[23]

When Cobb resumed command of Bate's artillery battalion, he relocated the batteries in accordance with the directive of General Breckinridge. Gracey's battery was detached and remained to the left of Bragg's headquarters; Mebane took position in the center of the division's new line; and the Washington Artillery was placed on two pieces of high ground north of Bragg's headquarters, at the right of Bate's division.[24] From these positions the battery could see, if not command, segments of two winding roads (Crutchfield to the south, Bird's Mill to the north) that crossed the ridge at that point.[25] The two pieces of ground, about seventy-five yards apart, appeared to project "beyond the general western slope of the ridge, with a slight depression on the right, which gave the advantage of enfilading fire in that direction." Cobb asked Slocomb to divide the battery, placing Chalaron on the right with two Napoleons and a James Rifle while Vaught took position on the left with similar pieces.[26]

Adolphe Chalaron did not like his post. A "rude parapet for artillery" existed there, but it proved "an obstacle to the proper handling of the guns." With Slocomb's permission, Chalaron hauled the pieces outside the work and placed them closer to the crest. Of greater concern was the absence of infantry support here, at least on or close to the projecting

23. *OR,* Vol. XXXI, Pt. 2, pp. 739–40; Davis, *Breckinridge,* 388–89.

24. When the order to countermarch came, Bate moved his division south, but only to a position where Finley's left reached the Crutchfield road immediately to the north of Bragg's headquarters. As a result, Bate was essentially the length of a division north of where he had been. *OR,* Vol. XXXI, Pt. 2, pp. 739–40; Vol. LII, Pt. 1, p. 96. JAC estimated his position as one-half mile right (north) of Bragg's headquarters. JAC to W. B. Hazen, May 4, 1878, in W. B. Hazen, *Narrative of Military Service* (Boston, 1885), p. 203.

25. "Now [about 1900] the main Bird's-mill road, and the one by which the electric railroad reaches the crest of the Ridge." Chalaron, "Missionary Ridge," Chalaron Papers, HTT. Crutchfield road formed the left of Bate's line. *OR,* Vol. XXXI, Pt. 2, p. 740.

26. *OR,* Vol. XXXI, Pt. 2, pp. 740–41; Vol. LII, Pt. 1, pp. 97–98; Chalaron, "Missionary Ridge," Chalaron Papers, HTT.

high ground that the right half-battery occupied.[27] This worried both Chalaron and Slocomb. According to Bate, this empty space was left at the request of Patton Anderson, who commanded the division to Bate's right. He wanted room for one of his brigades (Alexander W. Reynolds') to deploy. Reynolds, augmented by three of Finley's Florida regiments, was strung out below Bate, serving as the division's first line of defense. The plan was for Reynolds to fire one volley at the enemy when it attacked, then retire up the ridge and fill the space on Patton Anderson's left, abutting Tyler's Tennesseans.[28]

The Fifth Company was "barely in position" when, exactly at 3:40 P.M., a roar came from Orchard Knob as the six guns of Bridges' Illinois battery opened fire. This signaled the beginning of the attack against the Confederate center by the Army of the Cumberland. Thomas' men, about twenty-five thousand strong, four divisions of them, appeared. They seemed double that number. A few Confederate infantrymen sneaked off at the fearful sight of "at least eighty thousand men in the valley below." On they came, these men of Thomas', cheering and dashing straight for the base of Missionary Ridge. If this were not enough, Slocomb observed Yankee batteries that "had sprung into full play from various and unexpected points in the valley," providing cover fire support for the charging infantry.[29]

Then, to the astonishment and dismay of the gunners, Reynolds' North Carolina-Virginia brigade posted below, at the base of the ridge, "retreated up the hill and disappeared" in the rear. This was in accordance with Bragg's orders issued at 2 P.M., but the withdrawal split the command and degenerated into a panicky "climb for your life." The fleeing soldiers threw Finley's Florida troops (Vaught's infantry support) into confusion. Slocomb reacted to "this unusual timidity in our infantry" by

27. Chalaron, "Missionary Ridge," Chalaron Papers, HTT.

28. Defense in depth by lines of infantry was Hardee's idea, one borrowed from the revolutionary war hero Daniel Morgan. One of his favorite tactics when holding ground and outnumbered badly, Hardee would employ it again with great success at the Battle of Averasboro in March, 1865. See Nathaniel C. Hughes, Jr., *Bentonville: The Final Battle of Sherman and Johnston* (Chapel Hill, 1996), 33–34; Hughes, *Hardee*, 281–86. Unfortunately for the Confederates at Missionary Ridge, Breckinridge disagreed with Hardee's plan and countermanded Hardee's order. Failure to notify all subordinate unit leaders would disastrously compound the confusion. *OR*, Vol. XXXI, Pt. 2, p. 740; Vol. LII, Pt. 1, p. 97; Talley Autobiography, CCNMP; Davis, *Breckinridge*, 388; Cozzens, *Shipwreck of Their Hopes*, 254, 289.

29. Cozzens, *Shipwreck of Their Hopes*, 263; Sword, *Mountains Touched with Fire*, 270–71; *OR*, Vol. LII, Pt. 1, p. 97.

immediately opening fire and shooting as rapidly as possible at the enemy emerging from the woods. He did so not only to check the enemy advance but to "reassure our troops." The "well-directed and effective fire" from Vaught and Chalaron brought the Federal first line to a halt, forcing some to retreat behind the abandoned trenches at the base of slope, and others to go back upon their second line out of range of small arms fire.[30]

Thomas' men came on again, but this time "the slope in front was kept clear of the enemy by a rapid and effective fire." They gave up charging directly into Slocomb's guns, instead boring off to the right and left. This exposed some of them to enfilade fire from Chalaron on the right. For protection against this fire the enemy, a brigade under Brig. Gen. William B. Hazen took cover behind "a swell in the slope," a "depression in the ridge," to the right of Chalaron. From this point they climbed the ridge, momentarily safe in the dead space beneath the plunging and enfilading fire from the battery's pieces, and safe from musket fire from the crest.[31]

The Yankees came up quickly. When the blue infantry emerged suddenly from the deep gully or ravine, the astonished Confederate infantry offered little resistance. Thus, in a matter of a few minutes the Federals had gained the crest, "some 200 yards to my right," reported Slocomb, "the infantry at that point abandoning their works without a struggle, leaving in the hands of the enemy two or more pieces of artillery which were afterward turned upon my battery."[32] Bate could not believe his eyes. He saw colors on top of the ridge, but he believed them to be those of a Confederate unit. When he discovered the truth, he directed the right of Tyler's brigade to engage them.[33]

Meanwhile, the Federals attacked again directly up the slope, and once again, according to Bate, they were repulsed. General Bragg, however, wanted Bate to counterattack and drive off the enemy that had penetrated

30. JAC saw Hazen's Federals "seeking shelter behind a large cluster of our [CSA] log huts at the foot of the ridge." Hazen, *Narrative,* 203.

31. Chalaron, "Missionary Ridge," Chalaron Papers, HTT; Cozzens, *Shipwreck of Their Hopes,* 268–69, 275; *OR,* Vol. XXXI, Pt. 2, pp. 739–42; Vol. LII, Pt. 2, p. 97; W. B. Hazen to J. A. Chalaron, June 22, 1879, Chalaron Papers, HTT; JAC to W. B. Hazen, May 4, 1879, in Hazen, *Narrative,* 203.

32. The breakthrough point is designated by Wiley Sword as "Sharp's Spur," named after Confederate Col. Jacob H. Sharp, whose Mississippi brigade defended at this point. Sharp was not present, however, and the brigade was commanded at Missionary Ridge by Col. William F. Tucker. Chalaron, "Missionary Ridge," HTT; Sword, *Mountains Touched with Fire,* 285n.

33. For clear, compelling accounts of the breakthrough, see Sword, *Mountains Touched with Fire,* 284–95; and Cozzens, *Shipwreck of Their Hopes,* 268–88, 296.

to the top of the ridge. With no reserves and being hard-pressed to his front primarily by Maj. Gen. Phil Sheridan's troops, Bate responded by sending the remnants of A. W. Reynolds' brigade north toward those Federals clustered about their flag. The Confederate troops balked, however, and made only a halfhearted attempt to dislodge the enemy. In a few minutes "second and third flags were on the ridge near the same spot." Using Capt. Staunton H. Dent's cannon as support, the Federals formed a line of battle and attacked down the crest of the ridge, brushing Reynolds' men aside and breaking Bate's right flank.[34] Colonel Tyler was wounded, his Tennesseans routed. Almost simultaneously Union flags appeared on the crest to the left of Billy Vaught. Another breakthrough! Bate's infantry, fearing being surrounded, panicked and broke to the rear.[35]

At the point in the battle when the enemy had established themselves on the Confederate right and turned Dent's pieces against the Fifth Company, Slocomb considered withdrawing his guns. He would have been justified, he thought, "considering the defection of the infantry around me, the exhausted state of my limber chests and the difficulty of removing artillery from the ridge." His men were tired, dead tired. That day they would fire 675 rounds, according to Chalaron, more than they fired at Chickamauga.[36]

34. There is conflicting evidence about the battery to the north of Slocomb. The historical marker located there states that it was Capt. James Garrity's battery, and that his guns were captured and turned against the Confederates. Chalaron helped place these markers on Crest Road. It appears, nevertheless, that there was another battery positioned between Garrity and Slocomb—that of Staunton H. Dent. This is stated clearly by Patton Anderson in his official report and by A. M. Manigault in his Civil War narrative. Slocomb's report, unfortunately, does not identify the mysterious battery. John Hoffman, *The Confederate Collapse at the Battle of Missionary Ridge: The Reports of James Patton Anderson and His Brigade Commanders* (Dayton, Ohio, 1985), 42–43: Arthur M. Manigault, *A Carolinian Goes to War: The Civil War Narrative of Arthur Middleton Manigault,* ed. R. Lockwood Turner (Columbia, S.C., 1983); *OR,* Vol. LII, Pt. 1, p. 97.

35. Reynolds maintained that he "rallied most of his brigade on the crest and plugged the gap between Anderson's left and Bate's right. Nonetheless, most of his men either had regrouped behind Bate's division or disappeared over Missionary Ridge and out of the battle altogether." *OR,* Vol. LII, Pt. 1, p. 97; Vol. XXXI, Pt. 2, pp. 741–42; Vol. XXX, Pt. 2, p. 744; Talley Autobiography, CCNMP; J. E. Austin to J. A. Chalaron, August 27, 1875 (printed in unidentified clipping), Chalaron Papers, HTT; Connelly, *Autumn of Glory,* 275–76; Daniel, *Cannoneers in Gray,* 114–15; Sword, *Mountains Touched with Fire,* 273; Cozzens, *Shipwreck of Their Hopes,* 289, 301.

36. It is doubtful that the battery fired 675 rounds at Missionary Ridge as Chalaron maintained. This number works out to more than two chests of ammunition per gun, which means Slocomb would have had to resupply at least once on November 25 despite the adverse logistical conditions. J. H. Ogden III, to author, November 1, 1996.

Felix Arroyo, Number One (sponger) at his piece, "begged" the section commander to relieve him. They had been firing as rapidly as possible and Arroyo, fresh from his hospital stay, could continue no longer. The lieutenant obliged and Arroyo moved away from the piece, handing the sponge staff to his relief, John J. Boudreaux. Almost immediately the new Number One "fell down, having been shot through the neck." Another crew member took Boudreaux's place and Arroyo became Number Five, whose job of fetching rounds from the limber and bringing them forward to Number Two (loader) was "almost as tiresome." The company stubbornly held its position, nevertheless, "judging the battle as only begun." [37]

To defend themselves against the breakthrough in Anderson's sector, and to respond to the dangerous fire from Dent's four guns into their flank, Slocomb ordered Chalaron to change front to the right and engage the Yankees swarming about these guns. As Chalaron's men shifted the trails of their pieces, General Reynolds came up. He went to Cpl. Charles W. Withan's piece and started to sight the gun. The young Kentucky gunner, however, interfered and refused to move out of the way. "No sir," he said to General Reynolds. "No one sights this gun but its corporal." [38]

Slocomb knew he must have more ammunition. He sent for it, but only one limber chest was able to get through. To reach the battery from the caisson park on the east slope, limbers had to run a "gauntlet of the enemy's fire," since the road on which they had to move passed between the enemy and the battery. [39] It was a critical moment. Low on ammunition, the enemy closing on them from three sides, the Fifth Company needed a miracle. [40]

Before Chalaron's half-battery could fire a round, Federal gunners

37. *OR,* Vol. LII, Pt. 1, p. 97; Chalaron, "Missionary Ridge," Chalaron Papers, HTT; Arroyo Journal, WA Papers, HTT.

38. *OR,* Vol. XXXI, Pt. 2, p. 97; J. E. Austin to JAC, August 27, 1875, unidentified newspaper clipping; Chalaron, "Missionary Ridge," Chalaron Papers, HTT.

39. "Slocomb's caissons were at the bottom of the ridge—certainly to protect them, probably because the horses were so weak, because the roads/routes of travel were so few and so poor, and because the ridge was so narrow there wasn't a place on the top or the immediate back slope for the caissons. Note also that when he does go to resupply he is sending up only limbers and not the caisson bodies too, probably because of the conditions mentioned above." J. H. Ogden III, to author, November 1, 1996.

40. *OR,* Vol. XXXI, Pt. 2, p. 97; J. E. Austin to J. A. Chalaron, August 27, 1875, unidentified newspaper clipping in Chalaron Papers, HTT.

from down in the valley made a spectacular shot. The round, according to Chalaron, came from Orchard Knob. If this is correct, it came from the Fifth Company's nemesis—Bridges' Illinois battery, which had occupied Orchard Knob on November 25.[41] Apparently it was a single round and it struck with great effect, blowing up the limber chests of Chalaron's two Napoleons. The explosion was tremendous, seen and heard at all points on the battlefield. It blew the limbers and their carriages to smithereens.[42] It killed or disabled most of the horses and "so entangled the remainder as to require cutting them out of harness to save them." Gunner E. H. Wingate, a thirty-year-old North Carolinian, was among those blown off his feet by the concussion. "Burnt, mutilated," Wingate was "saved from death by being thrust head foremost into a barrel of molasses, abandoned by some commissary."[43] The disaster "added to the confusion and panic of the infantry." Finley's Florida troops supporting Vaught now bolted. Enemy flags appeared on the left as "thousands came swarming over the heights." All was lost.[44]

Slocomb determined to save what he could. He ordered the four guns that still had teams to limber up, and directed the crews of Chalaron's Napoleons to remain near their guns in hope that they might be needed to support a timely counterattack coming to their relief. For a moment this seemed to be the case. An organized Confederate regiment appeared on the crest in rear of the guns. Chalaron, Sgt. Thomas C. Allen, and Cpl. Charles A. Adams raced to meet them and in a few moments they had the infantry advancing toward the abandoned guns. Cuthbert Slocomb would always remember the sight: Confederate infantry in line of battle, following Chalaron, Allen, and Adams. The three placed themselves in the front rank joyfully and defiantly waving the colors of the Fifth Company. All was for nothing, however. The North Carolina soldiers halted before they reached the guns. Their column seemed to shiver, then broke apart in the "wildest confusion." They ran down the back of the ridge,

41. *OR,* Vol. XXXI, Pt. 2, p. 130; Sword, *Mountains Touched with Fire,* 184.

42. This calamity at Missionary Ridge led to the practice of burying the limber chest when in fortified or dug-in positions. Levy, "Memoirs," American Jewish Archives.

43. The cold molasses would have cooled Wingate's burns and thereby prevented further damage to skin tissue. Janet Newsom, R.N., to author, February 22, 1995.

44. *OR,* Vol. LII, Pt. 1, p. 97; Chalaron, "Missionary Ridge," Chalaron Papers, HTT; J. E. Austin to J. A. Chalaron, August 27, 1875, unidentified newspaper clipping in Chalaron Papers, HTT; Arroyo Journal, WA Papers, HTT; Pasco Diary, November 25, 1863, CCNMP.

dropping their own flag. Chalaron scornfully picked it up and thrust it in the hands of one of the infantrymen, then ran on to his forsaken Napoleons.[45]

In the meantime Slocomb had found three canister rounds. He had Chalaron's crews load the guns. Yankee infantry fired a volley at them at close range but they stayed at their work, pushing fixed rounds of canister down the tubes. The enemy, advancing all the while, closed to within thirty yards. Then, to their utter consternation, the gunners found they could not discharge their pieces. There were no friction primers.[46] Helpless, with the enemy upon them flank and rear, Slocomb shouted for his gunners to save themselves.[47]

Slocomb, Chalaron, and the two gun crews fled for their lives across the top of the ridge and dropped down into the hollow behind their position. There, before their eyes, they saw the four other pieces. With both of the roads on either side of the battery's position in the hands of the enemy, there was no chance to save the guns except by "plunging down the slope." Vaught and Leverich attempted to do so while Slocomb and Chalaron remained with the guns on top of the ridge. To Billy Vaught's dismay, the heavy pieces sank into the mud partway down the steep grade. Vaught decided to double-team. He unhitched the teams of the caissons and hitched them to the guns and directed all the gunners and drivers to put their backs to the wheels. He succeeded in getting two guns to the bottom of the slope and "partly up the opposite hill, all struggling with

45. It should be noted that Brig. Gen. Alexander W. Reynolds, who commanded the 58th and 60th North Carolina (consolidated), did not mention this incident in his report. Hoffman, *Confederate Collapse at the Battle of Missionary Ridge*, 74–75; *OR*, Vol. LII, Pt. 1, p. 98; Cozzens, *Shipwreck of Their Hopes*, 298–99.

46. Unfortunately for the Confederates, an innovative Yankee rifleman found a way to fire one of the loaded pieces. He poured the powder from a rifle cartridge into the vent, then "fired his Springfield rifle over the opening." Slocomb's canister went sailing into the fleeing rebels. *OR*, Vol. LII, Pt. 1, p. 98; Sword, *Mountains Touched with Fire*, 299; Cozzens, *Shipwreck of Their Hopes*, 299.

47. Bate, who watched Slocomb being overrun, stated in a letter to Chalaron: "it was impossible to escape capture otherwise than by leaving the guns." He added this pointed observation: "The dash of movement and close quarter fighting that characterized our late war, made it necessarily a fruitful field for the loss of field pieces. Their losses, while regretful, were not always censurable, but often pointed to the highest display of courage where the fight was hottest and most fatal. I once heard a captain of artillery boasting of having gone through the war without the loss of a gun. Upon close inquiry as to the battles he had been in I found that, as he expressed it, it was his 'good luck' not to have been in a single battle of note." W. B. Bate to J. A. Chalaron, June 10, 1891, Chalaron Papers, HTT.

might and main of men and horses." The other two guns were stuck fast, axle deep in mud.[48]

When he came upon the scene, Slocomb realized it was hopeless unless he could get infantry to help. He ran to the fleeing soldiers and commanded, begged, them to help him save the guns. They ignored him. "The enemy were now within forty yards, and my struggling men and teams were the only targets left to the volleys." Slocomb gave up. He ordered the guns unlimbered, "thereby saving my men, horses, and limbers." Lost, however, were all the guns and the six caissons.[49]

Lt. Charles G. Johnsen, all the while, had been stationed in the rear, in charge of the caissons. When the battle reached its height, he could stand it no longer. He ordered Sgt. John H. "Bully" Smith ("Hawkeye"'s brother) to take command of the caissons while he rode up to the crest where Bragg, his staff, and Randall Gibson were observing. Gibson grabbed Johnsen immediately and sent him to the left with a message to A. P. Stewart. When Johnsen found Stewart, the latter sent him on the run to help rally troops on the left that had been flanked and had broken. Johnsen succeeded in stopping a company of Georgians and placing them in a line across the top of the ridge. As he did so, he remembered there were troops from the 16th-25th Louisiana stationed at the bottom of the slope. While the Georgians organized themselves in an attempt to hold their blocking position, Johnsen raced down the slope and managed to extricate his Louisiana friends. When he got back to the top of the ridge, however, he saw disaster all about him and hurried back to the caissons. "I got the horses and limbers off with the wounded men except one limber that stalled in the creek." As the Fifth Company fled from Missionary Ridge, it appears all of the members except four took the Crutchfield road. The scene was one of shouting officers, confused, frightened men, and "shameful panic." As one fleeing rebel shouted to a comrade: "It was time to git!"[50]

48. Chalaron, "Missionary Ridge," Chalaron Papers, HTT; *OR,* Vol. LII, Pt. 1, p. 98; Cozzens, *Shipwreck of Their Hopes,* 300.

49. The pieces were captured in the hollow by Maj. Joab Stafford, 1st Ohio Infantry. *OR,* Vol. LII, Pt. 1, pp. 98–99; Cozzens, *Shipwreck of Their Hopes,* 300–301. J. H. Hallonquist in his report of "Guns, Caissons & Limbers lost in the late Battle and Retreat" shows Slocomb losing two James rifles, four Napoleons (twelve pounders), four caissons, and only one limber. Cobb lost four Napoleons, four caissons, and four limbers, while Mebane lost one caisson. Lt. Col. James H. Hallonquist CSR, RG 109, NA.

50. Arroyo Journal, WA Papers, HTT; C. G. Johnsen to JAC, September 18, 1894, Chalaron Papers, HTT.

THE BATTLE OF SLOCOMB

THE CONFEDERATES ran. They knew the Chickamauga bottoms lay ahead as well as the boiling, maddened creek itself, but they ran. "The road was full of waggons, of artillery, and of men. Officers were passing on horseback, yelling, 'Stop running boys, please face the enemy'; but their intention was to get away, as soon as possible, from this great danger." The confused, demoralized mass hurried on toward the single frail bridge across the surging stream. Adolphe Chalaron remembered the "blanched face of Gen. Bragg as he stood with some of his staff trying to arrest the rush of his troops to the rear. . . . His appeals were unavailing; the men passed on, many with curses on their lips to his address."[1] The first (and only) attempt to make a stand in this central sector came at a spot some one thousand to fifteen hundred yards behind the crest of Missionary Ridge. In effect it was a roadblock astride the Crutchfield road, the most direct escape route from Bragg's headquarters to the pontoon bridge across Chickamauga Creek.[2]

---

1. Arroyo Journal, WA Papers, HTT; Chalaron, "Missionary Ridge," Chalaron Papers, HTT.

2. Betts's map shows the crossing at Bird's Mill (also known as Mission Mill), located at the confluence of Spring Creek, East Chickamauga Creek, and West Chickamauga Creek. Two bridges

There are three versions of this Confederate rear-guard stand. Bate maintains that he and Bragg and "many subaltern officers" established such a line, then Bragg rode on east toward the bridge, requesting Bate to hold as long as possible and then retire across the creek and meet him at Chickamauga Station. Bate took immediate action, according to his report, throwing skirmishers of the 15th-37th Tennessee under Maj. J. M. Wall forward to the right of the road and sharpshooters from Austin's 14th Louisiana battalion to the left. Artillery was placed beside the road itself. Once he had the defensive position established, Bate entrusted the line to Gen. Jesse J. Finley and rode to the rear, where he established a second line in an open field near the junction of the Crutchfield and Bird's Mill roads, some five hundred to one thousand yards behind the Finley line. Once he felt confident about this second line, Bate raced back to join Finley, who had become "hotly engaged." Bate, Finley, and their men, fighting over an hour after nightfall, not only checked the Yankee advance but threw them back, "thus enabling a quiet and orderly withdrawal of that line." Bate's account is seconded by Bragg.

This version raises questions, however. The 15th-37th Tennessee upon which Bate relied was beset with serious morale problems. It had sustained high losses during the fight on the ridge proper, including its commander, and is believed to have been so disheartened that it is doubtful it could have fulfilled the mission attributed to it by Bate, especially under the leadership of the colonel of the 37th Georgia, whom Bate states exercised direct command of the remnants of this regiment and Tyler's brigade until he was wounded. Furthermore, all Florida troops that survived the fiasco that divided and decimated Finley's brigade on Missionary Ridge appear to have been employed as the nucleus of Bate's secondary line and were led by Lt. Col. A. D. McLean of the 6th Florida. Finley apparently left no report. If he had held active command of this delaying action on Crutchfield road, he would have been in charge of the Tennessee and Louisiana troops from Bate's and Gibson's brigades. This seems unlikely.[3]

Lt. Col. James J. Turner, 10th and 30th Tennessee, who took command of Tyler's brigade after Lt. Col. A. F. Rudler, 37th Georgia, was wounded,

---

are shown, just north of the mill. Chickamauga Park historian James H. Ogden III maintains that Betts's map is wrong. Mission Mill is located in the present-day Eastgate Center at Eastgate Mall, just south of Brainerd Road. The bridge used by Slocomb was a pontoon bridge located about three-quarters of a mile north of the mouth of Spring Creek.

3. *OR*, Vol. XXXI, Pt. 2, pp. 742–43, 665–66; John B. Lindsley, *The Military Annals of Tennessee* (Nashville, 1896), 503.

maintained that he halted the brigade on a ridge fifteen hundred yards east of Missionary Ridge and formed a line of battle across the road. There he was joined by Cobb's battery and some five hundred detached soldiers. "As all the generals had left and we were free to act independently, we concluded to stop the Federal forces at this point till darkness should arrest their advance." Providing indispensable service as skirmishers for Turner's line was Maj. Theodore D. Caswell's 4th Georgia Sharpshooters of Tyler's brigade. They soon became "hotly engaged," but succeeded in repulsing the enemy handily. It was then that Breckinridge appeared and ordered Turner to retire across Chickamauga Creek at once.[4]

Bate does not mention Turner, however, nor Caswell. Turner does not mention Bate (except an over-the-shoulder order "to follow on to the pontoon bridge"), nor Finley, nor Austin. Furthermore Turner states Tyler's brigade was "in good condition," as they retreated off Missionary Ridge whereas the historian of the 15th and 37th Tennessee reported it had sustained "very heavy losses." Moreover, brigade commander Tyler had been seriously wounded, as had his successor, Lieutenant Colonel Rudler. Cobb's battery, Turner's testimony notwithstanding, could not have played a role, having been overwhelmed and captured near Bragg's headquarters.[5]

A third and more plausible version of this sharp little rear-guard action just east of Missionary Ridge credits Cuthbert Slocomb. Six sources give this account, and they seem to be consistent. Felix Arroyo states that the company found a "very muddy place" along Crutchfield road, a place "where not a man living could have walked one step." At the end of the stretch was high ground, and "just there" the cannoneers found two abandoned pieces of artillery. Slocomb, accompanied by Ned Austin, decided they should make a stand. Austin deployed his sharpshooters while Slocomb swung the pieces about so they controlled the road. Since "the Federals could not do any manoeuvre, they had to abandon the pursuit." Slocomb himself reports: "With Lieutenants Vaught and Chalaron and part of my cannoneers I remained at the point where the first stand was made by our troops. Here we placed in position and manned during the fight which ensued several pieces belonging to different batteries." According to Louisiana Confederate historian and veteran John Dimitry of the Crescent Regiment, writing thirty-five years after the battle, credit for

4. Lindsley, *Military Annals of Tennessee,* 453.
5. *Ibid.;* Daniel, *Cannoneers in Gray,* 116.

the successful stand belongs largely to Cuthbert Slocomb. "Shall we not call it 'the battle of Slocomb,' and let it stand so in history, to the lasting credit of the valorous captain of the Washington Artillery?"[6]

It was Slocomb, according to Dimitry, who saw abandoned Confederate guns. "'Prepare those guns for action,' he shouted. . . . Each command, as it came down the slope, rushed forward, filled with new courage, to make that line formidable. Heroic Slocomb, as he stood with guns once more around him, smiled as he saw them served by his tried cannoneers. . . . It was an oasis of victory in that desert of defeat." Moreover, "it saved Bragg's army," enabling it, "on the half sunken pontoons, to cross [Chickamauga Creek] in safety."[7] Charles G. Johnsen, who was across Chickamauga Creek during the fight, seconded Dimitry's sentiments in an 1894 letter to Chalaron.[8]

Chalaron, who was present, states that "the first stand attempted after leaving the ridge was made possible by the members of this Company." They found the guns, prepared them for action, and "with the assistance of Major J. E. Austin a line was formed here, the Louisianians and other troops rallied, and after a sharp fight of more than an hour the progress of the enemy was checked."[9] Austin is emphatic in his account. As he and his sharpshooters retreated down the Crutchfield road, he encountered a "sad and sorrowful" Slocomb. "Well, Ned, I have lost my guns for the first time. . . . If your battalion had been there, it would not have happened." Pointing to the cannon he had found, he told Austin he had "a few rounds of ammunition, and if you will give me your support, I will right here on this hill, wipe out what happened on the other." Austin took one look at Slocomb's determined face and replied, "I am with you Slocomb, to the last."[10]

6. Arroyo Journal, WA Papers, HTT; J. E. Austin to A. L. Stuart, December 4, 1863, Confederate States of America Army Papers, Georgia Historical Society, Savannah; *OR*, Vol. LII, Pt. 1, p. 98; Evans, *Confederate Military History*, XIII, 189.

7. Ned Austin described the pontoons as a single bridge "of an indifferent character and construction." See J. E. Austin to JAC, August 27, 1875, unidentified newspaper clipping, Chalaron Papers, HTT.

8. Dimitry quoted in Evans, *Confederate Military History*, XIII, 189; C. G. Johnsen to JAC, September 18, 1894, Chalaron Papers, HTT.

9. Providing significant assistance were men from the 16th-25th Louisiana who acted as skirmishers and helped serve one of the pieces. See D. Gober to H. H. Bein, [December, 1863], C.S.A. Army Papers, Georgia Historical Society; Chalaron, "Missionary Ridge," Chalaron Papers, HTT.

10. J. E. Austin to JAC, August 27, 1875, unidentified newspaper clipping, Chalaron Papers, HTT.

They did not have a moment to lose. While Slocomb placed the pieces in battery, Austin split his command into wings, one supporting the guns, the other deployed as skirmishers about two hundred yards to their front. In a very short time the enemy appeared and lively skirmishing began. "On no battlefield of the war," recalled Austin, "did I see a more admirable exhibition of valor. We all felt his [Slocomb's] spirit of determination . . . enough to die." Bragg and Bate, according to Austin, heard the firing and came back. They saw the opportunity and reinforced Slocomb and Austin with a few hundred men, a number sufficient to repulse the Federals when they attacked in force. Then darkness mercifully intervened and closed the action of November 25.[11]

Bate received praise for his initiative in this final action of Missionary Ridge. Austin heard that this checking on Crutchfield road resulted in Bate's promotion to major general.[12] Cuthbert Slocomb deserved the honor, maintained Austin, "for the fight was made by him, upon his own volition, with his company and my battalion, unsupported, unsustained in the first onslaught by any other troops. I thought it, at the time," continued Austin, "to be a reckless determination on the part of Slocomb, and I steadfastly believe that he intended to die there rather than be driven from the position." Slocomb's stand on that road "saved our army."[13]

Under cover of darkness, Slocomb, Austin, and their makeshift command withdrew. Slocomb told Chalaron and Vaught to lead the men across Chickamauga Creek to the battery's wagon camp near Chickamauga Station.[14] There they rejoined Johnsen and another detachment that was protecting the battery's horses and limbers. In the meantime Slocomb met General Breckinridge on the pontoon bridge. Breckinridge, in a rather unnecessary order, asked the captain to keep his command together. Once he had gathered his men east of the creek, Slocomb put Vaught in charge,

11. *Ibid.* The Federals thrown back by Slocomb and Austin were Wagner's and Harker's brigades of Sheridan's division. Cozzens, *Shipwreck of Their Hopes,* 337–40.

12. Austin is partially correct. Probably Bate's performance at Chickamauga was a more important factor.

13. J. E. Austin to JAC, August 27, 1875, unidentified newspaper clipping, Chalaron Papers, HTT.

14. Chickamauga Station had begun life as "Pull Tight," Tennessee, so named "because of extreme tenacity of the mud." The depot was also known for having a general store and a fine saloon. Weston A. Goodspeed, ed., *History of Tennessee* (Nashville, 1887), 902.

and shortly after (about 2 A.M.) the battery (without any guns) started its march from Chickamauga Station. Slocomb, Chalaron, and twenty members stayed behind to help Mebane's battery.[15]

Throughout the remainder of that night and the following day (November 26) the company moved with Bate's division wagon train as it retreated southeast through Ringgold. Men would remember that night: "the cold was increasing every second," large fir trees had been set afire at fifty yard intervals, giving a lurid, almost ghostlike cast to faces. The knowledge that they had repulsed the Federals on Crutchfield road brought smiles to the members' faces, however. Their spirits, even under the most terrible circumstances, were never low for very long. All they needed was a spark. The stand at Crutchfield road provided that, and it was not long before "the Louisianans [were filling] their night march to Ringgold with music." Adding more cheer on that cold, dark tramp was Archie Taylor, a boy who had followed the battery into the battle of Missionary Ridge and spent most of the twenty-fifth bringing up ammunition. Archie played the comedian as they marched along, "imitating the antics of the fleeing and panic stricken troops as they left the ridge." The veterans loved his rendition and remembered it.[16]

This lightheartedness is remarkable. Despite the miserable weather, the widespread sickness, an unpopular unit reassignment, the low morale of the Army of Tennessee in general, and in spite of having participated in a military disaster, the Fifth Company kept its spirits high—so high that Archie Taylor and a young private named McIntyre wanted to join their ranks and fight beside them. No wonder the company was regarded as special.

On November 26, Slocomb led the battery into and beyond the village of Ringgold, through Taylor's Ridge to Dalton. They did not stop at Dalton, however, but continued south to Resaca. When they arrived in Re-

15. When the company set out for Resaca, this detail remained at Chickamauga to assist Captain Mebane at his request. They searched for Mebane throughout the early hours of the twenty-sixth, up until the time the depot was evacuated, but were unable to find him. Then they too fell in with the retreating army and managed to catch up with the Fifth Company before reaching Ringgold. Arroyo Journal, WA Papers, HTT; *OR*, Vol. LII, Pt. 1, p. 98; Cozzens, *Shipwreck of Their Hopes*, 348.

16. Another young man named McIntyre joined the company for the fight at Missionary Ridge, and he too spent the day toting spherical case and canister rounds. Evans, *Confederate Military History*, XIII, 189; Arroyo Journal, WA Papers, HTT; Chalaron, "Missionary Ridge," Chalaron Papers, HTT; 5WA Master Roster, WA Papers, HTT.

saca, they found Captain Cobb waiting for them. He ordered them to turn about and take their horses and limbers back to Dalton.[17]

Missionary Ridge had been a humiliating, costly experience for the Washington Artillery. They had lost their guns. Along with them four caissons had been destroyed or captured.[18] At least twenty horses had been killed, disabled or lost. Three men had been captured: the Irish driver Mike Sheridan, gunner Hugh D. McCown, Jr., and Charles Weingart. A Virginian who clerked in his uncle's clothing store before the war, young McCown would be sent to Rock Island prison. After being confined four months, he took the oath of allegiance and abandoned the war. Sheridan had had enough also. He took the oath and enlisted in the United States Army for frontier duty. Weingart, injured at Chickamauga when he was struck in the back with a "flying splinter," was back in action at his piece at Missionary Ridge. Along with McCown and Sheridan he was captured and sent to Rock Island. He would hold out longer than the other two, remaining in prison until the end of March, 1865, before he, too, took the oath.[19]

One man deserted at Missionary Ridge—A. F. Kibbe, a Louisianan who had gone to Texas before the war. There he had enlisted in the 3rd Texas Cavalry. When the regiment was dismounted, he, being underaged, transferred to the Fifth Company sometime during the fall of 1863. Before the year 1863 was out, two more members would be gone: New Orleans policeman Fred D. Goodwyn deserted at Dalton on December 22 and took the Federal oath a month later; teamster Robert J. Watson would go with him.[20]

No member of the unit had been killed, but seven had been wounded: Corporal Wingate; the meat cutter John Boudreaux; Pat Lacey, an Irish driver from Tipperary County and onetime New Orleans steamboat crewman who, when he had recuperated, would transfer to the Confederate

17. *OR,* Vol. LII, Pt. 1, p. 98; Chalaron, 5WA Itinerary, Chalaron Papers, HTT. Evidently Slocomb did not bring off the guns he used in the rearguard action west of Chickamauga Creek. Perhaps the battalions to whom the guns belonged reclaimed them and brought them off, or perhaps they were abandoned.

18. In this three-day fight at Chattanooga the Army of Tennessee suffered a terrible loss in ordnance: forty cannon and sixty-nine limbers and caissons. Cozzens, *Shipwreck of Their Hopes,* 389.

19. *OR,* Vol. LII, Pt. 1, pp. 98–99; 5WA Master Roster, WA Papers, HTT.

20. 5WA Master Roster, WA Papers, HTT.

navy; the eighteen-year-old gilder William H. Hall; surgeon Legaré's six-teen-year-old nephew from Illinois, Oscar, who also would be transferred upon his recovery and turned into a telegraph operator; Robert Giffen (the youngest son of Adam Giffen), who was seriously wounded in the leg; and Emile O'Brien, who had been grazed on the temple at Chicka-mauga and sustained a shoulder wound at Missionary Ridge. George W. Palfrey had not been wounded, but he had been sick a long time and became so ill the morning of the battle that he was sent to the rear "to guard the baggage." He would never be strong enough to return.[21]

Considering the spectacular explosion of the caissons and being vir-tually surrounded by the enemy, not to speak of the chaos of the rush down Missionary Ridge, losses on November 25 were exceedingly light. Nevertheless, when added to Glass's Mill, Chickamauga, and the camp miseries of October and November, the Fifth Company had suffered. Slo-comb's last strength report for 1863, dated December 14, showed the Washington Artillery numbering 93 effectives out of 118 present, with an aggregate present and absent of 193. As solace for their humiliation at Missionary Ridge the battery was issued two obsolete six-pounders and two unwanted twelve-pounder howitzers, with 142 rounds per gun.[22]

After he had made his report, Slocomb took leave and joined his wife, Abby. New Year's Eve found the couple on the north side of Lake Pont-chartrain. Abby was ill, desperately ill, according to one source. The Slo-combs needed medicine and money. Harry Baldwin, Slocomb's business partner, slipped out of New Orleans, hired a sailboat, and sailed across the lake. After he had delivered the medicine, updated his partner on business affairs, and given him some gold, Baldwin sailed back to the south shore. He had hoped to be concealed by the drizzle and low clouds, but the weather turned vicious. High winds overturned the boat and Harry Baldwin drowned.[23]

It took a patriot to look 1864 in the face.

---

21. WCDV to mother, December 3, 1864, Vaught Letters, HNOC; 5WA Master Roster, WA Papers, HTT.

22. 5WA Muster Roll, January 1–April 30, 1864, WA Papers, HTT: *OR*, Vol. XXXI, Pt. 3, p. 827.

23. Henry Fay "Harry" Baldwin was thirty-one years old, a native of Waterhouse, Massachusetts, who had been sent south for his health in 1852. He and Slocomb became partners in the hardware business in 1857 and seem to have prospered from the start. In that same year Harry's younger brother Albert came to New Orleans to make his fortune. The two brothers chose not to join the army when

(Continued)

war broke out and remained in New Orleans, Harry operating the hardware firm, Albert clerking for McStea, Value and Company. Harry, nevertheless, nominally belonged to a local cavalry outfit and is said to have contributed one hundred thousand dollars to the Confederate war effort in 1861. In 1863, after the Slocomb, Baldwin & Co. firm lost a boat (the *Laura Edwards*) to the Federal navy, Harry went to Washington and by means of his Boston business connections and influence was able to see President Lincoln, from whom he asked for, and received, restitution.

After Harry's death, Albert took over his affairs and operated Slocomb, Baldwin & Co. The younger Baldwin proved an extraordinary businessman and he and Cuthbert Slocomb formalized the partnership either in the summer of 1864 (see Chapter 13) or immediately following the war. When Slocomb returned home in May, 1865, he found that he was still a wealthy man. Indeed, in that year alone, Albert himself cleared seventy-five thousand dollars. Mary Francis Baldwin Stoddard, "The Baldwins," manuscript in possession of George Denègre, New Orleans.

11

BEES AND WASPS AND HORNETS

ON MARCH 6, 1864, a new recruit appeared—Phil Stephenson. A veteran of two-and-a-half years in the 13th Arkansas, he was one of Pat Cleburne's men. Young Stephenson could fight, no question about that, but he had been out of place in the rough company of Irish laborers in which he had found himself. His Arkansas comrades were older, hard-drinking, profane, uneducated, and totally unsuitable companions for this impressionable eighteen-year-old. Stephenson had a kind company commander from Virginia, Capt. Thomas C. Bartlett, who took a special interest in him. Bartlett happened to have a first cousin in the Fifth Company—Sgt. Thomas C. Allen—and he asked his cousin about allowing Stephenson to become a member of his gun crew of Piece Four. Thus it came to be that this well educated, refined, and somewhat frail young man from St. Louis enlisted in Slocomb's battery.[1]

1. Although a member of the 13th Arkansas since before the battle of Belmont, Stephenson, being underaged and protected somewhat by his older brother (the regimental adjutant), had never enlisted formally and therefore was free to enlist in the Fifth Company. Stephenson, *Civil War Memoir*, 163.

Phil Stephenson found the Washington Artillery a sharp contrast to Company K, 13th Arkansas Infantry. As he wrote his mother, "A nicer set of gentlemen I have never met with. They are all young men, their ages ranging from eighteen to twenty-five, sons of planters and residents of New Orleans." They were "city men . . . 'society men.' Most of them were French or of French descent. . . . The battery boys would go into battle or come out of a battle with a song or a jest," whereas the Arkansas infantry would go about the business of war "quietly, seriously but with equal fearlessness or resolution." He noted that the men of the Fifth Company were "gentlemen" and that they "were almost to a man of well-to-do families . . . boys, who, many of them, at home actually had help in dressing themselves! They had learned to put their hands to anything—cook, wash, clean the camp, dig breastworks—anything. They were sturdy, self reliant, tough, fearless, indifferent to hardship and danger, and 'gay as larks.'" Stephenson quickly noticed the distinct division between the gunners and the drivers. The latter were "a different grade of men socially. When hardships, marches, battles came, however, social lines played no part. Ragged and dirty, gentleman and plebeian looked alike. The army was a wonderful school of democracy."[2]

Soon after Stephenson joined the battery a blizzard struck, "the last compliments of a stern winter." Everyone felt dismal and depressed. Then, with the snow deep upon the Georgia landscape, there came a totally unexpected assault from trusted comrades camping beside them—Cobb's battery. They taunted the Fifth Company, "'Come out and fight!' No response. Our Louisiana boys were shivering and demoralized. They were not used to snow, and that was the biggest one most of them had ever seen! It was all very well for Cobb's men. They were Kentuckians and used to snow." A few (including the Missourian Stephenson) finally came out to engage the enemy, "but the rest kept close in their holes." "Come out and fight," again jeered the Kentuckians.

Suddenly, from one of the officers' tents came a familiar shout, "*I can't stand this any longer! Here boys, let's at them!*" And out roared a half-dressed figure, "stooping down as he ran, gathering snow and charging into the midst of the foe. It was Chalaron our peppery little 1st Lieutenant, hatless and his bald head shiny and red, while his Louis Napoleon moustache and imperial bristled up like the whiskers of a cat." Out tumbled

2. PDS to mother (Harriet Stephenson), July 1, 1864, P. D. Stephenson Letters, Museum of the Confederacy, Richmond, Virginia; Stephenson, *Civil War Memoir,* 163, 166–67.

the Fifth Company. After a tough scrap the members vanquished Cobb's men, then joined with them to attack Mebane's camp. The practice of fight-conquer-combine repeated itself throughout the day until the sport formalized into full-scale warfare, officers and all. The following day saw a "pitched battle." Generals gathered with their staffs in "grave conference," and began careful maneuvers to gain advantage of position and terrain. It was grand, great fun.[3]

Stephenson was so proud to be a member. "The 'W.A.' is known throughout the Confederacy," he wrote his mother, "and to have those two letters on your cap is to have a passport to the hearts of all southerners." The company's officers impressed him too. They "are considerate and always consistent in their conduct. . . . Captain C. H. Slocomb is one of the nicest men I ever met with, and I doubt whether there is a more accomplished officer in the army."[4]

Felix Arroyo shared Stephenson's view of Slocomb and recorded an incident that occurred during the bitter weather at Dalton.[5] "One day early in the morning it was very cold, Capt. Slocomb appeared at the door of our cabin and asked my messmates if we had already eaten our breakfast. We answered negatively. 'Then,' said he, 'I hope you will have enough for me.' We handed him a small bench on which he sat down. A few minutes after we offered him a cup of corn coffee, sweetened by some sorghum molasses, a piece of corn bread, and while eating we had a very jolly time."[6]

Apparently everyone, from general officer to private, felt warmly toward Slocomb and admired his proficiency as a battery commander. The artillery of the Army of Tennessee, however, was a different matter. Army commander Joseph E. Johnston and his corps commanders, Hardee and Hood, found it "unsatisfactory on account of defective armament, insufficient strength in animals and want alike of adequate chiefs and of suitable organization." Brig. Gen. William N. Pendleton, chief of artillery, Army of Northern Virginia, came to inspect. He believed the Fifth Company's six-pounders to be "nearly useless" and their twelve-pounder howitzers "scarcely more valuable." The battery horses were "certainly thin."

3. Stephenson, *Civil War Memoir,* 168–69; W. J. Worsham, *The Old Nineteenth Tennessee Regiment* (Knoxville, 1902), 108.

4. PDS to mother, July 1, 1864, Stephenson Letters, Museum of the Confederacy.

5. The encampment near Dalton was called Camp Graves in honor of their beloved and respected battalion commander Rice Graves. Casey, *Outline of Civil War Campaigns,* 67.

6. Arroyo Journal, WA Papers, HTT.

Some had died from exhaustion, others from disease, "subject as they are to excessive draft, injurious exposure and long fasting." The hard winter at Dalton was killing off the animals rapidly. The artillery branch itself needed reorganization, training, and refitting.[7] Johnston, immediately after taking command of the Army of Tennessee on December 27, 1863, had taken extraordinary measures to obtain the necessary animals, but had met with little success because of the shortage that existed throughout the Confederacy. Johnston also encountered scarcities in wagons, leather goods, and raw materials of all sorts, not to speak of the chronic ordnance nightmare of defective fuses and shells.[8]

Throughout the four months near Dalton the Fifth Company remained in Maj. Robert Cobb's artillery battalion, Bate's division, Hood's corps. It was not until April 3, 1864, that Bate's division and Cobb's battalion were moved to Hardee's corps.[9] The infantry with whom the battery would work remained basically the same—the Orphans under Lewis, the Floridians under Finley. A noticeable difference was that Bate had become a major general and now the division was called Bate's division rather than Breckinridge's, the latter having been removed following Missionary Ridge at the request of Bragg.[10] Brigade commander Robert C. Tyler was gone too, his November leg wound requiring amputation. He had been replaced by an ill-starred Tennessean, Col. Thomas Benton Smith. Smith was twenty-six years old and former commander of the 20th Tennessee. He was popular, with obvious leadership qualities, but could he handle a brigade?

Lines of authority regarding the artillery became blurred as Johnston centralized the command structure. Now each infantry division had its artillery battalion as before, each consisting of three four-gun batteries (Cobb's battalion was composed of the Washington Artillery, and Gracey's and Mebane's batteries). Each corps had an artillery "regiment" made up of three or four battalions (Hood had three, Hardee four).[11]

7. *OR*, Vol. XXXII, Pt. 3, pp. 684–86.

8. Daniel, *Cannoneers in Gray*, 125–31.

9. Cobb did not receive his commission as major until May, 1864. *OR*, Vol. XXXII, Pt. 2, pp. 590, 821, Pt. 3, pp. 687, 742; Casey, *Outline of Civil War Campaigns*, 72; Daniel, *Cannoneers in Gray*, 140.

10. Bate was assigned permanent command of Breckinridge's division at Dalton, February 27, 1864. *Senate Documents*, 59th Cong., 2nd Sess., No. 403, p. 70.

11. In addition there was a reserve regiment comprised of three battalions and the cavalry artillery, which had five batteries.

Hardee's artillery regiment contained "12 batteries, 48 guns, 742 horses, and 1,243 men." It was commanded by Col. Melancthon Smith, a West Pointer and a highly praised, dependable veteran of fights from Belmont to Missionary Ridge. Johnston's chief of artillery, now commanding the army's "battery brigade," was Brig. Gen. Francis A. Shoup, another West Pointer who had performed well under Hardee and who even had led an infantry brigade at one time. Although the reorganization promised centralization, able leadership, and more organizational regularity, the problem would be control. Who would exercise direct tactical authority over the battalions? The division commander or the artillery regimental commander? Bate or Melancthon Smith? "The result was ambiguity and confusion."[12]

Nevertheless, it was good to be back in Hardee's corps, even though it was under Bate, even though the company had been reduced to only four guns. Happier news came in April when the battery received four twelve-pounder Napoleons to replace the six-pounders and the howitzers. The members had great confidence in the brass smoothbore Napoleon, which was "accounted the best gun for all round field service then made. . . . We would not have exchanged them for Parrott Rifles, or any other style of guns. They were beautiful," thought Stephenson, "perfectly plain, tapering gracefully from muzzle to 'reinforce' or butt, without rings, or ornaments of any kind. We were proud of them and felt towards them almost as if they were human. . . . In the hands of Corporal Alex Allain, or Charlie Fox or Oscar Legaré and other gunners we faced many a Parrott rifle in artillery duels with confidence."[13]

Another happy surprise at Dalton was a brand new company flag. It had been made by the women of Mobile and sent up to Dalton.[14] Phil Stephenson loved it:

It was a beautiful flag—an oblong of white silk with the upper left hand corner a square of red and a maltese cross blue studded with state stars crossing the red. The rest of the flag (white) had the battles in which the command had fought

---

12. J. E. Johnston to JAC, June 30, 1875, Chalaron Papers, HTT; *OR*, Vol. XXXII, Pt. 2, pp. 590, 821, Pt. 3, pp. 643, 686–88, 696; Daniel, *Cannoneers in Gray,* 130–39.

13. A. Allain to A. Armant, August 14, 1903, Chalaron Papers, HTT; Stephenson, *Civil War Memoir,* 164–65; Casey, *Outline of Civil War Campaigns,* 72.

14. The original flag presented by Colonel Walton had been sent to Tom Blair's family in Mobile for safekeeping. Vaught somehow secured this flag and brought it to New Orleans after the war. "He naturally kept the matter very secret at the time," relates Chalaron, "and dying soon after the war, the existence of the flag was known only to his wife & children. It found its way to Texas where

placed in gilt letters one name below the other in parallel lines, thus breaking the monotony of the white with flashes of gold. Our flag was full of names. . . . The effect of this design, when the flag with its blood red corner and star spangled blue cross and stripes of glittering gold on the background of white when flung to the breeze especially in the sunlight, was striking in the extreme.[15]

The cold winter of 1864 finally passed. March with its unreliable, teasing weather, soon gave way to April, which proved as disappointing: cold and wet. Drill continued, however; indeed, it became even more frequent. Mock battles were held. Then during the second week in April the company moved its camp, becoming more fully integrated into Hardee's command. This interrupted the incessant drill and for a while the men found themselves "busy putting up stables, harness racks, corn sheds &c." Word leaked out to the privates that Slocomb had made application for the battery to accompany fellow Louisianan Brig. Gen. Thomas M. Scott's regiment west to the Department of Southwest Mississippi and East Louisiana, in effect becoming Scott's "flying artillery." The transfer was an appealing notion. Anything to be banded again with their fellow Louisianans. The request, however, was denied—to no one's surprise.[16]

Everyone seemed tired of waiting, ready for the fighting they knew was sure to come. General Sherman ended the suspense when he swung into action on May 5, 1864. During the following days, two of his armies under Maj. Gen. George H. Thomas and Maj. Gen. John M. Schofield moved up close to the defenses west and northwest of Dalton—Buzzard Roost Gap and Rocky Face Ridge, while a third army under Maj. Gen. James B. McPherson forced its way through Snake Creek Gap, flanking Johnston's position to the south. It was Sherman's intent to have McPherson cut the vital Western and Atlantic Railroad at Resaca.

---

resides one of his daughters, Mrs. Lawrence V. Elder." She informed Chalaron and was responsible for it being presented to Confederate Memorial Hall. The second flag, one of the Hardee battle flags, had "Fifth Company, Washington Artillery, N.O." inscribed inside the silver moon on the blue field. The banner Slocomb received at Dalton was the third flag and would serve the company throughout the remainder of the war. *CV,* XV (1907), 468; Kenneth A. Legendre to author, April 4, 1994; 5WA Master Roster, WA Papers, HTT.

15. Stephenson, writing from memory, came close. Actually the traditional St. Andrews cross was in the upper left-hand corner. Stephenson, *Civil War Memoir,* 293–94.

16. S. B. Newman, Jr., to M. Greenwood, Greenwood Papers, HNOC; Bergeron, *Guide to Louisiana Military Units,* 40.

In response Johnston sent Bate's division to occupy Buzzard Roost on May 7, along with A. P. Stewart's division from Hood's corps. The Fifth Company took position "on a short low ridge . . . about 600 yards directly in rear of Mill Creek Gap [Buzzard Roost]." The enemy did not launch a full-scale attack, however. "Only once did we get a shot at them," remembered Stephenson, "a column came within our vision—far back, almost out of range, and looked like a long *black* snake, slowly squirming along and finally turning its head to the right (our left). Now was our opportunity! Our Napoleons' muzzles were elevated, the shell fuses cut long, and away blazed one gun after another." The rounds flew far out into the distance. "We could see them burst and the long body of the snake lose its solidity and break into bits. Then came the yell from us. Then went another shot and another, until the reptile wriggled out of sight."[17]

McPherson in the meantime broke through Snake Creek Gap and advanced within a mile of the village of Resaca. It was a grand opportunity for the Union commander, a chance to trap Johnston in Dalton, but McPherson confronted too many unknowns and feared he might be entrapped himself. So he pulled back to the gap. Sherman rushed to join him with Thomas and Schofield, while Johnston, alerted that he might be cut off, withdrew during the night of May 12–13 from Dalton to prepared positions west of Resaca, arriving late in the afternoon of the thirteenth. Bate held the highest ground at Resaca, with Hindman of Hood's corps on his right and Cleburne on his right.[18]

On May 14 the Washington Artillery and Frank P. Gracey's battery found themselves positioned on a bald hill in the center of Bate's division with their pieces facing west and northwest. To the Fifth Company's right front was Joseph H. Lewis' brigade; Finley's was immediately to the front and left front.[19] Smith was in reserve. The battery went into action early

17. Zack C. Waters, "The Atlanta Campaign: Reports of William Brimage Bate," in *The Campaign for Atlanta and Sherman's March to the Sea,* ed. Theodore P. Savas and David A. Woodbury (Campbell, Calif., 1994), 206–207; Casey, *Outline of Civil War Campaigns,* 74; Albert Castel, *Decision in the West: The Atlanta Campaign of 1864* (Lawrence, Kans., 1992), 129, 131; Stephenson, *Civil War Memoir,* 172.

18. Waters, "Atlanta Campaign," 206–207; William R. Scaife, *Campaign for Atlanta* (Atlanta, 1985), 16–18.

19. Finley would be wounded at Resaca and not return until just before the Battle of Jonesboro. He was replaced by Col. Robert Bullock, commander of the 7th Florida, who had been captured at Missionary Ridge and exchanged. Waters, "Atlanta Campaign," 204.

in the morning and "continued to be engaged at intervals throughout the day." As the morning wore on and the sun became "scorching hot," skirmishing increased in intensity, with Yankee sharpshooters being particularly active. Federal Brig. Gen. Henry Moses Judah, unsupported, attacked to the right of Bate's sector and was sent reeling back. On came the divisions of Absalom Baird and Jacob D. Cox to meet similar fates. The battery watched this action for the most part, being "not directly assaulted." The one heavy attack (probably Baird's) on Bate's line was not pressed vigorously and was repulsed handily by Lewis's Orphans supported by Slocomb's guns. "At the time of a charge," recalled Stephenson, "both sides (those contiguous) would stop firing and look on."[20]

Sherman shifted his tactics. He brought up additional batteries, placing them on high ground behind the Union lines. From here they poured a murderous fire into the Confederate position. It seems that the Washington Artillery was a prime target. Many of the shells aimed at the Louisianans, however, fell upon Bate's helpless infantry surrounding them. Pvt. John S. Jackman of Lewis's brigade recorded that "the artillery has been playing the wilds with us. Several batteries are in our front, on a favorable hill for them, and have kept up a shelling all day. Slocum's pieces being unprotected, he has been unable to fire much—the sharpshooters as well as three batteries against him."[21]

The enemy fire increased drastically as the day wore on. A private in Tom Smith's brigade recalled it was "the most terrific artillery fire I was under in the war." Late in the afternoon of the fourteenth, a well-served six-gun enemy battery "upon a commanding hill" opened. "At first Slocum tried it single-handed against at least three batteries," but the Washington Artillery was outgunned. Armed with Parrott rifles, the enemy fire, particularly from this six-gun rifled battery, was rapid and accurate. Nevertheless, the fight continued for over an hour until the enemy gained dominance by demolishing two Napoleons. Slocomb and his men abandoned their pieces and took cover behind the hill. "Capt. Slocum [sic] and a gunner would occasionally slip up from behind the hill, the capt. loading a piece himself and the gunner would fire it, then they would both take shelter behind the ridge. Immediately a shower of shells would come flying

20. Washington Ives, *Civil War Journal and Letters,* ed. Jim R. Cabaniss (Tallahassee, 1987), 8; Davis, ed., *Diary of a Confederate Soldier,* 122–23; Castel, *Decision in the West,* 159–61; Stephenson, *Civil War Memoir,* 175.

21. Castel, *Decision in the West,* 161; Davis, ed., *Diary of a Confederate Soldier,* 124.

over, and would mow down the trees about his guns. . . . The sharpshooters, too, would turn loose at him at the same time."[22]

The Fifth Company dug in, working far into night. By dawn on Sunday, May 15, the battery was much better protected "behind an embra-
sured earth work," wrote Stephenson, "but on a bare knob of a hill, a
little below the summit, on the slope toward the enemy in a very exposed
position." Slocomb with his two remaining pieces "renewed the action"
early on Sunday, but according to Jackman, who observed the artillery
fight, it was futile—"too great odds against him." Thereafter the fire from
the Washington Artillery was intermittent. Yankee sharpshooters moved
up close and "had our embrasures so completely in their control that we
had been ordered to cease firing for a while." They "pestered us exceedingly like bees and wasps and hornets." Cpl. Sam Russell, a Virginian,
"was sitting down beside his gun [Piece Number One] sulking. The sun
was pelting down upon our unprotected heads, making inaction hard to
bear. Suddenly, with an oath [Russell] sprang behind his gun to sight it
'just to take one shot,'" and "like a flash" he was shot through the fore-
head. Toward evening, despite the terrible danger, Slocomb ordered detachments forward to man the two remaining guns and "a terrible artillery
duel" erupted. It was one-sided and over quickly. The Federals "dismantled one of our guns and so disabled the other as to render it unserviceable." The company hunkered down once again, the dead and
wounded "in our midst. . . . They could not be removed in day light."[23]

The battery horses remained exposed, however. Twenty would die at
Resaca, including Vaught's and Slocomb's mounts. Phil Stephenson
watched in horror as the captain's "handsome large chestnut sorrel"
walked around quietly, tethered "to a swinging limb of a tree, not far
behind our position until a shell cut him down. . . . Thoughtless it seemed,
in the Captain, to leave him there. Some of us remarked upon it at the
time." This was the captain's battle charger. His other horse he kept back
with the wagons. He would not risk Gypsy. "Gypsy was a magnificent
coal black mare, our Captain's favorite riding animal, blooded stock and
very sagacious. He never took her into battle, she was too valuable, but

22. W. J. McMurray, *History of the Twentieth Tennessee* (Nashville, 1904), 310; Davis, ed., *Diary
of a Confederate Soldier*, 124; 5WA Order Book, WA Papers, HTT; John S. Jackman, "From Dalton
to Atlanta," *Southern Bivouac*, I (1882–83), 323; Waters, "Atlanta Campaign," 208.

23. 5WA Order Book, WA Papers, HTT; Stephenson, *Civil War Memoir*, 175, 178; Ives, *Civil
War Journal*, 8.

for all other occasions and especially for drilling, or for reviews, Slocomb would be on Gypsy. Full of fire and speed, but as familiar with every evolution as himself, and responsive to each slightest touch of the rein."[24]

That Sunday night at 10 P.M. Bate's division quietly and carefully fell in behind Cleburne's and withdrew across the Oostanaula River, proceeded down the Calhoun road about five miles, and bivouacked. The bridges over which the army had crossed were now destroyed or removed. They could rest in safety for the moment.

Resaca had proven costly. Although Chalaron might contend "the Fifth Company never showed more coolness, more valor, nor more fortitude," Resaca had damaged the company's pride—all of their guns had been knocked out of action. Two required repair beyond the capability of the battery blacksmith and artificer. They were shipped to Atlanta and scrapped. There was little doubt that the battery, indeed Johnston's artillery, "had come off decidedly second best," contends Larry Daniel. "It could not match its opponent's rapid rate of fire or superior ordnance."[25]

The battery's dead in the two-day battle of Resaca included Cpl. Samuel F. Russell; the Kentuckian J. H. Simmons, who had just returned from detached duty in the Quartermaster Department; and William B. Stuart, a Marylander who was transported mortally wounded to Atlanta, where he would die June 10, 1864. Among the ten wounded was one of the company's best gunners, Charlie Fox, a twenty-two-year-old from Massachusetts; the wealthy Pointe Coupée planter Tony Barrow; Chalaron's younger brother, Jack; Cpl. Bob Frazer, another Kentuckian; and Charlie Percy.[26]

Percy was about twenty, from a planter family in Feliciana Parish. He had been wounded at Chickamauga, but had returned. This time he was sent to Buckner Hospital at Newnan, Georgia, west of Atlanta, where he became a "glad, bright presence." Nurse Fannie Beers noticed that her patient was embarrassed because he had lost his uniform. So she set about to help, and managed to outfit him with a "nice jacket and pants of gray." Percy was "pleased, but not yet quite satisfied, for the jacket was simply gray. He wanted it trimmed with [artillery] red." The resourceful Fannie

24. Stephenson, *Civil War Memoir*, 170.

25. Waters, "The Atlanta Campaign," 208; *OR*, Vol. LII, Pt. 2, p. 110; Daniel, *Cannoneers in Gray*, 145.

26. Apparently Pvt. Stephen A. Myers deserted at Resaca. 5WA Master Roster, WA Papers, HTT; Chalaron, "Washington Artillery in the Army of Tennessee," 220.

managed to come up with some red flannel and "trimmed the suit under his supervision. I can never forget how happy he was to get into this suit, or how he danced around me, pretending to go through the artillery drill, and to load and fire at imaginary Yankees." Charlie Percy would leave Buckner Hospital early in July and take his place once again at Piece Number Three.[27]

27. 5WA Master Roster, WA Papers, HTT; Beers, *Memories,* 122–24.

CAPTAIN, HAVEN'T I DONE MY DUTY?

JOHNSTON'S CONFEDERATES retreated through Calhoun toward Adairsville. Failing to find a suitable defensive position, they continued south, with Hood's and Polk's corps proceeding directly to Cassville and Hardee's to Kingston. Johnston prepared to surprise Sherman at Cassville and announced his plan to the Army of Tennessee. The night of May 19, 1864, however, Hood and Polk dissuaded Johnston and to the bitter disappointment of the entire army yet another withdrawal began before daybreak on the twentieth.

Hardee in the meantime had marched all night and reached the vicinity of Kingston the morning of the eighteenth, his men arriving "very tired." They then moved on east to Cassville, becoming the left of the Army of Tennessee. The Fifth Company had an excellent position at Cassville and had worked with feverish enthusiasm to complete their redoubts. When their works were nearly complete, about 2 A.M. on the twentieth, "Captain Sid. Hardee, of General Hardee's staff, rode up and ordered the work to cease, and the battery made ready to move."[1] They learned that John-

---

1. In a letter to the editor of the New Orleans *Daily Picayune,* June 14, 1874, Lt. Charles G. Johnsen wrote that the "only disappointment" felt by the battery toward Joseph E. Johnston was his "failure to give battle at Cassville after *issuing* the *battle order.*"

ston's plan of attack at Cassville "had been frustrated by General Hood."[2]

Bate's division crossed the Etowah River on the twentieth and retreated with Hardee's corps about eleven miles south to another strong position near Allatoona Pass. There they remained until May 23, when Johnston ordered Hardee's corps to move to Dallas, some fifteen miles southwest. They had had time to rest at Allatoona, however, and that lifted spirits.[3] One night they halted about 8 P.M. to cook rations. Felix Arroyo took the fresh meat they had been issued and began to boil it in a kettle. He reached in his haversack and pulled out a red pepper which he "had taken from a garden a few days before," and broke it in the kettle. Along came the Virginia schoolteacher, William "Mac" McGregor.

"You are already cooking your rations?"

"Yes," and Arroyo invited him to join him for some soup.

"Soup! Where the devil can you get any?"

"It will be ready very shortly," said Arroyo, and soon he grabbed Mac's cup and filled it.

McGregor found some cornbread in his haversack and munched it while he ate his soup. "You Frenchmen," he said, "are smarter than we are. We always throw away the water in which we boil our meat."

That incident reminded Arroyo of the evenings when members of the unit would gather in front of their tent: J. Winfield Scott, H. J. Boatner, Jessie Bryan, John Jamison, Louis Vincent, James Dabney, and McGregor were members of the mess and were there of course. Often they would be joined by Henry Ogden, Bob Frazer, the brothers Alex and "Fatty" Allain, and others. Sometimes Slocomb would come along and it appears he felt free to join them. Arroyo remembered a particular night when the captain dropped by and McGregor asked him why he would not get rid of so-and-so, dismiss him from the company. It seems that anytime a fight was about to start he "always had the belly ache." Slocomb did not reply. Their company officers were a good sort, believed Arroyo. When details were "organized for any sort of work, they would cheerfully apply their shoulders to the wheel and rest only when everything was done."[4]

The march from Allatoona to Dallas was sixteen miles—important miles because Sherman's forces under Thomas and Hooker were converging on the same point. Hardee's forces pushed, despite the casualness

2. Waters, "Atlanta Campaign," 208; C. G. Johnsen to J. E. Johnston, June 19, 1874, *SHSP,* XXI (1898), 318–19; Ives, *Civil War Journal,* 8–9.

3. Chalaron, 5WA Itinerary, Chalaron Papers, HTT; Scaife, *Campaign for Atlanta,* 29.

4. Arroyo Journal, WA Papers, HTT.

of Arroyo's soup account. They would stop and eat and rest, then be up at 2 A.M. to continue their tramp into the pitch black. The morning of May 25 found Hardee's corps blocking the Atlanta-Marietta road on high hills just east of Dallas. It proved a rather undramatic day for Bate's division, but farther east they heard a terrific racket as Hooker's XX Corps and Hood's corps fought it out at New Hope Church. This was a surprise. Phil Stephenson, indeed most of the battery after the missed opportunity at Cassville, did not expect a fight "before we reached Atlanta."[5]

Hooker's attack failed, as did a subsequent effort by Oliver O. Howard at Pickett's Mill on May 27. Now Johnston decided to hit back. He targeted Sherman's exposed right, sending Hood swinging out wide along Little Pumpkin Vine Creek. This ambitious flanking move was canceled, however, when the Federals drew back their right into a strong defensive position. It appeared that Sherman might not be pulling back just his right, but withdrawing his entire army, so Johnston directed Hardee to have a division sent forward to feel the Federal position. Bate's division, being on the extreme left, was chosen. If the enemy "is not in force," Bate was told, attack and seize the Union positions across Pumpkin Vine Creek. Confident that he confronted only a skirmish line, Bate disregarded contradictory intelligence and launched an all-out assault at 3:45 P.M. with his Florida and Kentucky brigades.[6] It was disastrous. Bate's men struck Maj. Gen. John Logan's entrenched XV Corps and were hurled back with heavy casualties—the Orphans losing over half the troops that crossed the creek. The debacle "savaged [the two brigades] and resulted in their loss of confidence in Bate." John S. Jackman of Lewis' brigade recorded in his diary that "the boys think Gen'l Bate—'Old Grits' as they call him—went to Gen'l Hardee and got permission to make the charge, reporting that only a Federal skirmish line was in front of his division. The boys generally know what is in front, and could have told Gen Bate better. He 'catches it' from all sides and quarters."[7]

The Fifth Company had a miserable position at Dallas. They "occupied

5. Davis, ed., *Diary of a Confederate Soldier,* 129; Stephenson, *Civil War Memoir,* 181–82; Castel, *Decision in the West,* 200–43.

6. Bate was assisted by the dismounted cavalry brigade of Brig. Gen. Frank C. Armstrong, Maj. Gen. William H. Jackson's division. Armstrong discovered that the enemy was in strength and relayed the news to Bate who attempted to abort the attack, but it proved too late to stop Robert Bullock and Joseph P. Lewis.

7. Ives, *Civil War Journal,* 9; Castel, *Decision in the West,* 245–46; Daniel, *Cannoneers in Gray,* 150; Waters, "Atlanta Campaign," 201, 212–15; Davis, ed., *Diary of a Confederate Soldier,* 133.

a bare rounded ridge . . . one of the worst positions we were ever in, opposite a high, densely wooded hill which commanded us." They had moved their guns up about noon on the twenty-fifth, "in broad day," and "viciously" dug in. "Hot and deadly it was, from the very first" as the Yankee cannon, with uncanny accuracy blasted their position. "Fatal hill!" For three days they dueled with enemy batteries across Pumpkin Vine Creek. The climax came on the twenty-eight, when Bate made his charge. Opposing the company were "two or more twenty-pound Parrott guns." Piece Three was hit by a twenty-pounder missile. "They were next to us," remembered Stephenson, "on our left, about 20 or 25 feet off, and I saw it all. One shell or solid shot entered the mouth of the gun, tore off parts of it and knocked the whole detachment right and left." As the shell struck Piece Three, "an awful shriek rang out into the air! Shall I ever forget it?" wrote Stephenson thirty-five years later. "It pierced high above the dreadful din. '*Oh-h-h Christ Almighty!*' . . . Voice of anguish in tones that froze the blood. It was Tom B. Winston. His legs were torn off just below the waist. As we went on fighting, a hasty backward glance saw him borne away on a stretcher, his face and mangled form covered, a shapeless, shrouded heap."[8]

Mac McGregor was struck in the side and also killed. Stephenson reflected on his fallen comrades:

Two men could hardly be more unlike than were these two men, joined together as common victims of one shot. Both city men, "gentlemen," but very different. Tom B. was the dandy of our company, a fixy, dressy, neat little fellow. It was the constant wonder of us all how he kept himself so clean. And how he managed nearly always to have a white shirt ("biled shirt" as it was called in camp). When he went into action he would carefully roll his cuffs back! And then, in his shirtsleeves, take the sponge staff in hand. He was No. 2 at the piece; McGregor (No. 3) stood right behind him, his padded thumb on the vent. McGregor was a school teacher, a tall, sallow-faced, bearded man of thirty or more, well educated, with a reserved, melancholy disposition. Good soldiers, both of them.[9]

Slocomb ran to Billy Sewell, who also was down and obviously hurt badly. As the captain knelt by him, Sewell reached up and put his arms around Slocomb's neck, "pulling his face near his." He asked him: "Cap-

8. Jackman, "From Dalton to Atlanta," 452; *OR*, Vol. LII, Pt. 2, p. 110; Stephenson, *Civil War Memoir*, 184.
9. 5WA Master Roster, WA Papers, HTT; Stephenson, *Civil War Memoir*, 184.

tain, haven't I done my duty?" Sewell died soon after.[10] The losses ran higher: Martin Mathis, who had been shot through the thigh at Chickamauga, was killed at Dallas, as was artificer John T. Beggs, who also had been wounded at Chickamauga. Beggs was yet another Virginian in the battery, a skilled mechanic, who had worked as a ship's carpenter in New Orleans before the war. Two members of the unit were wounded at Dallas: Cpl. Tim White and artificer John M. Davidson, a Scotsman who was related by marriage to Richard L. Pugh. Davidson was hit on the twenty-eighth; White had been wounded in an artillery duel on May 26.[11]

Two guns had been disabled: Piece Three, which had to be shipped off for salvage, and another gun that was restored to service by the company blacksmith. Slocomb could find solace only in reporting that "I have good reason to believe that [the enemy's loss] has also been very heavy." He knew this from having examined the abandoned Yankee works to his front, where according to Stephenson the men "found quite a number of graves." The battery had been economical with its ammunition at Dallas, having expended 198 rounds.[12]

Fortunately for the Fifth Company, over two weeks would pass before they became directly engaged again. During this time the Washington Artillery would move to Pine Mountain and take position close to the summit, to the right of Lt. René T. Beauregard's South Carolina rifled battery. There they dug in and kept improving their works night and day. "The trenches were our home. . . . They were broad, deep ditches, broad enough to sit in with our backs to the embankment and our legs stretched out to full length . . . little transverse ditches to drain them, sticks holding blankets stretched above us to keep off the sun and rain *sometimes* were allowed." Pine Mountain, however, was not a good position for the Fifth Company. Although it was excellent for observation, the salient in which they were placed enabled Federal batteries "to fire from every quarter except our exact rear upon its summit." It was here on June 14 that a number of horrified battery members witnessed corps commander Leonidas Polk being killed by a three-inch solid shot while observing from behind Beauregard's position.[13]

10. Entry by JAC in 5WA Record Book, WA Papers, HTT.

11. Chalaron and Slocomb disagree on the date White was wounded, Chalaron believing it occurred on the twenty-seventh. 5WA Master Roster, WA Papers, HTT; *OR*, Vol. LII, Pt. 2, p. 110.

12. *OR*, Vol. LII, Pt. 2, p. 110; Stephenson, *Civil War Memoir*, 186.

13. CHS to M. Greenwood, June 7, 1864, Greenwood Papers, HNOC; Stephenson, *Civil War Memoir*, 186, 189–91; Davis, ed., *Diary of a Confederate Soldier*, 141–42; Castel, *Decision in the West*, 276.

A fierce bombardment followed. Upon the advanced point held by the Washington Artillery the enemy poured "a perfect deluge of shot and shell." The Yankee guns "sent up to us one prolonged deafening roar, from what seemed to us at least a hundred guns! Imagine them in a semicircle . . . all trained upon you on that point! The sides of the mountain trembled." The Confederates attempted to respond, but they were out of range and impossibly outgunned. No place seemed safe as every man sought cover. One gunner, a Parisian named Barrail, a veteran of an uprising against Louis Napoleon and once a valued member of the company, had lost his nerve after Missionary Ridge. During this bombardment at Pine Mountain, Barrail took the opportunity to leave his post and find a safe spot where the caissons were parked. A shell found him, however, and tore off his head.[14]

There were more psychological casualties from this terrible position on Pine Mountain that was "exposed on all sides to a heavy and continuous shelling." The day after Polk's death and the great bombardment, orders came to evacuate the position. As the battery pulled out, Slocomb and Chalaron went back to the site to check that nothing had been left. They came across a mess gathered about a fire in a bombproof that Cpl. John Boardman "had built under the brow of the hill."[15]

Slocomb expressed his astonishment at finding them there, but the men gave the excuse that they were waiting because of food cooking on the fire. They assured the captain "that in a moment they would all rejoin" the column. Slocomb warned the men that they must hurry or risk capture. Then he and Chalaron rode off accompanied by bugler Andy Swain, whom Slocomb ordered to leave the fire and accompany him. A while later Pvt. Charles C. Cotting came racing back to the old line, determined to retrieve the haversack that he had left at the breastworks. Cotting saw the group still sitting around the fire despite Slocomb's admonition. He too warned them of the danger.

The result was that the Washington Artillery lost the entire group of six gunners. They would maintain afterward that they had fallen asleep and were not awakened when the battery moved out and had been captured by Yankee pickets, but Chalaron would prove unrelenting in his refusal to allow them to be readmitted to membership in the company after the war. All were carried as deserters although the Galpin brothers,

14. S. B. Newman, Jr., to M. Greenwood, June 17, 1864, Greenwood Papers, HNOC; Stephenson, *Civil War Memoir,* 191–95.

15. E. Fehrenback, John Boardman, and E. Charles to Officers and Members of 5WA, n.d., 1875, Chalaron Papers, HTT.

Frank and Samuel, the Frenchman Fehrenback, and Boardman would be imprisoned at Rock Island and not released until May, 1865. Edwin Charles would take the Federal oath shortly before the end of the war and be released. Edward Virtue would take the oath in October, 1864, and join the United States Army for frontier duty.[16]

Compounding this sorry episode was the wounding of Tim White on June 15. White had been hospitalized in Marietta since his injury at Dallas and chafed at the prospect of remaining out of action and away from the company. He finally secured his release from the hospital and made his way back, but was intercepted by the enemy near Gilgal Church and wounded again.[17]

On June 16, 1864, Johnston abandoned the Pine Mountain salient and pulled back the left of his line. The new position, in the form of an inverted V, was found untenable, however, because the center was dominated by George Thomas' artillery. It was here on June 18 that battery commander John W. Mebane was killed by a Yankee shell and replaced by Lt. J. W. Phillips. Of far greater importance to the company was the injury to Billy Vaught. Apparently it was during this temporary stand before retiring to the Kennesaw line that he was deafened by the concussion of an exploding shell. Vaught went on sick leave June 20, suffering from "neuralgia and deafness," and would never return to active duty, although he would be standing by his comrades at the surrender the following May. This was a terrible loss, "for he was a valuable officer," recalled Stephenson, who knew him only a short time and thought of him as "always cool and measured in temper, words, and deeds, of good judgment and fidelity."[18]

Once again, as Larry Daniel has pointed out, the "powerful Union artillery had influenced a retreat decision." That night after Mebane's death the Confederates fell back toward Marietta. Slocomb's battery was miserable. The rain had continued now for about two weeks. "About half

16. JAC to E. Fehrenback, John Boardman, November 6, 1875, Chalaron Papers, HTT; E. Fehrenback, John Boardman, and E. Charles to Officers and Members of 5WA, n.d., 1875, Chalaron Papers, HTT; E. Virtue statement, Confederate Personnel Documents, HTT.

17. 5WA Master Roster, WA Papers, HTT.

18. "Many of us were deafened temporarily," Stephenson remembered. "I myself was dull of hearing for some time after the war. I ascribed it for the most part to the experiences at Kennesaw. It must be remembered that it was almost like a shell exploding in a room, for we were in a 'room' [redoubt], lacking only wall and the ceiling. Our custom was to put cotton in our ears." Daniel, *Cannoneers in Gray,* 151; Castel, *Decision in the West,* 282–83; Ives, *Civil War Journal,* 11; Stephenson, *Civil War Memoir,* 199; C. Swett's Report, December 21, 1864, Inspection Records and Related Reports, RG 109, NA; 5WA Master Roster, WA Papers, HTT.

our company are sick," reported Cpl. Sam Newman, "from as much exposure, marching at night[,] building breastworks when not marching and remaining wet for 24 or 36 hours."[19]

Johnston's army fell back a short distance and established its Kennesaw line. This seven-mile front northwest of Marietta was anchored by Kennesaw Mountain itself with Polk's corps (now commanded by the veteran William W. Loring and soon to be led by A. P. Stewart) on the crest. Hardee's corps fanned out to the left and south on a line of hills overlooking Nose's Creek. It was a very strong position and for ten days the Army of Tennessee held Sherman at bay, frustrating him to the extent that he attempted a most uncharacteristic frontal assault on June 27, striking just to the left of Bate's line. The Washington Artillery, however, did not play a significant role in this costly repulse.[20]

It was a dangerous existence on the Kennesaw line. Newman wrote his friend Moses Greenwood that "they have two Batteries of Parrott guns (3 inch rifles) and one 24 pound howitser [sic] directly in front of our works about 700 yds distance, with an open field between us. We can see this works and men walking about, perfectly plain." He also told Greenwood of his own close call: "While standing at the breastworks in the rain with my oil cloth around me, a shell exploded near me, and a fragment about two inches square passed through my oil cloth near the thigh. It scared me pretty badly, and I am truly thankful for my escape." Moses Greenwood, the father of Milo Greenwood, who had been killed at Chickamauga, was important to the battery. Not only did he get packages through the lines—containing books, money, socks, and handkerchiefs for his friends Newman, Cotting, and others—but he sent vegetables and fruit up from Mobile. Often these perishables arrived spoiled, but Slocomb encouraged Greenwood to keep up the shipments: "Living as we do on Bacon & corn bread you may well understand the great need we have for vegetables."[21]

19. Daniel, *Cannoneers in Gray,* 151; S. B. Newman, Jr., to M. Greenwood, June 19, 1864, Greenwood Papers, HNOC.

20. Daniel, *Cannoneers in Gray,* 151; Castel, *Decision in the West,* 282–83; S. B. Newman, Jr., to M. Greenwood, June 19, 1864, J. H. Duggan to M. Greenwood, June 14, 1864, Greenwood Papers, HNOC; Scaife, *Campaign for Atlanta,* 41.

21. S. B. Newman, Jr., to M. Greenwood, June 26, 30, 1864, CHS to M. Greenwood, July 11, 1864, Greenwood Papers, HTT. Moses Greenwood was about fifty-six years old, a commission merchant from Massachusetts who had immigrated to Arkansas about 1840, thence to New Orleans. 1850 Census, Orleans Parish, Louisiana, 29; New Orleans *City Directory,* 1851, p. 81.

The day before Sherman's great frontal assault at Kennesaw, a shell struck in Phil Stephenson's redoubt. It hit the axle of Piece Four, exploded, and knocked down the crew like tenpins. Gunner Alex Allain was wounded in the arm and his brother "Fatty" was also injured. The bent axle made it unsafe to fire the gun, but Chalaron insisted it be "fired anyhow."[22]

Alex Allain won the admiration of Stephenson during one of their artillery duels on the Kennesaw line.

The saplings which formed the sides of our embrasure began to give way under the impact of shots, and the dirt behind them fell forward into it, threatening to fill it and so block the line and sweep of our fire. We were in the midst of a particularly fierce fight and would be practically muzzled by that bank of dirt forming fast before our gun.

Alex jumped up into the embrasure, into that focus of the shot and shell of the opposing battery and the bullets of sharpshooters and proceeded to repair it. He asked for an axe, straightened and drove down the upright posts, replaced the sapling behind them, and with a spade removed what dirt he could, and jumped down and resumed the sighting of our piece. I recall as yesterday how cool he was, how calm and pleasant his voice sounded as he gave directions to those of us who waited on him, and how unconcernedly he turned his back upon the enemy when the work required it. He was not touched.[23]

For his bravery and meritorious performance at Kennesaw, Allain would win his corporal's stripes. Young Oscar Legaré also was promoted for saving the the company flag, which waved defiantly over the battery breastworks. An enemy round snapped the flagstaff in two and Oscar climbed atop the redoubt and replaced it so fast that the enemy could not tell what had happened because of the smoke. Then they shot it down again, tearing it. This time the Yankees saw the banner tumble and gave "one long and loud cheer," but Oscar was on the parapet in no time at all and again replaced it.[24]

The stand at Kennesaw was costly—perhaps not in lives as at Dallas and Resaca, but Slocomb had lost Vaught and nine men wounded. Lt. Abe Leverich was wounded, but not severely. D. A. Rice had his jaw broken by a shell fragment, yet would be able to return before the Atlanta

22. A. Allain to JAC, August 3, 1875, Chalaron Papers, HTT; A. Allain to A. Armant, August 14, 1903, Confederate Personnel Documents, HTT.

23. Stephenson, *Civil War Memoir,* 197–98.

24. 5WA Master Roster, WA Papers, HTT.

campaign ended. Charles Staub was also struck in the head and would die of his wound within four months. Sgt. "Bully" Smith was hit in the side, Charlie Watt in the thigh, and corporals James F. Giffen and J. Winfield Scott were slightly wounded.[25]

Sherman resumed his turning movements at the end of June, compelling Johnston to abandon his formidable Kennesaw line and retire to a fortified bridgehead on the north bank of the Chattahoochee River. These defenses "were intended to be a very elaborate affair. . . . [General Shoup's] idea was to have a chain of heavy stockade forts connected by strong earthworks in the middle of which would be the salients for artillery."[26] The works were not completed, however, and had to be replaced with the customary redoubts and earth and log breastworks.[27] Ten quiet days passed here on the banks of the Chattahoochee; then on July 9, the Confederates awoke to the fact that Sherman had made a lodgment on the south bank some sixteen miles upriver at Roswell. They were flanked once again. On the night of July 9–10, the Army of Tennessee pulled out of their fortifications, crossed the Chattahoochee and retired south of Peachtree Creek about two miles north of Atlanta's fixed defenses.[28]

Phil Stephenson remembered the Chattahoochee crossing vividly: "It was a gloriously beautiful moonlight night." The men were subdued as they moved across the wobbly pontoon bridge. "With me the thoughts engendered were melancholy. The bloody struggles, the horrid scenes, the frightful passions at play, all of these made a dreadful contrast to the beauty all about us. What a monster man is!"[29]

25. *Ibid.;* CHS to M. Greenwood, July 11, 1864, Greenwood Papers, HNOC.

26. Joe Duggan maintained the forts were about 150 yards apart, the intervals being filled with a "strong picket fence of logs with loop holes." Stephenson, *Civil War Memoir,* 203–204; Castel, *Decision in the West,* 334; J. Duggan to M. Greenwood, July 3, 1864, Greenwood Papers, HNOC.

27. Staff officer William Palfrey wrote Moses Greenwood that Shoup "did not have time to complete his line of works as he wished, but it was sufficiently far advanced to receive the army. It was amusing to hear the remarks made by the men as they came in sight of the new line. Very few had any confidence in it. They are beginning to understand it now. . . . The idea was to let a small number hold the line so the rest can assume the offensive or be sent to meet any raid sent against our communications. Hardee and Cheatham like the line. . . . Hood was in favor of crossing the river. Hardee opposed it." W. Palfrey to M. Greenwood, July 6, 11, 1864, Greenwood Papers, HNOC.

28. Casey, *Outline of Civil War Campaigns,* 76; Castel, *Decision in the West,* 340.

29. Stephenson, *Civil War Memoir,* 204–206.

ODD SITUATION FOR A BATTERY

I T WAS leisurely at first. The Washington Artillery encamped about three miles north of Atlanta and since the heat was intense ("as oppressive as at home," according to Charles Cotting), they built "arbors of brush" to shield themselves from the sun. "We loll around, every one amuses himself as he thinks best to relieve the monotony of camp life. Fortunately for us Capt. Slocomb manages to get a number of Magazines &c. (old dates) which we busy ourselves in reading." [1]

Of course they sought out the young ladies in the neighborhood. One was "Miss Abby," a secret Unionist. Into her grove and yard "poured" the Fifth Company ("an army of black mounted cannon," as she expressed it). "An officer came up quickly and said, 'They are falling back and will soon fight at the breastworks. It will not be safe for you to remain here, madam.'"

Miss Abby was distraught and wept. Nervously she would pull a handkerchief out of her pocket and absently replace it, or would snatch "up my muslin dress every now and then, as I went from room to room, not

---

1. C. C. Cotting to M. Greenwood, July 18, 1864, Greenwood Papers, HNOC.

knowing what to do or where to go, what to save—if anything could be saved—or what to leave." The men, seeing her distress, made the decision for her. "They went into the parlor and had the carpet rolled up, pictures packed and many other things, before I knew it." Others "looked on piteously . . . and I heard one to say in a low voice, 'I tell you boys, if our army ever sets foot on Northern soil, we ought never to leave one house standing, to pay for such suffering as this.' My heart thanked them," thought Miss Abby, "for their sympathy, but I thought they little knew upon what a 'traitor' they were bestowing it." [2]

Despite such duplicity, camp days near Atlanta represented a magnificent change from the harshness of the Kennesaw line. The battery was "living in *clover.* Every day nearly we get quite a quantity of vegetables such as cucumbers, squashes, potatoes, tomatoes, onions, &c which together with our ration of bread and bacon make a sumptuous repast. The boys are all in excellent health and spirits." [3]

"General Bragg is in camp!" The word swept through camp July 17. Then a "startling rumor"—"Johnston is relieved!" The news "is dismissed in a moment, scoffed at as absurd," but repeated. "A feeling of uneasiness is discernible." Hours passed heavily, and then the rumor was confirmed: Johnston was dismissed on July 18. When the order was read aloud to the company, some members "wept like children, others seemed speechless, and others poured forth denunciations and curses upon our deluded and infatuated President." According to Phil Stephenson, mutiny "lifted its ugly head." The commander of his piece, the Virginian Tom Allen, "a superb soldier, mounted a stump and passionately advised going in a body to Johnston's headquarters to protest his leaving." Cooler heads prevailed, however, and the battery resigned itself to John Bell Hood as army commander. [4]

2. Mills Lane, ed., *Times That Prove People's Principles* (Savannah, 1993), 197. The diary of "Miss Abby" can be found in the Manuscript Library, University of Georgia, Athens. It remained a mystery for years until Thomas G. Dyer discovered the identity of the author—Cyrena Bailey Stone, a thirty-four-year-old native of East Berkshire, Vermont, and wife of Amherst W. Stone, a Vermont lawyer who had come to Georgia in the 1840s. See Thomas G. Dyer, "Georgia History in Fiction—Atlanta's Other Civil War Novel: Fictional Unionists in a Confederate City," *Georgia Historical Quarterly,* LXXIX (1995), 149–50, 152.

3. C. C. Cotting to M. Greenwood, July 18, 1864, Greenwood Papers, HNOC.

4. Johnston received the telegram from Richmond at 10 P.M. on the seventeenth. Castel, *Decision in the West,* 362; Stephenson, *Civil War Memoir,* 208–209; C. C. Cotting to M. Greenwood, July 18, 1864, Greenwood Papers, HNOC.

Immediately, it seemed, a grand opportunity presented itself to the new Confederate leader—a chance for victory, to reverse the slide of the Atlanta campaign. Sherman was sending Thomas' Army of the Cumberland across Peachtree Creek while McPherson and Schofield pushed south toward Decatur. Hood decided to exploit this great gap existing between Sherman's forces and drive Thomas "into the pocket formed by the juncture of [Peachtree Creek] with the Chattahoochee."[5]

Hood put his army in motion immediately. On the evening of the eighteenth, Hardee and Stewart moved to positions close to Peachtree Creek. There they encamped. Early the next morning Bate's division, on the right of Hardee's corps, began constructing breastworks. Then the division moved forward toward Peachtree Creek. They did not advance far, however, and soon returned to their works. Phil Stephenson and the Washington Artillery "spent the whole time struggling along behind an entrenched line of battle of our men (who never did get engaged) trying to get a 'position.' We went for perhaps two miles, and then went back again. There was no road and it was through thick woods. . . . Not a shot was fired along that whole line as I recall. Indeed, not even a sign of any enemy." Sgt. Maj. Washington Ives, one of Robert Bullock's Floridians (Bate's division), seconded Stephenson's memory of this curious nineteenth day of July on the west side of Peachtree Creek. Meanwhile the company could hear "fierce fighting . . . going on to our east at the time," but this fighting did not include Bate or his men.[6]

Hood's overall plan for July 20 had called for Hardee and Stewart to strike Thomas' left and center while Cheatham (temporarily in command of Hood's corps) would guard Hardee's right flank, thus interdicting the battlefield. The attack was to have been launched at 1 P.M. on July 20, but maintaining contact with Cheatham, who was drifting farther and farther to the right, caused constant realignment of the fronts of Hardee's and Stewart's corps, so it was not until 4 P.M. that the assault began.

Bate's division had a key role. It would be the enveloping element, attacking the enemy left and starting the "process of rolling up the Union line," as Breckinridge had done at Chickamauga. Bate, however, was no Breckinridge. He would lose his way, "flounder about," and be unable to locate the enemy. Knowing they were expected to attack, these blind grop-

5. Connelly, *Autumn of Glory,* 440; Castel, *Decision in the West,* 366–67.
6. Stephenson, *Civil War Memoir,* 213; Ives, *Civil War Journal,* 14.

ings, these senseless stop-and-start tactics, exasperated the troops of the division.[7]

As their part in this important flanking movement, the Fifth Company swung far to the right and rear with Bate's infantry, but soon became separated. Bate ordered Chalaron to take a section (Pieces Three and Four) and go forward to the skirmish line "to harass the enemy with artillery shots as they crossed the bridge" at a point where "the creek described a very pronounced curve, the bridge being at the point of the shoe. Our position was at the heel." Chalaron went into battery near the road "in a wood to the left side of a tobacco barn with an opening in front of us reaching to the water's edge."[8] He placed Sgt. Tom Allen and Piece Four next to the wall of the barn with Piece Three to his left and rear. From that point they could see the banners of the "enemy infantry in close order. For a while after opening my guns," Chalaron remembered, "I had some sport," their fire causing commotion in the Yankee column. Oscar Legaré, gunner on Piece Three, "shot with telling effect and was highly elated."

Suddenly there came a cannon shell from across Peachtree Creek. "The enemy were on the opposite bank which was high, a naked red clay bank. . . . We did not know they were there until a shot from a masked battery revealed it. . . . We could see nothing but their smoke when they fired." Chalaron had no infantry for support, no skirmishers in front, no pickets to warn him. He and his men, according to Stephenson, were totally surprised when the Federal battery atop that high bank opened fire. Chalaron and Stephenson disagreed about the range, the latter believing the Federals were less than a quarter of a mile away. Chalaron thought they were at least three times that distance. In any event, "within two discharges the enemy had determined our range." Chalaron maintained that he gave the order to limber to the rear immediately. Stephenson, to the contrary, remembered that Chalaron accepted the duel, stubbornly remaining in position, although "it was an unequal fight. . . . They could see every man of us."[9]

The Federals had sharpshooters too. "Will Tutt, who rammed and sponged, and I, who loaded, found it certain death to stand up," recalled

7. Connelly, *Autumn of Glory,* 440–41; Castel, *Decision in the West,* 372–78.
8. The road was probably the Brighton.
9. Stephenson, *Civil War Memoir,* 214–15.

Stephenson. So we crouched by the muzzle of our gun on either side, loading it in that position." To remain and fight, however, was madness, so, upon Chalaron's order, the section prepared to withdraw. Tom Allen's Piece Four limbered up first. As Piece Three prepared to do so, Legaré shouted to Chalaron "that he had a load in his gun . . . and he had dead range and begged to be allowed to fire. I yielded," remembered Chalaron. Oscar Legaré hurried and sighted the piece and gave the command to fire. The friction primer, however, failed. Number Four rushed to insert another and was about to jerk the lanyard when Oscar "stopped him." He wanted to make absolutely sure of the shot, so he leaned forward, carefully "resighted the piece." As Oscar was putting his eye to the breech, Chalaron yelled at him to hurry.

At that moment bright discharges came from across the creek. An instant later a round of spherical case struck Piece Three about a foot from Oscar's head, "dug a deep groove in the gun & exploded immediately." It killed Oscar instantly and mortally wounded Charlie Percy, crouching close behind Oscar, manning the trail of the piece—playful Charlie, the boy with Nurse Beers's new gray uniform with the bright red trim. "Alas!" wrote a saddened Phil Stephenson, "the two boys were torn to pieces, from the waist up. We found long strips of flesh high up on the trees behind them."

"Never again," declared a sobered Chalaron, "did I yield to requests for any delay in executing orders & I had many such demands for last shots." The section then retreated, gently placing its dead and dying upon limbers, "humiliated at the thought of withdrawing under fire and saddened at the great loss we had sustained." [10]

The battery fell back a good distance from Peachtree Creek, then, according to Stephenson,

threw down a fence skirting the road on our right (as we retreated) and faced to the front again. Tearing at great speed through the forest, we made for sounds of battle to our left front. Evidences of strife were all about us, dead and wounded men and horses, upturned limber chests, etc. . . . We seemed to be by ourselves ["strangely isolated"]—no infantry support whatever, just out in the woods in the hottest kind of contest. We were of little use at this new position. The day was

10. The account of this fight at the bend in Peachtree Creek is based on a notation by JAC on a letter of condolence from C. G. Johnsen to Oscar's uncle, Dr. J. Cecil Legaré, July 20, 1864; Chalaron Papers, HTT; and on Stephenson, *Civil War Memoir,* 214–15.

almost gone, and the fighting about us over when we got there. Night soon brought cessation.[11]

Thus ended the terrible day of July 20. Oscar was dead. Charlie Percy would not live a week, and Evans Ricketts had received a nasty wound from which he would die eight months later. Ben Bridge and Tony Barrow, the latter having been hit previously at Resaca, suffered lesser wounds and would recover.[12]

The battle of Peachtree Creek had been a miserable failure for the Washington Artillery and for Bate's division. The division did not become engaged with the Federals at all, although no division in the Army of Tennessee had a more important assignment. The battery seems to have spent the two days wandering about and, with the exception of Chalaron's unfortunate experience at the creek bank, does not seem to have fired a round.[13]

July 21 saw little improvement. Hardee moved three miles east-south-east, then Bate, who had been covering the movement of the corps, returned and reoccupied the front line. The Fifth Company, according to Stephenson, "did nothing but dawdle . . . going slowly in toward Atlanta. A part of this day was spent by some of us in a dismantled little house along the road side where I got a much needed nap, and where others spent the time scribbling over the whitewashed walls." At nightfall, July 21, things changed. "We soon found ourselves going rapidly towards the city. Odd, such a movement seemed, but we welcomed it. Anything was better than the aimless going here and there under the new leadership. There seemed a purpose." As part of a "large, swiftly marching column of men, and with a swinging gait in a short while [we] reached Atlanta."[14]

Hood planned to hit again. Using a stratagem reminiscent of the glory days in the Army of Northern Virginia, he would send Hardee's corps on a sweep through Atlanta and around McPherson's left flank. The original plan called for Hardee to march all night July 21 via Cobb's Mill until he reached McPherson's rear (near Decatur). Then he was to turn north and

11. Stephenson, *Civil War Memoir,* 214–15.

12. 5WA Master Roster, WA Papers, HTT.

13. Ives, *Civil War Journal,* 14; Waters, "Atlanta Campaign," 201; Daniel, *Cannoneers in Gray,* 157–58.

14. Ives, *Civil War Journal,* 14; Stephenson, *Civil War Memoir,* 215–16.

assail the Union left and rear. This plan was revised, however, giving Hardee latitude to use a shorter route and simply attack McPherson's left flank. Stewart and Cheatham would move inside the Atlanta defenses and join in the attack once they heard Hardee's guns.[15]

Bate's division, already tired from marching and counter-marching that day, struck out at dark "through Atlanta down the McDonough road for some miles, and then to Cobb's Mill . . . arriving at said [Sugar] Creek at 3 A.M., on the 22nd." They rested three hours and began their tramp once again, this time up the Fayetteville road toward Decatur. After moving east a short distance they halted and deployed parallel to the road. Bate formed the right of Hardee's four attacking divisions with his own right one-half mile west of the Parker house. Once off the road, however, Bate's men encountered dense woods and undergrowth. To have moved the Fifth Company, which was "the only artillery with me," through this jungle would have required an inordinate amount of time, so Bate ordered Slocomb "to take a left hand road which turned off in the neighborhood of Mrs [*sic*] Parker's and as soon as possible unite with the lines in the forward movement."[16]

It had been an exhausting but exciting night march for Slocomb's battery. They knew something big was afoot. "The moon was full and made it light as day. Our course was zig zag tending to the southeast corner of the town, and we passed through much of the residential portion." As was their custom, the company sang as they moved through the city— "Annie Laurie," "Anne Darling," and many other favorites. "The infantry before and after us caught the infection. . . . Not so the citizens of Atlanta. Those tall dwellings remained as close and silent as convents!"[17]

"We found ourselves by break of day, with our faces turned north on a straight, level, dirt road, skirted by thick woods on our left. Halts came, the men jamming up against each other each time (for they were sleepy) just like cars on a freight train. . . . No singing now." They halted at a farm house and Bate's infantry " 'left faced' and formed in two lines, facing the deep woods and stepping from the road, halted again just in the edge of the woods, 'dressing the line,' and awaiting orders." The battery, however, stayed in the road while the infantry went into the woods. Finally a courier arrived with orders and conferred with Slocomb. Then the

15. Connelly, *Autumn of Glory,* 445–46.

16. Waters, "Atlanta Campaign," 216–17; Scaife, *Campaign for Atlanta,* 60.

17. Stephenson, *Civil War Memoir,* 216.

battery started down the road once again, away from the division, guided by the courier. They proceeded toward Decatur a short distance, then turned left "into a little narrow road that came into the other diagonally from the northwest. This, followed for a short distance would place us so that by advancing from it to the front we would strike the right flank of our division." [18]

"But the courier kept going on and on, not leaving that little road. . . . Time passed. All about us was still, not a trace of our infantry. The assignment to position amounted to a march." Hungry and hot, members began to drift off into the woods on either side of the road, picking blackberries. They had traversed a mile at least and crossed "quite a good sized creek." [19] "Suddenly, the road took a turn and a shot rang out!" Phil Stephenson looked up and saw a Yankee picket dash off. "Then came shot after shot and men running back through the woods. Where were we?" [20]

They moved ahead about two hundred yards and discovered "wagons upon wagons! Army wagons. It was the vast wagon train of the enemy! . . . We had struck the enemy rear." Phil Stephenson could see animals feeding and men cooking. "Astonishing spectacle. Magnificent opportunity for cavalry or infantry. But what an astounding situation for a battery of artillery." Battalion commander Robert Cobb, who accompanied the Washington Artillery, rode forward to reconnoiter. "I can see his red head now," recalled Stephenson, "as he disappeared around a bend in the road—flaming red, both cap and hair." Cobb returned quickly and ordered Slocomb to retire, which the latter did, pulling back a few hundred yards to a good position where the battery unlimbered. Cobb sent back to division for instructions and waited while some "straggling infantry men who had followed us to overtake their commands were put out as pickets. Odd situation for a battery." Presently the courier returned and reported Wheeler's cavalry to their rear. The cavalry were surprised to learn the Washington Artillery lay ahead, supposing "that everything in front of them was 'Yankee.'" The battery was to return; Wheeler would deal with the enemy rear. [21]

Again they had wasted precious hours. Again they were far out of position. "Whose blunder it was, I cannot say—not Hood's this time,

18. *Ibid.,* 217–18.
19. Probably Sugar Creek.
20. Stephenson, *Civil War Memoir,* 218.
21. *Ibid.,* 218–19; for Wheeler's activities, see Castel, *Decision in the West,* 388–94.

however. I suspect," reflected Stephenson. "It was General Bate's. We told the cavalry of the unprotected park of wagons . . . and passed rapidly to the rear, for the battle was raging." Slocomb's men turned off the road to the right and fought their way through the woods, "having to 'blaze a way' for some distance with our axes. . . . After travelling a long, long distance," they came up behind Bate's line, "where we ought to have been all along." Slocomb went into battery "and stood ready for action the rest of the day, but of little use. We fired a few rounds, but were not in a position to do any execution." Bate vaguely reported that following the repulse of his infantry the Washington Artillery had come up and was "brought into play upon the lines of the enemy that He might occupy him in my front and prevent his reinforcing other parts of the line."[22]

Thus ended the battle of Atlanta, another fiasco, at least in the eyes of Phil Stephenson. Chalaron, in his numerous writings about the battery, seems to ignore July 22. Slocomb and his men might as well have been on furlough. Of course, one might argue that Atlanta (like Shiloh and Chickamauga) was purely an infantry battle, and could only have been an infantry battle because of the difficult terrain and lack of observation.[23] In any event, based on the scant information available, it appears the battery, indeed Cobb's battalion, was poorly managed on July 22. The fault probably lies, as Stephenson suggests, with Maj. Gen. William B. Bate. Bate's division, numbering only twelve hundred because of the losses at Dallas (for which his "Kentuckians and Floridians blame and hate him"), and straggling, approached the Federal lines "floundering through underbrush, muck, and knee-deep water." When he did attack, Bate was met with "a devastating cross fire of canister," and hurled back demoralized, out of action for the remainder of the day.[24]

Following the futility of July 22, Hardee's corps marched back into the Atlanta fortifications. Cheatham (once again a division commander since Stephen D. Lee had arrived and taken command of Hood's corps) and Cleburne manned trenches on the east side of Atlanta while Bate and the Washington Artillery were shifted to the opposite side of the city to support those works that were becoming progressively more threatened as

---

22. Stephenson, *Civil War Memoir,* 219–20; Waters, "Atlanta Campaign," 218.

23. The Federal artillery, as usual, played an important role, but they had the great advantage of being on the tactical defensive.

24. Castel, *Decision in the West,* 393–97; Ives, *Civil War Journal,* 70.

Sherman slid west and south. To thwart this encroachment, Hood, on July 28, once again pulled his troops out of their breastworks and attempted another flank attack, this time conducted by Lee and Stewart. The surprise assault (battle of Ezra Church) proved no surprise and failed dismally, accompanied once again by high loss. As Stewart's men prepared to march out to the attack, the 30th Louisiana and its "magnificent band" halted near the Washington Artillery. The band "commenced serenading us . . . Alas! many of these poor young men were hearing those airs for the last time." Both this regiment and the battery's old friends, the 13th and 20th Louisiana Consolidated, would suffer terrible losses a few hours later at Ezra Church. The Fifth Company, although acting more in the capacity of witnesses than participants, took solace in the knowledge that they had moved up and provided "a well directed" enfilade fire that "probably saved the rest of our troops." Nevertheless the battle was "a humiliating failure," leaving members of the battery with a feeling of "disgust, intense, intolerable to us all."[25]

During the month of August, 1864, Sherman steadily tightened his siege lines around Atlanta and bombarded the city.[26] "We took their steady shelling philosophically," remembered Stephenson, "and now and then returned it."[27] The battery itself was located in works directly in front of the John J. Thrasher home, a "splendid" two-story brick structure directly west of the city (on Ashby Street), equidistant between Atlanta and Ezra Church. Members of the company were no strangers at the Thrashers'. They had been visiting the home and the three Thrasher daughters since "before the investment of Atlanta and while we were around Marietta."[28]

When Sherman's artillery moved in close, however, the Thrashers fled their home and the city, leaving their property in the care of servants. It made a sumptuous battery headquarters and was enjoyed immensely by

25. Felix Arroyo Journal, Louisiana Historical Association Collections, HTT; see Castel, *Decision in the West,* 424–36; Stephenson, *Civil War Memoir,* 225–26.

26. On August 9, the Federals fired more than five thousand rounds into the city. Some of these were from thirty-pounder Parrott rifles added to a number of twenty-pounders already on hand. Daniel, *Cannoneers in Gray,* 161.

27. Hood's field artillery was down to only 125 rounds per gun. Daniel, *Cannoneers in Gray,* 163.

28. The affable speculator-politician Thrasher had made and lost several fortunes and was widely known for "big-handed hospitality." Stephenson, *Civil War Memoir,* 229–30, 242n; Arroyo Journal, LHA Collection, HTT.

Slocomb and his men alike. One morning, however, fellow Louisianan and cavalry brigade commander Col. John S. Scott, came by "and told us to vacate that building as soon as possible, because he wanted to establish his headquarters in it." According to Pvt. Felix Arroyo, Slocomb stubbornly held his ground, telling Scott that the Washington Artillery "had taken it first and that he intended to keep it." So the Thrasher home remained the palace of the Fifth Company and Colonel Scott "went away without saying another word. . . . Slocomb was the best hearted man that possibly could be found in this world," observed his worshiping gunner Arroyo.[29]

Cavalry actions indirectly affected the Washington Artillery about this time. On August 10, Wheeler left on a large-scale raid against Sherman's communications. This, of course, presented Federal cavalry with an opportunity and they rode south toward Macon attempting to cut the vital railroad that supplied Hood and Atlanta. To meet this threat, Hood ordered that infantry be mounted and for some of their mounts he turned to the artillery, taking battery horses in exchange for mules. Slocomb hitched the mules to the caissons, but this swap reduced efficiency and made drivers nervous. Yankee shells on several occasions "came near stampeding the mules."[30]

Four days before Wheeler left, Bate's division had its proudest day of the Atlanta campaign. Two Union corps attempted to swing west and south to cut the "last two remaining supply lines to Atlanta."[31] Hood countered by dispatching Bate's division to a position just north of Utoy Creek.[32] Bate's division was larger and stronger now, having been increased by the addition of Henry R. Jackson's Georgia brigade.[33] These troops (many of them green militia) and their inexperienced commander had been assigned when W. H. T. Walker's division was broken up after Hardee's July 22 failure.[34]

On August 6, Jacob Cox's division, XXIII Corps, assaulted Bate's works and was repulsed. Fragmented attacks by other units followed and

29. Arroyo Journal, LHA Collection, HTT.

30. W. Palfrey to M. Greenwood, August 11, 1864, Greenwood Papers, HNOC; Chalaron, "Slocomb's Battery in the Tennessee Army," Jackson Barracks Library, New Orleans.

31. Scaife, *Campaign for Atlanta*, 101.

32. Often referred to as "Eutaw Creek" by Confederates.

33. Jackson's brigade had been commanded by Brig. Gen. Clement H. Stevens, who was mortally wounded at Peachtree Creek.

34. Castel, *Decision in the West*, 423.

met with like results. Thus the purely defensive battle of Utoy Creek gave Bate (and Hood) reason to boast. It was a "brilliant fight," declared Bate, and the stubborn stand by the bold Tennessean and his men gave army commander Hood occasion to issue a special order commending particularly Tom Smith's brigade and the Orphans for their pluck and for their capture of three stands of Yankee colors. Casualties among Bate's Confederates, including the artillery, were very light. The role of the Washington Artillery at Utoy Creek is unknown and probably was minor since they are not mentioned in the official reports or by participants. Things quickly returned to their normal state along the line.[35]

Such was the state of things in the month of August, 1864. That month we spent in the trenches, under a fire of shot and shell and musketry, which, although not continuous, was heavy. So too, it was spent, under fire by the hapless people of Atlanta, mostly women and children.

The "ping" and "spit" and "sputter" and "drop" of bullets about you, the shriek and gobble and flutter of shells, all became monotonous, mere matters of routine in which interest and excitement flag, and life becomes a bore. The enemy did not press us. His energies were elsewhere, on our flank and rear. His work with us was merely to keep us there, to annoy and wear us out.[36]

Sherman's shells kept coming, eroding morale, claiming their victims. "Old Grits" Bate himself was the most conspicuous loss, being shot through the knee on August 12 "by a stray ball in our rear."[37] Hardee, though not wounded, was worn out. Humiliated by Hood's criticism and depressed over the continued slaughter of irreplaceable officers and men, he had to confront an insistent, even angry twenty-eight-year-old woman: Abby Day Slocomb. The captain's wife wanted her husband in Columbia, South Carolina, "if possible but for nine hours. I must see him on unfortunate business." Abby Slocomb, never a reticent woman as may be seen in her postwar correspondence with Chalaron, wrote not to Slocomb, not to Bate, but to corps commander Hardee. He responded that Slocomb "could not be spared at present," but Mrs. Slocomb persisted, resorting

35. Waters, "Atlanta Campaign," 219; Scaife, *Campaign for Atlanta,* 103–107; Castel, *Decision in the West,* 458–60; McMurray, *Twentieth Tennessee,* 323; Marshall, *Bate,* 136; *Senate Documents,* 59th Cong., 2nd Sess., No. 403, p. 73; Ives, *Civil War Journal,* 69.

36. Stephenson, *Civil War Memoir,* 228–29.

37. It is widely circulated that Bate received his wound during the battle of Utoy Creek. Ives, *Civil War Journal,* 69; Castel, *Decision in the West,* 483; Marshall, *Bate,* 136; *Senate Documents,* 59th Cong., 2nd Sess., No. 403, p. 73.

to at least two telegrams. Hardee, displaying great patience, wrote Slocomb that he would try to make arrangements as soon as possible. "I am anxious to do all in my power to oblige you both."[38]

Cuthbert Slocomb was beset by problems other than the routine operation and supply of the Fifth Company. Although the business matters to which his wife referred are unknown, he felt an obligation to the families of the men who had been killed or seriously wounded. The files of the Washington Artillery contain several letters conveying this. His letter to Oscar Legaré's mother, who was refuging in Thomaston, Georgia, reveals something of the character of the captain.

My dear Madam

Since the death of your son I have been anxious to write you expressing my deep sorrow and sympathy in your great calamity but have refrained from doing so until now when Time having possibly somewhat soothed the sharpness of your grief a few lines from me might not be intrusive.

Through this last campaign, Oscar had been more under my immediate notice than heretofore and I had become much attached to him.

He displayed a degree of courage & coolness on the field that in one of his years was extraordinary. During our Engagement at Kennesaw Ridge when the Enemy was firing upon us with great fury our Flag which was planted on the Breast Works was twice shot away. Each time before the smoke & dust had cleared off Oscar leaped up and replaced the flag in its position, doing it so rapidly as not to give the Enemy an opportunity of seeing the effect of his shot.

After being appointed Gunner it was a pleasure to watch that whilst all was excitement and noise around he would with the greatest coolness sight his gun, not seeming to care for what was going on around him—all his energies being bent upon making a good shot that would tell with effect upon the Enemy.

During all our long & fatiguing march from Dalton to this place he suffered no demoralization, his spirits were buoyant, nothing depressed him, he was at all times cheerful & ready to do his duty be it what it might be and was always to be found at his post.

His loss to us is great; to you it is irreparable. The strong love existing between he & yourself is too sacred from me to attempt to offer consolation. God alone can comfort & solace you in this dark hour. That He will cheer & sustain yourself & daughter will be the prayer of

Cuthbert H. Slocomb[39]

38. Abby D. Slocomb to W. J. Hardee, August 22, 1864, W. J. Hardee to CSH, August 24, 1864, Confederate Personnel Documents, HTT.

39. CHS to Mrs. Legaré, August 25, 1864, Confederate Personnel Documents, HTT.

Joseph Adolphe Chalaron
Photograph in author's collection

Washington Irving Hodgson
Photograph in author's collection

Charles Garrett Johnsen
Courtesy Howard-Tilton Memorial Library, Tulane University

Abram Inskeep Leverich
From Even More Confederate Faces *(Orange, Va., 1983),*
courtesy William Turner, LaPlata, Md.

Cuthbert Harrison Slocomb
From Even More Confederate Faces *(Orange, Va., 1983),*
courtesy William Turner, LaPlata, Md.

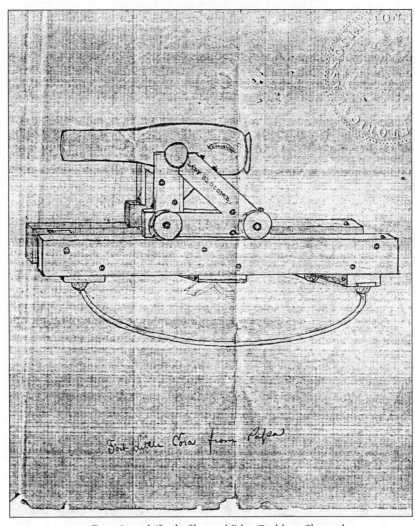

Drawing of "Lady Slocomb" by Cuthbert Slocomb
Courtesy Howard-Tilton Memorial Library, Tulane University

William Crumm Darrah Vaught
From Even More Confederate Faces *(Orange, Va., 1983)*
courtesy William Turner, LaPlata, Md.

Daniel Weisiger Adams
Photograph in author's collection

William Brimage Bate
Photograph in author's collection

John Cabell Breckinridge
Courtesy National Archives

Randall L. Gibson
Courtesy National Archives

Dabney Herndon Maury
From Even More Confederate Faces *(Orange, Va., 1983),
courtesy William Turner, LaPlata, Md.*

"Irate Tiger" logo
Courtesy AGO Military Archives, Jackson Barracks, New Orleans

14

JONESBORO

ON AUGUST 27, 1864, the shelling stopped, and "silence crept along the line leftward until it became general." Out sallied suspicious Confederate reconnaissance parties. The Yankees were gone, and "captured men reported Sherman in full retreat." On the twenty-eighth the Confederates advanced in heavy force and occupied the Union works, confirming the rumor. All the while General Hood tried to make sense of reports coming into headquarters and to prepare for any eventuality. As Hood was soon to learn, Sherman had boldly divided his army: twenty thousand guarded the Chattahoochee crossings and the railroad, the remainder (Maj. Gen. Oliver O. Howard's Army of the Tennessee and Jefferson C. Davis' XIV Corps) were in the act of swinging wide to the west, then south, intending to snap Hood's rail communications to Macon and West Point.[1]

Hood, of course, was aware of the implications, the dangers, of a

1. Schofield's XXIII Corps remained at East Point screening the great envelopment. See Scaife, *Campaign for Atlanta*, 108; Connelly, *Autumn of Glory*, 459–61; Castel, *Decision in the West*, 484–86.

Union sweep to the south, but intelligence was skimpy, contradictory, and wishful. "What Hood does not know," contends Albert Castel, "and, under the circumstances, cannot know is exactly what Sherman intends to do, where, when, and how." As Hood slowly became better informed, he dispatched Hardee with the combat weight of the army, two corps (his own and Lee's), to block Sherman's massive envelopment on the night of August 30. Hardee was "to take whatever measures you may think necessary" to protect the railroad, confronting the Federals either at the station at Rough and Ready or at the town of Jonesboro. Further developments required Hood to be more specific. He called Hardee back from East Point, Georgia, for a conference and ordered his lieutenant to proceed with his entire force to Jonesboro. There he was to attack the approaching Federal columns (reportedly two corps, but actually six were closing in) early in the morning and drive them back over the Flint River.[2]

Hardee's movement to Jonesboro, however, met with all manner of delay. The column was led by Bate's division, temporarily commanded by the able and experienced Tennessean Maj. Gen. John C. Brown. This division had been dispatched earlier (August 28) to Rough and Ready Station on the Macon Railroad, with Lewis' brigade going on ahead to Jonesboro. When the order came for Brown to continue on to Jonesboro with the rest of the division during the night of the thirtieth, they encountered Federal pickets near John Chambers' Mill. All evidence pointed to a Federal force a mile ahead. Brown, under advice from acting corps commander Cleburne, tried to avoid a night battle, veering left onto a "field road" running parallel to the railroad.[3] After considerable delay, Brown's men finally reached Jonesboro "at sunrise having marched all night long and having slept scarcely an hour in three nights." Slowly the remainder of Confederate force arrived on the field, but it was not until 3 P.M. that Hardee was able to launch his attack. All hope for surprise, though, had been lost and Union Maj. Gen. Oliver O. Howard had two corps entrenched and awaiting attack, with a third in close support.

Hardee's orders were to attack, and he did, but this fight against Howard proved to be a poor offensive effort by Hardee and the exhausted troops of the Army of Tennessee. Even Cleburne's reliable division (led

2. Scaife, *Campaign for Atlanta*, 108; Connelly, *Autumn of Glory,* 462–63; Castel, *Decision in the West,* 485–97.

3. Hardee delegated command of his corps to Cleburne while he assumed operational control of his own and Lee's corps.

by Mark P. Lowrey) went astray, hurling its strength against Judson Kilpatrick's dismounted cavalry rather than the flank of Howard's infantry, as ordered. Stephen D. Lee's corps attacked prematurely and met with disaster, while Cheatham's division (commanded by George E. Maney) halted indecisively in the midst of the attack and lost precious momentum. Before Maney's men could renew their assault, Brown had been repulsed, Bullock's Florida brigade losing 120 out of 700 effectives. The Yankee field batteries did particularly competent work in smashing this disjointed Confederate effort. The Washington Artillery on this pathetic first day's fight at Jonesboro appears not to have made an "artillery assault" but instead remained well to the rear of the infantry in temporary works, delivering long-range supporting fire.[4]

Hardee faced a crisis the following morning, September 1. Hood had ordered Lee's corps withdrawn, believing that Union troops under Schofield, who had broken the Macon & Western Railroad between Jonesboro and Atlanta, "were advancing on Atlanta . . . from the south." Therefore Hardee had to defend Jonesboro by himself. In an attempt to do so, he spread his one corps across a wide, two-corps front north and west of Jonesboro, hoping somehow to repulse an almost certain attack by Howard's three Union corps. Bate's division (Brown commanding) formed the center of Hardee's line with Cleburne on the right, his flimsy works sharply refused, and Cheatham's division (John C. Carter commanding) on the left.[5] To create an even greater imbalance in strength between the two opposing forces, Sherman dispatched an additional corps (David S. Stanley's IV Corps) "down the railroad from the northeast in an attempt to surround Hardee."[6]

Before Hardee's men could properly fortify, Sherman's troops began closing in, "not in assault," according to Phil Stephenson, "but with clouds of skirmishers, and with his overwhelming columns behind them." The Fifth Company was on left center of Brown's line, which had to contend with John Logan's XV Corps. "Like swarms of invisible bees the bullets buzzed about our heads, but there was no reply from us—we were working like beavers, throwing up works . . . 'taking' the deadly fire, and

---

4. Hughes, *Hardee*, 235–38; Castel, *Decision in the West*, 498; Scaife, *Campaign for Atlanta*, 108–109, 116; Ives, *Civil War Journal*, 70–72.

5. George E. Maney appears to have been relieved on the night of August 31–September 1, and this humiliation ended his service with the Army of Tennessee.

6. Scaife, *Campaign for Atlanta*, 110–12; Stephenson, *Civil War Memoir*, 232–33; Ives, *Civil War Journal*, 72.

many a fine fellow fell, shovel or pick in hand." At one point, with their works "not half up," the battery members needed to level off the irregular heaps of fresh earth and create embrasures in the parapet. To do this required that men mount the works with a shovel, exposing themselves to Yankee sharpshooters. If not done, the "works were useless," "the enemy in overwhelming numbers were close enough to rush us."

"Vincent, come up here," shouted Lt. Charles G. Johnsen, who commanded Piece Four. "There's no danger!" Louie Vincent, a young Philadelphian in the company, "sprang up [on the earth parapet], spade in hand," recalled Stephenson, "I do not think he had thrown but one spade full of dirt when a bullet struck him low in the back, which was partially turned to the foe, and traveled upward, exiting through the front of his shoulder." Louie fell into the arms of Johnsen and was laid "gently down on his side in the trench, the blood gushing in torrents from his mouth." Next to be hit was Sgt. Bob Frazer, who had just returned from the hospital, having recovered from his Resaca wound. Frazer was struck in the stomach by a sharpshooter's round and died that night.

The terrible day wore on and yet the enemy did not assault. Meanwhile the works grew stronger by the hour. Perhaps they might be able to hold, after all, optimists thought. Slocomb, knowing that his gunners were fighting "on empty stomachs," came up. "He was smiling (he had a sweet smile) and holding out a pone of cornbread. 'Boys,' said he, 'I'll divide.' At that instant, he was struck in the shoulder. A powerful thud it was, twirling him around like a top. He did not fall, but it knocked him breathless, and his face turned pale. We saw at once that he was badly hurt and led him away."[7]

Stephenson reflected about the incident. "A rare combination was our captain, of captivating qualities—his courage of the high kind, serene, dauntless; his temper gentle and sympathetic; his feeling for his men more like that of an elder brother than of a disciplinarian, although faithful in that respect, too. The incident itself throws light on his character, his thoughtful care of his men, his unselfish disposition to share with them the little he had."[8]

About 4 P.M. the Yankees attacked. Jefferson C. Davis' corps (three divisions) assaulted Cleburne's division and, after being repulsed twice,

---

7. Stephenson, *Civil War Memoir*, 233–35.
8. *Ibid.*, 235.

overran a salient in the line, bagging a brigade of Arkansas troops and many of Lewis' Kentuckians who had been assigned during the emergency to Cleburne's division.[9] In response to this crisis Hardee stripped his left, throwing every brigade into the breach and prolonging the right against yet another Federal corps (Stanley's IV Corps) groping to find and turn Hardee's right. Somehow Hardee's shifts of manpower, born of utter desperation, stiffened that flank sufficiently. The left, however, stood open. Carter's division was gone, so Jonesboro invited an enemy advance from the west. As a consequence of Hardee's desperate personnel scramble, John C. Brown's division, once the center, had become the left. Now, in an ultimate absurdity, they (minus Lewis' brigade) confronted the entire Army of the Tennessee—three corps.[10]

Phil Stephenson dreaded what was to come. The redoubt for his Piece Four had not been completed. Because of the Yankee sharpshooters, "there was not even the beginning of an embrasure. The gun had to fire into a wall of earth! The alarm was given, just as we were about to attempt the embrasure. . . . The pickets jump into the works with the words 'They're coming, boys. . . .' We of the battery throw away our friction primers and take slow matches for we do not choose to run any risks in such close quarters. . . . We blazed away—with solid shot and *blew out* a path for our firing! Our Lieutenant Johnsen knew, too, that there was some value in noise!"[11]

The attack, when it came, astonished the company. "It did not amount to anything, as they did not come within seventy-five yards of us. Our line was weak enough everywhere and ought to have been carried at any point. Our antagonist was cautious," Stephenson observed with high restraint. While Howard's Army of the Tennessee poked at them warily, the Washington Artillery could hear the terrible onslaught on the right. There seemed to be no way that Cleburne and Carter could maintain their positions. Indeed, rounds from a Federal battery enfilading Cleburne's lines, as well as musket fire, struck Brown's lines with killing effect. To their immense relief, the Fifth Company learned that the right, somehow, had been able to hold on, and before long, darkness arrived, becoming a most

9. The survivors of Lewis' Orphan Brigade would be mounted after Jonesboro to serve as cavalry until the end of the war.

10. Scaife, *Campaign for Atlanta*, 111–15; Castel, *Decision in the West*, 510–22; Hughes, *Hardee*, 239–40.

11. Stephenson, *Civil War Memoir*, 236–37.

welcome ally. At 10 P.M., in a magnificent separation, they slipped out of their trenches, under the very noses of Sherman's five corps, and stole away, down the Macon & Western Railroad toward Lovejoy's Station, seven miles south. There, one mile north of town, Hardee faced his exhausted corps about, looking defiantly north. Once again they broke out picks and spades and began to dig.[12]

Vincent and Frazer were dead. Forty-five-year-old Armant Delery had been mortally wounded and would die seven weeks later. Killed immediately had been Father Emmeran Blieml, a German Benedictine monk who had attached himself to the Fifth Company during the fighting at Atlanta. At the time of his death Blieml was administering last rites to Union Col. William Grace in front of the company's position. An enemy shell blew off his head.[13] The "Old Gentleman," Henry Ogden, left an account of Louis Vincent's burial, which probably occurred near Lovejoy's Station. "As we placed [Louie] in his grave a wild Texas regiment, noisy, joking, laughing, talking were passing by & the Enemy were giving shot & shell after them, but we finished our work even to fencing the grave with rails . . . in an old neglected churchyard."[14]

Injured during the two-day fight at Jonesboro were Irishman Mike Campbell and Cuthbert Slocomb. Slocomb's wound was serious, and he subsequently had a "narrow escape from death by gangrene." Taken by ambulance to Lovejoy's, he was sent to the Ladies General Hospital No. 3 at Columbia, South Carolina, where his wife Abby would nurse him as an outpatient from September 30 until his discharge on November 19.[15] When Slocomb was hit, command of the Fifth Company immediately devolved on Adolphe Chalaron. Popular, well respected and highly energetic, Chalaron had earned the right to lead the Washington Artillery. Perhaps one might criticize him for impetuosity, but no man, not even Slocomb himself, better represented the personality of the battery.

Chalaron and the Fifth Company had little time for adjustment. On September 2, Sherman dogged Hardee's retreating Confederates and pressed against the Lovejoy defenses, which were very strong. To destroy

12. New Orleans *Daily Picayune,* June 14, 1874; Connelly, *Autumn of Glory,* 464–65; Stephenson, *Civil War Memoir,* 238–39.

13. See Lindsley, *The Military Annals of Tennessee,* 289; Ed Gleeson, *Rebel Sons of Erin* (Indianapolis, 1993), 126–28; 5WA Master Roster, WA Papers, HTT.

14. H. V. Ogden to JAC, November 21, 1905, Chalaron Papers, HTT.

15. Chalaron, "Slocomb's Battery in the Tennessee Army"; 5WA Master Roster, WA Papers, HTT; Casey, *Outline of Civil War Campaigns,* 78.

this Confederate command Sherman realized that his options were either a bloody assault or time-consuming maneuvering, so he ordered the attack against Hardee to be suspended. On September 3, Stewart's and Lee's corps arrived at Lovejoy's and greatly strengthened Hardee's defenses. Two days later Sherman broke off the action and pulled his army back toward Atlanta. His men deserved a rest. The bloody four-month ordeal, which would be called the Atlanta campaign, was over.[16]

16. Castel, *Decision in the West,* 530–36.

15

THE PRICE OF IMMORTALITY

THE WASHINGTON Artillery remained at Lovejoy's Station almost three weeks. On September 19, 1864, they moved with the Army of Tennessee back to Jonesboro, then nineteen miles west to the village of Palmetto on the Atlanta and West Point Railroad, close to the banks of the Chattahoochee. There President Davis paid the army a visit, which, to no one's surprise, provided little encouragement. And there General Hardee left the army, which provided great discouragement.[1]

Along with the lofty discussions of grand strategy and key personnel, some reorganization of the army took place at Palmetto that directly affected the battery. Not only did they have a new, albeit temporary, commander in Chalaron, but Maj. Gen. Frank Cheatham took Hardee's place as corps commander. Within Bate's division (Bate himself would return October 10), the Orphans were gone—Lewis' Kentuckians would become mounted infantry; Frank Gracey's Kentucky battery, the Fifth Company's sister unit for so long, would depart with them.[2] Replacing Gracey would

1. 5WA Itinerary, WA Papers, HTT; Ives, *Civil War Journal,* 74; Horn, *Army of Tennessee,* 373–74.

2. *OR,* Vol. XXXIX, Pt. 1, p. 826. Frank Gracey had been wounded and battery command had passed to Lt. R. B. Matthews during the latter portion of the Atlanta campaign.

be Capt. René T. Beauregard and his South Carolina battery with whom the Washington Artillery had worked at Kennesaw. Thus Maj. Robert Cobb's artillery battalion now would consist of Beauregard's battery, J.W. Phillips' (formerly Mebane's) Tennessee battery, and the Fifth Company. Bate's infantry, very small in number and very short in officers, was familiar: Bullock's Florida brigade, Tom Smith's Tennesseans, and Henry R. Jackson's Georgians.[3]

After ten days at Palmetto, Hood's army, rested and somewhat reorganized, cooked two days' rations and "began moving towards Sherman's rear." On the twenty-ninth of September the men marched north twelve and one-half miles on a hot, steamy day and began crossing the Chattahoochee River. By October 1, they were moving toward Marietta, determined to snap Sherman's communications. The bulk of the artillery, however, did not accompany the army. In an effort to shorten his trains and travel light, Hood permitted only one battery to accompany each infantry division.[4] The Washington Artillery was chosen to march with Bate, the remainder of the battalion going north to the army's base at Jacksonville, Alabama.[5]

"The boys are in good spirits," Washington Ives of Bullock's Florida brigade reported. To be on the offensive once again was invigorating. Sherman was not surprised, however. He countered Hood by withdrawing all of his army from Atlanta (except the XX Corps) and setting out in pursuit. Hood and his men, nonetheless, successfully reached the Western and Atlantic Railroad, breaking miles of track between Acworth and Big Shanty. These veterans of Hood were covering familiar ground. "The whole country between Dalton and Atlanta seemed literally dug up! Dug up into parallel lines of entrenchments," Stephenson remembered, "in intervals of four to ten miles, and in length anywhere from five to fifteen. The effect of the sight of them, lying there silent and desolate was awe inspiring. Frowning and threatening they seemed." Rather than give battle to the pursuing Sherman and his big, powerful army, Hood turned west from Allatoona, swung well around Rome as if headed into Alabama or up into Tennessee, then veered north and east, and, on October 10, struck the railroad again, this time near Resaca. Continuing north toward Dal-

---

3. *Ibid.,* Pt. 2, p. 857; Daniel, *Cannoneers in Gray,* 167.

4. Hood would continue this questionable practice in the dash from Columbia to Franklin that November. Indeed, by that time, it would be one battery per corps. In fairness to Hood, one should bear in mind the shortage and condition of the army's horses.

5. Daniel, *Cannoneers in Gray,* 170; Thomas Robson Hay, *Hood's Tennessee Campaign* (Dayton, Ohio, 1976), 44–45.

ton (which he captured on October 13), he destroyed additional miles of track and pocketed small, isolated garrisons.[6]

In conjunction with the seizure of Dalton, Hood sent Bate's division on an independent mission north and west of town, to Mill Creek Gap (Buzzard's Roost). This break in Rocky Face Ridge was the likely route for an invasion of Tennessee, the place where the Fifth Company's Atlanta campaign had begun five months earlier. Mill Creek Gap, however, was protected by a Federal blockhouse. Bate was "to take the block-house in the gap and destroy the railroad."[7]

As Bate approached within three miles of Mill Creek Gap, he heard a locomotive moving north from Dalton toward the gap. Quickly he sent off his escort "with a man mounted behind each to cut the road and prevent the escape of trains from Dalton." The blockhouse that controlled the gap appeared formidable yet had to be reduced. Bate surrounded it with infantry and sent in two flags of truce. The Yankee defenders, apparently believing the besiegers were "merely cavalry," ignored these demands to surrender, so Bate decided to destroy the stubborn outpost. This effort would not require three brigades of infantry, however, so he put them to work destroying track. In the meantime he ordered his sharpshooter battalion to coordinate with the Washington Artillery in firing at the portholes of the blockhouse and suppressing the Federal riflemen attempting to fire through. The Yankees were well protected by timber four feet thick with earth of the same depth thrown up outside. Beyond the stout timber and earth fort was a ditch filled with water, easily covered by small arms from forty portholes.

Late in the afternoon, while the sharpshooters neutralized the Federals attempting to shoot out of the rifle ports, Chalaron and the Fifth Company moved up within point-blank range (two hundred yards). Concentrating the play of their pieces on one side of the fort, they "opened, and with a vengeance. Round after round was poured into them, mostly solid shot" until that side of the blockhouse was "completely torn to pieces." Not long after dark the garrison surrendered—some fifty men from Illinois. Twelve or fifteen of the gallant defenders were dead or wounded. It was a mission handled with dispatch, a credit to the gunnery of Abe Leverich and Chalaron. A great prize was the garrison's coffee supply.

---

6. Ives, *Civil War Journal,* 74; Stephenson, *Civil War Memoir,* 251; Henry D. Jamison, ed., *Letters and Recollections of a Confederate Soldier* (Nashville, 1964), 101; Connelly, *Autumn of Glory,* 477–83.

7. *OR,* Vol. XXXIX, Pt. 1, p. 826.

Gen. Billy Bate, however, "claimed" the coffee. "The Battery got the glory," Lt. Charles Johnsen would lament ten years later, "Bate the coffee."[8]

The next morning Bate burned the blockhouse and pushed forward three miles to Tunnel Hill, which he captured together with a cache of stores. The men took as much as they could carry and burned the remainder. They ripped up track between Tunnel Hill and Mill Creek Gap, then turned south, becoming in effect the rearguard of Hood's army. They marched toward La Fayette, Georgia, and there rejoined Cheatham's corps. Continuing west and south, the Army of Tennessee crossed into Alabama, paused at Gadsden for Hood to confer with department commander Beauregard, then set out again on October 22, but not to Guntersville where Beauregard expected the army to cross the Tennessee River, but west toward Decatur. At the latter point Hood's army delayed a day and a half while their commander pondered whether or not to attack the strongly defended river crossing. He decided to quietly pass by, then drifted farther west, reaching Tuscumbia, Alabama, on October 31. There Hood would remain attempting to resupply his bedraggled army. "Two [three] weeks passed at Tuscumbia. Weeks not restful nor helpful," complained Stephenson.

It had been a hard march across north Georgia and north Alabama. The weather had been miserable, the rations short (Phil Stephenson in his narrative would underline the word *starving*). The company's horses and mules, having been deprived of proper forage and shelter for so long, pulled their heavy loads with difficulty and suffered miserably.[9] Among the casualties of this long "forced march" from La Fayette, Georgia, to Tuscumbia, Alabama, was battalion commander Robert Cobb, one of many who became so ill they were no longer fit for field service. Cobb was hospitalized and replaced by Capt. René Beauregard, who ranked both Chalaron and Lt. J. W. Phillips, commander of Mebane's battery.[10]

At last, on November 13, Bate's division crossed the Tennessee River.

8. *Ibid.;* JAC to J. E. Johnston, July 20, 1875, Chalaron Papers, HTT; *CV,* IV (1897), 103; Casey, *Outline of Civil War Campaigns,* 80–81; Stephenson, *Civil War Memoir,* 254; New Orleans *Daily Picayune,* June 14, 1874.

9. The shortage of healthy animals for the army's artillery was critical—an estimated 360 would be needed "to supply the places of those broken down." Daniel, *Cannoneers in Gray,* 171.

10. It appears that Cobb never returned to active duty, although the battalion continued to bear his name until the end of the war. *OR,* Vol. XLV, Pt. 1, p. 742; Connelly, *Autumn of Glory,* 491; Stephenson, *Civil War Memoir,* 259–65; Casey, *Outline of Civil War Campaigns,* 81.

It was a tedious process, slowed by all manner of logistical and command complications. Indeed, it would take another week for the entire army to reach the north bank. Hood had swung so far to the west that Sherman had given up any idea of chasing him. Instead the Federal commander returned to Atlanta, leaving two corps (twenty-five thousand men) behind to help George Thomas defend against Hood's impending invasion of Tennessee. With the balance of his field forces (sixty-five thousand), Sherman turned southeast toward Savannah, Georgia, cutting loose from his communications and abandoning his hard-won prize, Atlanta.[11]

If Hood intended to interpose his army between George Thomas at Nashville and John Schofield (commanding the two corps detached by Sherman) in the Pulaski-Columbia sector, he seemed in no rush. While Lee and Stewart marched toward Columbia via the direct route through Lawrenceburg, Tennessee, Hood with Cheatham's corps made the tramp by way of Waynesboro, Tennessee, "a circuitous 103-mile route through the rugged Highland Rim country." This was "very poor country," complained Washington Ives. On November 24, the Florida private drew two small biscuits for his day's ration and was "very happy."[12] By November 25, Hood had established himself at Mount Pleasant, twelve miles west of Columbia. Here the country was rich, provisions plentiful. Hood and his troops approached Columbia leisurely, enjoying the hospitality of middle Tennessee. Then the Confederate commander deployed his three corps below the town, ringing Schofield's defenses which were backed against Duck River. When Hood made no attempt to assault, Schofield abandoned Columbia and crossed Duck River the night of November 27. The Union general found a ridge about a mile north of the riverbank and entrenched there, awaiting Hood's next move.[13]

Schofield was gone and snow was falling. Indeed it had been spitting snow since they entered Tennessee, but the Fifth Company did not seem to mind the cold. An optimism born of desperation pervaded the army, certainly Chalaron's battery. No matter that fifteen of the members were

11. 5WA Itinerary, WA Papers, HTT; *OR*, Vol. XXXIX, Pt. 1, p. 827; W. Palfrey to M. Greenwood, October 21, 1864, Greenwood Papers, HNOC; Hay, *Hood's Tennessee Campaign*, 56–60; Wiley Sword, *Embrace an Angry Wind* (New York, 1992), 57–74; Horn, *Army of Tennessee*, 379–83; Stephenson, *Civil War Memoir*, 259–65, 274.

12. "A biscuit anytime during the campaign readily sold for $1." Ives, *Civil War Journal*, 15.

13. Connelly, *Autumn of Glory*, 491; Sword, *Embrace an Angry Wind*, 95; Hay, *Hood's Tennessee Campaign*, 81–82.

barefooted, "refusing to go [to] the rear." They would press on, following the guns, "taking the chances of procuring shoes in one way or another." Besides, middle Tennessee, virtually unscarred by war, offered them "plenty to eat, sausage . . . and spare-ribs, butter and other good things—and cheap as they can be. Fine gobblers at two dollars—C.S. currency—apiece. Chickens twenty five cents each. Very funny but true." [14]

Schofield and his troops stubbornly remained on the north side of Duck River, ready to dispute any crossing at that point. A spirited cannonade ensued, resulting in the death of Hood's artillery chief, Col. Robert F. Beckham. [15] While the opposing forces took long-range shots at each other across the river, Hood, now fired with great energy, his eyes fixed on Nashville, decided to flank Schofield. Perhaps he could surprise him. Leaving Lee's corps to demonstrate at Columbia, Hood marched the bulk of the Army of Tennessee a few miles east and crossed Duck River at Davis' Ford on November 29. Once the infantry had crossed to the north bank, Hood raced to cut off Schofield at Spring Hill. Bate's division, as part of Cheatham's corps, formed part of this enveloping force and would play a crucial and controversial role in the ensuing debacle at Spring Hill. The Fifth Company would not. [16]

As in north Georgia earlier that fall, Hood again pared down his army for the dash to Spring Hill. Hood defined "light marching order" as cavalry and infantry. No trains and no guns, with only one battery to accompany each corps. And these batteries were to leave behind their caissons! For its artillery support, Stewart's corps would take along Guibor's Missouri battery. Cheatham was supposed to have the Fifth Company. [17]

But he did not. The company, true to Hood's directive, proceeded with the column as far as Davis' Ford (or Ferry), where the Army of Tennessee crossed Duck River. [18] There they stopped, however, apparently serving only to cover the crossing by the infantry or, perhaps, to control another ford or bridge located nearby. Chalaron, in the company itinerary, notes

14. Chalaron, "Slocomb's Battery in the Tennessee Army"; W. M. Palfrey to M. Greenwood, November 28, 1864, Greenwood Papers, HNOC.

15. See Daniel, *Cannoneers in Gray,* 172.

16. See Horn, *Army of Tennessee,* 387–89; Connelly, *Autumn of Glory,* 496; Sword, *Embrace an Angry Wind,* 14–47; Hay, *Hood's Tennessee Campaign,* 88–89.

17. Daniel, *Cannoneers in Gray,* 172.

18. For information about Davis Ford and the Davis Ford road that led north to Spring Hill, see William Bruce Turner, *History of Maury County, Tennessee* (Nashville, 1955), 314–15.

that the battery marched to "Davis Ferry & back" (to Columbia), some fourteen miles. While the Army of Tennessee sidestepped Schofield and dashed toward Spring Hill, "Where were the rest of us?" asked Phil Stephenson. "Coming on behind, or guarding bridges, etc. This last is what we (5th Co. W.A.) were doing! Six miles south of Columbia or 31 miles from Franklin, we were on the morning of the 30th of November, guarding a bridge over a little stream all by ourselves until about noon that day. A bright day it was and a lazy, quiet one for us."[19]

While the Washington Artillery lolled beside the bridge on that pretty sunny morning, their infantry comrades rushed north from Spring Hill to Franklin. There, at 4 P.M., the slaughter that would become known as the battle of Franklin began. It would be over except for occasional bright flashes in the dark by the time the Fifth Company arrived to help.[20] The battery members had tried their best. After receiving the order to hurry forward sometime after noon, the Washington Artillery raced north from Columbia. "The horses were put to a trot, and we gunners were put to it to keep up," recalled Stephenson. "The pike to Franklin was macadamized and graded, and the teams could make good time . . . [but] man after man dropped behind. The distance was long and the order urgent. There was no slackening of the pace for our fiery Lieutenant commanding, Chalaron . . . was always in for a fight." They could hear the roar of the battle ahead and about the time they passed Spring Hill they began to meet "ambulances filled with wounded." When they reached Winstead Hill overlooking the battlefield, it was dark as pitch. They stopped and pulled their Napoleons off the pike. They were too late.[21]

At dawn on December 1, the Fifth Company could view the horror of the battlefield spread before them. They went to work, spending most of that day helping bury the dead.[22] The next morning they limbered up and moved through Franklin with Bate's division, prepared to cross the Harpeth River and advance on Nashville. It was then, just as they were about

19. 5WA Itinerary, WA Papers, HTT; Stephenson, *Civil War Memoir,* 285.

20. For the disappointing participation of Bate's division at Franklin, see Horn, *Army of Tennessee,* 401; Sword, *Embrace an Angry Wind,* 181; 38–40; Hay, *Hood's Tennessee Campaign,* 125.

21. Phil Stephenson estimated that their arrival was between 8:00 and 9:00 P.M. Stephenson, *Civil War Memoir,* 285–86.

22. Washington Ives maintained, "It was impossible to bury all our dead in one day." Ives, *Civil War Journal,* 15.

to cross the Harpeth River, that Bate received special orders from General Hood directing him to take his division "with one battery of artillery, over to Murfreesboro . . . to destroy the railroad from Murfreesboro to Nashville, burning all the bridges and taking the blockhouses and burning them." Brig. Gen. Benjamin J. Hill with 150 Tennessee cavalry was to accompany this expedition.[23] This was to be Bate's second such venture in two months—a vote of confidence in Bate, certainly. No doubt the army commander Hood, not to speak of Bate, hoped that the threat to Nashville by the approaching Army of Tennessee might cause the Federals to abandon Murfreesboro. Bate's job then would be simply to walk in and take it.[24]

In accordance with Hood's directive, Bate turned his column sharply east on the road to Triune where they would encamp that night. The following day he headed his column north on the Nolensville pike, then east again using country roads until he reached the Wilkinson turnpike. The men followed this road until they were some five or six miles northwest of Murfreesboro. Then they bivouacked close to, but on the west side of, Overall's Creek, within easy striking distance of Murfreesboro.

It had been a pleasant two-day march, helping soften the shock of Franklin. The weather had brightened and the Washington Artillery noticed nice homes along the way, invariably with groups of girls waving handkerchiefs encouragingly from their front porches. There would be the usual banter at a distance; then, as the division column nudged forward, the girls at one home grew more curious and ventured down to the front gate. "Of course, those gay Louisianians gave them a yell," remembered Phil Stephenson, "but that was not enough. Some [men], who

23. Hill was a veteran infantry commander who had acted as provost marshal of the Army of Tennessee since the Atlanta campaign. He had been promoted to brigadier general two days before Bate left for Murfreesboro.

24. In his memoirs Hood states that Forrest was intended to be in command of the joint venture from the outset and that the infantry was specifically placed under his command. This does not seem to agree with either Hood's official report or with Forrest's report. Forrest declares that after being relieved by the infantry in front of Nashville on December 2, his objective became the destruction of "the railroad, block-houses, and telegraph lines leading from Nashville to Murfreesboro." He did not receive orders to move on Murfreesboro itself until December 4, and it was not until December 5 that Hood ordered Bate to place himself and his division under Forrest's control. J. A. Chalaron, "Hood's Campaign at Murfreesboro," *CV,* XI (1903), 438–39; *OR,* XLV, Pt. 1, p. 745; Vol. LXV, Pt. 1, pp. 654–55, 754–55; Stephenson, *Civil War Memoir,* 288–89, 291–92; John B. Hood, *Advance and Retreat: Personal Experiences in the United States and Confederate States Armies* (Bloomington, Ind., 1959), 300–301.

were not altogether scarecrows in appearance, crowded to the gate and with bows and doffing of old hats and smiles on their dirty faces made their acquaintance." The young women asked to see the company flag and the men obliged, unrolling it, smoothing out wrinkles, and displaying it for all to see. Phil Stephenson would recall the company banner that day in the bright Tennessee sun as "beautiful . . . striking in the extreme."[25]

"Old Grits" was worried. Bate had just learned from a captured Yankee vedette that Murfreesboro had not been evacuated as he and Hood had hoped, but that it remained garrisoned with five thousand to ten thousand Federals. It was common knowledge that the town's fortifications were strong, carefully engineered, and dominated by powerful Fortress Rosecrans, which bristled with cannon. Murfreesboro surely would be no Tunnel Hill. It seemed dangerous, if not ludicrous, even to venture too close, considering that Bate had only about one thousand men including Hill's cavalry. Washington Ives of Bullock's 4th Florida estimated Bate's infantry strength as Bullock with 200, Smith with 275, and Jackson with 250.[26]

Billy Bate was bold, and he was determined to succeed. Yet, at Spring Hill and at Franklin, Bate had seen firsthand General Hood's wrath toward bunglers, toward commanders who fell short of expectation. Therefore, despite his native impetuosity, and despite the protective umbrella afforded by Bedford Forrest being in command, Bate prudently notified Hood in Nashville of the situation at Murfreesboro and awaited instructions. Hood responded promptly. He was sending Forrest with cavalry and infantry to assist. In the meantime, he told Bate, keep the object of the mission (wrecking the railroad) paramount. Chalaron was worried also. The morale, the aggressiveness, of Bate's infantry, despite the words and actions of their leader, was highly questionable. "Demoralization was openly expressed by many." If it came to a fight, "I felt apprehensive of the loss of my guns."[27]

Once he received authorization from Hood, Bate decided to strike fast, without waiting for Forrest to come up. He told General Hill to ride south

25. *OR,* Vol. XLV, Pt. 1, p. 745; Ives, *Civil War Journal,* 17; Stephenson, *Civil War Memoir,* 292–94.

26. Ives, *Civil War Journal,* 17–18.

27. *OR,* Vol. XLV, Pt. 1, p. 745; Stephenson, *Civil War Memoir,* 294; Chalaron, "Hood's Campaign at Murfreesboro," 438.

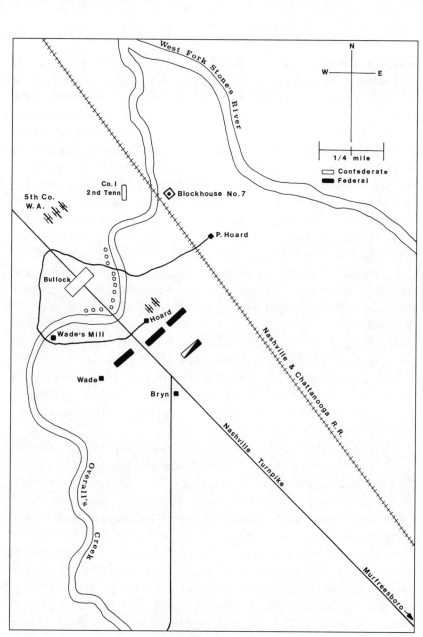

Battle of the Blockhouse, December 4, 1864
Adapted from David R. Deatrick, Jr., drawing
Map by Blake A. Magner

and demonstrate on both the Wilkinson and Salem pikes. He cautioned his cavalry commander to keep pickets on both his flanks, as if Hill had fifteen hundred men instead of 150. Meanwhile, early on December 4, Bate moved with his three infantry brigades and the Fifth Company away from Wilkinson and Salem pikes. They marched in the opposite direction, carefully keeping west of, and parallel to, Overall's Creek. His infantry went through fields and woods, down country lanes, "around the arc of the city," until they struck the Nashville-Murfreesboro pike, about five and one-half miles from Murfreesboro. Before noon Bate had pushed across the pike and come in sight of the Nashville and Chattanooga Railroad. There, close to the railroad, on the south side of Overall's Creek, was a blockhouse guarding the railroad bridge. "Its garrison were pluckily" firing as fast as they could at the approaching Confederates. Bate pushed on nearer the creek, placing Chalaron's guns within range of the blockhouse. He positioned three regiments of Bullock's Floridians on the Nashville road to resist an advance along the turnpike and to support Chalaron's guns. Company I, 2nd Tennessee Infantry was posted across the creek from the blockhouse. This unit was to prevent a crossing of the railroad bridge and act as snipers against the blockhouse. The 6th Florida was detached and assigned train-guard duty in the rear. Jackson's brigade also went to the rear and set to work tearing up track. Tom Smith's Tennesseans waited in reserve.[28]

Chalaron made a quick reconnaissance and reported to Bate that the blockhouse was "very strong." It stood some five hundred yards below the creek and according to Chalaron, because of "the limited range and impact of my battery of four smooth-bore Napoleon guns, I felt that it would take some time to reduce the place." Bate nevertheless ordered Chalaron to open immediately, so the latter went into battery left (north) of the Nashville pike, between it and the railroad, some eight hundred to one thousand yards from the blockhouse. The battery position was elevated and open, providing excellent observation, both of the blockhouse and of the pike bridge. The Murfreesboro side of Overall's Creek, however, was wooded and any movements of the enemy along this south side would be "screened, except along the pike."[29]

28. *OR*, Vol. XLV, Pt. 1, pp. 744–45; Stephenson, *Civil War Memoir*, 294–95; Chalaron, "Hood's Campaign at Murfreesboro," 439.

29. Chalaron, "Hood's Campaign at Murfreesboro," 439.

About noon Chalaron opened with all four pieces. Yankee skirmishers stationed between Overall's Creek and the blockhouse appeared to be few in number and fell back quickly. Hawkeye Smith and Charlie Fox quickly had the range: "practice excellent; almost every shot told." Earth packed around the fort "could be seen to fly; the lookout was knocked to pieces." Federal Lt. H. Milo Torrence, who commanded the blockhouse, reported seventy-two rounds were fired at the fort, "thirty-one of which struck the building—five in the lookout and twenty-six in the main building and its entrance way." No round penetrated the inner portion of the fort, however. Those that did hit the main structure broke through only the outer casing of the fortification.[30]

Not more than half an hour after engaging, Chalaron spotted Federal cavalry on the Nashville pike, advancing from Murfreesboro. He sent a few rounds their way. It was between 2:00 and 3:00 P.M.[31] The Yankee horsemen turned off to the right (east) toward the blockhouse, disappearing behind the curtain of woods. Chalaron notified Bate. Then he saw enemy artillery. It appeared to be one battery, advancing down the pike followed by "a low and dense cloud of dust"—infantry. Both disappeared into the woods. Again Chalaron notified Bate.

In no time at all enemy field pieces opened on the Fifth Company. The Federals were visible on the south side of Overall's Creek, between the blockhouse and Nashville pike—at a range of about eight hundred yards. Chalaron immediately shifted fire from the blockhouse to the enemy battery. "An exceedingly lively duel ensued between us, which lasted a long while." The Yankees had an advantage. As the sun dropped toward the tree tops, their guns faded into "the shadows of the dark bulky [brick] house behind them.[32] All we could see," Phil Stephenson recalled, "was a smeary blot a little darker than the rest. . . . No gun nor man was distinct, although not over 800 yards off." It was a sharp fight. "The aim of the opposing battery was very accurate and [Chalaron] kept us changing positions to break it."[33]

When the duel began, one of the gunners, Louey Seibrecht, a German boy from New Orleans, had been in the rear. He stopped behind a tree

---

30. *Ibid.,* 439–40; *OR,* Vol. XLV, Pt. 1, p. 635.

31. *OR,* Vol. XLV, Pt. 1, p. 635; Ives, *Civil War Journal,* 18.

32. According to Union accounts, the artillery was placed in the yard of the Hoard house.

33. Chalaron, "Hood's Campaign at Murfreesboro," 439–40; Stephenson, *Civil War Memoir,* 295, 170.

to "watch his chances to make a rush [back to his piece] between shots." He stepped from behind the tree, waved his arms and just then a shell exploded "full in his front." "It tore him literally to fragments." Phil Stephenson recalled another scene just to the rear of the company's position in the midst of this deadly artillery action. "How perfectly under control our horses were through all that close firing . . . the drivers and limber chest and horses of our piece 4 as they appeared at one of our stationary moments, the men sitting or half-reclining on the ground at their horses' heads, the horses quietly standing in their tracks, heads to front, the reins in the men's hands, all directly in range and only fifty yards or so behind the guns and that deadly duel in progress."[34]

The Washington Artillery finally managed to suppress the enemy guns and turned their fire on the enemy infantry, who had availed themselves of the Fifth Company's preoccupation and massed at the creek bank near the railroad bridge in preparation for forcing a crossing.[35] Still another body of Federals now threatened to dash over the turnpike bridge. Over they came. Splashing through Overall's Creek at several points to the east, they made lodgements on the north side of the creek. Soon the badly outnumbered Floridians, their brigade commander Robert Bullock severely wounded, abandoned the creek bank entirely.[36] Bate brought up Smith's reserve brigade, "but they got no farther than my pieces," complained Chalaron, "and huddled up around them to such an extent as to impede [the guns'] rapid handling." Indeed, most of the Tennesseans appeared to be "mixed with the disorganized Floridians in the depression in my rear, and all was confusion around me."[37]

To further confound matters, Lt. Abraham B. Schell, a reliable officer who commanded Bate's Whitworth rifle detachment, came running from the left front, where he and his Company I, 2nd Tennessee Infantry, had been stationed along the creek bank, guarding the battery's left flank and

34. Stephenson, *Civil War Memoir*, 302, 170.

35. None of the 8th Minnesota Infantry, stationed near the blockhouse, ever crossed the creek. Only two companies of this regiment were sent to the right, while the remainder of the regiment formed on the bank of the creek near the blockhouse and railroad bridge.

36. Only the 174th Ohio Infantry and skirmishers from the 61st Illinois Infantry actually crossed Overall's Creek. It appears the Floridians were pushed back by this single Federal regiment, but they were outnumbered and the 174th was a new regiment, fat with eager recruits.

37. Chalaron, "Hood's Campaign at Murfreesboro," 439–40; Ives, *Civil War Journal*, 18; Stephenson, *Civil War Memoir*, 295–96; *OR*, Vol. XLV, Pt. 1, p. 750; McMurray, *Twentieth Tennessee*, 343; D. W. Sanders, "Hood's Tennessee Campaign," *Southern Bivouac*, IV (1885), 113.

fighting a mini-battle with Yankee skirmishers crowding the opposite bank. "Look out, Chalaron," Schell cried. "The enemy's cavalry are forming on your left to charge you on the flank!"

Chalaron saw them four hundred yards off, "just starting at a rapid pace toward my left and rear." He yelled at Abe Leverich, who commanded the left section, to shift his guns on the cavalry and load with canister. Chalaron himself helped reposition Piece Four, "rushing through the affrighted mob of our infantry." He then turned to his right section and ordered Charles Johnsen to limber up. Desperately Chalaron sought to hurry Johnsen's guns to the rear and back on line with Leverich, a ninety-degree change of battery front. "Through the falling veil of darkness loomed up the enemy's line of horses, madly coming at us, unchecked by Leverich's canister. There was no time to halt, to come into battery, to do anything but meet the clash. . . . Turning to Johnsen, I said, 'Leverich has failed to check them! They're on us! Have you a weapon?' 'Not a penknife,' [Johnsen] replied; and I raised my sword arm to guard my head from an expected saber stroke." [38]

Horses raced by. But, to Chalaron's astonishment, he saw empty saddles! "Thirty or forty horses, riderless, but aligned, sweeping like a whirlwind past us." On they rode, these riderless mounts, through the intervals between the pieces, into the milling, demoralized infantry, creating chaos behind the guns. One round had smashed the Yankee charge and blown a host of riders off their horses. A blast from Piece Four with "a double-shotted load of canister full into the faces of a column of cavalry charging down upon our rear, not 50 paces off!" [39]

The abortive cavalry charge had had its effect, nonetheless. Those who remained of Smith's and Bullock's infantry "could not be controlled. The panicky spirit was still in them, the dread of being trapped." They fled. "The few that had not already run hung in disorganized fragments about

38. Chalaron, "Hood's Campaign at Murfreesboro," 439–40; Stephenson, *Civil War Memoir,* 297–98.

39. Stephenson, *Civil War Memoir,* 297; *OR,* Vol. XLV, Pt. 1, p. 745; Owen, *In Camp and Battle,* 415. Despite Chalaron's claim that the single discharge from two of his guns stopped the charge of the 13th Indiana Cavalry, there is a more probable cause. David Deatrick, who has studied extensively the December, 1864, skirmishes around Murfreesboro, suggests: "As the Federal Cavalry was maneuvering along the creek bank in an effort to flank the Confederate artillery, they were mistaken for Confederates by the 8th Minnesota. As they began their charge they were met with a volley from the flank and rear. . . . It is also unlikely that a blast of canister would not harm twenty of the horses which were subsequently captured by the Confederates." David R. Deatrick, Jr., to author, June 12, 1996.

us."[40] No matter. Thanks to Leverich, the immediate danger was past. Chalaron had Johnsen send shrapnel in the direction of the retreating Federal cavalry while Leverich limbered up and took a new position some 150 yards to the right and rear of Johnsen. From there Chalaron opened fire on "the enemy infantry that had crossed the pike bridge and driven off our infantry in my front."[41]

"Our infantry fled at once, deserting us shamefully," related Phil Stephenson. "But the men of our battery had never at any time lost their heads, neither officers or privates. With disgust and indignation in our hearts, we kept by our guns."[42] When Leverich opened on the approaching Yankee infantry, Chalaron had Johnsen's section displace, retiring the two Napoleons 150 yards to the rear and left of Leverich; when Johnsen opened fire from there, Chalaron retired Leverich toward the Nashville pike. Soon there were no more bullets coming at the battery. They were out of range of the enemy infantry who had crossed the creek. At that point, before the Yankees could reform and push out a line of battle toward the isolated battery, Chalaron ordered the Fifth Company to cease firing.[43] They limbered up and moved off, up the Nashville pike in search of the division. Fortunately for them, the Yankees showed no disposition to follow.[44]

An unexpected boon from the Washington Artillery's stand at Overall's Creek had been the capture of twenty healthy Union cavalry horses. As these mounts tore through Chalaron's position, they were caught by alert men stationed in the rear to tend the caissons and ambulances. All the horses they captured "bore the number 13 branded on their haunches," designating them the property of the 13th Indiana Cavalry, who had made

40. Stephenson, *Civil War Memoir,* 299.

41. The union infantry were the 61st Illinois and 174th Ohio. Chalaron, "Hood's Campaign at Murfreesboro," 440.

42. Stephenson, *Civil War Memoir,* 299.

43. Bate's report of the fight at Overall's Creek appears to be a study in misrepresentation. He certainly credits the Washington Artillery with "conspicuous and most effective gallantry," but leaves the impression that the enemy cavalry and infantry were repulsed handily by Tyler's and Jackson's infantry who arrived just in time to save the day. He does not attempt to explain why the three infantry brigades rapidly made their way at least a mile (infantryman Washington Ives maintains it was three) to the rear and threw up field works. *OR,* Vol. XLV, Pt. 1, p. 440; Ives, *Civil War Journal,* 18; Chalaron, "Hood's Campaign at Murfreesboro," 440.

44. Stephenson, *Civil War Memoir,* 299; Chalaron, "Hood's Campaign at Murfreesboro," 440; Casey, *Outline of the Civil War Campaigns,* 83; Sword, *Embrace an Angry Wind,* 295–96.

the flank attack.[45] This charge, although broken and repulsed by a perfect shot by Leverich, did succeed, nevertheless, in routing the remainder of Bate's infantry, driving them as well as the Washington Artillery from their threatening position behind Overall's Creek.

There had been losses. Seibrecht was dead. John Berry, who had been wounded at Atlanta and hospitalized, was wounded again. A minié ball struck him in the jaw and throat, and he had to be left behind to the mercy of the enemy. Cpl. J. W. Scott, who also had rejoined the battery after a wound at Kennesaw, was hit but managed to get off the field, as did E. H. Wingate, who was "shot through the lungs" yet miraculously was able to walk away. Driver Henry Miller, a German immigrant, was horribly wounded—"a shell burst in his very lap and *scooped out the whole lap,*" reported Stephenson. His brother John refused to leave him. They remained there near the creek with John Berry awaiting capture and prison.[46] A number of others including Chris Wild were slightly wounded and retired from the field successfully. Seven battery horses had been killed, Chalaron noted, and 217 rounds fired, 76 at the blockhouse.[47]

Chalaron headed to the rear, riding in front of his guns and caissons. He saw "Old Grits" and his staff in the distance and rode up to them. "It's Chalaron!" cried a staff officer. Bate greeted Chalaron and said, "I am so sorry you have lost your guns." The battery commander answered "in no amiable mood: Lost my guns? No, sir, I have not lost my guns!"[48]

Phil Stephenson reported their encounter somewhat differently. The infantry was busy constructing hasty field fortifications when the battery arrived. When he saw Chalaron, Bate rode up to him "and grasping his hand, said, in an agitated voice, 'Lieutenant, you have immortalized yourself. *You have saved my division!*' To which that peppery little Frenchman replied curtly and with refreshing frankness, '*I know I have.*' A broad grin overspread the faces of our boys at Bate's words and the answer he got, and we were disposed at the time to remark, that 'If saving Bate's Division was the price of immortality, it was dirt cheap!'"[49]

45. Chalaron, "Hood's Campaign at Murfreesboro," 440.
46. The Millers were released from Camp Chase in mid-May, 1865. Berry would return to New Orleans in June.
47. 5WA Master Roster, WA Papers, HTT; Chalaron, "Hood's Campaign at Murfreesboro," 440; Stephenson, *Civil War Memoir,* 302–303.
48. Chalaron, "Hood's Campaign at Murfreesboro," 440.
49. Stephenson, *Civil War Memoir,* 300.

16

EVERY MAN FOR HIMSELF

AFTER 10:00 P.M. the night of December 4, following the engagement at Overall's Creek, Bate pulled back farther, placing his division just south of Smyrna, Tennessee, behind Stewart's Creek. He had been unsteadied by the vicious sally by the Murfreesboro defenders and was apprehensive that he might be cut off from Hood's army by yet another bold thrust by the enemy down the Nashville pike. Morning brought relief, nonetheless, and Bate's thoughts returned to the offensive, the obligation of fulfilling his mission. He advanced up the pike toward Nashville intending to attack the blockhouses at Smyrna and Read's Branch, but the garrisons fled at his approach, so, without a fight, Bate's men were able to burn the blockhouses and bridges as well as destroy several miles of railroad.[1]

General Forrest came on the scene and turned Bate about. They would attack Murfreesboro, he said, with sufficient force this time. Bate and his men started south again and marched back to and across Overall's Creek

---

1. McMurray, *Twentieth Tennessee,* 343–44. The blockhouse at Smyrna was evacuated by order of Gen. George Thomas. An order to evacuate all the blockhouses along the railroad had been sent, but most never received it because of the proximity of the Confederate cavalry.

on December 6. The blockhouse the Fifth Company had hammered two days earlier fell into their hands without much of a fight. Things looked good. Bate built defensive works and pushed forward skirmishers "as near to the works around Murfreesboro as practicable." More infantry came up during the late afternoon of the sixth—two small, battle-weary brigades: Joseph B. Palmer's Tennesseans (Stevenson's division) and Claudius W. Sears's Mississippians (French's division). Accompanying them were two veteran artillery units: Guibor's Missouri battery and Fenner's Louisiana battery. Counting his two cavalry divisions, Forrest's total command now numbered about six thousand of combined arms, mostly cavalry. Still it was an impressive strike force—on paper.[2]

The morning of December 7, Forrest climbed a tree near the Nashville pike to observe. He noticed far in the distance a column of Yankee cavalry and infantry in motion south of Murfreesboro, apparently heading west toward Salem. Forrest dropped from the tree, hurriedly mounted, and led his escort company in front of the Confederate pickets, riding dangerously close to Fortress Rosecrans itself. Once he had completed this risky reconnaissance, he returned and explained an idea he had conceived. Let the enemy come out of the Fortress Rosecrans to attack us, as they had done on December 4 at Overall's Creek, and as they appeared to be doing at the moment. He wanted to lure them even closer. Let Bate and the infantry stand on the defensive and hold off their attack while Forrest's cavalry dashed in behind the Yankee infantry, cutting them off so that they might be surrounded and destroyed or, if more feasible, the cavalry could drive directly into Murfreesboro itself. According to Phil Stephenson, there was another element to Forrest's plan: Bate's infantry and the Fifth Company were to engage the enemy, then "withdraw a little distance after slight resistance, so as to decoy the enemy still further from his base."[3]

Bate and Palmer shared a strong position south of Overall's Creek,

2. *OR,* Vol. XLV, Pt. 1, pp. 745, 755–58; McMurray, *Twentieth Tennessee,* 343–44; Ives, *Civil War Journal,* 18; Jamison, *Letters and Recollections,* 177; Robert O. Neff, *Tennessee's Battered Brigadier: The Life of General Joseph B. Palmer* (Nashville, 1988), 112–13; Sword, *Embrace an Angry Wind,* 296; Andrew N. Lytle, *Bedford Forrest and His Critter Company* (New York, 1960), 360–61; Stephenson, *Civil War Memoir,* 307.

3. Chalaron, "Hood's Campaign at Murfreesboro," 439–40; Thomas Jordan and J. P. Pryor, *The Campaigns of Lieut.-Gen. N. B. Forrest and of Forrest's Cavalry* (New Orleans, 1868), 632–33; McMurray, *Twentieth Tennessee,* 344; John A. Wyeth, *Life of General N. B. Forrest* (New York, 1899) 550; Lytle. *Bedford Forrest,* 360; Stephenson, *Civil War Memoir,* 306.

with Palmer on a hill facing Fortress Rosecrans and Bate entrenched to his right. When he spotted the Federal column leaving Murfreesboro, Forrest's thoughts, as always, turned to the offensive and tactics of movement. He sent Abraham Buford's cavalry division with horse artillery toward Murfreesboro and shifted his infantry south to receive the Yankee enveloping force in a position of their choice rather than await the Federals in front of Fortress Rosecrans.[4] Bate and Palmer abandoned their newly constructed works and marched south toward the Wilkinson pike.[5]

Bate knew the route, having used it three days before. He also knew a good position facing a large open field just east and south of Overall's Creek, immediately below Wilkinson pike. So he set his troops in motion at once and quickly had them at the designated spot. There the infantry set to work constructing log barricades. Sears held the right, Palmer the center, and Bullock's Floridians (now commanded by Maj. Jacob A. Lash) the left. Jackson and Tom Smith were back a short distance, in reserve on Wilkinson pike.[6]

The enemy column observed by Forrest turned out to be a reconnaissance in force commanded by Maj. Gen. Robert H. Milroy, former general officer in the Army of the Potomac, who had been disgraced and removed from active duty for his miserable performance at Winchester, Virginia, in June, 1863. Milroy was burning for revenge and an opportunity to redeem himself. It was Milroy who had commanded the aggressive attack against Bate on December 4, and he was eager for a repeat performance. Forrest could not have wished for a more overly aggressive Union leader, nor one more likely to fall into his trap.

On came Milroy, 3,325 strong—seven infantry regiments, a cavalry regiment, and a battery. They advanced southwest over Salem Pike, crossed Stone's River, then swung sharply north across the Triune-Murfreesboro road, continuing north on a road that connected with Wilkinson pike.[7] After marching half a mile on this road, Milroy veered obliquely northwest, heading his column directly toward what he believed

---

4. Buford's cavalry had been picketing the road to Lebanon and were already east of Murfreesboro.

5. In his report Bate states that he crossed Overall's Creek while moving into position. If this is correct, it must mean that he and Palmer moved north on the Nashville pike and down the west side of Overall's Creek until they reached Wilkinson pike. This seems an unlikely route, however, indirect and needlessly time consuming. *OR*, Vol. XLV, Pt. 1, p. 746.

6. *Ibid.*, 746, 755; Jordan and Pryor, *Campaigns of Forrest*, 632–33; Neff, *Battered Brigadier*, 113–18; McMurray, *Twentieth Tennessee*, 344.

7. Gresham Lane.

was Forrest's right flank.[8] This was fine. Instead of being positioned perpendicular to the pike, the Confederate infantry were aligned at almost a forty-five-degree angle from the Wilkinson pike southwest to Armstrong Branch, a tributary of Overall's Creek. So Milroy's advance, although it appeared to aim directly for the Confederate flank, would actually strike them frontally. As if it were once again the days of 1862, it seems the Fifth Company and one of the other batteries were advanced in front of the infantry. This placement was at the request of Gen. T. B. Smith, who had sent a staff officer back to Forrest to ask specifically that the Washington Artillery be brought up.

As Chalaron and his men moved into position, Brig. Gen. Lawrence S. "Sul" Ross's cavalrymen were retiring from the front, having been "tolling the enemy on, and were coming back on the pike to give way to us of the infantry and artillery."[9] It was just as the two commands met that Archie Bennett, at Stephenson's side, "sank down to the ground." The startled Phil Stephenson tried to help Archie get to his feet, "but help was in vain. He was shot in the stomach and mortally hurt. We gave him to the ambulance corps and rushed on. He died that night." Mystified, Stephenson had no idea where the bullet came from. No enemy was in sight. "I heard no musketry."[10]

When the blue-jackets did appear, the Confederate cannoneers were ready and opened fire, stopping Milroy's advance to the northwest. The Confederate artillery had deflected the enemy line of attack. Milroy and his men backed off and disappeared into thick woods. Many of the Confederates (especially Bate) believed that they had withdrawn to Murfreesboro. Milroy, however, had no such notion. Instead, he took advantage of the cover of the woods to shift north and change front, making the Wilkinson pike the axis of his attack, thus threatening the Confederate left.[11]

As Milroy changed front and advanced west along the Wilkinson pike, Forrest countered by transferring Sears's infantry from the right to the left of his line and ordering up Jackson from reserve. Jackson and Sears took position too far to the left, however, leaving a gap that Forrest di-

---

8. *OR,* Vol. XLV, Pt. 1, pp. 613–17; Sword, *Embrace an Angry Wind,* 296.

9. Ross was posted at the crossing of Stone's River on the Salem pike. Milroy's artillery (13th New York Light) drove him away from the bridge, thus permitting the Federal infantry to cross. Ross then fell back to Salem, allowing Milroy to turn north unmolested.

10. Stephenson, *Civil War Memoir,* 310.

11. *OR,* Vol. XLV, Pt. 1, pp. 617, 619, 627.

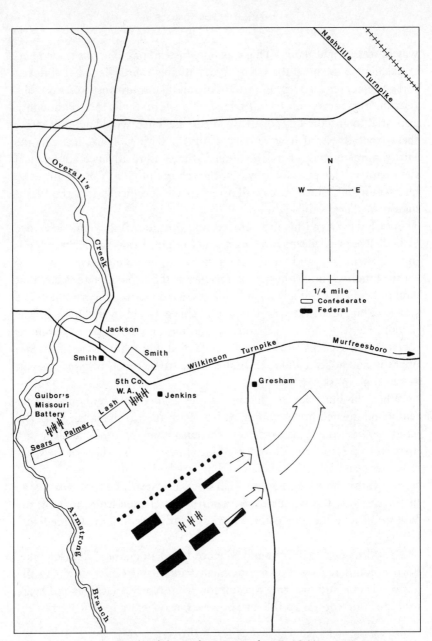

Battle of the Cedars, December 7, 1864
Adapted from David R. Deatrick, Jr., drawing
Map by Blake A. Magner

rected Tom Smith to fill. Milroy now attacked, the brunt of his assault falling on the advancing Smith. Forrest shifted Jackson and Sears to the right to help Smith, which they did with some success, according to Bate, crumpling Milroy's right flank.

The Fifth Company, after helping disrupt Milroy's initial approach, had withdrawn from their advanced post according to plan and taken their place in Forrest's main line of battle. When the enemy skirmishers appeared, attacking down the line of Wilkinson pike, Bate's infantry gave way, not deliberately as planned, but precipitously. "Their officers got them stopped just before they actually got in our midst, and reformed." The artillery batteries again limbered to the rear, according to plan, states Stephenson, but "as soon as Bate's men saw us withdrawing, they began to waver and to thin out rapidly." Milroy's men saw this confusion in the Confederate ranks and charged again, "with loud cheers, with splendid audacity." Then, to the astonishment of Forrest and the artillerymen, the Confederate infantry collapsed. The breakthrough seems to have begun with Lash's Florida troops, according to Washington Ives of the 4th Florida. "The whole command ran about the same time," he recorded in his diary, and soon "the infantry was in full retreat." Stephenson stated that it was "shameful to relate" that the "main line, Bate's men, behind works though they were, jumped up without scarcely the firing of a gun, and taking to their heels, came back upon us and around us pell mell as we were retiring. . . . That was the worst thing I ever saw Southern men do in battle. I hate to record it, but it is true."[12]

Desperately Forrest attempted to stop them, as did Bate, but to no avail.[13] Chalaron recklessly took it upon himself to reverse the situation. He decided, "without orders I suspect," declared Stephenson, that a little

12. In his official report Bate minimizes the panic of the Confederate infantry. He relates how he with Jackson's and Smith's brigades stayed in position parallel to Wilkinson pike, "where I remained without molestation until ordered by Forrest to move across the creek and join him which I did leisurely." On the other hand, Bate points his finger at Forrest's cavalry, accusing them of not being "seriously engaged" and failing to provide intelligence about Milroy's movements. Stephenson, *Civil War Memoir*, 307; Chalaron, "Slocomb's Battery in the Tennessee Army"; *OR*, XLV, Pt. 1, pp. 746, 755; Sanders, "Hood's Tennessee Campaign," IV, 113; Sword, *Embrace an Angry Wind*, 297; McMurray, *Twentieth Tennessee*, 345; Ives, *Civil War Journal*, 18; William T. Alderson, ed., "The Civil War Diary of Captain James Litton Cooper, September 30, 1861, to January, 1865," *Tennessee Historical Quarterly*, XV (1956), 141–74.

13. This is the famous incident where Forrest reportedly shot a Confederate color bearer "running for dear life." Wyeth, *Life of Forrest*, 552; Jordan and Pryor, *Campaigns of Forrest*, 633.

canister might stem the tide. While the infantry fled, the Washington Artillery advanced and unlimbered. Pieces Two and Four fired "one or two rounds of canister into the faces of the enemy who were now almost upon us (not over fifty or sixty feet off) and checked them for the moment." Then, to their horror, the Fifth Company saw Milroy's infantry "coming out of a long stretch of woods that ran parallel to the pike (our only line of exit) . . . not over three or four hundred yards off! We were caught in a right angle, the foe both in front and flank!" Bate's infantry had taken flight, and the two pieces and their crews were all alone—except for Forrest.

"Take those guns away from here," shouted Forrest. "That was all we were waiting for! In a flash, they were limbered up, and we started back." Pieces One and Three had a head start and "made good their escape." Leverich's section, Sgt. Jim Browning's Piece Two and Tom Allen's Piece Four, "tore down the pike" after them, "running a gauntlet of fire that every instant drew nearer and nearer." Phil Stephenson, running beside Piece Four, looked back over his shoulder and saw Forrest. There he was, alone, "sitting motionless on his horse. How he escaped I know not." [14]

Abe Leverich looked for help. Those of Bate's infantry who were visible seemed preoccupied with re-forming. Guibor's battery fired a few shells but seemed to do little harm to the advancing Federals. [15] There was to be no help.

Ahead the enemy had broken across the pike and blocked the route of escape. To turn off into the woods "meant the wedging of our guns among the trees and their certain loss." Leverich had no other choice, however. Off the road went the teams pulling the two pieces. "We had not gone, I suppose, twenty steps, when the wheels of both pieces were jammed between the trees, but not a man left his post. We stayed by our guns making strenuous efforts to loose them! Every horse was soon shot down, several men also." Yankees closed in, some firing, some "yelling 'Halt, Halt!' . . . Our hearts and eyes were on our guns—our beloved guns!" The Irish driver Bill Dooley fought like a madman trying to cut the harness of "disabled horses to save his piece. The enemy shot him at point blank. . . .

---

14. Stephenson, *Civil War Memoir,* 308.

15. Phil Stephenson was uncertain, but believed it was Fenner's battery that tried to help. More likely it was Guibor's battery, as most accounts have the Missourians in battery near the bridge over Overall's Creek.

It was all over in a flash." Leverich shouted, "Boys, save yourselves! Every man for himself!"[16]

Phil Stephenson blamed Chalaron. He "no doubt thought that by running his guns to the front, [Bate's infantry] would rally on him, and so save the day! It was a gallant act, a most chivalrous act and won applause from all who heard of it, but an act that cost us dear. He sacrificed half his battery. . . . The whole thing was a fiasco."[17]

Not only had the Washington Artillery lost Pieces Two and Four with most of the horses, but the company had two men wounded and captured: Henry J. Marks and Bill Dooley (whose leg would be amputated by Federal surgeons). Also captured were Henry Hardy and another Irish driver, Andy Hopkins.[18] Probably the only thing that saved Forrest and Bate from a worse fate, according to historian T. R. Hay, was the success of Abraham Buford's cavalry division, which penetrated Murfreesboro and caused a pandemonium that resulted in the immediate recall of Milroy's victorious force.[19]

The night of December 7–8, 1864, would be long remembered. The Fifth Company retired with Bate's division a few miles north behind Stewart's Creek. Filled with rage and shame over losing their two pieces, the members, as they trudged north toward Stewart's Creek, turned on Bate's men. They had been enchained to these men for a year, these cowardly infantry "whose base conduct had brought this disgrace upon us. We cursed them without measure as they slouched along. Nay, heaped up execrations upon them until we were exhausted. I was never given to profanity," recorded Stephenson, who would become a Presbyterian preacher after the war, "but this was an occasion when I joined in! Tears, indeed, rolled down our eyes as we denounced them. Not one of them resented it. I do not remember a single word in reply."[20]

16. 5WA Master Roster, WA Papers, HTT; Wyeth, *Life of Forrest*, 552; *OR*, Vol. XLV, Pt. 1, pp. 746, 755; Stephenson, *Civil War Memoir*, 309; Chalaron, "Washington Artillery in the Army of Tennessee," 221; Casey, *Outline of Civil War Campaign*, 83.

17. Stephenson, *Civil War Memoir*, 310.

18. 5WA Master Roster, WA Papers, HTT.

19. For many years this Forrest-Milroy fight of December 7 was referred to as the Second Battle of Murfreesboro, using the name given the conflict by the Confederates. As early as 1870, however, published Federal reports referred to the engagement as the battle of the Cedars. This designation has prevailed. Hay, *Hood's Tennessee Campaign*, 141; David R. Deatrick, Jr., to author, June 12, 1996. The action on December 4 was and continues to be referred to, as the engagement at Overall's Creek.

20. Stephenson, *Civil War Memoir*, 311.

The Washington Artillery remained at Stewart's Creek for two days—caught, as it were, in some disturbing Arctic dreamworld, between Murfreesboro and Nashville, between Forrest and Hood. Archie Bennett died at 4 A.M. on the eighth. Chalaron assembled the company just off the Murfreesboro road, where they buried him between two trees, each slashed with five notches. They gave his effects to Archie's personal servant, William, who would take them back to his father in Florida. It was difficult digging Archie's grave. The temperature had plunged since midnight and it had begun to snow and sleet. The wind howled and stung. By morning the ground seemed like rock. The men huddled together as they stood around Archie's shallow grave.[21]

The weather worsened. On December 9 a heavy snowstorm struck. The temperature dropped to ten degrees and the wind grew even more piercing. "Our artillery carriages are frozen in the ground," wrote Capt. Thomas Key, an Arkansas battery commander, "and ice half an inch thick coats my brass guns." Nothing moved that did not have to. Washington Ives wrote on December 12, "I know [today] was the coldest day I ever experienced. . . . Many were frost bitten and the ice was so thick that the weapons did not disturb it." The temperature fell below zero, perhaps ten degrees below.[22]

As if to add deliberately to the company's sufferings, an order came from General Bate on December 9 directing that the battery be ready to move with his division to Nashville. The men, who sat or lay shivering "with no shelter but open flies," appealed to Chalaron to ask Forrest to "retain Slocomb's Battery with his forces." Anything to get away from Bate. Chalaron did go, announcing that he spoke for all the members of the battery. As he stood there, making his case in Forrest's tent, who should enter but General Bate.

"You here, Chalaron?" Bate asked.

"Yes, General, I have received your order, and my men not wishing to

---

21. Archie Bennett's body would be recovered by the family the following spring and brought to New Orleans, where Dr. Palmer presided at his funeral. 5WA Master Roster, WA Papers, HTT; C. H. Slocomb to A. T. Bennett, Sr., January 15, 1865, WA Papers, HTT; Chalaron, "Slocomb's Battery in the Tennessee Army"; Hay, *Hood's Tennessee Campaign*, 141; Sword, *Embrace an Angry Wind*, 303.

22. Hay, *Hood's Tennessee Campaign*, 141; Ives, *Civil War Journal*, 18; Daniel, *Cannoneers in Gray*, 175; Sword, *Embrace an Angry Wind*, 303; Chalaron, "Slocomb's Battery in the Tennessee Army."

return to the army with your division, I have come to ask General Forrest to keep my battery with him."

Chalaron proceeded to explain how his men felt. Bate "expressed regret" and promised Chalaron that "he would do [the battery] justice in his report of the fight before Murfreesboro." Chalaron remonstrated, but Forrest intervened: "Lieutenant, I can do nothing in this matter, you are attached to General Bate's division and are subject to his orders." To appease Chalaron, Bate allowed the Fifth Company to march and camp apart from the infantry as they moved to Nashville, so long as the battery "reached the division's position with the main army, by the 12th of December." [23]

The Washington Artillery started out for Nashville on December 10. The country "looked as desolate and dreary as a desert," thought Stephenson. The Nashville pike, according to Chalaron, "was a sheet of ice and as slippery as glass." The awful wind "full in the face . . . struck us, raging down that bleak road, stiffening and benumbing our limbs." Men "would huddle together in the wake of each wagon to escape the new foe. The condition of the drivers became pitiable," remembered Stephenson. "What they had to endure was terrible. One [driver] lost all control of his limbs, and a sudden jolt of his horse tumbled him off as though he was frozen stiff. He fell under the wheels of the gun and had one foot crushed." Phil Stephenson himself became desperate during the march. He had lost his blanket during the melee at Overall's Creek, replacing it with a "thread-bare saddle blanket" he found beside the road. Now he could not sleep and could find no warmth, no place to hide from the wind and ice. "Unless I could get more covering, I would die." So, "shoeless, hatless, blanketless," he disobeyed orders and straggled across the countryside searching house to house for a blanket. [24]

Despite this terrible war with nature, on December 12 the Fifth Company, including Phil Stephenson (replete with a heavy mackinaw a kind lady had given him), reported to General Bate "at the division's position on the line of Cheatham's Corps, that formed the right of Hood's army fronting Nashville." They lay "in mud, snow-slush, sleet and ice," remembered Chalaron, behind the infantry until the morning of December 15,

23. Chalaron, "Slocomb's Battery in the Tennessee Army."

24. Stephenson, *Civil War Memoir,* 312–18; Chalaron, "Slocomb's Battery in the Tennessee Army."

when Captain Beauregard moved them to the top of Rain's Hill, "immediately in front of Fort Negley which easily commanded our insignificant works." Rain's Hill, located just south and west of Nolensville pike, provided magnificent observation, nevertheless. In the distance one could see the capital, Murfreesboro pike, and Fort Negley.[25]

On the morning of December 15, at 8 A.M., the enemy attacked the Confederate right. Frank Cheatham, commanding that sector, rode up to the summit of Rain's Hill to observe. "His whole staff was with him, and they formed a conspicuous target." The enemy gunners at Negley "had our range exactly," and Cheatham "had not been there five minutes before a shell was sent plump into their midst." Cheatham was knocked to the ground, at least one horse was hit, and the little group of horsemen were scattered unceremoniously. "Much to our satisfaction," declared Chalaron, for they were "drawing too much attention upon us from Fort Negley." Some of these shells passed over the company's redoubts and "came near stampeding the mules that were hitched to our caissons."[26]

These attacks against the Confederate right came to nothing.[27] The two guns of the Fifth Company, Sgt. David W. "Hawkeye" Smith's Piece One and his brother "Bully" Smith's Piece Three, both commanded by Lt. Charles Johnsen and Chalaron, were not engaged, and their detachments spent the morning ducking shells from Fort Negley and listening to disquieting booms from the left of the army.[28] There a powerful and well-coordinated flank attack had sent Stewart's corps reeling backward, badly defeated. Darkness alone appeared to have saved Hood's army from calamity on the fifteenth.

Hood moved quickly to establish a new line about a mile south, extending along a series of hills from Franklin pike on the right past Granny White pike on the left. To the left Hood dispatched Bate's division, and subsequently Cheatham's entire corps. The Fifth Company left Rain's Hill

25. Stephenson, *Civil War Memoir*, 319–20; Chalaron, "Slocomb's Battery in the Tennessee Army."

26. Stephenson, *Civil War Memoir*, 319–20; Chalaron, "Slocomb's Battery in the Tennessee Army."

27. A second attack by Maj. Gen. James B. Steedman's division came at 11 A.M. but was repulsed handily.

28. "Detachment" was a more common Civil War parlance than "crew." 5WA Order Book, WA Papers, HTT; Chalaron, "Slocomb's Battery in the Tennessee Army"; Sword, *Embrace an Angry Wind*, 331–43; Horn, *Army of Tennessee*, 412–25.

before dark and began their long, tiring march of four miles to Hood's extreme left.[29] It was dark, deep December dark, when Chalaron met Bate on Granny White pike. Bate ordered him to take his two remaining guns forward and continue down the pike until he encountered one of the three infantry brigades, "which he supposed were in front." There Chalaron was to await further orders.

Chalaron rode ahead, his guns and wagons trailing. After traveling about three hundred yards on Granny White pike, he was startled by a shot. It was a Union picket. Chalaron wheeled his horse about and galloped away; "otherwise I would have run right into the lines of the enemy with my guns." After he had halted and alerted the Fifth Company, Chalaron rode back to Bate and reported the alarming news that there were no Confederate pickets ahead on the pike. Somehow, "the division had gotten into place in the dark on unknown ground," thus making it "impossible for it to take advantage of the best natural defenses of the locality." It made little difference actually. According to Bate and Chalaron it was impossible to bring the guns on line because the intervening "cultivated low ground was an obstruction through which even the ambulances could not pass. . . . Hence the artillery was left in the rear for the night."[30]

The morning of December 16 found Bate on line, the left of his division resting on Shy's Hill, some six hundred yards west of the Granny White pike. Tom Smith was on the left, Lash's Floridians in the center, and Jackson on the right. Hooked to Bate's left flank was the brigade of Matthew D. Ector, bent back in a tortured manner, almost a right angle, from the point where it touched Smith. Beyond Ector ran the lines of the remainder of Cheatham's Corps.[31] Thus Bate held a dangerous salient in Hood's line with no hope of friendly interlocking fire that might help cover his front. Hood faulted Cheatham for this "grave neglect."[32]

---

29. As at Atlanta on July 22, when his flank attack was delayed, Bate would move slowly and in some confusion. He himself blamed his tardiness on darkness and marshy fields. *OR,* Vol. XLV, Pt. 1, p. 748.

30. Chalaron, "Slocomb's Battery in the Army of Tennessee"; Sword, *Embrace an Angry Wind,* 347–49; *OR,* XLV, Pt. 1, p. 748.

31. Paul H. Stockdale, *The Death of an Army: The Battle of Nashville and Hood's Retreat* (Murfreesboro, Tenn., 1992), 63.

32. Wiley Sword contends, contrary to Chalaron, that Ector's brigade was in reserve behind Edward C. Walthall on Bate's right, not extending Bate's left to connect with Otho F. Strahl's brigade, although Sword's map does show Ector in that position. Chalaron, "Slocomb's Battery in the Army of Tennessee"; Sword, *Embrace an Angry Wind,* 349, 364; Hay, *Hood's Tennessee Campaign,* 156.

Immediately behind this angle in the Confederate line formed by Ector and Bate lay open fields, "horses and men sinking with every movement, in the loose-thawed earth," and in this space the batteries of Chalaron and Beauregard waited until Bate ordered them up.[33] At 8 A.M. on December 16, the Federal guns opened "from many points and commanding elevations" in Bate's front. Indeed, his position was totally enfiladed—hit from front, from east and west, as well as in reverse.[34] Enemy rounds from every direction arced over the infantry's hasty works and struck in the park where the artillery and much of Hood's wagon train waited helplessly. Battalion commander Beauregard and Chalaron sat in the saddle side by side, the rump of Chalaron's mount "touching the head" of the Fifth Company's lead horses. Beauregard saw a shell curving toward them over the lines and alerted Chalaron. They both bent low on their horses' necks and the round passed just over Chalaron, killing "the battery horse behind mine."[35] Here, in this vulnerable pocket, "massed in great confusion so as to be hopelessly in each other's way, were most of the ordnance wagons and ambulances," remembered Stephenson, "as well as many of the quartermaster and commissary trains of our whole army." Chalaron recalled that "we of the artillery, caught in that mesh of wagons felt useless and helpless. . . . We had to take our share of their shelling, stand and take it in impotent rage and disgust."[36]

It seemed to Chalaron that at least fifty enemy guns were firing, their ammunition supply apparently inexhaustible. As the morning wore on the Federal attack on Hood's right seemed to be contained, but a substantial Union cavalry force had driven in behind the Confederate left and threatened Granny White pike. To counter this enveloping move, Hood pulled Ector's brigade out of line and sent it to the left rear to support the beleaguered cavalry division of Brig. Gen. James R. Chalmers. This resulted in Bate's already attenuated line of infantry having to stretch to cover Ector's sector. If this were not disheartening enough, even more troops continued to be withdrawn from the Confederate left. Three brigades from Cleburne's division headed south to combat the encircling

33. It is believed J. W. Phillips' battery was in this congested wagon park as well, at least until early afternoon.

34. "One battery alone fired almost six hundred rounds on Cheatham here during the day." Horn, *Army of Tennessee,* 416; Daniel, *Cannoneers in Gray,* 177; Connelly, *Autumn of Glory,* 511.

35. Chalaron, "Slocomb's Battery in the Army of Tennessee."

36. Stephenson, *Civil War Memoir,* 323, 327–28; Chalaron, "Slocomb's Battery in the Army of Tennessee."

Yankees. Meanwhile, to Bate's right, Daniel H. Reynolds' brigade from Edward C. Walthall's line also pulled out at 3:15 P.M. and was sent down Granny White pike to assist Ector. Thus, by 4 P.M. Bate was confronted with having to defend a line along the western and northern slopes of Shy's Hill far beyond the capability of the manpower available. Moreover, his position was completely dominated by Federal rifled guns that had been moved up very close shortly after noon. At the same time murderous cross fire by Yankee sharpshooters kept Bate's infantry ducking and unable to strengthen their works, which, as at Missionary Ridge, "did not command the slope." It was a recipe for disaster.[37]

Flush into this vulnerable position smashed the division of Federal Brig. Gen. John McArthur, any one of whose three brigades equaled or exceeded Bate's division in number. This frontal onslaught was overpowering, not to speak of random bullets striking into Bate's line from the rear, where Cleburne's men fought off Yankee cavalry. "Bate was in a nutcracker," observed Wiley Sword, "with his weakened line entirely unsupported. Hood, a few hours earlier, had taken away his only reserves." Bate's line shattered like a porcelain dinner plate. His men, utterly demoralized, fled the field, leaving not only their weapons but hundreds of comrades, including Gen. Tom Smith, Major Lash, and General Jackson, to be captured.[38]

Bate's artillery battalion was never a factor at Nashville, either on the fifteenth or the sixteenth. Perhaps it was the mushy ground, as he claimed; perhaps he had his hands full strengthening and making sense out of the weak line he had been assigned. His artillery, nevertheless, appears to have been forgotten, certainly neglected. Undoubtedly the terrain impeded their use, but this seems an inadequate explanation. Chalaron, "literally chafing with rage," according to Phil Stephenson, "dashed up again and again to A. P. Stewart . . . and implored him 'for God's sake to give him a position.'" In any event, no one called for the battalion's guns until about the time (mid-afternoon) Reynolds' brigade had been pulled out of line. It was then, according to Chalaron, that Bate sent for a section of Beauregard's battery and planted it on Lash's line so as to cover the front of the Floridians and the left of Edward C. Walthall's division. The Yankee fire was so heavy by that time that pieces had to be reloaded "by drawing

37. Hay, *Hood's Tennessee Campaign*, 160; *OR*, Vol. XLV, Pt. 1, p. 749.
38. Sword, *Embrace an Angry Wind*, 369–74; Marshall, *Bate*, 156–58; Chalaron, "Slocomb's Battery in the Army of Tennessee."

them aside with the prolonge, to the protection of the parapet."[39] Chalaron received orders, probably about the same time, to "plant my two Napoleons on a terrace that formed the first rise from the open ground to the range of hills that ran parallel to and in rear of Bate's, Walthall's and Loring's line." Placed that far to the rear, having to fire over the wagon park or over the infantry works at targets they could not observe, the battery was destined to be about as useful at Nashville as it had been at Franklin.[40]

The Washington Artillery was now east of the Granny White pike, directly behind William W. Loring's division, Stewart's corps, which was also just east of the pike. There they would stay for the remainder of December 16, largely inactive, "firing a few long range shots," overly mindful of the frail, thinning line and the "thickening fray to our left and rear." The furious 4 P.M. bombardment of Bate's position and the "deafening roars of musketry" directed at his works "announced a determined assault." Suddenly the remnants of the division appeared in full flight attempting to escape "that fatal pocket." Organization disappeared amid "the wildest disorder and confusion." At this moment Phil Stephenson saw General Bate trying to rally small squads from the panic-stricken mob. Bate was mounted "on his little white pony and swinging his crutch" wildly in a furious but futile attempt to command their attention.[41]

As the infantry collapsed, Chalaron sought to save his two pieces, "taking them up and over the hills by a road that followed the terrace on which they stood." Seizing every horse possible (and strays seemed to be running everywhere), the battery harnessed them to the guns. They managed to climb part way up that steep road only to find it blocked by "abandoned wagons and ambulances. . . . The bewildering disorder, the constant upsetting of wagons and consequent choking up of the way, the deafening uproar, the wild countenances of men, the almost hopeless chance of escape, these things," remembered Stephenson, "robbed the stoutest hearts of fortitude." Chalaron pleaded with passing infantry to help shove the two guns up the hill to safety, but it was useless. General

---

39. The prolonge was a stout rope used to connect the lunette of the carriage and pintle hook of the limber to move the piece short distances without limber. Jacob D. Cox, *The March to the Sea* (New York, 1906), 118.

40. Chalaron, "Slocomb's Battery in the Army of Tennessee"; *OR*, Vol. XLV, Pt. 1, pp. 748–49; Hay, *Hood's Tennessee Campaign*, 162.

41. Chalaron, "Slocomb's Battery in the Army of Tennessee"; Sanders, "Hood's Tennessee Campaign," IV, 174–75; Stephenson, *Civil War Memoir*, 332.

Cheatham also ordered infantry to assist with the guns, "but even his words were of no avail." As enemy fire on the company's rear and flank "showed that he was closing around us, General Cheatham told me to save my men, limbers and teams and abandon the guns."[42]

They unharnessed the animals and Abe Leverich led the column out and over the high hill while Chalaron remained with Bully and Hawkeye Smith and some of their crews. They spiked pieces One and Three, threw them off their carriages ("dismounted them"), and broke the carriage wheels.[43] Then they ran for their lives, "the enemy firing at us from three sides." Under this fire some continued up the road while others attempted to climb the steep hill. Chalaron himself clung to the mane of his mare and she, through "extraordinary exertions," carried him up and over, "her four shoes torn off in her scramble over the rocks." After allowing her to rest, Chalaron "threw her bridle reins over my shoulder and led her . . . along the ridge towards the Franklin Pike," safe from the bullets of the enemy. Finally he reached the pike and discovered Phillips "standing in battery to cover the retreat of our disorganized troops." There, with Phillips' battery, Chalaron "found my teams, limbers, officers and most of my men." Stephenson saw Hood here. Stewart and Cheatham were with him. Hood "seemed overwhelmed by his defeat and sat on his horse, a picture of despair—his head sunk on his breast, reins dangling loosely. . . . If anyone looked 'whipped' that day, our unfortunate leader certainly did."[44]

The Washington Artillery remained with Phillips' battery as the debris of the Army of Tennessee swept past them down the Franklin pike. They learned that the rear guard protecting Franklin pike was composed of elements of Henry D. Clayton's and Carter L. Stevenson's divisions of Lee's corps. Randall Gibson's Louisiana brigade had been particularly noticeable in its role in establishing a defensive position.[45] It was only a matter of time, however, before "this undaunted rear guard was forced

42. Stephenson, *Civil War Memoir,* 326, 330; Chalaron, "Slocomb's Battery in the Army of Tennessee."

43. Among the men staying behind for this dangerous work were acting Cpl. Tim White, Pvt. Kenneth Robertson, and Phil Stephenson. K. Robertson to JAC, June 14, 1875, Chalaron Papers, HTT; Stephenson, *Civil War Memoir,* 331.

44. Chalaron, "Slocomb's Battery in the Army of Tennessee"; Stephenson, *Civil War Memoir,* 334.

45. Of crucial importance in keeping Granny White pike open was D. H. Reynolds' Arkansas brigade, which displayed exemplary initiative. Hay, *Hood's Tennessee Campaign,* 162–63.

back to our position." Darkness had fallen, and under its friendly protection the Fifth Company and the rear guard were ordered to retreat toward Franklin. They proceeded through the black night, drenched by a cold and pitiless rain, braced for further attacks by pursuing Federals. On they fled past Brentwood and halted near Hollow Tree Gap, "about six miles from Franklin." They seemed safe for the moment. Apparently the Yankees were just as tired and wet and miserable. Perhaps they might be able to escape George Thomas' juggernaut after all. They pulled their blankets tight against their bodies and tried to sleep an hour or so, knowing that at dawn they must flee south once again.[46]

46. Chalaron, "Slocomb's Battery in the Army of Tennessee"; Stanley F. Horn, *The Decisive Battle of Nashville* (Baton Rouge, 1991), 149–50.

17

DROWNED RATS

THE SKY pelted cold rain on what remained of the Army of Tennessee. The sun hid its face. The rain would continue all day December 17 as the great "mob like column," once a proud army, slushed south through frozen mud toward Franklin. Federal cavalry under the energetic and determined Gen. James H. Wilson pressed the Confederate rearguard, "charging at every opportunity and in the most daring manner," reported Gen. Stephen D. Lee. "It was apparent that they were determined to make the retreat a rout if possible." Again and again Wilson's troopers attempted to cut behind the rearguard or attack it head on. It was a running fight all day as the Confederate main column struggled to find sanctuary, to put the Harpeth River between them and their tormentors.[1]

The Confederates had started their march before dawn. The climax that bitter winter day would come before noon when Wilson with approximately three thousand men slashed toward the pontoon bridge at Franklin. Randall Gibson and his brigade of about five hundred troops fought them off as long as they could, then, virtually surrounded, fled

---

1. *OR,* Vol. XLV, Pt. 1, pp. 740–56.

across the bridge.[2] Pioneers from Lee's corps managed to destroy both the railroad bridge and the pontoon bridge in the nick of time, placing the rushing Harpeth River between the Confederates and their relentless pursuers. But only for the moment—other Yankee cavalry units had forded the river west of town, and by early afternoon Wilson's forces had captured the city and were battling Lee again just below the town.[3]

Slowly Chalaron's command reassembled after crossing the Harpeth. Men caught up; some who had fled to Franklin on stray horses and mules were overtaken. Tim White rode in, resplendent in a Yankee "calvaryman's full outfit," and others appeared, having wandered the countryside. As the battery continued its tramp south from Franklin to Spring Hill, they passed small squads of men, remnants of regiments, brigades. Phil Stephenson saw one of these battered units, not over one-hundred strong, standing by the roadside in the rain.

"What command is this?" he asked.

"This is all that is left of the Louisiana Brigade," replied "one of these with head bandaged, destitute of hat or shoes but still retaining his gun." Gibson's brigade had been punished badly for their gallant stand on the Harpeth, with many wounded, many captured.[4]

After bivouacking at Spring Hill the night of December 18, the Fifth Company pushed on the following day for Columbia. The march that day was terribly difficult. "There was no moving off the pike," for the mud in the fields and woods-alongside was like quicksand. The pike itself was bad enough, congested with vehicles and thousands of sullen men. Equipment of all sorts, including rifles, littered the roadside, the trash of soldiers who had lost hope. "Progress was snail-like," recalled Chalaron, in the mud and slush. Rain continued, "changing at times into a sleet, and towards evening the weather was freezing cold." Finally, as they lay on the banks of the Duck River, stalled, helpless, shivering, "awaiting the completion of the pontoon bridge, the hours were more bitter with suffering from the cold than any we had yet endured."[5]

---

2. Assisting Gibson were some of Abe Buford's cavalry and Capt. Hiram M. Bledsoe's Missouri battery.

3. See Sword, *Embrace an Angry Wind,* 394–401; Stockdale, *Death of an Army,* 119–25; *OR,* Vol. XLI, Pt. 1, p. 703.

4. Stephenson, *Civil War Memoir,* 36–39.

5. Chalaron, "Slocomb's Battery in the Army of Tennessee"; Hay, *Hood's Tennessee Campaign,* 171.

By midnight on the nineteenth, all were across the Duck River. At last a deep, swollen stream separated them from their enemy. "We breathed free."[6] Hood knew better. It was only a question of time before Wilson's cavalry would cross above or below. Then the bluecoats would be pouring over the river, eager for the kill. So the Army of Tennessee evacuated Columbia on the twentieth and marched south on the Pulaski pike. The elements continued to punish the weary retreating column—heavy rain, then sleet. On the morning of the twenty-first the members awoke to a snow-blanketed countryside.[7] The temperature dropped sharply. They had to push on, nevertheless. On December 22, 1864, Thomas' pursuing infantry, thousands of them, began crossing the Duck River.[8]

Scenes from the awful retreat from Nashville caught in a man's memory like glass slivers. When he recalled the march, Chalaron would see the face of Cpl. D. A. Rice, gunner of Piece Three. "He had been wounded in the head at Kennesaw Ridge" so that it was "impossible for him to close one eye, and the cold striking it, kept it with flowing tears continually, [tears] that froze and formed a pendant icicle six inches long at times." Also trudging along with them was E. H. Wingate, shot through the chest at Overall's Creek, and hospitalized in Franklin. He had left his bed when the army passed through, "determined to make his way out or die in the attempt to escape prison." Chalaron mounted Wingate on one of the horses and assigned a man to help hold him up in the saddle.[9]

The Washington Artillery encamped six miles below Columbia on the south side of Richland Creek. Even the march to that bivouac had to be made in hard rain and sleet, but no matter. Now they were happier men. Not only had they been fed in Columbia, but they met on the road their old captain, Cuthbert Slocomb, who had been absent since September 1, nearly four months. "The spirits of the men arose again at the sight of his face," declared Stephenson, "for we were all devoted to him." "He was again with his dear company," Chalaron agreed, "imparting life, energy, and hope to officers and men." Slocomb, after a conference with Bate,

6. Chalaron, "Slocomb's Battery in the Army of Tennessee."

7. Union surgeon George E. Cooper stated, "Probably in no part of the war have the men suffered more than in the month of December, 1864." *OR*, Vol. XLI, Pt. 1, p. 111; Stockdale, *Death of an Army*, 143.

8. Sword, *Embrace an Angry Wind*, 410.

9. Chalaron, "Slocomb's Battery in the Army of Tennessee."

took charge of the artillery battalion, and Chalaron remained in command of Slocomb's battery.[10]

On December 22, as they stayed encamped below Columbia, orders came for all battery horses and mules to be turned in—they were needed to haul the pontoon train.[11] So Chalaron had the drivers bring the caissons and limbers onto the bridge over Richland Creek. There they dumped all the ammunition into the water. "The limbers and caissons were then taken back [to camp], piled up and set fire to." This was painful, of course. Saving these vehicles had required effort and sacrifice. All for nothing, some would say.[12]

This was the understandable mentality that pervaded the army—that had pervaded the army since Atlanta. Desertion had become common. War weariness had taken the heart out of the determined, the patriotic. It would reach epidemic proportions in January, 1865.[13] The Fifth Company, however, lost only one man from desertion during the late fall and winter.[14]

The Army of Tennessee set out once again the following day, heading for Bainbridge, a little village on the Tennessee River. There Hood planned to construct a pontoon bridge and cross. Below Pulaski, however, good roads ended. The country grew hilly, sparsely settled, and inhospitable. In the terrible cold, battery members tended to scatter since the "limbers and teams were no longer there as a rallying point." Indeed, marching order for the army itself had broken down. The men who kept together did so "not from [a sense of] duty but from necessity. The officers had lost interest as well as the men."[15] All along the road from Pulaski to the Tennessee River (some forty miles), one could find the debris of a demoralized army—broken-down wagons, baggage, and rifles. Perhaps most

10. Stephenson, *Civil War Memoir*, 38–39; Chalaron, "Slocomb's Battery in the Army of Tennessee"; Capt. Charles Swett to Maj. Gen. Arnold Elzey, December 21, 1864, Inspection Records and Related Reports, RG 109, NA.

11. Officers and noncommissioned officers retained their horses.

12. Chalaron, "Slocomb's Battery in the Army of Tennessee."

13. See Stephenson, *Civil War Memoir*, 346–48.

14. Two men were lost on the retreat. Irish driver Mike Campbell was captured on December 16 at Nashville as the Fifth Company fled entrapment. He would be imprisoned until the summer of 1865. John Gillespie, a teamster, appears to have deserted, being captured in Limestone County, Alabama, on December 31. He would take the Federal oath and enlist in the Union army. 5WA Master Roster, WA Papers, HTT; John Gillespie CSR, RG 109, NA.

15. Stephenson, *Civil War Memoir*, 346.

alarming of all were abandoned boats, scattered here and there, boats that everyone knew were needed for the pontoon bridge. Someone else would tend to that. They passed them by, trudging on, numb to their fate.[16]

The men had the highest hopes for crossing the Tennessee on Christmas. First, however, Shoal Creek had to be waded, and they found the ford "wide, deep, and dangerous." Many splashed into the icy water "with their clothes on, and many divested themselves and bore their duds high above their heads to keep them dry." Chalaron crossed Shoal Creek riding side by side with Maj. Ned Austin; Phil Stephenson jumped up behind Bully Smith and held on to the sergeant tightly. The little mule they were riding managed to get across with its double load. Stevenson only got his legs wet. But they did not cross the Tennessee on Christmas. They spent the day "drenched, like drowned rats from the icy waters of that creek, men huddled together on that little strip of land," patiently waiting, afraid the Yankees might appear any hour, constantly being assured "that the pontoon bridge would be completed in the morning, and that another day would see us safely over the swollen Tennessee."[17]

The Fifth Company did cross the Tennessee River on the twenty-sixth, "having taken about twelve days to accomplish the retreat of about 120 miles from Nashville."[18] Once on the Alabama side, Chalaron and several members of the battery helped perform a task crucial to the safety of the army. Federal gunboats under Admiral S. P. Lee had appeared several miles downriver, jeopardizing the pontoon bridge and the army's escape. To meet this crisis Cheatham sent Phillips' battery, the only one in the battalion with guns, downriver.[19] Chalaron and some of his men went along to help Phillips. They went into battery on a bluff from which they opened fire on the gunboats. "This fire, and that from another Confederate battery on the other side of the river," caused Lee to stop, cease firing, and withdraw. It is generally believed that if the admiral had persisted, his boats could have reached the fragile pontoon bridge, certainly

16. Following a rearguard action at Richland Creek by Edward C. Walthall's troops, "The enemy infantry relinquished the pursuit, and from here on, Wilson's pressure diminished steadily." Chalaron, "Slocomb's Battery in the Army of Tennessee"; Horn, *Army of Tennessee*, 420.

17. Stephenson, *Civil War Memoir*, 344; Chalaron, "Slocomb's Battery in the Army of Tennessee"; Owen, *In Camp and Battle*, 415; Stockdale, *Death of an Army*, 155.

18. They crossed at a point opposite Bainbridge, Alabama, near present-day Muscle Shoals.

19. Hood had suffered a terrible loss of ordnance during the Tennessee campaign, losing 59 of 124 guns. Daniel, *Cannoneers in Gray*, 180.

brought it within range of their guns. Thus the Army of Tennessee and John Bell Hood by the narrowest of margins "had avoided a fatal coup de grâce."[20]

Forty-five men began the march from the Tennessee River bridgehead to Tuscumbia, then turned northwest, tramping along the Memphis and Charleston Railroad toward Iuka, Mississippi, where they were told there would be food. Until then "it was literally a race with starvation."[21] They did receive rations ("only a cracker to each man," according to Stephenson) at Cherokee Station before they reached Iuka, and this seemed to have sufficed, enabling them to march on to Burnsville, Mississippi, about ten miles past Iuka. There they left the Memphis and Charleston, marching southwest to Rienzi, Mississippi, on the Mobile and Ohio Railroad, about twenty miles south of Corinth. It was on their arrival at Rienzi, or perhaps a day or two before, that the Fifth Company first heard the rumor that all batteries that had lost their guns were to assemble at Columbus, Mississippi, where they were to be re-equipped. They were to march to Columbus (about one hundred miles south) beside the railroad. The men of the Washington Artillery, however, were broken down. After marching part of the way to Tupelo, Chalaron went to corps commander Frank Cheatham.[22] He told the general that his battery was unable "to march a step further, as forty-five of them were bare-footed." He requested that they be permitted to take the train. The general sent a staff officer to inspect. He confirmed Chalaron's statement, and Cheatham allowed forty-three of the company to take the cars. "With the others," wrote Chalaron, "I marched to Columbus."[23]

The infantry of the Army of Tennessee halted and encamped at Tupelo between January 7 and 12, 1865, with Cheatham's corps being the last to arrive. There the Fifth Company would bid farewell to this army with

20. For a complete account, objectively and eloquently presented, of the retreat of Hood's army from Nashville to the crossing at Bainbridge, see Sword, *Embrace an Angry Wind,* 385–421. Chalaron, "Slocomb's Battery in the Army of Tennessee"; 5WA Itinerary, WA Papers, HTT.

21. Stephenson, *Civil War Memoir,* 344–45; Chalaron, "Washington Artillery in the Army of Tennessee," 221.

22. Chalaron's account ("Slocomb's Battery in the Army of Tennessee") gives the location of this incident with Cheatham at Corinth. It seems more likely that it would have occurred at Rienzi, probably the point where the stretch of serviceable track began, or at Tupelo itself.

23. Chalaron's itinerary shows that he marched cross-country after reaching Rienzi, forty-five miles southeast to Fulton, Mississippi, then southeast again seventy-five miles to Columbus, apparently bypassing Tupelo. Stephenson, *Civil War Memoir,* 348; Casey, *Outline of Civil War Campaigns,* 85; Chalaron, "Slocomb's Battery in the Army of Tennessee"; 5WA Itinerary, WA Papers, HTT.

which it had served two and one-half years. The company, with most of the army's artillerists, continued on toward Columbus, sixty miles south. For those who rode the train it proved a harrowing experience. They were placed on open flat cars. "We almost perished again!" remembered Stephenson. "Many had frozen feet and hands. Several men rolled off the cars in the night and were frozen to death (some of them Yankee prisoners)."[24]

The Washington Artillery "had hoped for winter quarters at Columbus, but that was not to be. We remained in our little fly tents, at the open end as big a fire as we could get wood to make, the back and sides banked and closed with earth." Not that they were entirely forgotten. The women of Eutaw, Alabama, some fifty miles southeast of Columbus, held a concert for the benefit of the Fifth Company and Abe Leverich, who appears to have been in attendance, returned to his comrades armed with a most welcome letter on pink stationery. In delicate script a woman of Eutaw wrote Cuthbert Slocomb, telling him that the concert had been a great success, the proceeds being $340 and twenty-nine pairs of socks.[25]

The Fifth Company remained in Columbus throughout January. Then it was decided that they would go to Mobile, where their new commander, Maj. Gen. Dabney H. Maury, was to assign "the light artillerists from the Army of Tennessee on duty as infantry." He assured "both officers and men that such assignment is only temporary, and they will be returned to the proper arm of the service as soon as guns can be obtained for them." They left Columbus for Mobile during the first week of February, 1865. Again they traveled by flat car, again they traveled in rain and sleet. Twenty-four hours it took them—"seventy-five men per car—no platform rails, no seats. 'Twas barely standing room," Chalaron remembered, "and from that train many an exhausted soldier dropped upon the track that night."[26]

At last they reached Mobile. Their long trek from Nashville had ended. Surely happier times awaited them.

---

24. Horn, *Army of Tennessee*, 421; Stockdale, *Death of an Army*, 170; Sword, *Embrace an Angry Wind*, 425; Stephenson, *Civil War Memoir*, 352.

25. Stephenson, *Civil War Memoir*, 353; S. Morgan to CHS, February 15, 1865, WA Papers, HTT.

26. Daniel, *Cannoneers in Gray*, 182–83; *OR*, Vol. XLIX, Pt. 1, pp. 1047, 953; New Orleans *Times-Democrat*, May 29, 1883.

18

ANXIOUS TO DO AND TO DARE

ITH HOOD'S army smashed and driven from Tennessee, rich operational opportunities lay open for the Federals in the Deep South. By the middle of March, 1865, they pressed overwhelming cavalry forces into central Alabama, seeking to destroy the Confederates' vital depots and ordnance works at Selma. All the while, one of the North's ablest generals, Edward R. S. Canby, commander of a gigantic department extending from Missouri to Louisiana, and from Texas to Florida, set about collecting sufficient forces to lay siege to Mobile. On March 20, assisted by twenty ships and leading an army of about twenty-six thousand men, Canby began active operations against Mobile and its defenses.[1]

Lt. Gen. Richard Taylor, commanding the Confederate Department of Alabama, Mississippi, and East Louisiana, struggled to counter these iron combinations of the enemy. To resist Canby's attack against Mobile, Taylor relied on Maj. Gen. Dabney H. Maury, a good soldier and a realist.[2]

---

1. T. Michael Parrish, *Richard Taylor: Soldier Prince of Dixie* (Chapel Hill, 1992), 406, 430–36; Arthur W. Bergeron, Jr., *Confederate Mobile* (Jackson, Miss., 1991), 167–74.

2. Phil Stephenson recalled that the men called Maury "Puss in Boots" because "half of his diminutive person seemed lost in the huge cavalry boots he wore and which were the vogue." Stephenson, *Civil War Memoir,* 358–59.

Thoroughly familiar with the natural strengths and weaknesses of his position, Maury knew effective defense required more than sturdy yet passive fortifications. He needed more troops, especially veteran soldiers, as many as Taylor could provide.

Taylor did his best. To assist Maury he had dispatched in February three brigades from the Army of Tennessee, including Randall Gibson's Louisiana brigade. In addition, he ordered artillerists at Columbus, all of those belonging to batteries without guns, to Mobile. Although Taylor had intended these men to be used as infantry, Maury wanted them to man his heavy guns already positioned in prepared works on both sides of Mobile Bay. In the meantime, however, batteries such as the Washington Artillery were issued muskets and began learning infantry drill. With these additional troops Taylor had provided from the Army of Tennessee, Maury's force at Mobile totaled about nine thousand.[3]

Nothing to it, thought Phil Stephenson. "We caught on to the infantry drill in no time." And, as winter closed, it was as infantry that they paraded through the streets of Mobile. "In that review we gained applause from the citizens lining the streets," remembered Stephenson, "for the straightness of our 'front' as we swept by in double platoons. 'There goes the 5th Co. W.A.,' came whispers from the pavement, and out of the corners of our eyes we could see the smiling ladies."[4]

Not long after they arrived in Mobile, word reached the Fifth Company that Joseph E. Johnston once again had been assigned to command the Army of Tennessee. An excited Cuthbert Slocomb, representing the wishes of the Washington Artillery, and after having formally consulted them, made an eloquent appeal directly to Johnston himself:

The announcement of your reinstatement to command in the field, has filled us with new hope, & stimulated our desire to serve again under you. We therefore pray, that you will use your influence to have the 5th Company Washington Artillery fitted up as a Light Battery and ordered to report to you. We are at present manning heavy Guns at this place, an occupation very contrary to our wishes, and to the active life we have always led on the front since entering the service. Our spirits are chafed at lying here idle whilst the Army we have fought with from Shiloh to Nashville, is encountering new dangers & facing its old foe.

If in the course of three years hard & incessant service, we have deserved well of the Confederacy, let our reward be a prominent position in the front of Battle in the coming struggle. Strong in our faith of ultimate success, and anxious to do

---

3. Liddell, *Liddell's Record,* 194–95; Bergeron, *Confederate Mobile,* 168–69.
4. Stephenson, *Civil War Memoir,* 358.

and to dare everything for its accomplishment, a compliance with our request, though it may not add to the respect, affection and devotion we entertain for our own General, will ever be remembered by us with pleasure & thankfulness.[5]

This impassioned request, however, fell victim to the perils of the 1865 Confederate mail service and never reached Johnston. When a copy of the letter was furnished him after the war, Johnston remarked, "Nothing that I have read in the last 10 years has touched my heart like the copy of that application."[6]

Mobile offered an easygoing existence initially, at least until March 20, although the Fifth Company as infantry-artillery did serve "double duty handling siege guns and muskets." Passes to town were liberally provided by Chalaron, Leverich, and Johnsen, and the men were quick to savor the delights of the city. There coffeehouses and "iron-clad" pies and the theater, indeed, simply the sanity of civilian life, offered diversion and hope immeasurable. The men would crowd into the theater, tossing aside concerns about the five-dollar admission charge as if they were millionaires. They would boo and hiss the rickety heroes and cheer mightily the heavily rouged heroines. They endured gladly five acts of *Richelieu or the Conspiracy* and sighed like the schoolboys they were while viewing *Faint Heart Never Won Fair Lady.* Sometimes they would be entertained by the local band in the city park; sometimes, when they wanted quiet and thoughtful solitude, they would take the "shell road" and walk along Mobile Bay for miles, imagining Federal warships anchored near the "lower" bay and wondering "when they were coming."[7]

It was also good to be back with the Louisiana brigade. Once again full of defiant "Try Us" spirit, the Fifth Company vowed to capture the first Yankee field battery they met, so "that the Washington Artillery may be refitted."[8] In the meantime the company (Chalaron commanding) would serve as one of the three batteries in Cobb's artillery battalion (Cuthbert Slocomb commanding). With them were their old friends from Capt. J. W. Phillips' Tennessee battery. Replacing Beauregard's South Carolinians (who had gone east at the request of Beauregard's father) were

---

5. CHS to J. E. Johnston, March 4, 1865, 5WA Order Book, WA Papers, HTT.

6. Slocomb's plea was endorsed by Chalaron, Leverich, and Johnsen for the company. New Orleans *Times-Democrat,* May 29, 1883.

7. Stephenson, *Civil War Memoir,* 357–58; William C. Brown Diary, February, 1865, Chattanooga-Hamilton County Bicentennial Library, Chattanooga.

8. JAC, 1882 speech, quoted in Owen, *In Camp and Battle,* 415.

an interesting mix of Georgians and Marylanders commanded by Capt. William L. Ritter. Ritter's battery, however, was a veteran Army of Tennessee outfit and quite capable.[9]

Maj. Robert Cobb had been absent since October, 1864, and would not return to command his battalion. Yet Slocomb was never promoted to Cobb's position and the battalion was never called Slocomb's Battalion, even in Maury's table of organization of March 10, 1865. Slocomb, nevertheless, commanded the battalion from December, 1864, until the fall of Spanish Fort the following April, giving credence, one would suppose, to Washington Artillery legend that Slocomb consistently refused all opportunities for advancement. The captain saw his primary responsibility throughout the war as the welfare and proper conduct of the Fifth Company.

On March 20, 1865, in response to an urgent request from Brig. Gen. St. John R. Liddell, second in command at Mobile, General Maury sent "his entire infantry force across the bay" to Spanish Fort and put them at Liddell's disposal. When Liddell boldly ventured forth to attack the far stronger Canby, the Federal commander continued to maneuver, veering off to the north and threatening Fort Blakely, the seizure of which would interpose a heavy Union force between Spanish Fort and Mobile. This was intolerable, of course. To preempt that threat, Liddell immediately occupied the Blakely defenses himself with the bulk of his infantry, leaving Randall Gibson with the remainder to defend Spanish Fort, Mobile's other earthen strongpoint on the eastern shore of the "upper" bay. Gibson's command would consist of his own Louisiana brigade (commanded by Lt. Col. Robert H. Lindsay), Bryan M. Thomas' brigade (Alabama militia), and 360 artillerymen, in all some 1,800 effectives.[10]

The only approach by water to Mobile "was a narrow and tortuous channel marked out by stakes" that ran past Spanish Fort, then by Blakely. "All the rest of the bay, where deep water was," according to Stephenson, "was filled with torpedoes, and a variety of obstructions." Spanish Fort itself was a string of redoubts on sand bluffs overlooking the bay. These

---

9. Ritter's battery represented the residue of the Third Maryland Artillery Company, at one time a ship's detachment that had been captured at Vicksburg and, following their exchange, consolidated with Stephens' Georgia battery. Names usually associated with these two batteries are Capt. Henry B. Latrobe and Capt. John B. Rowan. *OR*, Vol. XLIX, Pt. 1, p. 1047.

10. Bergeron, *Confederate Mobile*, 175; *OR*, XLXI, Pt. 1, pp. 1046–47; Liddell, *Liddell's Record*, 194; Casey, *Outline of Civil War Campaigns*, 86.

badly eroded fortifications had been built by the Spanish in the eighteenth century. On the site of this old fort Maury built three earth redoubts, one on each end and one in the center, connected to each other by rifle pits. Their purpose, facing inland rather than out over the Mobile Bay, was to protect Spanish Fort against land attack. Water batteries would take care of any Yankee ships that might try to force their way up the narrow channel.

Spanish Fort was formidable. Its left rested on a great marsh, believed to be impassable, and its right on the Apalachee River. Within the three redoubts Maury had placed thirty cannon, and he had mined the land approaches with "sub-terra shells." The position was vulnerable, however. The thirty-five hundred yards of works were thinly manned while the redoubts themselves provided little if any mutual fire support.[11]

The Fifth Company, ninety strong, came over to Spanish Fort on March 24 and became the garrison for the center redoubt, which they immediately dubbed Fort Blair in honor of their beloved lieutenant lost at Glass's Mill. In all they had eight pieces of ordnance. Their big gun was an eight-inch Columbiad that they named "Lady Slocomb." Their other guns, two Napoleons and one three-inch rifle, they called "Lady Vaught," "Cora Slocomb" (for the captain's infant daughter), and "General Gibson."[12] Two of their four Coehorn mortars bore the less exalted names of "Theresa" and "Louise" in remembrance of the peanut- and apple-vending girls at the coffeehouse in Mobile. Fort Blair faced the interior or marshlands. "Before us," remembered Phil Stephenson, "arose gloomy woods like a wall, distant some thousand yards or so. The intervening space had been cleared off by our men. Already our pickets were thrown far into those dark woods."[13]

Randall Gibson demanded hard work from the garrison of Spanish Fort. He had them thicken and deepen the redoubts, improve the rifle

11. Stephenson, *Civil War Memoir,* 358–59; Dabney H. Maury, "Defense of Spanish Fort," *SHSP,* XXXIX (1914), 135; *OR,* XLIX, Pt. 1, p. 314; Casey, *Outline of Civil War Campaigns,* 86–87. For a detailed description of the defenses of Spanish Fort, see George S. Waterman, "Afloat—Afield—Afloat," *CV,* VIII (1900), 53–54.

12. After World War I, Cora Slocomb, then the Countess de Brazzia of Italy, and her husband, an officer in the Italian army, were entertained at Jackson Barracks by the Battalion Washington Artillery.

13. Phil Stephenson called the Coehorn mortar "Terrance" (or "Peanuts") rather than "Theresa." J. W. Patton to CHS, March 24, 1865, WA Papers, HTT; unidentified newspaper clipping, WA Papers, HTT; Stephenson, *Civil War Memoir,* 359.

pits, and construct bombproofs away from the guns to be used as "magazines, temporary hospital, and living quarters." [14] The Federals tightened their lines around Spanish Fort on March 27. Gibson slowed them with a counterattack, but the Yankees were too powerful and by that evening had "completed the investment." In the process, however, "Slocomb knocked one of the enemy's batteries all to pieces," Gibson reported. "We are all in good spirits, and confident." Enemy assaults at sunset on the twenty-seventh were also repulsed handily, with Thomas' inexperienced Alabama reserves performing "handsomely." [15]

Gibson was no fool. He realized the odds. He sent off his horses and wagons the night of the twenty-seventh and requested additional ammunition and entrenching tools. During the following days the Yankees emplaced their field batteries and closed their siege lines from one thousand to three hundred yards—perfect sharpshooter range and an easy distance over which to mount an infantry rush. The determined enemy, complained Phil Stephenson, "devoted their especial attention to our embrasures and poured a steady stream of bullets through them from early morn till dewy eve. Mining and counter-mining began." To defend themselves, the company resorted to closing the embrasures with sheets of iron "an inch or so thick and about 3 feet square. These screens (wood as well as iron) were sufficient to resist the sharpshooters' bullets." Soon they became "speckled all over with the white splotches" from minié balls. "When the guns were ready to run out, the 'curtain' was withdrawn from an aperture to let our cannon speak." [16]

Eventually even this game of death became boring. Henry Férand, "for diversion," stuck his red kepi just over the shield and looked back at his batterymates grinning. A ricocheting round, however, wiped the grin off the face of this veteran who had been wounded previously at Glass's Mill and should have known better. The bullet struck him in the hip "and gave him a furlough which lasted to the end of the war." Phil Stephenson would

14. "We cut down great trees," reported Stephenson, "rolled the trunks over the mouth, then put a layer of brush and dirt, then came another layer of heavy logs crosswise, then a layer of brush and dirt, until the roof was six to eight feet thick." Stephenson, *Civil War Memoir,* 360.

15. Bergeron, *Confederate Mobile,* 175–76; Stephenson, *Civil War Memoir,* 360; *OR,* Vol. XLIX, Pt. 2, pp. 1161, 1163.

16. Bergeron, *Confederate Mobile,* 176; Stephenson, *Civil War Memoir,* 360; Waterman, "Afloat—Afield—Afloat," 53; Maury, "Defense of Spanish Fort," 135; *OR,* Vol. XLIX, Pt. 2, pp. 200–201; Mobile *Register,* March 19, 1891.

see Férand in June—he was "still on crutches, and his face was pale and worn with suffering, and he had a hard time getting along." [17]

The diabolical sharpshooter fire took a higher and higher toll as the Yankees pressed through the line of rifle pits and up closer against Fort Blair itself. It reminded the members of June, 1864, except that here at Spanish Fort the sharpshooter fire was more severe. One of the Yankee rounds inflicted a freakish double wound, cutting its way through the cheek of Abe Leverich (an injury that would bother him the rest of his life) and then continuing on and lodging deep in Cpl. James F. Giffen's shoulder. It was Leverich's second wound, Giffen's third. The company officers saw them fall. Out rushed Slocomb, Chalaron, Johnsen, and Billy Vaught, who had recently rejoined the battery. [18] They helped Leverich and Giffen into Slocomb's tent, then moved them to a nearby bombproof. Soon after reaching this haven, however, they saw a Yankee "fuse shell" land at the doorway and roll inside. "Not a syllable was uttered." The officers flattened themselves against the earth walls and hid in corners while Orderly Sgt. John Bartley reached down and grabbed the spinning, hissing, "unwelcome visitor" and tossed it out. [19]

"Artillery duels became a daily occurrence, our 'head logs' were constantly knocked down, bruising and crippling us." [20] During one of these duels on March 29, there was a direct hit on Charlie Fox's gun. Metal chunks and slivers tore into the quiet Marylander Ned McIlhenny, killing him. McIlhenny had just received a "long-expected letter from his widowed mother" and, in celebration, had stepped up to the parapet with his musket to take a shot "at the nearest foe." Stephenson recalled that he "got a glimpse of his face as he fell, a face of agony. Alas, no time for thought, sorrow or sympathy. Time only to move his body out of the way so that the gun could be worked." [21]

Canby's Yankees labored furiously. The first days of April saw them

---

17. Gibson reported that "the works from Redoubt 3 [Fort Blair] were placed so far back on the retreating slope that the infantry could only command its crest, but not the ravine beyond." *OR,* XLIX, Pt. 2. p. 314; Stephenson, *Civil War Memoir,* 362–63.

18. It is not known when Vaught rejoined the battery—probably when they came to Mobile—but it is doubtful that he saw any active duty because of his deafness. Chalaron was clearly second in command at Spanish Fort and until the surrender. Waterman, "Afloat—Afield—Afloat," 22.

19. *Ibid.,* 24.

20. Philip D. Stephenson, "Defense of Spanish Fort," Philadelphia *Weekly Times,* July 26, 1894.

21. New Orleans *Daily Picayune,* September 20, 1899; Stephenson, *Civil War Memoir,* 363.

bringing up more guns and shifting their lines closer and closer. Zigzag approach trenches ran everywhere, it seemed. Fort Blair was pounded. "For the first ten days my artillery, aided by well-trained sharpshooters, was able to cope with that of the enemy," Gibson stated, "sometimes silencing his guns, and often broke up his working parties in handsome style." The eight-inch Columbiad Lady Slocomb alone fired 144 shell, 18 solid shot, 13 grape, and 6 canister during the ten-day siege and, according to Chalaron, beat back or checked the Federal rush on March 27.[22] The Lady Slocomb, of course, became "from the start a target for an incessant and pitiless fire" from sharpshooters and artillery.[23]

As the days wore on, however, Canby's strength and determination told. "I never saw such digging as the enemy does," Gibson reported to Maury. "He is fast converting his advanced skirmish line into his main line." Meanwhile the Federal fleet "kept up a well-directed and heavy fire in our rear and mortars dropped over the whole surface." These mortar shells were "huge fifteen-inch bombs, so large that we could see them with the naked eye shortly after leaving the mortar's mouth," remembered Stephenson, "see them as they arose up into the air, describe a graceful curve and then begin hurrying with vicious impetus down full upon us."[24]

The Washington Artillery fought back in any and every way it could devise. Charlie Fox, one of the finest of the Napoleon gunners, also became expert in handling the Coehorn mortars, "little fellows about 15 inches long, but throwing almost a 12 pound shell."[25] One day while firing "Louise," Fox "kicked higher than a kite a poor fellow in one of the Yankee pickets pits." When Fox shot at the pickets, the men made sure to watch, expecting "coats, hats, etc., to rise into the air after the explosion."[26]

The enemy endured these antics of the Fifth Company. They knew their day was coming, and soon. A Yankee picket called out, "Say, Reb, your mortars have injured us a little, but tomorrow we are going to shell you. . . . Then you will tell me how you like ours." Sure enough, on April

22. Ordnance report, March–April, 1865, WA Papers, HTT.

23. New Orleans *Daily Picayune,* September 20, 1899.

24. *OR,* Vol. XLIX, Pt. 2, p. 1194, Pt. 1, p. 315; Stephenson, *Civil War Memoir,* 363.

25. Maury had about forty of these small mortars cast in Mobile. He also had some wooden mortars made of gum stumps, hollowed out to eight-inch and ten-inch calibre, "then hooped with iron and lined with sheet iron," intending them to be used with light charges and at short range against the enemy rifle pits. Maury, "Defense of Spanish Fort," 135.

26. Waterman, "Afloat—Afield—Afloat," 54; Stephenson, *Civil War Memoir,* 360–61.

4, the Federals retaliated, unleashing their heaviest bombardment yet. It began at 5:30 P.M. and lasted two hours. Even the citizens of Mobile could hear the terrible firing, "not a moment elapsing between the booming of 'heavy artillery.'" It seemed as though Fort Blair was their special target.[27] According to Chalaron, a round from a twenty-pound Parrott rifle, probably fired by the Black Horse Battery, 18th New York Artillery, struck the Lady Slocomb on the right trunnion. Almost simultaneously another shell from the position of Battery L, 1st Indiana Artillery, hit, "passing under the gun, between the cheeks of the carriage, and shattered the elevating screw. The gun was thus doubly disabled." The gun crew wedged the gun in place, however, "menacingly deceiving the enemy as to its condition." Under cover of darkness, Chalaron ordered the gun dismounted and thrown down the bluff along with its shattered carriage.[28] On the night of April 6, with the help of one-hundred infantry tugging at ropes, another carriage and Columbiad would be dragged up to the redoubt to replace the Lady Slocomb.[29]

The April 4 "firing was so rapid," Gibson reported to Maury, "we could not estimate accurately the number of guns. Colonel Patton, Captain Slocomb, and myself estimate [the enemy's] guns at about thirty and his mortars at twelve."[30] Despite the growing power of the Federals, Gibson remained confident, defiant. "The enemy's batteries are very heavy, but they can never take this place with them. All's well."[31]

The fearful pounding taken by Fort Blair prompted Dabney Maury to

27. Arroyo Journal, LHA Collection, HTT; Bergeron, *Confederate Mobile*, 178; *OR*, Vol. XLIX, Pt. 2, p. 1199.

28. Long after the war the Lady Slocomb would be rescued by Chalaron and others and returned to New Orleans. There on September 19, 1899, it was dedicated as a monument to Cuthbert H. Slocomb and the "men who gave their lives for its defense." Chalaron, the spirit behind its reclamation, provided the dedicatory address. Powell Casey mused in more recent times, "On each business day thousands of New Orleanians drive down Camp Street past the Confederate Memorial Hall with never a glance at the building or at the 8-inch Columbiad cannon resting on the small lawn." Evans, *Confederate Military History*, XIII, 158; Casey, *Outline of Civil War Campaigns*, 87.

29. New Orleans *Daily Picayune*, October 1, 1883, September 20, 1899; Casey, *Outline of Civil War Campaigns*, 88.

30. Col. Isaac W. Patton, 22nd Louisiana Infantry, commanded the regiment instrumental in the defense of Mobile for the previous year. Patton's men became heavy artillerists and helped garrison not only Spanish Fort but the Huger and Tracy batteries. See Arthur W. Bergeron, Jr., "The Twenty-Second Louisiana Consolidated Infantry in the Defense of Mobile, 1864–1865," *Alabama Historical Quarterly*, XXXVIII (1976), 204–13.

31. *OR*, Vol. XLIX, Pt. 2, p. 1199.

pay them a visit. He proposed to Slocomb that the Fifth Company be relieved by a fresh battery. "I told him they had been overworked and needed rest," said Maury, "and other companies not yet engaged stood ready to take their place." Slocomb asked Maury if he might "submit the question" to the men. When he returned, he said, "General, the company, grateful for your kind intention, desire to hold this position to the end. We respectfully decline to be relieved." The Washington Artillery impressed Maury. Even among the veteran companies in Spanish Fort— Lumsden's, Barry's Lookout battery, Phillips', Fenner's, the Eufaula battery, and others—"the flower of our Western army"—the Fifth Company "was conspicuous for fine conduct even in this fine command. . . . They had been holding the most advanced and exposed redoubt for more than a week of incessant action, fighting by day, fighting and working by night." [32]

Slocomb's battery stayed. The enemy moved in even closer. With their masses, Spanish Fort was vulnerable to the sudden charge. Randall Gibson, of course, was aware of the peril. He stated to Maury that "my men are wider apart than they ever were under Johnston or Hood. My works not so strong as they ordinarily were and the enemy in larger force, more active, and closer." "I found by the 8th of April," reported Gibson, "that all my artillery was about silenced; that the enemy had greatly increased his; that his working parties greatly re-enforced at every point and carefully protected against sorties, were pushing forward at a rate that would bring them up to our main works." It became apparent that he "could no longer hold the position without imminent risk of losing the garrison." Spanish Fort was rapidly becoming a death trap, casualties were mounting fearfully. [33]

Just before nightfall on April 8, Canby unleashed a tremendous bombardment, employing all fifty-three of his siege guns. To attempt to respond meant instant death. The Confederates in Spanish Fort ducked, then hid in their bombproofs, then fled outside the works, "scattered in the open space behind them." Phil Stephenson remembered "the unbroken roaring of artillery, the yelling, shrieking and exploding of the shells, the bellowing boom of the mortars, the dense shroud of sulphurous smoke

32. Maury, "Defense of Spanish Fort," 131–32.
33. *OR*, Vol. XLIX, Pt. 1, p. 316, Pt. 2, pp. 1191, 1204; Scott Diary, April 6, 1865, Chattanooga-Hamilton County Bicentennial Library.

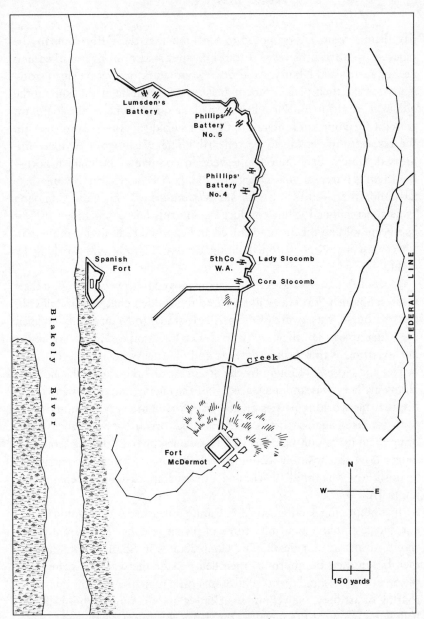

Spanish Fort, March, 1865
Adapted from J. A. Chalaron drawing
Map by Blake A. Magner

thickening around us." Armageddon had come: "The uproar of the damned was about us. Men hopped about, raving, blood bursting from ears and nostrils, driven stark crazy by concussion."[34]

The Yankees "did all this to get us in a 'proper frame of mind' for their assault." When the blue infantry came against Fort Blair, however, they were beaten back handily, "evidently a feint." The main attack came on the Confederate left. The Yankees drove up to the fort, beating back Gibson's feeble counterattacks easily, then broke into the works, capturing the Lookout battery, several hundred yards of trenches, and hundreds of Confederates.[35]

Fortunately for the remaining defenders of Spanish Fort, after the Yankees had overwhelmed the left end of their line, they stopped and entrenched. Could they not see that the works in several places had been leveled, the guns silenced? "Why they did not come right on and take us too we could never understand." Gibson realized that this breakthrough, if exploited, "would have enabled [the enemy] to cut off our retreat." No alternative existed but to abandon Spanish Fort immediately.[36]

As they prepared to leave Fort Blair the company flag was committed for safekeeping to Orderly Sgt. John Bartley. He sewed it carefully and tightly around his body. Meanwhile the men spiked their guns and disabled the carriages. All was accomplished by 9 P.M. About 10 P.M. the Fifth Company abandoned the redoubt, leaving just before the rear guard (Colonel Lindsay and the 16th-25th Louisiana).[37] When they received the order to evacuate, the cannoneers jumped over their works and ran to-

34. Bergeron, *Confederate Mobile*, 180–81; William L. Cameron, "The Battles Opposite Mobile," *CV*, XXIII (1915), 305; Brown Diary, April 8, 1865, Chattanooga-Hamilton County Bicentennial Library; Stephenson, *Civil War Memoir*, 364; Edgar Jones, "History of the 18th Alabama Infantry," Alabama Department of Archives, Montgomery.

35. One of the first Confederate counterattacks was conducted by the Fifth Company's old friends, the 14th Texas Cavalry (Dismounted), Ector's brigade. They had come over to Spanish Fort to replace Bryan Thomas's green reserves. During the first week in April they provided sharpshooter defense for the battery much in the manner of Ned Austin's battalion. In 1899, when the Lady Slocomb was brought to New Orleans, the Texans graciously shared in the event, providing funds to purchase the granite base. JAC to Members of WA Camp #15, UCV, n.d., Chalaron Papers, HTT. Brown Diary, April 8, 1865, Chattanooga-Hamilton County Bicentennial Library; Bergeron, *Confederate Mobile*, 181.

36. Bergeron, *Confederate Mobile*, 181; Stephenson, *Civil War Memoir*, 365; *OR*, Vol. XLIX, Pt. 1, p. 316; Maury, "Defense of Spanish Fort," 134–35.

37. 5WA Master Roster, WA Papers, HTT; *SHSP*, XI (1883), 329; *CV*, XV (1907), 468; Casey, *Outline of Civil War Campaigns*, 90; New Orleans *Daily Picayune*, September 20, 1899.

ward the beach (the rear of Spanish Fort) and reached the edge of the marsh. "And there, to our amazement, we found the beginning of a treadway."[38] It was eighteen-inches wide, "three or four feet above the marsh and one mile long." "We passed so close to the enemy's pickets stationed in the marsh," Phil Stephenson remembered, "that we could hear them talking, and right under the nose of their battery." The men took off their shoes, turned under or tossed away any articles that might glitter or clang, and carried their muskets low, on the side away from the Federals.

The narrow little walkway ended on the Apalachee River, where steamers waited to ferry them across to Battery Huger. The Fifth Company lowered themselves from the flimsy bridge and waded waist deep in water and muck to reach the boats, which they boarded along with Gibson's infantry. First they sailed to Battery Huger, then on to Blakely. On the beach at Fort Blakely many of them waited, perhaps an hour, while their superiors debated their fate—would they remain and help defend Blakely or continue on to Mobile? Fortunately for the Washington Artillery it was determined that they should re-embark and sail on to Mobile. Less than twenty-four hours later Blakely would be overrun in a massive simultaneous assault by four Union divisions, a disaster bitterly coincident with Lee's surrender at Appomattox.[39]

The stand at Spanish Fort had proved costly to the Washington Artillery. McIlhenny and the Pennsylvania-born carpenter Benjamin R. Miller had been killed. Eleven had been wounded, including Chalaron himself, the former drayman and company driver John R. Abbott, the German bookbinder William C. B. Matthews, driver Thomas Kehough, Edward S. Turpin, the New York–born artificer F. M. Thompson, Alphonse Rost, and James R. Dailey. Several of the wounded would be captured either at Fort Blair or in the following days at hospitals in Mobile. The wounded and captured would include Abe Leverich.[40]

The Fifth Company flag, however, was safe. Bartley protected it

38. This footbridge had been built at Maury's direction before Spanish Fort was attacked.

39. General Liddell had given Gibson as much help as possible to facilitate the dangerous evacuation of Spanish Fort. A few years later Liddell would think back and contend angrily that he could have held Blakely if he could have retained the Spanish Fort garrison. This seems farfetched. *OR,* Vol. XLIX, Pt. 1, p. 316, Pt. 2, pp. 1217–19; Arroyo Journal, WA Papers, HTT; Bergeron, *Confederate Mobile,* 181, 184–87; Maury, "Defense of Spanish Fort," 131; Stephenson, *Civil War Memoir,* 366–68; New Orleans *Daily Picayune,* September 20, 1899; Liddell, *Liddell's Record,* 195–96.

40. 5WA Master Roster, WA Papers, HTT; New Orleans *Daily Picayune,* September 20, 1899.

throughout the harrowing evacuation and carried it back to New Orleans. There he turned it over to Slocomb, who preserved it until his death. It passed to his widow Abby, who in turn presented it to Confederate Memorial Hall.[41]

In Mobile the day following the fall of Spanish Fort, the day Blakely braced for the coming onslaught, the Fifth Company was refitted as a light battery. General Maury provided the men with two three-inch rifles and two twelve-pounder Napoleons and assigned them to Maj. Henry C. Semple's battalion. They were to report to Semple at Camp Beulah, where they would receive horses, harness, and all the required artillery accoutrements.[42] When Blakely was overrun on the ninth, General Maury knew there was no longer hope of defending Mobile. He began evacuating the city on April 10 and left the morning of the twelfth, marching north with 4,500 men, including Semple's three batteries.[43] A regiment of Canby's troops occupied the city that afternoon without meeting any resistance.[44]

The Washington Artillery, as part of Maury's column, marched north from Mobile thirty-seven miles to Citronelle, Alabama, following the line of the Mobile and Ohio Railroad. The Federals showed no inclination to pursue, so Maury's command "sauntered on from day to day in the balmy spring air" to Meridian, Mississippi. There they left the railroad and marched on in leisurely fashion to Cuba Station, Alabama, about twenty-five miles east of Meridian. It was common knowledge that negotiations for surrender were being conducted between Taylor and Canby. In recognition of the inevitable, they named this bivouac at Cuba Station, their final encampment, "Camp Farewell."

It was during this time, on the march north and the sojourn at Cuba Station, that the company received a high compliment from the cranky

41. 5WA Master Roster, WA Papers, HTT; *SHSP,* XI (1883), 329; *CV,* XV (1907), 468; Casey, *Outline of Civil War Campaigns,* 90.

42. Camp Beulah was located about four miles from Mobile on the Spring Hill road. It was established in July, 1862, by the 18th Alabama Infantry when that unit was dropped off at Mobile as Bragg's army passed through en route to Chattanooga. A. W. Bergeron, Jr., to author, August 1, 1995. *OR,* Vol. XLIX, Pt. 2, p. 1223; J. A. Brown to CHS, April 9, 1865, 5WA Order Book, WA Papers, HTT; Owen, *Outline of Civil War Campaigns,* 416.

43. Semple's battalion consisted of the "3rd Missouri Artillery" (probably the Jackson Light Artillery–Saint Louis Light Artillery consolidated company), Capt. Thomas F. Tobin's Tennessee battery (the old Memphis Light Artillery, which had seen much service in the Trans-Mississippi) and the Fifth Company.

44. Bergeron, *Confederate Mobile,* 189–91.

but well-respected Semple. He wrote Slocomb an unusual, unsolicited note stating that he had always admired the Washington Artillery, "*one of the very best companies*" in the Army of Tennessee. "But it is not the least of its claims to distinction," Semple continued, "that in a season of depression, and of almost universal demoralization, it has steadfastly preserved its discipline, and has been as honorably careful of the property agreed to be surrendered to the U.S. as if it were to be used by them for immediate action."[45]

The men of the Fifth Company remained at Cuba Station until May 6, when they received orders to return to Meridian, marching at 5 A.M. on the seventh. This, the final tramp of the battery and of the soldiers of the Army of Tennessee, would be led by Semple's artillery followed by the infantry. They made the twenty-one-mile march to meet their conquerors and were pleasantly surprised when they were spared a ceremonial surrender. "Everything was perfectly businesslike and humdrum[,] no excitement, no disorder. The Federal troops were kept well in hand, were not allowed to insult us, and they showed no disposition to do so." The Fifth Company turned over their guns, then waited patiently.[46]

On May 10 each member received his parole. The gracious victors then permitted the Washington Artillery to ride the cars on the Mobile and Ohio back to Mobile. There at the depot Chalaron formed them, called the men to attention, and presented the company to General Canby, whom Lieutenant Johnsen overheard say to another officer, "There is the noblest body of men that ever lived." Canby handed a document to Confederate Capt. Will Steven, who had arranged their transportation from Meridian. This was the same Will Steven, private and gunner, who had been too badly wounded at Shiloh to see further field service and who, later in the war, had become a member of General Taylor's staff, then his chief quartermaster. Armed with authority from General Canby, Steven,

---

45. Maury struggled during this time to keep his command together, to give it some semblance of order. Desertion and disorder were rampant. H. C. Semple to CHS, May 7, 1865, 5WA Order Book, WA Papers, HTT; Chalaron, 5WA Itinerary, Chalaron Papers, HTT; *OR*, Vol. XLIX, Pt. 2, p. 1244.

46. The surrendered guns were: Piece 1: three-inch rifle, maker Skates & Co., Mobile, 1862; Piece 2: Napoleon, Macon Arsenal, 1863, No. 34, weight 1,170 lbs.; Piece 3: Napoleon, Columbus Arsenal, 1864, No. 39, weight 1,221 lbs.; Piece 4: Napoleon, Columbus Arsenal, 1864, No. 31, weight 1,220 lbs. 5WA Order Book, WA Papers, HTT. Stephenson, *Civil War Memoir*, 371; Richard Taylor, *Destruction and Reconstruction* (New York, 1879), 222; *OR*, Vol. XLIX, Pt. 2, pp. 1270, 1275, 1286.

who made all the arrangements, joined his comrades as they marched from the depot to the Mobile wharves. There they boarded a steamer provided by the good offices of Canby.[47]

Lt. Charles Johnsen could not bear the agony. Once he had embarked, he went over to the capstan, leaned against it, placed his head against the cold iron, and cried. "An old Quarter Master of the Illinois regiment came up to me and in the kindest vein said, 'My son, what is the matter?' I told him I had nothing to live for, that I wish I had died on a victorious battle field." The old Yankee then told the young Rebel "that our defeat was our victory and I would live to thank God for it. I have lived to see that day." On May 14 the steamer reached New Orleans and tied up at the end of "the New Basin." Eighty-seven officers and men stood in ranks there on the wharf, their eyes on Cuthbert Slocomb, waiting for the captain to release them from their duties and disband them.[48]

Slocomb had brought them home. In his pocket he carried a sheet of Washington Artillery stationery, still crowned with the irate tiger's head and the motto, "Try Us." It bore the signatures of the men facing him. In this statement, which they had prepared at Cuba Landing, they wished to thank him for having declined promotion and military honors "to abide by the fortunes of your old command, to look after their comfort and share their hardships. . . . We shall ever feel proud of you as Captain . . . and never cease to be grateful."[49]

Slocomb dismissed them. The company broke ranks, bid each other good-bye, and sought their different ways through the streets of New Orleans, the city they had left thirty-eight months before—on that pretty afternoon in March when they rolled their bright, shiny six-pounders aboard the train bound for Tennessee.

47. Canby won the gratitude and respect of many Confederates for his kindness and accommodation at the time of surrender. Confederate Personnel Documents, HTT; Liddell, *Liddell's Record,* 197, 199; Chalaron, 5WA Itinerary, Chalaron Papers, HTT.

48. Stephenson, *Civil War Memoir,* 371; 5WA Muster Rolls, April–May, 1865, WA Papers, HTT; C. G. Johnsen to JAC, June 8, 1891, Chalaron Papers, HTT; Casey, *Outline of Civil War Campaigns,* 32, 90; 5WA Master Roster, WA Papers, HTT.

49. Address of officers and men of 5WA to CHS, May 6, 1865, 5WA Order Book, WA Papers, HTT.

EPILOGUE

They would reunite, these members of the Fifth Company, less than a year after the surrender. At a meeting in New Orleans on April 20, 1866, Slocomb, Chalaron, Leverich, Johnsen, and forty-five other members established the Relief Association, Fifth Company, Washington Artillery. This benevolent organization had dues of fifty cents per month, a constitution, and bylaws.[1] Two months later they made the association publicly known by advertising in the New Orleans *Times*. Those who might wish to join were asked to contact Henry V. Ogden, treasurer, at the office of the Crescent Mutual Insurance Company, with which Ogden had become

---

1. The Battalion Washington Artillery would not be reorganized until almost ten years later. Walton was elected colonel, and Chalaron, commander of Company B. In 1877 the battalion purchased four ten-pounder Parrott rifles, two twelve-pounder howitzers, sabers, and muskets. The following year they became part of the Louisiana State National Guard. As members of the National Guard, the Washington Artillery served with distinction in six wars and became the artillery of the 256th Infantry Brigade, Louisiana National Guard, which is a unit within the 5th Infantry Division at Fort Polk, Louisiana. The headquarters as well as the archives of the Washington Artillery are at Jackson Barracks in New Orleans. Battalion Washington Artillery, *Washington Artillery Souvenir* (New Orleans, 1894), 33; Casey, *Outline of Civil War Campaigns*, 89, 31–32; Owen, *In Camp and Battle*, 424.

affiliated as the resident secretary of the Globe Insurance Company of Liverpool and London.[2]

Ogden, "the best soldier," "the Old Gentleman," became highly successful after the war. He was instrumental in raising the funds for and designing the conspicuous Battalion Washington Artillery monument that was erected in Metairie Cemetery. Eventually he moved to Wisconsin, where he would die at eighty-five after completing a study of the cottonseed oil industry of the South.

The captain also prospered, and he and his wife Abby built a magnificent home on Esplanade Avenue. He would die suddenly, however, in 1873 at the age of forty-one, known more by his fellow citizens of New Orleans for his charitable deeds than for his wealth.[3] It is stated in his obituary that while helping rescue the poor who had been driven from their homes by a flood, he contracted the disease that killed him.[4] "One can almost say he has given his life to help the poor and needy."[5] Truly, this modest man's character and life remained consistent to the end, inspiring those about him.[6]

Slocomb certainly inspired Adolphe Chalaron throughout their association, and Slocomb's death prompted Chalaron to contact all the members of the Fifth Company, requesting information for the history of Slocomb's battery that he would attempt to write but never complete. Chalaron remained the central rallying figure for the battery, its spokes-

2. WA Papers, HTT; New Orleans *Times,* June 18, 1866.

3. Slocomb's partner, Albert Baldwin (1834–1912), would become a merchant-prince of the postwar era, a leading banker and involved, it is said, in fifty businesses. Dividing his time between residences and offices in New Orleans and New England, he came to enjoy national prominence.

4. Always enormously popular, Slocomb declined to become a candidate for mayor in March, 1866, but agreed to go as a delegate to the ill-fated 1866 convention of the Democratic Party convened by President Andrew Johnson in Philadelphia.

5. New Orleans *Daily Picayune,* February 1, 1873.

6. Slocomb "left a large estate to his only child, Cora. He named as Cora's guardian his friend and comrade-in-arms, Tom Bayne. During one of my [Charles Bayne] visits to Italy, I spent a couple of days at Brazza, the castle near Udine of Cora Slocum's husband, the Conte di Brazza Savorgnan. A silk United States flag on its staff occupied a corner of the Salon. It was of the size a regiment would carry. Cora told me that one of her school friends from New England had recently visited her, and, remarking on the flag, said: 'Well, well, Cora Slocomb di Brazza, it is certainly a pleasure for a patriot like me to find so conspicuously displayed in the Salon of an Italian Countess, the flag of my country.' Then she added, facetiously: 'It is especially gratifying in view of the fact that the Countess who displays it is the daughter of a former rebel against the United States! And where did you get that flag, Cora?' Said Cora: 'My father captured it at the Battle of Gettysburg.'" C. Bayne, "Tom Bayne Is Wounded."

man, and representative. Although he failed in business and was continually embarrassed by debt, Chalaron would allow nothing to divert him from preserving the memory and traditions of the Washington Artillery. In time he came to have a broader mission. From 1875 until his death in 1909, probably no figure in Louisiana was more important in veterans' affairs. He was a popular speaker at reunions. He established monuments, marked battlefields, and could be counted on as a defender of "the Cause" and the honor of the defenseless. Even after he had aged, one could still see Chalaron, as Phil Stephenson remembered him, throwing back the flap of his tent and charging out, bright faced, ready to do battle. "Peppery" is a marvelous adjective for the man.

The quiet Charles Johnsen worked hard after the war and established his own manufacturing plant, but would eventually fail financially. Abe Leverich, on the other hand, succeeded in business but became depressed after the deaths of his brother and his mother, whom he worshiped. A maid found him late one afternoon in December, 1896, after he had lunched at the Cotton Exchange, seated at the window overlooking a busy street, with a bullet in his head.

Billy Vaught fell over the side of a steamboat and drowned in 1870. W. Irving Hodgson died at the age of sixty-three, well respected and prosperous, a popular New Orleans social and political figure. Dr. Cecil Legaré became a hero in the terrible 1878 yellow fever epidemic, going to Memphis to help out, as did batterymate Dr. Warren Stone, Jr., who "left his home and large practice" to fight the fever in Brunswick, Georgia, traveling "about from one grief stricken village or town to another, giving his service gratuitously."

Gordon Bakewell became a respected Episcopal clergyman in New Orleans. Phil Stephenson settled in Virginia, where he served small Presbyterian churches in that state and in Pennsylvania. When he was fifty, Stephenson would sit in his manse study on Sunday afternoons and fill eight ledger volumes with memories of his boyhood adventures. A number of the company, such as Eugene May and Anthony Sambola, became prominent, contributing figures in their communities. Richard Salter became a New York capitalist, while William Freret built a national reputation as an architect and Thomas Bayne as a lawyer. Some, such as the Allains and Barrows, returned to plantation life, enjoying wealth and privilege.

Bully and Hawkeye Smith drifted back to New Jersey. Tom C. Allen died of pneumonia, less than six months after the surrender, in a room in the St. James Hotel where he served as desk clerk. Some of the men became laborers, some policemen, two barbers. Sam Newman, Jr., an outraged political activist, found himself armed once again, fighting in the anti-Republican riot at Liberty Place, where he was killed September 14, 1874. Some never adapted to civilian life and bounced from job to job, generally ending their lives in poverty. Others killed hope and opportunity with liquor. Some spent their lives in pain. Leverich did. So did Felix Arroyo. In 1873, not long after Slocomb died, Arroyo's old wounds revisited him suddenly. He would endure the next twenty years "a helpless cripple," blind and humiliated, longing for death.

What can be said, then, about this group of men, this company of artillerists and their seminal experience in the Civil War? For one thing, the Fifth Company, Washington Artillery of New Orleans, was a large battery, much larger than the other companies in the battalion, much larger than comparable units in both the Army of Tennessee and the Army of Northern Virginia. One hundred and sixty members of the Fifth Company had left New Orleans for Tennessee, and to that number were added 215 who either joined or were assigned. When the surgeons, the cooks, and those who served but were never enlisted are included, the number rises to 418. If one adds those who appeared on the 1861 rolls but never saw active duty, the total climbs to nearly 500. Of the 418 who served, 50 were killed, died of their wounds, or died of disease; about 100 were wounded; and 36 deserted. The men were in battle or under fire 121 days and 77 nights. They marched 3,285 miles and traveled by rail 2,939 more. They fired 5,906 rounds of ammunition and had 143 battery horses killed.[7]

What else should be said of these men who fired so many rounds and marched so many miles? First Lt. John H. Bingham, of Douglas' Texas battery, a respected battery of the Army of Tennessee, wrote, "Slocomb's Fifth Company, Washington Artillery, of New Orleans, was well known by the whole army, and was, in fact, the pride of the artillery corps."[8] Bragg thought well of them. So did Johnson and Hardee. They were recognized as a cohesive, well-disciplined organization that fought boldly and tenaciously. They were conspicuous at Shiloh and performed well at

7. Chalaron, 5WA Rosters, Chalaron Papers, HTT; 5WA Order Book, WA Papers, HTT; Owen, *In Camp and Battle,* 424; Casey, *Outline of Civil War Campaigns,* 32, 89.

8. *CV,* V (1897), 306.

Perryville, where they enjoyed clear fields of fire. Although without Slocomb and fragmented into sections, they fought in commendable fashion at Murfreesboro. They had a turkey-shoot at Jackson and at Chickamauga attempted to stand down a mass of Federal artillery.

Following the death of battalion commander Rice Graves and the advent of William Brimage Bate, however, the members of the Fifth Company repeatedly found themselves in poor or wrong positions and served without distinction. One might point out that as the war wore on, the enemy's artillery grew in efficiency and effectiveness, whereas that of the Army of Tennessee declined. The Fifth Company was badly overmatched in the Atlanta campaign and reluctantly went underground. They dawdled at Atlanta and were mauled at Jonesboro. For a time, at Overall's Creek and the second battle at Murfreesboro, old times seemed to have returned and the company grew cocky again, only to be sacrificed to the weakness of their own infantry. Fortunately, Spanish Fort gave them the opportunity to redeem themselves. They took it.

The Confederacy possessed no finer soldiers than this company of the Washington Artillery. They sought glory in Virginia with the four other companies of their battalion, but it was not to be. Instead they were issued the hard rations of those who followed Bragg and Johnston and Hood. In good faith and in the spirit of their battery commander, they became proud members of the Army of Tennessee, "Try us," they would shout. And they would be tried, over and over. These men, this Fifth Company, could be counted upon to do their duty, and do it with enthusiasm and style.

APPENDIX A

ROSTER OF THE FIFTH COMPANY

Adolphe Chalaron made perhaps two dozen lists of individuals who served in the battery during the war. He carefully distinguished those who had been elected to membership in the Battalion Washington Artillery before the war, those who still belonged when the company was reorganized in February, 1862, those who left for the front in April, 1862, those who were present at the surrender, those who had deserted, and those who had been casualties. Perhaps the premature death of Slocomb prompted his exactitude. On July 1, 1875, Chalaron sent a circular to as many members of the battery as he could locate, informing them that he intended to publish a history of the company and giving each of them a questionnaire to complete. He explained in a letter to Gen. Henry R. Jackson the necessity for reconstruction of the battery's history and roster, the company "having lost all of its official papers at Nashville."[1]

The roster that follows, however, is probably more inclusive than Chalaron would have desired. Individuals appear who used the Fifth Company as a convenience and served only a short time. Also listed are names of men who never fought for the Confederacy, much less the Fifth Company,

1. JAC to Henry R. Jackson, July 20, 1875, Chalaron Papers, HTT.

but who appeared on the company rolls at one time or another. Also included are men who claim to have belonged to the company, some who were members in name only, some who were temporarily transferred into the battery, some belonging to other units who temporarily pitched in to help Slocomb and his boys man their pieces, and some who belonged to no other military command but decided to fight for a while with the Fifth Company. There are about sixty such individuals.

Then there are the unnamed and unlisted servants, black and white—at least three dozen of them, perhaps as many as fifty—who shared the hardships and dangers of the Fifth Company. Their names would have been included had I been able to locate them.

The resulting list has been assembled from various sources, all of which, it must be emphasized, only amplify Chalaron's forty-year work of loving yet obsessive record keeping. Some of the records are contradictory, many are confusing. Documents utilized include the Compiled Service Record of each individual; the Fifth Company morning reports, minute book, order book, and muster rolls; the bound volume *Record of Deceased Members;* the list compiled by Abe Leverich prior to leaving New Orleans; postwar applications for admission to the Fifth Company Association; A. B. Booth's *Records of Louisiana Confederate Soldiers;* obituaries, notices, and other accounts appearing in New Orleans newspapers Clement A. Evans' *Confederate Military History;* biographical sections of histories of New Orleans and Louisiana; the *Washington Artillery Souvenir;* New Orleans city directories; the 1860, 1870, and 1880 Louisiana censuses; the interment records of New Orleans cemeteries; pension lists; the records of the Nicholls Old Soldiers Home; and a carefully preserved clothing issue book that provides age, physical characteristics, occupation, and place of birth of 149 members.[2]

A partial attempt has been made to indicate the campaigns and battles in which an individual participated. I decided to severely limit such, however, giving only an indication in many instances. For a much more complete record one must examine Chalaron's master roster at Tulane University.

For the sake of brevity, documentation in the roster has been virtually eliminated. This was a difficult, regrettable determination. To have provided such, however, would have expanded this large battery roster into

2. Locations of these sources appear in the bibliography.

a book of its own. Also, obvious terms and certain terms that appear with great frequency have been abbreviated:

A.D.C.	Aide de Camp	5WA	Fifth Company,
appt.	appointed		Washington Artillery
arty.	artillery	inf.	infantry
bn.	battalion	k	killed
brig.	brigade	NO	New Orleans
BWA	Battalion Washington Artillery	NSH	Nicholls Soldiers Home
c	captured	p	paroled
ca.	circa	prom.	promoted
cav.	cavalry	Q.M.	Quarter Master
co.	company	r	residence, resided
CSN	Confederate States Navy	regt.	regiment
d	died	transf.	transferred
div.	division	USN	United States Navy
e	enlisted	w	wounded

ABBOTT, JOHN R. Driver.
Born *ca.* 1837 in Orleans Co., N.Y. Expressman in NO. Gray eyes, dark hair, fair complexion; e 3/6/62, NO; detached 6/64 with ordnance train, but returned; w Spanish Fort, 4/4/65; present at surrender and p 5/10/65, Meridian, Miss., returning with 5WA to NO, where he became a book-keeper, Planters Press; d 3/15/06, NO; and buried in Army of Tenn. tomb, Metairie Cemetery.

ADAMS, CHARLES ALLEN. Cpl.
Born 5/27/45 in Philadelphia, Pa., (according to death certificate); said to have been son of Commodore Adams [Allen?], USN. Student in Pointe Coupée Parish; brown eyes, dark hair and complexion, 5'7"; e 3/6/62, NO; appt. cpl. 7/24/62; commended for Murfreesboro by Vaught; w at Missionary Ridge; absent on sick leave at surrender. Nephew of Mary Allen, daughter of Charles W. Allen, who first owned Longwood; lived 1900–1920 in Pointe Coupée Parish at Longwood. Never married; no children; manual laborer at time of pension application 8/5/04; eventually inherited Longwood. d 2/6/35 (age 89) in Pointe Coupée.

ADAMS, JAMES H. Pvt. Driver.
Born England. e 3/9/62, NO; c 1863; after the war resided in NO, where he was a policeman.

ADAMS, S. H. Pvt.
Member of Co. D. 1st. Ala. Bn. of Arty.; temp. assigned to 5WA.

ALLAIN, ALEXANDER PIERRE "ALEX." Cpl.
Born *ca.* 1844 in West Baton Rouge Parish, La., son of Theophile Allain and Aspasie LeBlanc; student at Bardstown, Ky.; returned home to north Baton Rouge and e 3/6/62, NO; gray eyes, black hair, dark complexion, 5'10½"; brother of V. F. Allain; prom. to cpl. for his service at Kennesaw Ridge, where w; in all 5WA battles and campaigns; p 5/10/65, Meridian, Miss. After war, sugarcane and rice planter, West Baton Rouge, Plaque-mines, and St. Charles Parishes; moved in 1889 to Albania Plantation, St. Mary Parish; d 5/30/10, St. Mary Parish; buried in Army of Tenn. tomb, Metairie Cemetery. Married Jeannie Georgine Proctor, who d 12/27/37.

ALLAIN, VILLENEUVE FRANÇOIS "FATTY." Pvt.
Born West Baton Rouge Parish *ca.* 1839, son of Theophile Allain and Aspasie LeBlanc; clerk; gray eyes, light hair and complexion, 5'6"; brother of Alex; e 3/6/62, NO; w and c at Perryville, 10/8/62; exchanged; w at Kennesaw Ridge, 6/64; absent, sick, at surrender; d 8/29/19;[3] married Sara Turnbull Lobdell (d 2/4/26).

ALLEN (ALLYN), OSCAR E. Pvt.
e 3/10/62, NO; r Fauquier Co., Va.; transf. from Co. H, 20th La. Inf., 4/63; detailed in Pioneer corps by Gen. Bragg; c near Chickamauga, 9/20/63; imprisoned at Camp Douglas, Ill. until release 6/14/65. After war, r NO; occupation in 1873 was either a furniture dealer or a patrol-man; listed as a shoemaker, 1893.

ALLEN, THOMAS C. Sgt.
Born 1839 in Fauquier Co., Va.; clerk in NO, 1860; blue eyes, brown hair, fair complexion, 5'11"; e 3/6/62, NO; in all battles and campaigns; prom. to cpl., 5/7/62; prom. to sgt. 11/1/62; mentioned for gallantry at Missionary Ridge; reduced to ranks by court-martial at Tullahoma, 1863; reappt. sgt. 5/4/63; p 5/10/65, Meridian, Miss.; d of pneumonia, 1/29/66

---

3. New Orleans *Times Picayune,* August 30, 1919; yet Record of Deceased Members of the BWA gives date of death as November 9, 1881, in Bayou Goula, La.

at St. James Hotel, NO, where he worked as a clerk. Funeral by Dr. Benjamin Palmer. Buried in Girod St. Cemetery, NO.

ANDERSON, JOHN ROBERT. Pvt.
Born *ca.* 1845 in Clay Co., Mo.; clerk; blue eyes, light hair, fair complexion, 5'8"; e 6/1/63, Mobile; k by cannonball at Glass's Mill, 9/19/63.

ANTHONY, JOHN W. Pvt.
e 5/13/62, Corinth, Miss.; recog. for conspicuous conduct at Murfreesboro by being named to Roll of Honor; w by cannonball at Murfreesboro, 12/31/62; d of wounds 1/4/63.

ARMANT, AGRICOLE F. Pvt.[4]
Born *ca.* 1844 in NO; student; r St. James Parish; gray eyes, brown hair, light complexion, 5'10"; e 4/15/62, Corinth; messmate of PDS; in all battles and campaigns; absent at surrender, furloughed; p 6/13/65, New Iberia, La. Bookkeeper in NO after war; r in St. John the Baptist, La., 1899.

ARNOLD, WILLIAM THOMAS. Pvt.
Born 7/19/36 at St. Bernard Parish, La.; seaman; blue eyes, light hair, fair complexion, 5'8"; e 6/24/62, Morton, Miss.; Glass's Mill, Chickamauga; hospitalized in Newnan, Ga., 11/12/63; transf. to Co. A, 1st Bn., Duke's regt., Ky. Cav.;[5] spent last months of the war in the defense of Petersburg; p 4/9/65 at Appomattox. After war, teller at American Exchange National Bank in Dallas, Tex.; eventually prom. to vice president; d 12/27/27, Dallas; buried in Metairie Cemetery.

ARROYO, ARTHUR. Pvt.
Born 1825 in St. Charles Parish, La., a descendant of an old Spanish family. Lawyer. Gray eyes, dark hair and complexion, 5'10½"; e 6/1/63, Jackson, Miss., giving age as 40. Discharged 8/31/63, unfit for service; d 7/19/75, NO.

ARROYO, CHARLES. Pvt.
e 1/1/62; r NO; p 5/10/65, Meridian, Miss.; d 8/4/69, age 40.

ARROYO, FELIX. Pvt.
Born St. Charles Parish, La., 7/24/25, son of Laure Delery and Patrice

4. Phil Stephenson refers to him as Henry in his *Civil War Memoir,* 166.

5. Reported as killed as member of Forrest's cavalry according to Record of Deceased Members, 5WA, HTT.

Joseph Arroyo; educated Spring Hill College and Jefferson College; note clerk at Canal Bank in NO; with Merchants Mutual Insurance Co.; then sugar agent for firm of Henry & Arroyo; married Leontine Garidel; during Butler's occupation of NO required to take USA oath or register as enemy of the USA; refused to take oath and sent beyond the lines in 5/63; hazel eyes, light hair, fair complexion, 5'11"; e 6/1/63, Mobile; w at Chickamauga, 9/19/63; hospitalized in Marietta; returned for Missionary Ridge and Atlanta campaign; p 5/10/65, Meridian, Miss. After war, entered service of the Merchants Mutual Insurance Co., NO, as marine clerk; d 8/18/91, NO. Buried in Army of Tenn. tomb, Metairie Cemetery.

ATKINSON, W. H. Pvt. 12/61.

AVIN, J. R. Pvt.
Member of Culpepper S.C. Battery, temp. assigned to 5WA.

BAILEY, C. P. Pvt.
Born *ca.* 1834 in Worcester Co., Mass.; clerk, attorney's office, NO; e 6/24/62, Tupelo, Miss.; k Chickamauga, 9/19/63; brother served in Union army and was k at Port Hudson.

BAKER, ALDEN H. Pvt.
Born *ca.* 1844 in Escambia, Fla.; student; r Greenville, Ala.; blue eyes, brown hair, fair complexion, 5'11"; w Blackburn's Ford, Va.; on 5WA rolls, March–April, 1865; p 5/10/65, Meridian, Miss. After war, clerk and collector of customs, NO.

BAKER, M. A. Pvt. 12/61.

BAKEWELL, ALEXANDER GORDON. Orderly Sgt. and Lay Chaplain.
Born 1822 in Louisville, Ky.; attended Elizabeth College in England; returned to U.S. in 1839; director of English commission house, NO; e 3/6/62, NO, as orderly sgt. and lay chaplain; present at Shiloh and Corinth; discharged at Clear Creek, Miss., 6/4/62, over age; ordained by L. Polk after being wounded, becoming chaplain for 28th Miss. and 8th Miss. Bn. Consolidated. After war, minister of Trinity Chapel Episcopal Church, NO; chaplain general of the Louisiana Division, U.C.V., d 2/22/20, NO; buried in Metairie Cemetery. Married Sophie Cuvelier.

BANFIL (BANFILL, BANFIELD), JOSEPH W. Pvt.
Born *ca.* 1841 in Mason Co., Ky.; gray eyes, dark hair and complexion;

5'4½"; e 3/6/62, NO; c 9/62, during Kentucky campaign; exchanged 11/1/62; deserted near Jackson, Miss., 6/16/63; took USA oath, 8/18/63.

BANNISTER, RINALDO J., JR.[6]

BARRIEL (BARRAIL, BANAIL), A. Pvt.
Born *ca.* 1830 in France; hatter in NO; black eyes and hair, dark complexion, 6'; e 10/27/62, Knoxville, Tenn.; with battery thereafter until k at Pine Mountain, 6/19/64; buried in Georgia Confederate Cemetery, Marietta.

BARROW, ALEXANDER DOUGLASS. Pvt.
Born *ca.* 1837 in La.; son of Wylie Micajah Barrow and Cordelia G. Johnson; reared in Watertown, N.Y. and educated at Columbia College, Columbia, S.C.; returned to La. in 1859 and settled on Barrowza Plantation; farmer; blue eyes, light hair, fair complexion, 6'; e 8/12/61, NO; joined 5WA 11/2/63, La.; present at Battle of Murfreesboro; transf. to 13th La. Inf. and prom. to 2nd Lt., 3/23/64; r Port Allen, West Baton Rouge Parish, La., 1890; d 1/28/03; buried in Magnolia Cemetery, Baton Rouge. Married Lise Victorine Duralde.

BARROW, CORDELIUS JOHNSON "TONY." Pvt.
Born 9/3/45 in St. Francisville, La., son of Wylie Micajah Barrow and Cordelia G. Johnson; attended Mississippi Military Institute at Pass Christian and LSU at Alexandria; farmer in Pointe Coupée Parish; blue eyes, light hair and complexion, 5'8"; e 7/4/63, Bolton, Miss.; w in the shoulder and leg at Resaca, 5/14/64 and hospitalized; w in shoulder at Peachtree Creek, 7/20/64; returned from hospital to participate in Jonesboro, Tennessee campaign, and Spanish Fort; p 5/10/65, Meridian, Miss. After war, planter in West Baton Rouge Parish; worked for the railroad, Nashville; merchandizer and postmaster, Port Allen; eventually prospered, accumulating large land holdings; active in public affairs; d 9/13/24

6. Bannister and his father have been confused with each other. Young Bannister never served in the Fifth. He enlisted May 26, 1861, in the Second Washington Artillery, fought with them in Virginia, received a gunshot wound in the left hip, and was captured at Williamsport, Maryland, on July 6, 1863. After hospitalization at Harrisburg, Pennsylvania, and Baltimore, he was exchanged at Point Lookout on December 24, 1863. Bannister "drowned in the Mississippi River on 3/8/64 while on [parole] furlough"; born La.; age 25; occup. cooper; r NO; single.

Bannister, Sr., was an officer in the Fifth Company in late 1861, but was not reelected when the battery was formally organized February 24, 1862. He remained behind when the battery left New Orleans and transferred to the Sixth Company, Washington Artillery.

and buried in Magnolia Cemetery, Baton Rouge. Married Martha Johnson Robertson.

BARSTOW, WILLIAM R. Commissary Sgt.
Born in New York City, 1831; clerk; hazel eyes, light hair and complexion, 5'9"; e 3/6/62, NO; present on all rolls from 9/1/64–4/65; detailed with Maj. Ayers, Chief Q.M., Army of Tenn., 9/64, order of Gen. Hood. After war, partner in Byrnes & Barstow, wholesale grocers, commission merchants, agents for tin plate, NO; d 1/30/88.

BARTLEY, JOHN. Orderly Sgt.
Born ca. 1840 in Louisville, Ky.; clerk; blue eyes, brown hair, light complexion, 5'8"; r NO; e 3/6/62; commended for action at Shiloh; prom. to orderly sgt., 11/17/62 at Allisonia, Tenn.; in all major actions of battery; p 5/10/65, Meridian, Miss. After war, listed as clerk at Fassman Cotton Press, NO, 1873.

BARTON, B. G. Pvt. 12/61.

BAYLE (BAYLEY, BALE), JAMES. Driver.
Born ca. 1836 in Devonshire, England; gardener; dark eyes and hair, light complexion, 5'6"; e 3/6/62, NO; k Chickamauga, 9/20/63—leg shot off, close to body.

BAYNE, THOMAS LEVINGSTON. Pvt.
Born 8/4/24 in Jones Co., Ga., son of Charles Bayne and Elizabeth Bowen. Moved to Butler Co., Ala. as a child. Graduated from Yale in 1847 (valedictorian, Skull and Bones); read law with Thomas A. Clarke, NO; became partner with Clarke in 1850; e 3/6/62, NO; married Anna Maria Gayle and among groomsmen were John Slidell and James Campbell; "middle size, slight frame, with fair complexion." w and commanded, Shiloh, 4/6/62; discharged as unfit for further field service, 7/16/62. Became an assistant with the rank of captain of artillery to brother-in-law, Josiah Gorgas, in the ordnance department, 9/62, Richmond; prom. to lt. col. and headed newly created Bureau of Foreign Supplies in 1863; played role vital to the Richmond subsistence and commissary departments, advised secretary of war, and worked with agents in Bermuda and Nassau.[7] Also worked closely with secretary of treasury, and had direct access to the president himself.[8]

7. See OR, Series IV, Vol. II, p. 660; Vol. III, pp. 89, 783, 1071.

8. Richard D. Goff, Confederate Supply (Durham, N.C., 1969), 180. For information on Bayne's direction of the Bureau of Foreign Supplies, created in March, 1864, by President Davis and Secretary of War James A. Seddon, see Shackelford, George Wythe Randolph, 111–12, 126–27.

Surrendered in Charlotte, N.C. After war, resumed practice with Clarke; became a partner in law firms of Clonk, Bayne & Renshaw, 1873; and Bayne, Denègre & Bayne, 1893; served as vice-president, American Bar Association; d in NO, 12/10/91.

BEEBE, MARCUS JINENS. Pvt.
Born *ca.* 1842 in NO; student; e 3/6/62, NO; present through Missionary Ridge; absent 1/64–4/65; furloughed; transf. to CSN late 1864 and became master's mate; d in NO, 8/93.

BEGGS, JOHN T. Cpl. artificer.
Born *ca.* 1837 in Botetourt Co., Va.; ship carpenter; hazel eyes, dark hair and complexion, 6'; elected 4th Artificer, 2/62; e 3/6/62, NO; commended for Shiloh; prom. to cpl., 6/21/62; w at Chickamauga, 9/20/63, and again at Dallas, 5/28/64; d 7/10/64 in a hospital in Atlanta; buried Oakland Cemetery, Atlanta.

BEHAN, FRANK A. (J.) Pvt.
Born *ca.* 1843 in La., son of John Holland and Katherine Walker Behan; clerk; e 2/1/62, Richmond, Va. in 4WA; temp. assigned to 5WA from 4WA; p 5/10/65, Meridian, Miss. In 1892 was president of Crescent Jute Mfg. Co. in NO.

BEIN, GEORGE. Driver.
Born *ca.* 1835 in Baden, Germany; barber; brown eyes, dark hair and complexion, 5'8"; e 8/18/61, Camp Moore, La.; transf. from 11th La., 4/1/63; deserted 4/11/65 at evacuation of Mobile. After the war r NO where he was listed as a barber in 1873.

BELLANGER, ALFRED "ALF." Cpl.
Born *ca.* 1828 in Quebec; clerk in NO; e 3/6/62, NO, and elected caisson cpl.; brown hair, fair complexion, gray eyes. w (lost left hand) at Shiloh and discharged, 4/20/62, as unfit for service, by order of Gen. Bragg.

BELSOM (BILSON, BELSON), DROUSIN. Pvt.
Born *ca.* 1840 in St. Charles Parish; planter; blue eyes, light hair and complexion, 6'; e 6/1/63, Mobile; r Jefferson City, La.; in all battles and campaigns until surrender; p 5/10/65, Meridian, Miss.

BELSOM (BILSON, BELSON), FELIX. Pvt.
Born *ca.* 1844 in St. Charles Parish; planter near Jefferson City, La.; hazel

eyes, dark hair and complexion, 5′6″; e 6/1/63, Mobile, p 5/10/65, Meridian, Miss.; in all battles and campaigns until surrender. In 1899 r NO.[9]

BELSOM (BILSON, BELSON), JOSEPH, JR. Pvt.
Born *ca.* 1837 in St. Charles Parish, La.; clerk; hazel eyes, dark hair and complexion, 5′10″; e 6/1/63, Mobile; k Chickamauga, 9/19/63, when shot through both arms and the body.

BENNETT, ARCHIBALD T., JR. "ARCHIE." Pvt.
Born *ca.* 1840 in Apalachicola, Fla.; clerk; hazel eyes, dark hair and complexion, 5′10″; e 3/6/62, NO; in all battles and campaigns until k at 2nd Murfreesboro, 12/7/64.[10]

BENSON, CHARLES. Pvt.
Born NO; 19-year-old photographer; e 6/1/63 in Mobile (refugee from NO); brown eyes, dark hair, and fair complexion, 5′4″; deserted at evacuation of Mobile, 4/11/65; after war r NO where he was a carriage builder.

BERGAMINI, A. Pvt. 12/61.

BERRY, JOHN R. Pvt.
Born in Canton, Miss., 1836; moved to NO, in 1849; steamboat man 10 years, then policeman; e in the Confederate Guards Response battalion;[11] fought at Shiloh and Corinth; hospitalized and discharged; baked bread for sick soldiers; e 5WA, 9/3/62; w and c 7/25/64; hospitalized at No. 2 USA General Hospital, Chattanooga; exchanged. w and c (had been left behind) at Overall's Creek, 12/4/64; imprisoned at Camp Chase. After war, a baker, NO; owned wholesale grocery house, 1893; d 12/21/07, NO; buried in Metairie Cemetery.

---

9. He is mistakenly shown as having been buried in a mass grave in Evergreen Cemetery, Murfreesboro, Tennessee.

10. CHS wrote Bennett's father from Columbus, Mississippi: ATB w 12/7/64 and died 4 A.M. 12/8. Buried him on right side of M'boro-Nashville pike north of Squire Bridges house, 10¼ mi from Murfreesboro between two trees with five notches each. Creek runs between grave and house. Brought back to NO at close of war and funeral by Dr. Palmer on 5/22/65. Shot through chest with minié ball. His boy William with him & took care of his effects. CHS to Archibald T. Bennett, Sr., January 15, 1865, WA Papers, HTT.

11. Confederate Guards Response battalion, one designation for the 16th Louisiana battalion, was organized in New Orleans March 6, 1862, and engaged at Shiloh. A month later it was combined with a Florida infantry battalion, which is sometimes referred to in individual military service records as the Florida Battalion. The 16th Louisiana was also designated as the 12th Battalion.

BLACKWELL, WILLIAM. Pvt.
Born *ca.* 1839 in East Feliciana Parish, La.; coppersmith; gray eyes, dark hair and complexion, 5'9"; e 10/8/63, Mobile; hospitalized 11/17/63; p 4/26/65, Durham Station, N.C.[12] After war, r NO where he was a bartender; d at NSH, 7/3/12 and buried in Greenwood Cemetery.

BLAFFER, JOHN AUGUSTUS. Pvt.
Born 7/26/38 in NO; merchant; e Co. G, 1st La. as 2nd Lt. resigned and e as private in 5WA, 3/6/62, NO; present through 4/30/62; discharged 7/62; provided substitute (P. Ryan). After war, r NO; owned J. A. Blaffer & Co., dealer in hops, malt, cork & brewers supplies; bottlers of ale, porter, cider, wines, and liquors. In 1893 became a brick and lumber co. owner; president of the Lumberman's Exchange and president of the Society for Prevention of Cruelty to Children; d 2/15/20, NO and buried in Metairie Cemetery. Married Clementine A. Schneider, who d in 1898.

BLAIR, THOMAS MCMILLAN. Sgt.
Born 8/3/39 in Spring Hill, Ala. Clerk in NO in 1860. Blue eyes, dark hair, light complexion, 5'10"; e 3/6/62, NO; commended for Shiloh; prom. to 2nd Lt. 6/8/62; c Perryville; exchanged 11/1/62; k Chickamauga, 9/19/63; Bible and sash at CSA Museum, NO.

BLIEML, EMMERAN, O.S.B. Chaplain.
Born 9/19/31 in Ratisbon, Bavaria, Germany; emigrated to the USA and became a Benedictine monk in Pa., then a priest in Ky. and Tenn.[13] An excellent horseman, Father Blieml, despite the opposition of his bishop, became chaplain with the Irish 10th Tenn. Inf. He "kept with our battery on Ga. campaign, especially above Atlanta. Was killed in our Battery during the Battle of Jonesboro," 9/1/64.[14]

BOARDMAN (BOURDMAN), JOHN. Cpl.
Born *ca.* 1843 in Hancock Co., Miss. River pilot. Black eyes, dark hair and complexion, 6'; elected to 5WA 9/19/61; e 3/6/62, NO; prom. to cpl., 11/1/62; c (deserted) Pine Mountain, Ga., 6/16/64; imprisoned at Rock

---

12. CSR shows him paroled May 18, 1865, in Augusta, Georgia.

13. JAC could not remember his name. He recalled a Father "Blumer" or "Blumier," born in Holland.

14. Another account has Blieml's head torn off while administering the sacrament of extreme unction to the dying Union colonel William Grace. See Lindsley, *Military Annals of Tennessee*, 289; Gleeson, *Rebel Sons of Erin*, 126–28.

Island; released 5/30/65. Riverboat captain in 1893; d 9/19/21 and buried in Lafayette #1, NO.

BOATNER, H. (HUDSON?) J. Pvt.
Born *ca.* 1833 in Assumption Parish where he became a planter. Hazel eyes, light hair, fair complexion, 5'8"; e 5/13/62, Corinth, Miss.; w at Murfreesboro, 1/2/63 (two fingers shot off), but remained with 5WA at Jackson, Chickamauga, Missionary Ridge, through Atlanta and Tennessee campaigns, Spanish Fort; p 5/10/65, Meridian, Miss. In 1885 r Lafourche Parish.

BOUDREAUX, JOHN J. Pvt.
Born *ca.* 1838 in NO; butcher; black eyes and hair, dark complexion, 6'; e 6/1/63, Mobile; r NO; in all battles and campaigns; p 5/10/65, Meridian, Miss. After war, r NO; listed as a laborer, 1873; as a foreman at the NO Elevator & Warehouse Co., 1893; d 12/7/35; buried in the Catholic cemetery, Donaldsonville, Ascension Parish, La.

BOYDEN, A. Pvt.
e 3/6/62, NO; commended for Shiloh; on rolls through 6/62; discharged at Tupelo, Miss. 7/29/62, over age.

BOZDEN, A. Pvt. 12/61.

BRECKINRIDGE, STANHOPE PRESTON. Asst. Surgeon.
Born 4/20/41 in Louisville, Ky.; graduated from Centre College; e as asst. surgeon, 4th Ky. Inf.; on staff of J. S. Marmaduke; surgeon of 2nd Ky. Mounted Volunteers; fought at Murfreesboro; assigned to 5WA, 10/31/63, in camp at Missionary Ridge; remained with wounded at Missionary Ridge and c; exchanged 1/31/64; sick and sent to Genl. Hosp., Army of Tenn., Dalton; spring, 1864, reported to director of hospitals, S. H. Stout; transf. to Richmond, Va., and in charge of one of the principal hospitals. After war, physician in La. and Miss.; retired in Chattanooga, Tenn.; d 3/14/87, Chattanooga; buried in Louisville, Ky.

BREVARD, ALBERT H. Pvt.
Born *ca.* 1845 in Jackson, Mo.; student; refuged with relatives in Bladen Springs, Ala.; 5'9"; e 7/3/63, Mobile; in all 5WA battles and campaigns thereafter. p 5/10/65, Meridian, Miss. Drowned near Cape Girardeau, Mo., in 1875.

BREVARD, JOHN GAYLE. Pvt.
r NO; acute dysentery, 9/63; p 5/10/65, Meridian, Miss.; 1875 manufac-

turing guns, hardware, plows and nails in Vicksburg, Miss. d before 1903; married Mary Welch. Probably brother of A. H. Brevard.

BREWERTON, ALFRED WEST. Pvt.
Born *ca.* 1826 in Leeds, England. Printer in NO; gray eyes, light hair, fair complexion, 5'8"; e 6/1/63, Mobile (refugee from NO); in all campaigns thereafter; p 5/10/65, Meridian, Miss. After war, printer in NO.

BRIDGE, BEN, JR. Pvt.
Born *ca.* 1842 in NO. Clerk in NO. Brown eyes, dark hair and eyes, 5'8"; e 3/6/62, NO; hospitalized 7/9/63 at Jackson, Miss.; w at Peachtree Creek; in all battles and campaigns; member of crew of 8" gun at Spanish Fort, March–April, 1865; p 5/10/65, Meridian, Miss. After war, clerk at Bridge and Son, NO.; d 9/24/78, NO; buried in Army of Tenn. tomb, Metairie Cemetery.

BRINDLEY, L. D. Pvt.
Born *ca.* 1834, Louisville, Ky.; clerk; black eyes, dark hair, light complexion, 5'10½"; e 6/1/63, Mobile; r NO; hospitalized 9/27/63 at Floyd House and Ocmulgee Hospital, Macon, Ga. with syphilis; rejoined at Jonesboro and continued through Tennessee campaign and Spanish Fort. p 5/10/65, Meridian, Miss. After war, patrolman in NO.

BROADWELL, CHARLES B. Pvt.
Absent at surrender; transf.; after war, clerk at D. W. C. Sanford, NO.

BROCARD, LEONICE "LEON." Pvt.
About fifteen years old. Member of 1st Chasseurs à Pied, Louisiana Militia; c NO, 10/26/62; sick at time of exchange. On the field at Chickamauga and "insisted upon serving with the Battery and was killed while assisting at one of the guns," 9/20/63; shot in the mouth; never formally enlisted in 5WA.[15]

BROWN, GEORGE E. Pvt.
Born *ca.* 1838 in Woodburn, Ill. Clerk. Gray eyes, dark hair, light complexion, 5'9"; e 5/14/62 at Corinth; w Chickamauga, and slightly w, at

15. CHS's report: "Where every man in the company did his duty so nobly it is impossible to discriminate, I cannot refrain from expressing my admiration of the bravery of Leon Brocard, a youth of 16, who volunteered his services as the battery was going into action, and nobly met his death in performance of a self-imposed duty." *OR,* Vol. XXX, Pt. 2, p. 230.

Resaca, 5/14/64; "absent sick from 28th Feby 1864 until end of the war"; employed St. Mary's Hospital, La Grange, Ga., 7/64; absent sick at surrender; furloughed by medical board, 4/5/65; p Pass Manchac, La., 5/18/65.

Browning, James L. (M.) "Jim." Sgt.
Born *ca.* 1839 in Sumner Co., Tenn. Clerk in NO; Blue eyes, auburn hair, light complexion, 6'1"; e 3/6/62, Grand Junction, Tenn.; prom. to sgt., 8/16/63; in all battles and campaigns; p 5/10/65, Meridian, Miss.; d in Tex. in 1896.

Bruce, N. L. Cpl.
Member of old BWA; clerk; elected 6th cpl., 2/14/62; e 3/6/62, NO; slightly w Shiloh and discharged 5/13/62, disability. After war, salesman for John N. Gould, NO.

Bryan, Jessie (Jesse) A. Pvt.
Born *ca.* 1837 in Montgomery Co., Tenn.; gray eyes, light hair, fair complexion, 5'10"; e 11/9/63, Selma, Ala.; on rolls 1864; discharged 1/23/65, unfit for service, disability. After war, clerk at Toledano's, NO. In 1899 r Houston, Tex.[16]

Buckner, Newton "Newt." Pvt.
e 3/6/62, NO; discharged 6/23/62; transf. to 7th (10th?) La. where he became a lt. After war, merchant in NO where he d 10/22/99.

Buffier, E. Pvt.
e after leaving NO.

Bull, William Izard. Asst. Surgeon.
Born *ca.* 1838; r Charleston, S.C.; served from 9/64; with 5WA Tennessee campaign and Spanish Fort; assigned specially to 5WA 4/29/65 at Cuba Station, Ala.; p 5/10/65, Meridian, Miss.

Burns. See Byrnes.

Burns, James. Sgt.
Born Mulklow Co., Ireland; 5'8"; laborer; illiterate; e 3/6/62, NO. w at Shiloh; c on retreat from Jackson, Miss., 7/63.

Burrows, F. Pvt.
Born *ca.* 1841 in England. e, apparently, 6/11/63; appears in company clothing issue book.

16. One source lists him as having died in 1896.

BUTTS, JOHN F. Pvt.
Born 1837 in South Hampton Co., Va. To NO in 1849; raised by uncle; became a clerk; gray eyes, light hair, fair complexion, 5'8"; e 3/6/62, NO, in Crescent Regt.; transf. to 5WA, 6/62; participated in all actions until became ill and detailed to med. director, Army of Tennessee, 10/19/63, being "unfit for action." With medical dept. until the surrender. After war, chief clerk of city comptroller's office, NO; d 11/5/04.

BYRNES (BURNS), JAMES. Driver.
Born *ca.* 1840 in Ireland; laborer; r NO; single. e 3/6/62, NO; w 4/62 in fights around Corinth; c (deserted according to Chalaron) during evacuation of Jackson, Miss., 7/16/63; present on rolls March–Oct., 1864; detached for duty at Fort Craig. After war, partner in Byrnes & Barstow, wholesale grocers, commission merchants, and agents for tin plate, NO.

BYRNES (BURNS), JOSEPH. Wagoner.
Born *ca.* 1840, Meath Co., Ireland; gray eyes, dark hair and complexion, 5'8"; slightly w at Shiloh, 4/7/62; missing, "deserted," on retreat from Jackson, 7/16[26]/63.

CALMES, W. N. Cpl.
Member of old BWA; clerk; elected 3rd cpl., 12/14/62; e 3/6/62, NO; on roll 4/30/62; absent on outpost duty; discharged Tupelo, Miss., 7/16/62, over age; re-enlisted; present May–June, 1863. After war, cashier at Sinnott & Adams, NO. d Atlanta, 9/16/94, age 72.

CAMPBELL, A. MICHAEL. Driver.
Born Ireland *ca.* 1840; laborer in NO; hazel eyes, dark hair and complexion, 5'6"; e 3/6/62, NO; w Shiloh, 4/6/62; in Corinth, Ky., campaign, Murfreesboro, Jackson, Glass's Mill, Missionary Ridge, Atlanta campaign (w Jonesboro, 9/1/64), and Tennessee campaign (c Nashville, 12/16/64); imprisoned at Camp Chase, Ohio, and was in prison at surrender. After war, fireman at the NO Gas Works.

CAPON, PHILLIP "PHIL." Pvt.
Born *ca.* 1842 in Kent Co., England; clerk in NO; hazel eyes, black hair, dark complexion, 5'7"; e 8/1/63, Morton, Miss.; w at Chickamauga; d "suddenly of congestive chills" in camp at Dalton, Ga., 3/8/64. "This man had served with Slocomb as servant from his departure from NO for Virginia & with him until he enlisted in Company." Buried in Westhill Cemetery (CSA section), Dalton, Ga.

Carey. Driver.
Shot in hip at Shiloh, 4/7/62.

Carpenter, John D. F. Pvt.
Born *ca*. 1844 in NO. Resident of Tangipahoa, La. Transf. from 9th Bn., La. Cav.; e 12/13/62, Camp Moore, La. c Port Hudson. 5WA roll shows as furloughed 2/65 by examining board, Montgomery, Ala., for 60 days; present 4/30/65 and p with battery 5/10/65, Meridian, Miss. Living in NO in 1899.

Carter, G. W. Pvt. 12/61.

Casey, William. Blacksmith, Artificer.
Born *ca*. 1823 in Kilkenny Co., Ireland; blacksmith in NO; blue eyes, dark hair, light complexion, 5'8"; "Temp. loaned from 20th La. Inf., order of Gen. Anderson, to 5WA at Corinth and served with them at Shiloh where he won commendation. Returned to regiment, 4/12/62, but reassigned 5WA, being an A 1 Blacksmith and mechanic," and served until returned to 20th La., 12/63. After war was a foundryman in NO; d at NSH 10/22/99 and buried in Greenwood Cemetery, Metairie, La.

Chalaron, Henry. Pvt.
Born 1/31/41 in NO; clerk in NO; brown eyes, black hair, dark complexion, 5'6"; e 3/5/62, NO, in Co. D, Crescent Regt; transf. to 5WA in Tupelo, 7/62; all battles and campaigns; p 5/10/65 at Meridian, Miss. Returned to NO; d 10/31/13, NO; buried Metairie Cemetery. Married Ida Frances.

Chalaron, Jacques Antonio "Jack." Pvt.
Born *ca*. 1839 in NO; clerk; r NO. e 3/5/62, NO, in Co. D, Crescent Reg; transf. 5WA at Tupelo, 7/62; w Resaca, 5/14/64; 7/22/64 sent to rear sick. Detailed in fall, 1864, as clerk in office of Maj. Rawle, chief of artillery, District of Central Alabama, until surrender; p 5/10/65, Meridian, Miss.; d NO, 3/20/95 and buried in St. Louis #3 Cemetery.

Chalaron, Joseph Adolphe. 1st Lt.
Born 1/24/36 in NO; grad. from Louisiana College; clerk in mercantile trade; hazel eyes, black hair, dark complexion, 5'5; e BWA 8/61 and elected jr. 2nd Lt., 2/14/62; prom. to sr. 2nd. lt. 6/9/62, replacing Hews; became jr. 1st. lt. 6/13/62 when Vaught moved up to sr. 1st. lt. Served in every battle and campaign, having horses killed under him at Murfrees-

boro and Glass's Mill; assumed command of 5WA on the field at Jonesboro, 9/1/64 and remained in command until the surrender, despite being w at Spanish Fort; p 5/10/65, Meridian, Miss. After war, planter; became president of Hope Insurance Co.; beset with financial difficulties; presided over the Board of Pensions for La.; secretary, Louisiana Historical Association and UCV; led fund-raising efforts for Battle Abbey in Richmond. d 7/24/09, NO; buried in Army of Tenn. tomb at Metairie Cemetery. Married Marie Labarre of NO who d prior to 1909.

CHARLES, EDWIN. Cpl.
Born *ca.* 1842 in NO; student; dark complexion, dark hair, gray eyes, 5'9½" tall; elected 6th caisson cpl., 2/62; e 3/6/62, NO; "returned to ranks at his own request," 5/7/62; c ("deserted") 6/16/64 on retreat from Pine Mountain; imprisoned at Rock Island Barracks, Ill.; took USA oath 3/23/65; r (426 Camp St.) NO in 1873, but no occupation listed.

CHURCH, D. W. Pvt. 12/61.

CHURCHILL, W. C. 1st Cpl., 12/61.

CLARKE, JAMES, JR. Cpl.
Born c. 1844 in Louisville, Ky. Clerk in NO. Gray eyes, light hair and complexion, 5'10"; e 3/6/62, NO; all campaigns of 5WA; prom. to cpl., 2/28/64; p 5/10/65, Meridian, Miss. Returned to NO.

CLAYTON, JOHN. Driver.
e 3/6/62, NO; w at Shiloh, 4/6/62; discharged 7/16/62, disability; re-enlisted; c on furlough at NO, 10/21/62; exchanged 2/23/63; after war was a drayman in NO.

CLAYTON, W. W. Pvt.
e 3/6/62, NO; clerk; discharged 5/62, disability.

CLERC, JOHN P. Pvt.
Born *ca.* 1832 in Alsace, France; confectioner in NO; hazel eyes, light hair and complexion, 5'8"; e 3/6/62, NO; transf. from Orleans Guard Battery at Tupelo; sent to hospital sick 7/18/63–8/31/64; present otherwise; p 5/10/65, Meridian, Miss.

CLOPTON, D. Pvt.
Member of Co. D, 1st Ala. Arty. Bn.; temp. assigned to 5WA.

COHEN, LEWIN HENRY. Pvt. Asst. Surgeon
Appt. by secretary of war to rank from 9/24/62 and ordered to report to
Gen. Bragg. Served 9/62–spring/64 with 5WA, although with Polk's corps
and engineers most of 1863; returned to 5WA by 12/63.

COHOEN, W. H. Pvt.
Member of Co. D, 1st. Ala. Arty. Bn.; temp. assigned to 5WA.

COLEMAN, F. J. Pvt. 12/61.

COLLINS, ANDREW. Pvt.
Born 2/15/40, Lafourche Parish; planter in Lafourche Parish; blue eyes,
light hair and complexion, 6'; e 1/12/63, Tullahoma, Tenn.; received slight
w in side at Battle of Resaca; Atlanta and Tennessee campaigns, Spanish
Fort; p 5/10/65, Meridian, Miss. After war, merchant and planter residing
in Port Vincent, La.; d 9/5/09 and buried in Metairie Cemetery.

COMMANDEUR, N. Pvt.
Born ca. 1826, Louisville, Ky.; lawyer; e 8/26/63, Montgomery, Ala.;
Chickamauga, Missionary Ridge, Atlanta and Tennessee campaigns; c
and p, Eufala, Ala., while on detail. On roll for March–April, 1865, as
detailed for 30 days by order of Gen. Maury; after war was lawyer
in NO.

CONRAD, PAUL. Pvt.
Born 12/31/40 in NO; wholesale grocer; r Biloxi, Miss.; member of Chasseurs à Pied (w at Fraser's Farm, Sharpsburg, and Bellefield); "assigned
for duty with company at his own request," by Col. Thos. Taylor commanding Post at Mobile, 4/10/65; present March–April, 1865, roll; p
5/10/65, Meridian, Miss., "& obtained transportation to Biloxi Miss."
Elected asst. secretary of finance committee, NO City Council, 1867; later
worked with Louisiana State Lottery Co.

CONVERSE, FRANK M. Pvt.
Born ca. 1845 in NO; student; gray eyes; e 3/25/64, Mobile. On rolls
through April, 1865; furloughed in Feb., 1865, by Hood; p 5/10/65, Meridian, Miss. r NO, 1899.

COOK, J. B. Pvt.
Member of Co. D, 1st. Ala. Bn. of Arty., temp. assigned 5WA.

COTTING, CHARLES CHAUNCEY. Pvt.
Born 7/11/38 in NO; cashier in jewelry establishment when war broke

out; joined the Beauregard Rifles; became an officer in the state militia; 5/11/62, joined 5WA; Jackson, Chickamauga, Atlanta and Tennessee campaigns, Spanish Fort; w Mill Creek Gap; p 5/10/65, Meridian, Miss. After war, salesman for A. B. Griswold & Co., jewelers, NO; d 6/15/12, NO; buried Girod Cemetery, NO; reinterred at Metairie Cemetery. Married Agnes M. Kilpatrick.

COTTING, SAMUEL AUGUSTUS BELDEN. Pvt.
Born ca. 1845, NO; clerk; e 3/3/65, Mobile; on rolls March–April, 1865; p 5/10/65, Meridian, Miss.; d 6/23/67; buried Girod Cemetery, NO.

COTTRAUX, ETIENNE P. Pvt.
Born 9/45, NO; clerk; e 6/5/63, Mobile; Jackson, Chickamauga, Missionary Ridge, Atlanta and Tennessee campaigns, Spanish Fort; w twice; p 5/10/65, Meridian, Miss. After war, salesman for Small & Co., NO, "oldest coffee merchant" in city; in charge of fitting out La. troops during Spanish American War; Pickwick Club; d 3/11/06, NO; buried in Metairie Cemetery. Married Genevieve Duval.

COTTREAUX, STEPHEN J. Pvt. (Etienne P. Cottraux?)
Born ca. 1844, NO; clerk; gray eyes, light hair and complexion, 5'7"; e 6/63, Mobile; r NO; p 5/10/65, Meridian, Miss.

COVEY, D. H. (J. H., S. H.). Pvt.
e 3/5/62, NO; detached 7/26/62; became clerk with Gen. Sam Jones.

COX, J. J. Sgt.
Member of Culpepper Battery; temp. assigned to 5WA.

CRAWFORD, J. T. (GEORGE W.?) Pvt.
e 3/6/62, NO; w severely, Farmington 5/8/62; absent wounded, May–June, 1862, roll; discharged 6/62, disability.

CRAWFORD, WILLIAM A. Pvt.
Born ca. 1827 in Philadelphia, Pa.; clerk; e 6/1/63, Mobile; w Chickamauga, 9/20; hospitalized & furloughed there for 30 days, 10/4/63; deserted from furlough.

DABNEY, JAMES W. Pvt.
Born ca. 1833, Shelby Co., Tenn.; clerk in NO; blue eyes, dark hair and complexion, 5'10"; transf. from Crescent Regt. at Tupelo, 7/16/62; w and c Perryville, 10/8/62; exchanged 12/4/62. Murfreesboro, Jackson, Glass's Mill, Missionary Ridge, Atlanta campaign, detailed with wagons during

Tennessee campaign, Spanish Fort; p 5/10/65, Meridian, Miss.; 1873 was salesman for Stauffer, Kent & Co. in NO; r Bonham, Tex., 1885.

DAIGLE, (JAMES, JOSEPH) LOUIS D. Pvt.
Born *ca.* 1841 Assumption Parish; clerk; gray eyes, dark hair and complexion. e 6/1/62, Cedar Creek, Miss.; transf. from Orleans Guard Battery; k Chickamauga, 9/19/63.

DAILEY (DALEY, DALY), JAMES R. Driver.
Born *ca.* 1838 in NO; warehouse man; gray eyes, dark hair, light complexion, 6'; e 3/6/62, NO. Shiloh, Corinth, Kentucky campaign; with ordnance 1/19/64; w Spanish Fort, 4/4/65 and admitted to General Hospital Nott, Mobile; deserted 4/11/65, during evacuation of Mobile. After war, driver in NO.

DANIELL (DANIELS), CHARLES W. Pvt.
Born *ca.* 1837, Savannah, Ga.; planter; blue eyes, light hair and complexion, 5'11"; e 3/24/63, Tullahoma; present until departure for Mississippi; sent to hospital and furloughed for three months; prom. to capt., Read's-Maxwell's battery, Savannah, Ga., 1863. After war, clerk and asst. master mechanic, Mobile and Texas Railroad, NO.

DAPREMONT (DAPREMANT, DAPREMENT), LOUIS. Pvt.
Born *ca.* 1831, NO; clerk in NO; blue eyes, light hair and complexion, 5'8"; e 6/1/63, Mobile; Jackson, Glass's Mill, Missionary Ridge; transf. to 30th La. Inf., 1/1/64.

DAVIDSON, JOHN MERRYMAN. Artificer.
Born in Inverness, Scotland; attorney in NO; cousin by marriage of Richard L. Pugh; gray eyes, brown hair, dark complexion, 6'; elected 5th artificer, 2/62; e 3/6/62, NO; commended for action at Shiloh; severely w and discharged, 4/23/62; reenlisted 6/1/63; discharged 7/16/62 (over age); again reenlisted; w Dallas, 5/28/64; absent on furlough at surrender; p 6/7/65, Shreveport; r Hawaii in 1899.

DAVIS, SAMUEL J. Driver.
Born *ca.* 1842, Rome, N.Y.; painter in NO; blue eyes, dark hair, light complexion, 5'6"; e 3/6/62, NO; slightly w Shiloh, 4/7/62; c (7/62[?]) and exchanged 11/1/62 near Vicksburg; Corinth, Murfreesboro, Jackson, Glass's Mill, Missionary Ridge; absent on sick roll, 9/64; p 5/10/65, Meridian, Miss. After war, carpenter in NO.

DAVIS, WILLIAM A. H. Cpl.
Member of Culpepper Battery, temp. assigned to 5WA. After war, book-keeper, Fulton Warehouse, NO.

DAY, HENRY. Driver.
e 3/6/62, NO; Shiloh, Corinth; discharged, 7/16/62, over age.

DEBARDELOBEN, F. H. Sgt.
Member of Co. B, 1st Ala. Bn. of Arty.; temp. assigned 5WA.

DELERY, ANATOLE. Pvt.
Born 1822, NO; clerk; brown eyes, dark hair and complexion, 5'3"; e 6/1/63, Mobile; Jackson, Glass's Mill, Missionary Ridge, Atlanta campaign; detailed during Tennessee campaign; returned for Spanish Fort; p 5/10/65, Meridian, Miss. After war, clerk at Slocomb, Baldwin & Co. NO; d in NO at Shakespeare Alms House, 1/26/01; buried Metairie Cemetery.

DELERY, ARMANT. Pvt.
Born 1819, St. Charles Parish; clerk; e 6/1/63, Mobile; Jackson, Glass's Mill, Missionary Ridge, and Atlanta campaign; w Jonesboro, 9/1/64; d Macon, Ga., 10/22/64; buried Rose Hill Cemetery, Macon.

DEMERRITT, JOHN W. 1st Sgt.
Member of old BWA; e 3/6/62, NO; k Shiloh, 4/6/62.

DENÈGRE, JOSEPH "Joe." Sgt.
Born 3/3/39, NO; clerk; hazel eyes, light hair, dark complexion, 5'7"; e 3/6/62, NO; prom. to sgt., 4/11/62, for gallantry at Shiloh; Corinth, Kentucky campaign, Murfreesboro; prom. to capt. in ordnance dept., spring, 1863, and brought to Richmond to assist his friend T. L. Bayne in the operation of the Bureau of Foreign Supplies. "He declined a War Department mission to Europe a few months before the surrender because he was unwilling to leave while disaster threatened Government and friends"; d of tuberculosis 7/21/68 at Pau, France.[17] Brother of George Denègre, who married Bayne's daughter, Edith.

DEVERAY (DAVERNAY, DEVANY, DEVANEY, DEVERNAY), JOHN. Driver.
e 3/6/62, NO; Shiloh, Corinth; discharged 7/16/62, over age.

17. For an account of the activities of Denègre, Bayne, and Seixas in Richmond, see Bayne Autobiography, SHC; New Orleans *Picayune*, August 18, 1868. See also Shackelford, *George Wythe Randolph*, 139, 209n.

DICKS, J. L. Pvt.
Member of Bradford Battery; temp. assigned to 5WA.

DIVINE, W. W. Pvt. 12/61.

DIX, J. L. Pvt.

DOHERTY, L. M. Pvt.
On roll for Sept.–Oct., 1862; sent from camp at Knoxville sick, 10/30/62; Jan.–Feb., 1863, sick in Chattanooga; "absent at surrender."

DOOLEY, WILLIAM M. Driver.
Born in King's [Offaly] Co., Ireland, 1836; blacksmith in NO; blue eyes, light hair and complexion, 5′6″; e 3/6/62, NO; slightly w Shiloh; present during Kentucky campaign and all battles until w (lost leg) and c 2nd Murfreesboro, 12/7/64. Imprisoned Camp Chase; released 6/13/65. After war, drayman in NO; admitted to NSH, 3/27/84; d 9/25/85, NO; buried Army of Tenn. tomb, Metairie Cemetery.

DOWNING, J. B. Pvt.
Born ca. 1840 in NO; planter; gray eyes, dark hair, light complexion, 6′; e 11/7/63, Missionary Ridge, and fought with battery there; prom. to lieut., 9 Miss. Bn. of Sharp Shooters.

DUGGAN (DUGGIN), JOSEPH HENRY. Sgt.
Born Norfolk, Va. ca. 1834, but lived in NO "from infancy." e 3/6/62; w at Shiloh, 4/6/62, where commended for performance; prom. to sgt., 5/7/62; Corinth; c 7/62; exchanged; transf. to Fenner's battery, 8/18/62; prom. to captain of ordnance. After war, was a general commission merchant, secretary of the Louisiana Oil Co.; secretary-treasurer, Cotton Crushers Association; served as treasurer, BWA, 1877–91; d 9/27/91, NO; buried in Metairie Cemetery.

DUGGAN, MARTIN F. Pvt.
Born c. 1840 in NO; moulder; gray eyes, dark hair, light complexion, 5′6″; e 3/9/62, NO; transf. from Florida Battery; Kentucky campaign, Murfreesboro, Jackson; k at Chickamauga, 9/19/63.

EASTMAN, MIDDLETON. Pvt.
e 3/6/62, NO; discharged, 3/62, order of Gen. Bragg and sent back to NO. After war, employed at Eastman & Son, building materials, NO.

EASTON, T. B. Pvt. 12/61.

ELDRIDGE, S. H. Pvt.
Born *ca.* 1846, Arcole, La.; student in Arcadia, La.; e 11/3/64, Camp Moore, La.; Overall's Creek, 2nd Murfreesboro, Nashville, and Spanish Fort; p 5/10/65, Meridian, Miss.; r Amite City, La., 1899.

ELFER, J. ADRIAN [?] A. J. [J. A.]. Pvt.
Born *ca.* 1842; clerk; hazel eyes, black hair, dark complexion, 5'7"; e 10/8/63, Mobile; absent at surrender, sick leave. After war, clerk in NO; r there 1899.

ENGMAN, PETER W., JR. Pvt.
Born *ca.* 1842 in NO; clerk; hazel eyes, brown hair, fair complexion; e 8/1/63, Morton, Miss.; hospitalized, Jackson, Miss., 9/3/63; d of disease in hospital, 8/24/64.

ETTER, G. D. Pvt.
e 7/8/64, Mandeville, La.; r NO; p 5/10/65, Meridian, Miss.; returned to NO with 5WA; r Augusta, Ga., 1899.

FAHNESTOCK, A. MORRIS. Cpl.
Born *ca.* 1837 in Harrisburg, Pa.; clerk in NO; gray eyes, light hair and complexion, 5'8"; e 3/6/62, NO; commended for Shiloh; prom. to cpl., 4/11/62; Corinth; resigned cpl. appointment at Perryville; burned face at Murfreesboro; Jackson, Glass's Mill, Missionary Ridge; detailed 3/6/64, as clerk for Maj. Preston (inspector of arty.), by order of Gen. Johnston; unfit for field service.[18] Also assisted Dr. J. C. Legaré and Generals F. A. Shoup and W. W. Mackall; After war, listed as clerk, Charles G. Johnsen & Co., NO, 1873; r NO many years; d 8/7/84 at home in Pass Christian, Miss. Married Sallie Webb who d 10/2/71.

FALSE. See FOLSE.

FARRELL, MICHAEL. Driver.
Born *ca.* 1837 in Canada; e 3/6/62, NO; Shiloh, Corinth, Kentucky campaign, Murfreesboro, and Jackson; deserted at evacuation of Jackson, Miss., 7/16/63; after war, was special officer, NO National Banking Assoc.; d 1/22/85 in NO; r 40 years.

FARRELL, RICHARD. Driver.
Born 1833 in Waterford, Ireland; hazel eyes, dark hair, fair complexion,

---

18. One account lists him as "absent; to CSN."

5'9"; e 3/6/62, NO; Shiloh, Corinth, Kentucky campaign, Murfreesboro, Jackson; deserted at evacuation of Jackson, Miss., 7/16/63; after war, was laborer in NO; d 11/24/84.

FEHRENBACK (FAHRENBAN, FERENBACK, FEHRENBACH), NICHOLAS EDWARD. Cpl.
Born 5/20/42, Paris, France; e 3/6/62, NO; Shiloh, Corinth, w and c Perryville; exchanged 11/1/62; badly burned at Murfreesboro, 12/31/63; Jackson, Chickamauga, Missionary Ridge, Atlanta campaign; c ("deserted") at Pine Mountain, 6/16/64; imprisoned Rock Island until 5/20/65; d 5/31/81, Chatawa, Miss.

FEINHOUR (FEINOUR, FERNOUR), EDWARD C. Pvt.
Born *ca.* 1844 in Baltimore, Md.; clerk in NO; gray eyes, dark hair, fair complexion, 6'; member of Crescent Cadets, La. militia, 9/26/61; e 3/6/62, NO; Corinth, Kentucky campaign, Murfreesboro, Jackson, Glass's Mill, Missionary Ridge, and Atlanta campaign; messmate of PDS; sent to hospital sick from Lovejoy's Station; present at Spanish Fort; p 5/10/62, Meridian, Miss.; returned to NO with company where he would reside, listing himself as a "speculator" in 1873; d 5/31/81; buried in Catholic Cemetery, Chattawa, Miss., although has name plate in Army of Tenn. tomb, Metairie Cemetery.

FÉRAND, HENRY. Pvt.
Born *ca.* 1832 in NO; clerk; e 6/1/63, Mobile (refugee from NO); Jackson, w at Glass's Mill, Missionary Ridge, Atlanta and Tennessee campaigns, w Spanish Fort, 4/5/65.[19] p 5/10/65, Meridian, Miss. Brown eyes, dark hair and complexion, 5'10"; returned to NO with 5WA.

FERNANDEZ, S., JR. Pvt. 12/61.

FITCH, J. B. Pvt. 12/61.

FITZGERALD, JOHN. Pvt.
Born *ca.* 1841, NO; painter; gray eyes, black hair, dark complexion, 5'9"; e 6/1/63, Mobile. Served at Jackson and retreat to Morton, then sent to hospital 9/1/63; absent sick until end of war; d 4/17.

FITZWILLIAMS, DENNIS J. Pvt.
Born *ca.* 1843 in Ireland; clerk in NO; gray eyes, dark hair and complex-

___

19. Chalaron gives date of second wounding as February 28, 1865.

ion, 5'7"; e 8/11/61, NO. Chalaron does not list him as present at any engagements. Apparently sick and hospitalized throughout war. Absent at surrender; p 7/19/65, Houston, Tex.

FLETCHER, JOHN. Bugler.
e 3/19/62, Grand Junction, Tenn.; At Shiloh, but "not enlisted"; left battery at Clear Creek, 6/4/62; after war was carpenter in NO; d 9/05.

FLOOD, PATRICK HENRY. Pvt.
Born *ca.* 1835 in NO; painter; hazel eyes, black hair, dark complexion, 5'8"; e 6/1/63, Mobile; became ill, 6/63, although he served at Jackson and retreat to Morton; hospitalized, 9/1/63, in Mobile where he d 12/11/63; buried Magnolia Cemetery, Mobile.[20]

FOLSE, CHARLES N. Artificer.
Born 4/17/29 in Assumption Parish; sugar planter in Assumption; hazel eyes, black hair, dark complexion, 5'8"; e 6/1/62, Clear Creek, Miss. (transf. from Orleans Crescent Battery); Perryville, Murfreesboro, Jackson, Chickamauga, Missionary Ridge, Atlanta and Tennessee campaigns, Spanish Fort; p 5/10/65, Meridian, Miss.; returned to NO with 5WA. Operating Waverly Plantation, Assumption Parish, 1875; r Lafourche Parish, 1899; d 4/13/02.[21] Married Oville Truxillo who d 1/99.

FOREMAN, L. (ARTHUR L.?) Surgeon.
Appt. by secretary of war, 6/2/63, and reported to Gen. Bragg; attached to Wright's Ga. battery in late 1862. "With Battery at Dalton, and I think through Johnston's Georgia campaign until Hood's departure for Tenn." Also serving with 2nd Ky.

FOX, CHARLES WILLIAM "CHARLIE." Cpl.
Born 1/28/42 in Newburyport, Mass.; to NO, 11/59; clerk for steamship line; 5'8", fair complexion, light hair; e 3/6/62, NO, in Co. B, 10th La., then transf. to 5WA; Corinth, Kentucky campaign, Murfreesboro, and Jackson; prom. to cpl., 8/6/63; Glass's Mill, Missionary Ridge, Atlanta campaign (w in left arm at Resaca, 5/14/64); rejoined 5WA from hospital at Florence, Ala.; Overall's Creek, 2nd Murfreesboro, Nashville, Spanish Fort (in charge of special detachment manning 64-pounder, Redoubt #3); p 5/10/65, Meridian, Miss. After war, clerk at Heath, Lara & Heath,

---

20. Chalaron gives date of death as December 14, 1863.
21. Date of death may have been January 9, 1899, in New Orleans.

1873; clerk with house of Woodward Wright Co. (13 years); railroad clerk; employed in the custom house; clerk of sewerage and water board, 1908; sales mgr. of J. H. Mengen and Sons (marine hardware suppliers), 1913; r for a time at NSH; d 11/10/22, NO; married Henrietta Palmer, then Anna Monieg (d 11/23).

FOX, MICHAEL "MIKE." Pvt. Teamster.
Born in Meath Co., Ireland, *ca.* 1827; laborer in NO; gray eyes, dark hair, dark complexion, 5'2"; e 12/21/61, NO; attached 20th La., 10/12/62; returned to 5WA 7/14/63; Jonesboro; absent on rolls, 2/25/65 (furloughed by Gen. Hood); present 4/30/65 as teamster, ordnance train of battery. p 5/10/65, Meridian, Miss. Returned to NO with 5WA.

FRAE. See FROY.

FRAISER (FRASHER, FRAZER), JAMES T. Pvt.
Member of Co. B, 1st Ala. Bn. of Arty.; temp. assigned to 5WA.

FRASER (FRAZER), JOHN Y. Pvt.
Born 1837 in Columbiana Co., Ohio; clerk; gray eyes, dark hair, light complexion, 5'7"; e Confederate Guards Response, 3/6/62, NO; transf. to 5WA; Shiloh, Corinth, Kentucky campaign, Murfreesboro, Jackson; w Chickamauga, 9/20/63 (bullet in wrist); hospitalized, Atlanta, 9/25/63; prom. to lieut. in Read's-Maxwell's battery, Savannah, 1864. After war, clerk, NO; d Charity Hospital, NO, 1/22/93.

FRAZER (FRAZIER), ROBERT W. "BOB." Sgt.
Born 1844 in Winchester, Ky.; clerk; brown eyes, dark hair and complexion, 5'10"; e 3/6/62, NO; elected 4th cpl., 2/62; prom. sgt., 6/4/62; w Resaca, 5/14/63; w fatally Jonesboro, 8/31/64; d 9/1/64; buried in City Cemetery, Lexington, Ky.

FREILER (FRAILEY, FRESLER), JOHN. Pvt.
Born *ca.* 1842; r Tangipahoa Parish; e 11/20/63, Mobile. Joined company on retreat to Dalton; Atlanta and Tennessee campaigns, Spanish Fort. p 5/10/65, Meridian, Miss.; in 1908 was proprietor of Live Oak Plantation, Greensburg, La.; state legislator; d Presbyterian Hosp., NO, 4/25/17, and buried Greensburg. Married Dora Ludwig.

FRERET, GUSTAVE J. "GUS." Pvt.
Born *ca.* 1843 in NO; clerk; gray eyes, light hair and complexion, 5'6"; e 6/1/63, Mobile. Jackson and retreat to Morton; listed as sick on 10/63

roll; present 12/63; at Genl. Hosp., "Cantey," in spring, 1865, with frost-bitten feet. "Absent at surrender, sick furlough." After war, bookkeeper, NO; d 4/13/82; buried in Army of Tenn. tomb, Metairie Cemetery.

FRERET, WILLIAM ALFRED. Artificer (Pvt.)
Born 1/19/33, NO; son of Mayor William Freret and Fanny Salkeld; educated in England; an established architect when war broke out; e in 5WA, 3/6/62; 1st artificer at Shiloh and Corinth; detached at Tupelo, 6/17/62 and transf. to engineers, reporting to Gen. John Pegram; transf. later to staff of Gen. E. Kirby Smith, where served greater part of war.[22] At engagement at Rogers' Farm, "he was prom. for gallantry on the field by General Smith in person"; present at the battle of Richmond, Ky., occupation of Frankfort, Pleasant Hill, Saline River, and Camden; during Red River campaign, prom. to capt.; advanced to major of engineers and finally to lieutenant colonel. p at Shreveport. After war, returned to NO; appt. state engineer, 1866; became capt. and chief engineer, Shreveport, La.; resumed architectural practice; appt. supervising architect of the U.S. Treasury Department, 1887; d 12/5/11; buried in the Army of Tenn. tomb, Metairie Cemetery.

FROEMN (FROEM), L. Surgeon.
To rank from 7/15/62 and with Polk's corps, 12/62; surgeon with 5WA at Dalton, 12/63; attending CHS on 9/1/64, although on duty at Gen. Shoup's Hdq.

FROY (FROYE, FROZE), JACOB. Pvt.
Born ca. 1833 in Baden, Germany; shoemaker in NO; hazel eyes, black hair, dark complexion, 5'5"; e 8/29/61, Camp Moore; w Shiloh, Farmington; transf. to 5WA from 20th La. as driver; Murfreesboro, Jackson, Chickamauga, Missionary Ridge; returned to 20th La., 12/16/63.

GAGLE.
Joined after leaving NO.

GAINES, ALONZO. Pvt.
Born ca. 1831 in Bourbon Co., Ky.; clerk in NO; gray eyes, dark hair and complexion, 5'7"; e 6/1/63, Mobile; Jackson, Glass's Mill; detached to

---

22. "For gallant conduct in the field on the 30th ult., you are hereby appointed 1LT of Arty in Prov. Army of the Confederate States." John Pegram to W. Freret, September 21, 1862, Chalaron Papers, HTT.

General Hardee to work as clerk with Maj. Sykes, purchasing commissary; p Gainesville, Ala.; d 1869.

GALPIN, FRANK H. Pvt.
Born *ca.* 1840 in NO; clerk; hazel eyes, dark hair, light complexion. e 10/8/63, Mobile; joined 5WA at Missionary Ridge; w in shoulder at Resaca, 5/14/64.[23] c ("deserted") Pine Mountain, Ga., 6/13/64; imprisoned at Rock Island; released 5/23/65.

GALPIN, SAMUEL. Pvt.
Born *ca.* 1843 in NO; r NO; dark eyes and hair, fair complexion, 5′9″; e 8/12/61, NO, transf. to 5WA from 1st La., 11/1/63; Missionary Ridge and opening of Atlanta campaign; c ("deserted") Pine Mountain, Ga., 6/15/64, and imprisoned Rock Island.

GANNAWAY, CHRISTOPHER COLUMBUS. Pvt.
Appt. by secretary of war, 6/2/63 and served as "floater" in Breckinridge's div.; "Asst. Surgeon of Cobb's Btry., attached to 5WA at Dalton for a while."

GARLAND, WILLIAM H. Pvt.
r Summitt, Miss.; e 1WA; temp. assigned to 5WA, 3/63; p 5/10/65, Meridian, Miss.

GAYLE.
Served at Corinth; furloughed "on Doctor's report as hurt in foot." Perhaps same Gayle, 7th La., discharged 8/61 as "opium eater."

GEIGER, F. H. Pvt. 12/61.

GIBSON, ROBERT. Q.M. Sgt.
Born *ca.* 1838 in New York City; clerk in NO; hazel eyes, dark hair and complexion, 5′9″; e 3/6/62, NO; prom. to Q.M. Sgt., 7/5/62, Tupelo; "Remained at his post with the company in the field throughout all its campaigns, though suffering repeatedly from awful rheumatisms"; p 5/10/65, Meridian, Miss.; returned to New York where he d 6/4/76.

GIFFEN, JAMES FORTESCUE. Cpl.
Born 6/11/39 in NO, son of Adam Giffen; attended Harvard; left before graduation to join 5WA; e 3/6/62; w Shiloh, but served at Corinth; prom. cpl., 5/7/62; Kentucky campaign, Murfreesboro; prom. to sgt., 1/21/63;

---

23. Chalaron shows Samuel Galpin, rather than Frank Galpin, being wounded at Resaca.

Jackson, Chickamauga, Missionary Ridge, Atlanta, and Tennessee campaigns; w seriously Spanish Fort, 4/5/65, acting in capacity of sgt. major of Cobb's bn. of arty.; c at fall of Mobile and prisoner at surrender; also slightly w at Kennesaw Ridge. r NO after the war; entered hardware import business (Giffen & Co.); moved to Ky. for several years, becoming secretary of the Louisiana Sugar Planters Assoc. Appt. assist. appraiser for the port of NO by President Grover Cleveland; d 6/11/93 in NO. Married Louise Elizabeth Wallis who d 4/30/32.

GIFFEN, ROBERT C. Pvt.
Born *ca.* 1843 in NO, youngest son of Adam Giffen; medical student; gray eyes, light hair and complexion, 5'7½"; e 3/5/62 in Crescent Regiment and transf. to 5WA at Tupelo, 7/62; Kentucky campaign, Murfreesboro, Jackson, and Glass's Mill; hospitalized 10/8–10/22/63, Floyd House and Ocmulgee Hospital, Macon, Ga.; w Missionary Ridge, 11/25/63; hospitalized and detailed by secretary of war with provost marshal at Oryka, Miss.; after war, was druggist in NO; d 5/1/76 in NO.

GIFFIN, WILLIAM BUTLER. Sgt.
Born *ca.* 1837 in NO; son of Adam Giffen. e 3/6/62, NO; r St. Martinville, La.; elected 4th sgt. 2/62; mortally w Shiloh, 4/6/62 (struck by shell in leg); d 7/12/62 in NO.

GILBERT, JOHN. Pvt.
Member of Co. D, 1st Ala. Bn. of Arty.; temp. assigned to 5WA.

GILES, GEORGE H. Pvt.
Born NO *ca.* 1842; clerk in NO; gray eyes, dark hair, fair complexion, 5'6"; e 8/12/61, NO, in 1st La. Inf.; transf. to 5WA 11/7/63; Missionary Ridge, Atlanta and Tennessee campaigns, Spanish Fort. p. 5/10/65, Meridian, Miss. Returned to NO with 5WA. A George Giles listed as carpenter in NO, 1873; d 12/19/75, NO.

GILLESPIE, JOHN. Pvt. Teamster.
Born *ca.* 1828 in Christian Co., Ky.; painter in NO; blue eyes, dark hair, light complexion, 5'5"; e 11/9/63, Missionary Ridge. Present on roll, 8/31/64, as teamster; c Limestone Co., Ala., 12/31/64; took USA oath and enlisted in U.S. Army, 3/20/65 at Chicago.

GILLON (GILLAN), GEORGE. Driver. Cook.
e 3/6/62, NO; Shiloh and Corinth; discharged, 7/16/62, over age.

GOLDSMITH, T. (F.?). Pvt. 12/61.

GOLLMER, WILLIAM. Pvt.
Born in Wurtemburg, Germany, 9/17/41; located in NO, 1853; carpenter; blue eyes, light hair and complexion, 5'5"; e 3/9/62, NO, in CSA Response (Florida battery); transf. to 5WA, 7/16/62; c Perryville; exchanged and fought at Murfreesboro; sick in hospital, Tullahoma, spring, 1863; Jackson, Glass's Mill, Missionary Ridge, Atlanta and Tennessee campaigns, Spanish Fort; p 5/10/65, Meridian, Miss.; returned to NO with 5WA; a William Gollmer is listed as a porter in NO in 1873; d 10/12/97 of abdominal cancer, in NO; buried Lafayette Cemetery #1, NO.

GOMEZ, JAMES F. Pvt.
Born May, 1844, in NO; clerk; gray eyes, dark hair and complexion, 5'8"; e 6/1/63, Mobile (refugee from NO); Jackson, Glass's Mill; sent to hospital, 9/24/63; absent as sick, "unfit for field service," and detailed to Surg. S. H. Stout, med. div., by Gen. Johnston, 4/29/64; d 11/19/84.

GOODWYN (GOODWIN), FRED D. Pvt.
Born ca. 1833, in New York City; policeman in NO; brown eyes and hair, light complexion, 5'5"; e 3/9/62 in 16th La. Inf. Bn. ("Florida Bn") at NO; transf. to 5WA, 7/16/62, Tupelo; Kentucky campaign, Murfreesboro, Jackson, Glass's Mill, Missionary Ridge; deserted at Dalton, 12/22/63; took USA oath 1/4/63.

GORDON, HENRY "HARRY." Pvt.
Born 1846 in NO; clerk; black hair, brown eyes, dark complexion, 5'2"; e 11/25/63, Mobile; joined 5WA on retreat from Missionary Ridge and served throughout Atlanta and Tennessee campaigns, Spanish Fort; returned with 5WA to NO where d 1/21/73.

GREEN, BENJAMIN HILDRETH, JR. Sgt.
Elected 2nd sgt. about 12/61; e 3/6/62, NO; shot through body at Shiloh, 4/7/62 and died from wound very soon thereafter. Buried Girod Street Cemetery, NO.

GREENWOOD, MILO (MOSES?), JR. Pvt.
Born ca. 1830 in Worcester, Mass.; son of Moses Greenwood; vice-president, Greenwood & Son, Factors and Traders Ins. Co. e 5/8/62, Corinth; Kentucky campaign, Murfreesboro, and Jackson; w Chickamauga, 9/20/63; foot was amputated at the instep. Thought to be "doing very

well" on 10/4, but died the following day; buried in Georgia Confederate Cemetery, Marietta.

GREENWOOD, PHILLIP P. Pvt.
Born NO, *ca.* 1847; r Alabama; student; gray eyes, fair complexion, light hair; trying to join 5WA, spring, 1864; e 3/28/65, Mobile; Spanish Fort; p 5/10/65, Meridian, Miss.; after war, was clerk in NO.

GUNTER, A. Pvt.
Member of Co. B, 1st Ala. Bn. of Arty.; temp. assigned to 5WA.

HALL, C. J. Pvt.
Member of Co. D, 1st. Ala. Bn. of Arty.; temp. assigned to 5WA.

HALL, L. Asst. Surg.
"Assigned to Battery after promotion of Asst. Surg. Legaré." Served July–Oct., 1863; relieved by medical director, 10/15/63.

HALL, WILLIAM H. Pvt.
Born 1845 in Morton, Miss.; gilder; blue eyes, brown hair, light complexion, 5'1"; e 8/21/63, Morton, Miss.; w Missionary Ridge, 11/25/63, but served Atlanta and Tennessee campaigns; present at surrender; p 5/10/65, Meridian, Miss.

HALSEY, W. S. 5th Cpl., 12/61

HAMILTON, GEORGE W. Pvt.
Born *ca.* 1843 in Lawrence Co., Ala.; farmer; hazel eyes, dark hair, light complexion; e 10/11/63, Monroe, Miss.; transf. to 23rd Miss. and returned 4/64; absent at surrender.

HANEY, JOSEPH HANCOCK. Pvt.
Born 3/5/35, Seneca Co., Ohio; civil engineer, Van Buren Co., Ark.; e 7/12/61, Camp Walker, Ark. in 3rd Ark.; discharged 8/30/61; joined 5WA as volunteer 5/27/62 at Corinth; e formally on 6/16 at Tupelo; Kentucky campaign, Murfreesboro; 6/7/63, employed by Gen. Breckinridge at Jackson to survey and map vicinity. Discharged by prom. to 2nd lt., Engineers, 6/11/63; prom. to 1st lt., then capt., spending the remainder of the war in the Trans-Mississippi; surrendered at Shreveport. After the war, returned to Ark. and continued work building the Little Rock and Fort Smith Railroad; in 1904 employed as city engineer by the city of Little Rock, having r since at least 1875; d 8/12/04; buried in Mt. Holly Cemetery, Little Rock. Kept war diary.

Hanley (Hanly), William P. Driver.
e 3/6/62, NO; discharged 7/16/62, over age; after war was broom maker in NO.

Hardy, Henry (William Henry?). Pvt.
e 7/4/64 Chattahoochee River; c 2nd Murfreesboro, 12/7/64.

Harmm, B. M. Pvt.
Member of Co. D, 1st. Ala. Bn. of Arty.; temp. assigned to 5WA.

Harris, J. T. Sgt.
Member of Co. D, 1st Ala. Bn. of Arty.; temp. assigned to 5WA.

Harrison, William. Pvt.
e 6/26/64, Kennesaw Mountain; sent to hospital sick, and k en route in railroad accident, 7/10/64.

Hartnett, Casilear Joseph "Caz." Pvt.
Born 1/42 in England, stepson of Thomas H. Shields of NO; clerk; e 3/6/62, NO; k Shiloh, 4/6/62.

Harvey, Charles M. Pvt.
Born *ca.* 1826, Vermont,[24] son of Delia Oakes and James P. Harvey; unmarried merchant in NO; e 3/6/62, NO; discharged disability, 7/16/62 (fractured ankle); returned Jan.–Feb., 1865; d NO, 3/19/14 and buried in St. Patrick's Cemetery, NO.

Hayes, Mike. Pvt.
Born *ca.* 1833 in London, England; plasterer in NO; gray eyes, light hair and complexion, 5'5"; e 3/9/62, NO, in Confederate Guards Response battery; transf. to 5WA, 7/16/62, Tupelo; Kentucky campaign and Murfreesboro; c (deserted) on retreat from Jackson, 7/16/63; sent to Snyder's Bluff, Miss., 7/30/63.

Haynes (Hays), John. Driver.
e 3/6/62, NO; deserted 3/8/62, "prior to departure."

Hayward, W. B. Pvt.
Born *ca.* 1844 in NO; student; r Mississippi City, Miss.; e Enterprise, Miss.; p 5/10/65, Meridian, Miss.; operated cotton press; served on Board of Health, NO; r NO, 1899.

24. Obituary shows Harvey born in New Orleans.

HAZARD, JOHN B. Pvt.
Born *ca.* 1833, Washington Co., Ala.; bookkeeper, Shelby Co., Ala.; gray eyes, light hair, fair complexion, 6'; member of Crescent Rifles; participated in capture of Baton Rouge arsenal, 1/61; to Virginia as member of Dreux's bn.; sent to Ala. with chills and chronic fever; joined Crescent regt. and w at Mansfield; joined Roddy's cav.; transf. to 5WA by order of secretary of war, 10/4/63, Missionary Ridge; Atlanta and Tennessee campaigns, Spanish Fort; p 5/10/65, Meridian, Miss.; r Covington, Ky., 3/97; r Mooresville, Ala., 1899–1903.

HEDGES, J. H. H. Ordnance Sgt.
Born *ca.* 1837 in Va., son of the Rev. Dr. C. S. Hedges; merchant in NO and member of old BWA; e 3/6/62, NO; Shiloh, Farmington, Corinth; "Hedges" says Vaught, "has got a discharge on a surgeon's certificate of disability. Were I as fat as he is, I should be *ashamed* to sign my name to an application for a discharge." Transf. to ordnance dept., CSA. "During the last two years of the war he was made superintendent of the Powder Mills at Selma." p 5/10/65, Meridian, Miss. After the war, druggist, NO; traveling salesman for White Lead and Oil Co., St. Louis; d 6/15/12 at NSH in NO and buried in Army of Tenn. tomb, Metairie Cemetery. Married Kate Dorsey of Ill.

HENDERSON, H. L. Pvt.
e 3/6/62, NO; transf. to 6WA; absent at surrender.

HENDERSON, VICTOR EVANS. Pvt.
e 3/7/64, Dalton, Ga.; detached as clerk for Gen. Beauregard; on rolls 9/64–4/65 but furloughed sick leave; absent at surrender, sick leave; r after war in Harrison Co., Tex., where he was physician. Wife's name was Annie.

HENDERSON, WILLIAM D. Pvt.
e 3/6/62, NO; Shiloh and Corinth; detached for duty at Hospital Depot, Corinth, 5/18/62, by order of Gen. Beauregard; returned to 5WA late July, 1864, and served at Jonesboro; detached again 9/64 to Capt. J. S. Storey, by order of Gen. Hood; absent at surrender, detailed; r NO, 1873, and partner in Jackson, Kilpatrick & Henderson, importers and dealers in salt; later shown r in Dallas, Tex., as employee in general freight department of Texas and Pacific Railroad.

HENNING, WILLIAM H. Pvt. 12/61.

Sgt. in command of 5WA reserves and "chairman and chief instructor"; left in NO, 3/8/62.

HEWS, EDSON L. "ED." 2nd Lt.

Born *ca.* 1839; clothing salesman in NO; member of old BWA (joined 1858); elected sr. 2nd lt., 6/27/61; reelected 2/14/62; Shiloh; resigned with Hodgson, 6/17/62, at Cedar Creek, Miss. After war, partner in Pierson & Hews, men's clothing and furnishings store; charter member of the Louisiana Club; member of the Chess, Checkers, and Whist Club; member of some of the carnival organizations; d 4/18/05; buried Metairie Cemetery. Married Josephine "Jo" Pierson.

HIGGINS, STANFORD. Orderly Sgt.

Born *ca.* 1842; clerk; e 3/6/62, NO; elected 2nd cpl., 2/62; commended for Shiloh where w, 4/7/62; prom. to orderly sgt., 8/26/62; prom. to 1st sgt., 11/17/62; d 6/9/63 of typhoid pneumonia at Eagleville, Tenn.

HILL, ALFRED. Pvt. 12/61.

HODGSON, WASHINGTON IRVING. Capt.

Born 11/27/33, Louisville, Ky., son of sea captain, Henry Hodgson, and socially prominent Jane Josephine Howard. Educated in Kentucky and at Eaton Seminary, Tenn.; at age 14, moved to NO; was clerk with a hardware company, and in 1857 joined firm of James B. Walton, "the well-known auctioneer." Joined BWA, 1851; as 1st lt. of 4WA, remained in NO and organized reserve corps which evolved into 5WA when BWA went to Va. in 1861. Elected capt. 6/27/61; reelected at formal organization of 5WA, 2/2/62. Led 5WA at Shiloh; relinquished command to Vaught 6/4/62; resigned 6/13/62. Served during remainder of the war on staff of Gov. Henry W. Allen, and in Trans-Mississippi Department. After the war, worked for Walton, until 1869; opened auctioneering and real estate firm with Charles D. Nash, which in 1885 became W. I. Hodgson & Son. Elected councilman and an officer in Crescent City Democratic Club. d 3/14/96; buried in Lafayette Cemetery #1, NO. Married Annie F. Hames.

HOERNER, JULIUS. Pvt. 12/61.

HOLME, FRED. Artificer.

Elected 6th artificer, 2/62; e 3/6/62, NO; discharged, 7/16/62, over age.

HOLMES, CURTIS. Commissary Sgt.
Born *ca.* 1836 in Plymouth, Mass.; clerk in NO; gray eyes, brown hair, light complexion, 5'6"; e 3/6/62, NO; seriously w at Shiloh where commended for service; prom. to commissary sgt., 9/64; served in all battles and campaigns; p 5/10/65, Meridian, Miss.; d 1898, Plymouth, Mass.

HOPKINS, ANTHONY "ANDY." Driver.
Born *ca.* 1835 in Ireland; e 3/8/62, NO; transf. from Fla. Bn. (16th La.), 7/15/62; Kentucky campaign; severely w and c, Murfreesboro, 1/2/63; sick, could not be transf. for exchange; hospitalized in Chattanooga; absent at surrender, disabled. After war, private watchman, NO; r NO, 1899.

HOPKINS, OCTAVE. Pvt.
Born La.; e 3/27/62, Grand Junction, Tenn.; w Shiloh, 4/6/62; on rolls, Jan.–Feb., 1863, as absent, sick; cotton factor and merchant in NO after war.

HOPPER, JOHN. Pvt.
On roll, 1/4/64.

HORTON, S. J. Sgt.
Member of Co. D, 1st. Ala. Bn. of Arty.; temp. assigned to 5WA.

HULL, FRANCIS B. "FRANK." Pvt.
Born Miss.; e 3/23/64, Dalton, Ga.; r Jackson, Miss.; p 5/10/65, Meridian, Miss.; Atlanta and Tennessee campaigns, Spanish Fort; after war, "steamboat man" on Mississippi; located in Jackson, Miss., by mid-1880s.

HUMBERT, PAUL. Cpl.
e 9/13/61, Donaldsonville, La., in Donaldsonville arty.; temp. assigned to 5WA, 4/14/65, at Meridian, Miss.

HUMPHREYS, JOHN B. Pvt.
Born *ca.* 1832, Lake Charles Parish, La.; planter; gray eyes, auburn hair, fair complexion, 5'10"; e 3/6/62, NO; prom. 2nd lt., 1st La. Arty., 2/17/63; p 5/10/65, Meridian, Miss. r NO, 1899.

HYDE, FRANK. Pvt.
Born 1841; r Orleans Parish; fair complexion, light hair, blue eyes, 5'7"; e 6/17/64, Marietta, Ga.; c Nashville, 12/16/64; imprisoned at Camp Chase; released 6/13/65.

JAMES, THEODORE A. Lt.
Elected lieut., WA reserve co. (late 1861?); evidently not reelected when 5WA formally organized 2/24/62.

JAMESON (JAMISON, JAMIESON), JOHN J. Sgt.
Born *ca.* 1839, Alexandria, Va.; clerk in NO; gray eyes, light hair and complexion; e 3/6/62, NO; elected 1st cpl. 2/62; Shiloh, Corinth; prom. 5th sgt., 6/4/62; prom. 4th sgt., 6/21/62; returned to the ranks at own request, 8/6/63; present at surrender; p 5/10/65, Meridian, Miss.; after war, merchant, Alexandria, Va.; d 1/21/99, Bluefield, West Va.

JANIN, LOUIS. Pvt.
Native of France; lawyer and co-owner of sugar refinery with Judah P. Benjamin; member of 2WA until temp. assigned 5WA, 4/6/65, Mobile; after war, lawyer in NO; married Miss Covington.

JARREAU, J. Pvt. 12/61.

JARREAU, L. Pvt. 12/61.

JOHNSEN, CHARLES GARRETT. 2nd Lt.
Born 1833 in Vicksburg, of Danish descent; moved to NO where he became cotton merchant; e 3/6/62, NO; r St. Joseph, Tensas Parish, La.; as private commended for performance at Shiloh; commended for Murfreesboro; prom. 2nd Lt. 10/2/63; Atlanta and Tennessee campaigns, Spanish Fort; p 5/10/65, Meridian, Miss. After war, commission merchant, NO; in 1876 owner of the NO Machinery Depot, Foundry and Machine Shops; eventually business failed. As a Republican, appt. by President Benjamin Harrison supt. of Custom house; d 11/2/93, Mandeville, La., and buried there.

JONES, CLEMENT F. (B.? T.?) Cpl.
Born Kent Co., Md.; physician; e 3/6/62, NO; commended for Shiloh; prom. cpl., 11/19/62; appt. asst. surgeon, 5/10/63, Wartrace, Tenn.; transf. to Cleburne's division, then Wheeler's cavalry.

JONES, JAMES. Pvt.
Member of Co. D, 1st. Ala. Bn. of Arty.; temp. assigned to 5WA.

JONES, THOMAS. Pvt.
Member of Co. B, 1st Ala. Bn. of Arty.; temp. assigned to 5WA.

JORDAN (JOURDAN), JOHN (JAMES). Driver.
e 3/6/62, NO; present at Shiloh, Corinth; left sick at Red Sulphur Springs,

Tenn., 3/63, on march into Ky.; "never since been heard from"; deserted, 9/18/63, Red Sulphur Springs.

JORDAN, W. A. Artificer.
Elected 3rd artificer, 2/62; e 3/6/62, NO; discharged 7/16/62, over age; r NO after war and listed as builder.

KAISER, GABRIEL. Pvt.
e 3/6/62, NO; Shiloh, Corinth; present on rolls, 5/62–10/62; deserted, 5/12/62, according to Chalaron.

KEHOUGH (KEHOE, KEHO), THOMAS. Driver.
Born *ca.* 1834 in Waxford Co., Ireland; clerk in NO; gray eyes, dark hair and complexion, 5'6"; e 12/21/61, Camp Lewis, La.; transf. to 5WA; present at Jackson; hospitalized 7/18/63 and absent until 4/64; teamster on forage train through Atlanta and Tennessee campaigns; w Spanish Fort, 3/28/65; p 5/10/65, Meridian, Miss. Returned to NO.

KELLY, DANIEL "DAN." Pvt. 12/61.

KELLY, PATRICK "PAT." Driver.
Born Roscommon Co., Ireland *ca.* 1840; laborer in NO; dark eyes, hair, and complexion, 5'7"; e 3/6/62, NO; hospitalized 7/25/63, "unfit for field service"; detailed, 1/1/64–4/30/64, to surgeon Stout, medical director; on rolls 5/64–4/65 as absent, sick; p 5/11/65, Mobile; after war, was either candy maker, laborer, or saloon worker in NO.

KEMP, J. W. Cpl.
Member of Co. D, 1st. Ala. Bn. of Arty.; temp. assigned to 5WA.

KENNER, MINOR, JR. Pvt.
Born 1841, son of Stephen M. and Eliza Davis Kenner. e 3/6/62, NO; Shiloh, Corinth; prom. cadet, CSA, 11/21/62; Nov.–Dec. 1862, with Marshall's battery; reports to Gen. Buckner's hdq. 2/23/63 as engineer; prom. to 2nd lt., Engineers, 12/19/63; became adjutant, 1st La. Heavy Arty., Mobile; p Meridian, Miss., 5/13/65.

KENNETT, L. M., JR. Pvt.
Born *ca.* 1833 in Carrolton, Ill.; hazel eyes, light hair and complexion, 5'7"; e 6/1/63, Mobile (refugee from NO); detached, order of Gen. Bragg, to Capt. J. P. Horback (Chalmers' div.) on Q.M. duty, "unfit for field service"; p 5/11/65, Gainesville, Ala.

KENT, JOHN R. Pvt.
Born *ca.* 1844, Clinton, La.; farmer in Tangipahoa Parish; blue eyes, light hair and complexion, 5'8"; e 9/1/63, La Fayette, Ga.; w Resaca, 5/14/64; absent on rolls, 9/1/64–2/28/65; furloughed by order of Gen. Hood; p 5/10/65, Meridian, Miss.; after war, salesman for J. L. Dunnica & Co., NO; r. Kentwood, La., 1899.

KEYES, PATRICK "PAT." Pvt.
Born 1817; gray eyes, dark hair, light complexion, 5'8½"; e 6/20/63, Jackson, Miss., as substitute for R. L. Pugh; deserted (c) on retreat from Jackson, 7/16/63.

KIBBE (KIBBIE, KIBBLE), A. F. Pvt.
Born *ca.* 1842 in Vermillion, La.; stock raiser; blue eyes, light hair and complexion, 5'11"; e 9/16/61, Houston, Tex.; temp. transf. from 3rd Tex. Cav., being dismounted; deserted at Missionary Ridge, 11/25/63.

KNIGHT, G. F. Pvt. 12/61.

KORNDOFFER, R. Pvt. 12/61.

KRUMBHAAR, WILLIAM BUTLER. Pvt.
Born Philadelphia, Pa.; clerk; e 3/6/62, NO; after Shiloh, detailed with Maj. George Williamson, Asst. Adj. Gen., Gen. Leonidas Polk, 4/15/62; prom. 1st lt. arty., 11/17/62; organized and commanded Krumbhaar's-Stafford's battery in Trans-Mississippi, seeing action in the Indian Territory and Ark. Prom. to capt., 4/2/63, and major, 8/17/64; served with Gens. J. B. Magruder, T. H. Holmes and E. Kirby Smith; surrendered 5/65 in Shreveport, cmdg. 6th Arty. Bn., Dept. of Trans-Mississippi; after war, owned W. B. Krumbhaar & Co., prop. Penn Cotton Press.

LACEY (LACY), PATRICK "PAT." Pvt.
Born *ca.* 1828 in Tipperary Co., Ireland; steamboat man in NO; blue eyes, light hair and complexion, 5'7"; e 9/11/61, Camp Moore, La.; Jackson, Chickamauga, Missionary Ridge; transf. back to his regt., 12/63; transf. to CSN, 4/11/64, by order Gen. J. E. Johnston; after war, was foundryman in NO.

LACY, THOMAS. Driver.
e 3/6/62, NO; present, May–June, 1862; discharged 7/16/62, over age.

LAMARE, JUST M. Pvt.
Born *ca.* 1843 in Assumption Parish; "compositor"; blue eyes, fair com-

plexion, dark hair; e 6/1/63, Mobile; Jackson, Glass's Mill, Missionary Ridge, Atlanta and Tennessee campaigns. c on furlough, 3/8/65, in Ascension Parish; p 5/17/65 in NO; d 2/22/25, and buried in St. Patrick Cemetery, Donaldsonville, LA.

LAMB, A. M. Pvt.
Member of Culpepper S.C. battery; temp. assigned to 5WA.

LAW, GEORGE H. Pvt.
Born ca. 1839 in Howard Co., Mo.; clerk; e 6/5/62, Cedar Creek, Miss. Kentucky campaign, Murfreesboro, Jackson, Glass's Mill, Missionary Ridge; transf. to CSN ca. 8/64; r Cuero, Tex., 1899.

LEAHY (LAHEY, LEAHEY), JOHN. Driver.
Born ca. 1843 in Tex.; gray eyes, light hair, fair complexion, 5'7"; e 9/11/61, Camp Moore, La. in 13th La.; transf. to 5WA temp. as driver, 10/12/62, and remained on rolls July–Oct., 1863; Murfreesboro, Jackson, retreat to Morton, Glass's Mill, Missionary Ridge; returned to 13th La., 12/16/63.

LEARY, JOHN. Driver.
e 3/6/62, NO; though seriously w at Shiloh, 4/7/62, named first chief of caissons, 6/4/62; sent from Corinth to hospital at Holly Springs; still hospitalized through 10/63; d as result of wounds.

LEARY, T. Driver.

LECKIE, HENRY. Cpl.
e 3/6/62, NO; commended for Shiloh; appt. cpl., 4/23/62, Corinth; present on May–June, 1862, rolls; discharged at Tupelo, 7/16/62, over age; after war, cotton factor in NO.

LEE, WILLIAM A. Pvt.
e 8/18/62 at Camp Moore; temp. attached 10/12/62.

LEGARÉ, JOHN CECIL. Asst. Surgeon.
Born S.C.; graduated NO School of Medicine; owned "Souvenir Plantation" (on present site of Godchaux Sugar Co. at Reserve, La.); organized and became lt. of Avoyelles Rifles; mustered out of service; surgeon at Camps Moore and Lewis; joined 5WA, 3/6/62, in NO; appt. surgeon 9/26/62; 1/31/63 became sr. surgeon, Adams' brig., Breckinridge's div. (Chalaron: prom. from asst. surg. to surg., 7/8/63); became medical inspector of D. H. Hill's corps; assigned to medical director of hospitals,

S. H. Stout, 2/5/64; assign. Frank Ramsay Hospital, Thomaston, Ga.; later in hospital in Richmond, Va. After war, practiced medicine, NO, until moving to Ascension Parish in 1870; to Memphis during yellow fever epidemic, 1878; awarded medal for his services; appt. postmaster in Donaldsonville by President Benjamin Harrison, and later "the melter and refiner of the United States mint" at NO; apparently living in Abilene, Texas in 1897; d 5/31/05; buried in Metairie Cemetery. Married Eliza Mauran.

LEGARÉ, OSCAR A. Cpl.
Bn. 1847 in Alton, Ill.; nephew of Dr. J. C. Legaré; telegraph operator; gray eyes, light hair and complexion, 6'2"; e 6/12/62, Tupelo; Kentucky campaign, Murfreesboro; detached as telegraph operator by General Bragg, 1/11/63; returned for Chickamauga and w at Missionary Ridge, 11/25/63; Atlanta campaign; prom. cpl. at Kennesaw Ridge; k Peachtree Creek, 7/20/64; buried in Macon, Ga.

L'ESTRADE.
"Not enlisted, who served with the Battery during some of its engagements."

LEVERICH, ABRAM INSKEEP "ABE." 2nd Lt.
Born in NO ca. 1836, son of Emile Leverich, a prominent cotton merchant; educated in NO and at Flushing, Long Island; returned home and clerked at father's office; gray eyes, light hair and complexion, 5'10"; e 3/6/62, NO; prom. 1st sgt., 4/7/62; prom. orderly sgt., 6/4/62; prom. 2nd Lt., 7/24/62; w Kennesaw; severely w in cheek at Spanish Fort, 4/5/65; c when Mobile fell; prisoner at surrender. After war, clerk at Jary & Gillis, NO; in 1887 became partner, Gillis, Leverich & Co.; d 12/14/96; buried in Metairie Cemetery; president of Pickwick Club; bachelor, although one source lists Theodosia Braswell as wife; sister was Mrs. B. F. Eshleman.

LEVERICH, HENRY. Pvt.
Born ca. 1847 in NO, son of Emile Leverich and brother of Abram I.; student; e 4/7/65, Eutaw, Ala.; 5'10", fair complexion, dark hair, blue eyes; p 5/10/65, Meridian, Miss. After war, secretary of the NO and Lake Railroad; d 3/8/95.

LEVIE, C. A. Pvt.
Born ca. 1841 in NO; clerk; hazel eyes, dark hair and complexion, 5'11";

e 10/8/63, Mobile; present on rolls until 10/63; transf. to 22nd La. Arty which was captured at Vicksburg. After war, clerk in NO.

LEVY, LIONEL L. Pvt.
Born 1828 in Charleston, S.C. Mother was sister of Judah P. Benjamin; educated at Bingham's school in N.C. and Univ. of N.C. (grad., 1848); studied law in uncle Judah Benjamin's office; began law practice in NO; dark eyes, hair, and complexion, 5'3"; e 1/61 Crescent Rifles and participated in capture of arsenal at Baton Rouge; e 3/6/62, NO; commended for Shiloh; Kentucky campaign; prom. to Judge Advocate Lt. Gen. T. H. Holmes's military court, 12/26/62, with rank of captain of cavalry; continued in this duty until end of war, serving under Holmes's successor, Kirby Smith; surrendered with Gen. Taylor and p Meridian, Miss. After war, returned to NO and resumed law practice (Cotton & Levy); retired, 1890; d 11/20/1900.

LEYSTER, C. A. Pvt.
Transf. from 15th Miss. inf.

LOBDELL, JAMES ALEXANDER. Pvt.
Born 1847 in NO; member of 2WA; temp. assigned to 5WA, 4/6/65, in Mobile; after war, clerk in NO; admitted to NSH, 7/5/97.

LOGAN, HENRY. Pvt.
Born *ca.* 1845 in NO; student who r at Mississippi City, Miss., when he joined 5WA at Spanish Fort; present March–April, 1865; p 5/10/65, Meridian, Miss.; although returned to Mississippi City, was a shipping clerk in NO, 1873.

LONG, PATRICK "PAT." Driver.
Born Ireland; e 3/6/62, NO; present March–April, 1862; k Shiloh, 4/7/62.

LONSDALE, HENRY H. Pvt.
e 3/6/62, NO; Shiloh, Farmington, acting as company clerk; discharged 5/23/62, disability; after war, coffee broker in NO.

LYNOTT (LYNOT), THOMAS. Driver.
e 3/6/62, NO; present, March–April, 1862; Shiloh and Corinth; discharged 7/16/62, disability.

LYSTER, C. A. Pvt.
Member of 15th Miss.; temp. assigned to 5WA.

MABRY, A. G. Sgt.
Member of Co. B, 1st Ala. Bn. of Arty; temp. assigned to 5WA.

McCORMACK (McCORMICK, McCARMACK), HUGH. Driver.
e 3/6/62, NO; Shiloh, Corinth; c Perryville, 10/8/62; imprisoned at Lou-isville; took USA oath.

McCORMACK (McCORMICK), JOHN M. Pvt.
Born Kildare Co., Ireland, *ca.* 1837; 5'8", blue eyes, fair complexion, dark hair; tanner [tinner] in NO; e 3/9/62; transf. to 5WA from Fla. bn., 7/16/62; c during Kentucky campaign; exchanged 11/1/62; Jackson, Glass's Mill, Missionary Ridge, Atlanta and Tennessee campaigns; de-serted at Mobile during evacuation, 3/11/65 (Chalaron shows date of 4/11/65). After war, either constable or printer, NO; d 1/22/78, NO.

McCOWN, HUGH D. Pvt.
Born Hancock, western Virginia, *ca.* 1841; to NO in 1857; clerk in uncle's clothing store; e 3/6/62, NO; Shiloh, Corinth, Kentucky campaign, Mur-freesboro, Jackson, Chickamauga; c Missionary Ridge, 11/25/63; impris-oned Rock Island and took USA oath, 3/19/64. After war, became partner with uncle in R. Sproule & McCown clothing store; bought out uncle and operated the store as sole proprietor; also bought out competitors, Pierson & Hews; director of the Crescent Insurance Co.; d 5/17/01, NO; buried in Metairie Cemetery.

McDONALD, JOHN. Pvt.
e 3/6/62; k Shiloh, 4/6/62.

McDONALD, PETER A. Pvt.
Born Ireland *ca.* 1835; r Biloxi, Miss.; e Co. A, St. Paul's Bn., CSA, and then served in Co. C, 1st La. (CSA) Zouaves and as adjutant of this battalion; detached from Zouaves during summer, 1864; probable year began service with 5WA; p 5/10/65, Meridian, Miss. After war, dry goods clerk in NO; r Nicholls Soldiers Home, admitted being listed as a member of 5WA; d NSH, 5/6/04; buried Greenwood Cemetery, Metairie, La.

McDONALD, THOMAS. Driver.
Born *ca.* 1839, New York City; boilermaker; blue eyes, light hair, fair complexion, 5'9"; e 3/9/62, NO, in Confederate Guards Response Bat-tery; transf. to 5WA 7/16/62, Tupelo; w and c Murfreesboro, 1/2/63; re-joined for Jackson, Glass's Mill, Missionary Ridge; deserted at Mobile, 4/11/65.

McGREGOR, WILLIAM "MAC." Pvt.
Born *ca.* 1833, Hancock Co., Va.; teacher in NO; e 3/5/62, NO, in Crescent regt.; transf. to 5WA, 7/26/62; Kentucky campaign, Murfreesboro; hospitalized Jackson, Miss., 6/4–6/12/63; returned to battery at Dalton; k Dallas, 5/28/64.

McILHENNY, EDWARD S. "NED." Cpl.
Born *ca.* 1843 in Baltimore, Md.; clerk; gray eyes, dark hair, light complexion, 5'8"; member of Crescent Cadets La. Militia, 9/26/61; e 3/6/62, NO; Shiloh, Corinth, Kentucky campaign, Murfreesboro, Jackson, w Chickamauga; Missionary Ridge, Atlanta and Tennessee campaigns; appt. cpl., 1864; k Spanish Fort, 3/29/65.

McINTYRE, [?].
Not e; served with 5WA during some engagements; "at Missionary Ridge on the field & brought up ammunition."

McKNIGHT, MILTON. Pvt.
Born *ca.* 1832; e 3/6/62, NO; w slightly at Shiloh, 4/7/62; Corinth, Kentucky campaign; deserted at Crab Orchard, 10/14/62, on retreat from Kentucky.

McMILLAN (McMILLIAN), ROBERT W. (J.) Pvt.
Born *ca.* 1843 in Mobile, Ala.; clerk; brown eyes, red hair, fair complexion, 5'7"; e 6/28/62, Tupelo; sent to hospital sick 11/29/63 and detached to medical dept. (Surgeon Erskine, Hood's corps), 3/4/64; p 4/28/65, Greensboro, N.C. After war, partner in McMillan Bros. (commission merchants and western produce), NO; d 3/5/20, NO. Married Henrietta Milfenburger.

McNAIR, HENRY M. Pvt.
Born *ca.* 1832 in NO; planter; hazel eyes, dark hair and complexion, 5'11"; e 4/2/62, Corinth; Shiloh, Corinth, Kentucky campaign, Murfreesboro; transf. to Boone's La. battery, 3/9/63; c Port Hudson, 7/63. After war, employed by J. H. Mille & Co., NO; general agent, Southern Life Ins. Co. of Memphis; d 11/7/67 at his home near Fort Adams, Miss.

MACREADY (MACRADY, MCAEREDY, MCACREDY), LAWRENCE. Cpl.
Born *ca.* 1835 in NO; clerk; black eyes and hair, dark complexion, 5'4"; e 3/6/62, NO; 3rd caisson Cpl.; shot through thigh at Shiloh, 4/6/62; discharged for disability, 4/23/62; reenlisted 6/21/63; after Chickamauga, sent to rear sick and disabled by old wounds; transf. to medical dept.;

detailed to Surg. A. L. Breysacker, Hardee's corps; 5/64, detached to chief commissary, Army of Tenn.; p 4/28/65, Greensboro, N.C.; admitted NSH 11/17/02; d 5/2/13 in NO and buried in Metairie Cemetery.

MAGNOR, WILLIAM. Pvt.
Member of Co. B, 1st Bn., Ala. Arty.; temp. assigned to 5WA.

MAILLEN (MALLIU, MALLIEN), FRANK. Pvt.
e 3/6/62, NO; Shiloh, Corinth; discharged 7/16/62, over age.

MANNION (MANNAHON), PATRICK "PAT." Pvt.
Born ca. 1836 in Galway Co., Ireland; blue eyes, brown hair, dark complexion, 5'7"; e 9/11/61, Camp Moore; transf. from 13th La., 10/12/62; served with 5WA in Murfreesboro, Jackson, Glass's Mill, Chickamauga, Missionary Ridge; returned to 13th La., 12/16/63.

MARKS, HENRY J. Pvt.
Born 1843 in NO. e 12/31/61, Springfield, La.; r NO; w and c 2nd Murfreesboro, 12/7/64; imprisoned Camp Chase; p 5/18/65; r Starhill, La., 1899; d 2/25/99 in NO.

MARQUET (MARQUIT, MARQUETTE), LOUIS. Pvt.
Born County Derry, Ireland; e 3/6/62, NO; r St. Martin Parish; present March–April, 1865; p 5/10/65, Meridian, Miss.; d 2/28/93 in NO.

MARTIN, WILLIAM P. Pvt.
Born 1833; e 2/24/61, NO; r NO; present on all rolls; p 5/10/65, Meridian, Miss.; d 2/28/93, NO.

MASS (MAAS), B. VAN. Pvt.
e 11/21/63, Mobile; r Tangipahoa Parish; joined 5WA on retreat from Missionary Ridge; Atlanta and Tennessee campaigns. p 5/10/65, Meridian, Miss.; returned to NO; living in Biloxi, Miss., 1899.

MASSENA. See MUSSINA.

MATHER, HENRY J. Cpl.
Born ca. 1842 in NO; student; member of old BWA; brown eyes, dark hair and complexion, 5'9"; e 3/6/62, NO; Shiloh, Corinth, Kentucky campaign, Murfreesboro, Jackson, Glass's Mill; prom. cpl. and guidon of the battery following Lovejoy's Station, 9/64; Tennessee campaign, Spanish Fort; p 5/10/65, Meridian, Miss. After war, bookkeeper in NO; d in Tex.

MATHIS, LOUIS. Pvt.
Born 3/2/37, NO; clerk; brown eyes, dark hair and complexion, 5'9"; e 3/6/62, NO; Shiloh, Corinth, Kentucky campaign, Murfreesboro, Jackson, Glass's Mill, Missionary Ridge, Atlanta and Tennessee campaigns, Spanish Fort; p 5/10/65, Meridian, Miss. After war, secretary, then president of the Lafayette Fire Ins. Co., NO; d 9/5/03; married Elizabeth Kopp.

MATHIS, MARTIN. Pvt.
Born ca. 1835 in NO; clerk; gray eyes, light hair and complexion, 6'; e 3/6/62, NO; Shiloh, Corinth, Kentucky campaign, Murfreesboro, Jackson; w at Chickamauga 9/19/63, and sent to hospital; returned to open Atlanta campaign; w Dallas, 5/28/64 and d 7/4/64.

MATTHEWS (MATHES, MATHEWS, MATTHEW), WILLIAM C. B. Pvt.
Born ca. 1841 in Germany; bookbinder in NO; e in CSA Response but transf. to 5WA, 7/16/62, Tupelo; Kentucky campaign, Murfreesboro, Jackson, Glass's Mill, Missionary Ridge, Atlanta and Tennessee campaigns; w Spanish Fort, 4/4/65; p 5/10/65, Meridian, Miss. After war, returned to NO; d 8/15/06, NO; buried in the Army of Tenn. tomb, Metairie Cemetery.

MAY, EUGENE. Pvt.
Born Davis Co., Ky., 8/23/44, son of Thos. Isaac May and Hester Johnson; during childhood moved to NO where he was educated; medical student in NO; weighed over 210 pounds, gray eyes, light hair and complexion, 6'; e 3/6/62, NO; Shiloh, Corinth, Kentucky campaign, Murfreesboro, Jackson; prom. cpl. 8/6/63; Glass's Mill, Missionary Ridge; on rolls, Jan.–April, 1864, as detailed to Surg. J. C. Stickney, medical purveyor, Hardee's corps; transf. to CSN, appt. master's mate, 7/20/64. After war, clerk at Wheelock, Finlay & Co. (importers), NO; active participant in the BWA, commanded Battery B. president of the Firemen's Charitable Assoc.; secretary, Army of Tenn. Assoc.; elected clerk of superior criminal court and recorder of mortgages for Parish of Orleans; resigned latter office to become a druggist; d in NO, 6/17/01, as result of fall from horse; buried in Metairie Cemetery. Married Victoria N. Richards, who d in 1882; then Martha L. Cunningham.

MEADER (MEADOR), HERMAN S. L. Cpl.
Born ca. 1841 in Prussia; clerk in NO; e 3/9/62, NO, in Crescent Regt.; transf. to 5WA 7/16/62, Tupelo; prom. cpl., 1864; w Atlanta, 8/15/64;

participated in Hood's Tennessee campaign and Spanish Fort; p 5/10/65, Meridian, Miss. After war, partner in Clark & Meader (grocers); d 3/6/08, Greenville, S.C.; buried in Metairie Cemetery. Married Susie Lee Equen who d 1/11/02.

MERCIER, A. Pvt. 12/61.

METSLER (METZLER, METZLAR, MITGLES), JOHN. Pvt.
Born *ca.* 1838 in NO; blacksmith; e Confederate Guards Response Battery; transf. to 5WA, 7/16/62, Tupelo; c Perryville, 10/8/62; exchanged 11/1/62; in all battles and campaigns of the battery; p 5/10/65, Meridian, Miss.; after war, blacksmith in NO.

MILLER, BENJAMIN R. Pvt.
Born Pittsburgh, Pa., *ca.* 1829; black eyes, dark hair, 5'10½"; carpenter; e CSA Guards Response; transf. to 5WA, 7/16/62; k Spanish Fort, 3/30/65.

MILLER, DAVID C. Pvt.
Born *ca.* 1841 in Pinckney, Ohio; clerk in NO; gray eyes, light hair and complexion, 5'7"; e 3/6/62, NO; hospitalized 7/11/62, Jackson, Miss., but soon recuperated and participated in battles and campaigns; 11/13/63 appt. caisson cpl.; absent without leave and reduced to ranks, 12/20/63; p 5/10/65, Meridian, Miss.; d 10/28/74, Carrollton, La.

MILLER, HENRY. Pvt.
Born *ca.* 1841 in Germany; clerk in NO; brown eyes, dark hair and complexion, 5'10"; transf. from Confederate Response Battery, 7/16/62, Tupelo; Kentucky campaign, Jackson, Glass's Mill, Chickamauga, Missionary Ridge, Atlanta and Tennessee campaigns; w and c Overall's Creek, 12/4/64; imprisoned at Camp Chase, until 6/65, then paroled; d 6/23/78, NO.

MILLER, (MILLEN), JOHN. Driver.
Born 1840 in Germany; hazel eyes, dark hair, fair complexion, 5'10"; r NO, 1852; clerk; joined Washington Light Infantry (state troops), 3/6/62; e 6/63, Mobile (where refuging); Jackson, Glass's Mill, Chickamauga, Missionary Ridge, Atlanta and Tennessee campaigns; c Overall's Creek, 12/4/64; imprisoned Camp Chase; returned 6/10/65 to NO where he d 6/78.

MITCHELL, G. W. Pvt. 12/61.

MITCHELL, JOSEPH H. Pvt.
r NO; p 5/10/65, Meridian, Miss.; after war, cartman in NO; r NO, 1899.

MOORE, DANIEL. Driver.
e 3/6/62, NO; Shiloh, Corinth; discharged 7/16/62, over age.

MOREL, FRED. Pvt.
Born ca. 1831 in NO; printer; hazel eyes, dark hair, fair complexion, 5'5½"; e CSA Guards Response; transf. to 5WA, 7/16/62, Tupelo; Kentucky campaign, Murfreesboro, Jackson, Glass's Mill; k Chickamauga, 9/20/63.

MORGAN, B. W. Pvt.
Co. D, 1st Ala. Bn. of Arty.; temp. assigned to 5WA.

MORRIS, ROBERT. Pvt.
p 5/15/65.

MUELLER, W. C. C. Pvt. 12/61.

MURPHY, WILLIAM R. Pvt.
Born ca. 1839 in Miss.; bookkeeper, NO; e 3/6/62, NO; commended for performance at Shiloh; w Glass's Mill by gun carriage; furloughed 30 days from 11/7/63 and returned to NO; published as deserter, 12/14/63 at Dalton. After war, bookkeeper, NO.

MURRAY, JAMES R. Pvt.
Sent to hospital 11/29/63 and then transf. to CSN.

MURRAY, JOEL. Pvt.
e 5/13/62, Corinth, Miss.; present on rolls, May–June, 1862.

MURRAY (MURRY), JOHN R. Pvt.
Born ca. 1842 in Albany, N.Y.; clerk in NO; gray eyes, dark hair, light complexion, 5'4½"; e 12/4/62, Shelbyville, Tenn.; Murfreesboro, Jackson, w Glass's Mill, Missionary Ridge; hospitalized 11/29/63, then transf. to CSN, Mobile.

MURRAY, ROBERT. Pvt.
Discharged at Tupelo, 7/62, disability.

MUSSINA (MASSENA, MESSINA), EDWIN. Pvt.
Born ca. 1840, NO; clerk; gray eyes, dark hair and complexion, 5'3"; e 3/6/62, NO; Shiloh, Corinth, Kentucky campaign, Murfreesboro, Jackson, Chickamauga, Missionary Ridge, Atlanta campaign; detailed follow-

ing Lovejoy's Station, 9/15/64, with Capt. J. D. Hill, cmdg, scouts, by order of Gen. Hood; absent thereafter.

MYERS (MILLES), STEPHEN A. Pvt.
e 8/10/61, Madison, Ark., in Co. D, 13th Ark. Inf.; with 5WA at Missionary Ridge and Dalton; shown on 13th Ark. rolls as "teamster in Washington Artillery," 2/28–4/30/64; returned to 13th Ark.; c or deserted at Resaca; reported in USA post and prison hospital, Alton, Ill. with "int. fever and typh. malaria," 5/26–11/7/64; laborer, NO. 1873.

NEWMAN, SAMUEL BROOKS, JR. Cpl.
Born *ca.* 1843 in Natchez, Miss., son of well-known NO cotton merchant, Samuel B. Newman, and Jane Miller; student; blue eyes, light hair and complexion, 5'6"; e Crescent Cadets La. Militia, 5/12/63, Camp Moore, La.; Jackson, advance to Vicksburg, and retreat to Morton; sent to hospital, 9/63–12/63; Atlanta and Tennessee campaigns, Spanish Fort; p 5/10/65, Meridian, Miss. After war, worked with father in S. B. Newman & Co., cotton factors; activist with White League and k in Liberty Place riot, 9/14/74; buried "Washington Cemetery in NO" (probably Lafayette #1 or #2).

NEWMAN, WILLIAM J. Pvt.
Born *ca.* 1843 in Natchez, Miss.; student; e 5/15/63, Camp Moore, La.; Jackson, Glass's Mill, Chickamauga; 10/3/63 sent to hospital in Shelby Springs, Ala., where d of acute diarrhea, 11/7/64; buried Willow Mount Cemetery, Shelbyville, Tenn.

NISH, GEORGE F. Pvt.
Born *ca.* 1838 in England; e 3/9/62, NO in 16th La.; transf. to 5WA, 7/15/62; present, Sept.–Oct., 1862; c ("deserted") Perryville, 10/8/62.

NORRIS, ROBERT. Driver.
Born *ca.* 7/4/29 in NO; cooper; hazel eyes, dark hair, light complexion, 5'4"; e 3/6/62, NO; Shiloh, Corinth, Kentucky campaign; w Atlanta, 8/25/64; detailed for hospital duty, but discharged for medical reasons (unable to use right hand), 3/7/65; in hospital at Marion, Ala. at surrender. After war, watchman, NO.

NYE, JAMES M. Pvt. 12/61.

O'BRIEN, EMILE J. Sgt.
Born *ca.* 1842 in NO; hazel eyes, black hair, dark complexion, 5'10"; e

3/6/62, NO; second caisson cpl.; prom. to sgt. 4/7/62 and commended for Shiloh; w Chickamauga (grazed on temple by shell); w Missionary Ridge, 11/25/63; sent to rear because of wounds and transf. to Trans-Mississippi, 12/23/63; prom. to 2nd Lt., 1st La. Regular Arty., 4/27/64; p 5/10/65, Meridian, Miss. After war, proprietor of O'Brien & Co, cotton press, NO; active in Pickwick Club; participated in Liberty Place riot, 9/14/74; d 4/1/14; buried in Army of Tenn. tomb, Metairie Cemetery.

O'Brien, John J. Pvt.
A "non-exchanged prisoner"; joined in Meridian, Miss., 5/2/65; r NO; p 5/10/65, Meridian, Miss.

O'Brien, R. M. Color sgt., 12/61.

O'Donnell, John. Driver.
Born Ireland; e 3/6/62, NO; k Shiloh, 4/6/62.

Ogden, Henry Vining. Pvt.
Born ca. 1823 in Haddington (St. Lawrence Co.), N.Y.; manager, Liverpool and London and Globe Insurance Co., NO; gray eyes, sandy hair, light complexion, 6'1"; e 5/15/62, Corinth; transf. from Co. E, CSA Guards Response (on rolls March and April, 1862); discharged 7/62, over age; reenlisted as substitute for Sgt. E. Putnam; Kentucky campaign, Murfreesboro, Jackson, Chickamauga, Missionary Ridge, Atlanta and Tennessee campaigns, Spanish Fort. p 5/10/65, Meridian, Miss. After war, affiliated with Crescent Mutual Ins. Co., NO, 1866; in 1891 was resident secretary in NO of Globe Ins. Co., Liverpool and London; instrumental in the erection of Washington Artillery monument in Metairie Cemetery; r Milwaukee, Wis. ca. 1895; d 9/1/10; buried in Army of Tenn. tomb, Metairie Cemetery. Wife's name Caroline.

Ogden, Wallace. Pvt.
Born ca. 1830 in St. Lawrence Co., N.Y.; broker in NO; blue eyes, light hair and complexion, 5'10"; e 8/26/61, Camp Moccasin, La.; e 5WA Kentucky campaign, 8/26/62; Murfreesboro, Jackson, Chickamauga, Missionary Ridge, Atlanta campaign, Spanish Fort; prom. sergeant of ordnance, Cobb's battalion of artillery, 9/64; p 5/10/65, Meridian, Miss. After war, partner in DeBuys & Ogden stock & exchange brokers; d 3/15/84, NO.

Osborne, J. T. 3rd Artificer, 12/61.

O'SULLIVAN, BERNARD. Driver.
e 3/6/62, NO; Shiloh, Corinth; discharged, 7/16/62, over age.

OUTTLAW, R. L. Pvt. 12/61.

PALFREY, GEORGE WASHINGTON. Pvt.
Born *ca.* 1843 in NO; attended schools in NO and Bridgewater, Mass.; clerk; r Mississippi City, Miss.; e 3/6/62, NO; Shiloh, Corinth, Kentucky campaign, Murfreesboro, Jackson, Chickamauga; missing at Missionary Ridge (left for hospital) 11/25/63; p 5/10/65, Meridian, Miss. After war, accountant for Norwood & Richards, cotton factors and commission merchants, NO; secretary-treasurer of the NO Water Supply Co. and secretary-treasurer of the National Rice Milling Co.; d 1/5/13, NO, age 70; married Elizabeth Harrison.

PALMER, BENJAMIN MORGAN. Chaplain.
Born 1/25/18 in Charleston, S.C., son of the Rev. Edward Palmer; attended Amherst College and Univ. of Ga.; theological training at the seminary at Columbia, S.C.; 1841 pastor 1st Presbyterian Church, Savannah; ordained by Ga. presbytery; 1/43–12/56, pastor of 1st Presbyterian Church, Columbia, S.C., and taught at the seminary; 1856 r NO, pastor of 1st Presbyterian Church; elected moderator of the first general assembly of the Southern Presbyterian church 12/61; joined 5WA soon after Shiloh, as chaplain without commission; served only in camp, preaching in all divisions in the Army of Tennessee; rendered hospital duty in Columbia, S.C., and assisted in forwarding supplies to troops. After war, returned to 1st Presbyterian Church, NO; became chaplain-general, with rank of lt. col., on staffs of the commanders of the La. division, UCV; 2/8/87, honorary member of Army of Tenn. Assoc. of NO; married Mary A. McConnell.

PARTOFF, CHARLES. Pvt. 12/61.

PERCY, CHARLES R. "CHARLIE." Pvt.
Born *ca.* 1844 in East Feliciana Parish; planter; brown eyes and hair, fair complexion. e 8/18/61, Camp Moore; fought at Belmont and Shiloh with another regiment, probably 11th La.; joined 5WA at Tupelo, 7/62; Kentucky campaign, Murfreesboro, Jackson; w Chickamauga, 9/19/63; w Resaca, hospitalized in Newnan, Ga; mortally w Peachtree Creek, 7/20/64; d 7/26/64.

Pevey, F. Pvt.
Member of Co. B, 1st. Ala. Bn. of Arty.; temp. assigned to 5WA.

Phelps, H. J. Pvt. 12/61.

Phillips, W. Edgar. Pvt.
e 5/14/62, Corinth; d of disease in Jackson, Miss., hospital, 6/3/62; buried Greenwood Cemetery, Jackson.

Pierson, Jerry G. (J. J.?) Lt.
Elected jr. 1st lt. in WA Reserve Company, 12/61; not reelected when 5WA formally organized 2/24/62. After war, detective and captain, NO Metropolitan Police.

Pike, Z. M. Pvt. 12/61.

Ponder, John. Pvt.
Born 1849 [?] in Wilmington, Del., reared in Atlanta, Dalton, and Calhoun, Ga.; e 2/15/64, Kingston, Ga. and served until surrender; bugler during last year; p 5/10/65, Meridian, Miss., After war, r NO except 3 yrs in Wilmington in employ of Roach ship yards; in NO, asst. engineer for Cromwell steamship lines, then chief engineer at Charity hospital; d 12/17/21, NO; buried in Greenwood Cemetery, Metairie. Married Elizabeth McEaree.

Powell (Prowell), J. W. [R.?] Asst. Surgeon.
"Followed Battery out of Kentucky & acted asst. medical officer after capture of Asst. Surg. J. C. Legaré at Perryville & until his exchange. . . . Present with company until its departure from Wartrace Tenn for Jackson Miss."[25]

Pugh, George W. Pvt.
Born Assumption Parish, *ca.* 1831; gray eyes, light hair and complexion, 5'7"; planter in Assumption Parish; e 5/14/62, Corinth; Kentucky campaign, Murfreesboro, Jackson; slightly w, Chickamauga 9/20/63; Atlanta and Tennessee campaigns, Spanish Fort; p 5/10/65, Meridian, Miss.; returned to NO with company; d 1/27/90, Assumption Parish.

Pugh, John Eaton. Asst. Surgeon.
Born 6/29 in Assumption Parish; physician; e 5/4/62, Corinth; Kentucky campaign and Murfreesboro; assigned 12/31/62 to 1st & 3rd Fla.; at

25. Powell does not appear in Booth's lists or in the compiled service records of the company. J. W. Powell, chief surgeon on the staff of A. P. Hill, has not been established as the same individual.

Hurricane Springs Hosp., 4/16/63; prom. asst. surgeon, CSA, 6/2/63; d 2/27/06, Oakley Plantation, Assumption Parish; buried (probably) near Napoleonville, La.

PUGH, RICHARD LLOYD "DICK." Pvt.
Born 1837 in Lafourche Parish; son of Thomas and Eliza C. Foley Pugh; planter; blue eyes, dark hair, fair complexion, 5'8"; graduate of Centenary College, Jackson, La.; purchased Dixie Plantation (upper Lafourche Parish) and its slaves at auction in 1860; e 3/6/62, NO; Shiloh, Corinth, Kentucky campaign, Murfreesboro; absent without leave, May–June, 1863; furnished a substitute (Pat Keyes), 6/63; moved to Rusk, Tex., and rejoined his family; younger brother of Robert Pugh; brother-in-law of Willis P. Williams. d 7/24/91.[26] Married, Mary Louise Williams, 2/61.

PUGH, ROBERT. Pvt.
Born 1834 in Assumption Parish; son of Thomas and Eliza C. Foley Pugh; brother of Richard L. Pugh; planter and lawyer. Blue eyes, black hair, dark complexion, 5'6"; e 3/6/62, NO; r St. Landry Parish; transf. from 8th La; acting as A.D.C. to Col. Randall L. Gibson at Shiloh; Corinth, Kentucky campaign, Murfreesboro, Jackson, Chickamauga, Missionary Ridge, Atlanta and Tennessee campaigns; fractured arm, Demopolis, Ala., 10/3/64; p 5/10/65, Meridian, Miss.; d 8/14/87.

PUGH, ROBERT LAWRENCE. Pvt.
Born ca. 1842 in Assumption Parish; son of Col. William W. Pugh; planter; blue eyes, light hair and complexion, 5'9"; e 5/14/62, Corinth; c Kentucky campaign; exchanged 11/1/62; Murfreesboro, Jackson, Chickamauga; hospitalized, 9/19/63; absent sick; on staff of Gen. F. T. Nicholls, 1864; present on rolls, Jan.–April, 1864; after war, planter in Assumption Parish; d 7/24/91, Woodlawn Plantation, Assumption Parish;

PUTNAM, EMMETT. Sgt.
Born ca. 1833; e 3/6/62, NO; appt. 5th cpl., 2/29/62; prom. sgt., 6/21/62; discharged 8/26/62, having furnished a substitute (H. V. Ogden). d 12/8/71, NO.

REICHART (REICHERT, RICHARD, RICHART, REICHARD), EMILE F. Pvt.
Born ca. 1843 in Bavaria, Germany; bookbinder in NO; gray eyes, light

---

26. Died at Leighton, Louisiana, on July 20, 1885, according to Lathrop, "A Confederate Artilleryman," 373.

hair and complexion, 5′6″; e 3/6/62, NO; Shiloh, Corinth, Kentucky campaign, Murfreesboro; Jackson; k Chickamauga, 9/19/63.

REID, JOHN W. Driver.
k Murfreesboro, 1/2/63.[27]

RETLICH[?], CHARLES. Pvt. 12/61.

REWARDE (REVARTE, REVART), GUSTAVE. Pvt.
Member of 12th La. Cav.; temp. assigned to 5WA.

RHODES, E. Pvt.
e 4/9/62, Greenville, Ala.

RICE, D. A. Sgt.
Born *ca.* 1832, Franklin Co., Ala.; merchant in NO; e 6/18/62, Tupelo, Miss.; Kentucky campaign, Murfreesboro, Jackson; prom. cpl., 8/6/63; Glass's Mill, Missionary Ridge, Atlanta campaign; w Kennesaw Ridge, 6/27/64; returned for Jonesboro and Tennessee campaign: prom. sgt., 3/65; p 5/10/65, Meridian, Miss.; d Tensas Parish.

RICHARDS, HENRY M. Pvt.
Born *ca.* 1838 in Wilcox Co., Ala.; gray eyes, auburn hair, fair complexion, 5′11″; e 5/12/62, Corinth; discharged 12/11/62, disability; after war, engineer in NO.

RICHARDS, WILLIAM H. Pvt.
Born *ca.* 1833 in NO; clerk; gray eyes, brown hair, fair complexion, 5′11″; e 3/9/62, NO; transf. from Crescent Regt., 7/26/62; Kentucky campaign, Murfreesboro, Jackson; prom. artificer, 8/63; Glass's Mill, Missionary Ridge, Atlanta and Tennessee campaigns, Spanish Fort; p 5/10/65, Meridian, Miss. After war, salesman, M. W. Smith Co., NO.

RICHARDSON, FRANK LIDDELL. Pvt.
Born 7/28/43 in Wilkerson Co., Miss.; son of Francis D. and Bethia F. Liddell; r St. Mary Parish; student at Centenary College; blue eyes, light hair and complexion, 5′10″; e 9/11/61, Camp Moore, La. in 13th La.; transf. to 5WA, 1/16/63; absent, sick at hospital in Chattanooga with dysentery; discharged 4/13/63, disability; reenlisted and c 11/63 while serving in 2nd La. Cav.; paroled and exchanged; surrendered 6/4/65, Al-

27. See Chalaron, Master Roster, HTT: READ, JOHN W., d NO, 12/26/24; READ, W. J., Pvt., d NO, 12/26/24, son of John W. (No mention of 5WA; no age given.)

exandria, La. After war, lawyer in NO; commanded co. of men in Liberty Place riot, 9/14/74; mason and member of Pickwick Club; d 12/9/20, NO; buried in Metairie Cemetery. Married Josephine Moore.

RICKETTS, EVANS. Pvt.
Born *ca.* 1842, NO; clerk; gray eyes, light hair and complexion, 5′6″; e 3/6/62, NO. Shiloh, Corinth, Kentucky campaign, Murfreesboro, Jackson, Chickamauga. Furloughed 40 days, 11/21/63; w Peachtree Creek, 7/20/64; d from wounds, 3/25/65.

ROBERTSON, KENNETH. Pvt.
Born 10/15/47 near Huntsville, Ala.; student; Marion, Ala. Fair complexion, dark hair, dark eyes, 5′7″; joined 5WA at Rough and Ready Station, 8/29/64; Jonesboro, Tennessee campaign; c on retreat from Tennessee, 12/64 (1/4/65) at Tuscumbia, Ala.; imprisoned Camp Chase; released 6/13/65; in 1875 superintendent of Keystone Iron Co., Easton, Pa.; in 1899 r Mancelona, Mich.

RODGERS, J. C. Pvt. 12/61.

ROGERS, D. D. Pvt.
Listed as refugee from NO who enlisted in Mobile when 5WA passed through en route to Jackson.

ROST, ALPHONSE. Pvt.
r NO; e 5/6/64, Dalton; Atlanta and Tennessee campaigns, w Spanish Fort, 3/30/65; hospitalized at Genl. Hospital "Cantey" in Mobile; p 5/10/65, Meridian, Miss.; returned to NO with company.

RUFFIER (RUFFLIER), EDWARD. Cpl.
Born *ca.* 1841, NO; clerk; black eyes, dark hair and complexion, 5′6″; e Mobile, 6/1/63 (refugee from NO); Jackson, Glass's Mill, Missionary Ridge, Atlanta and Tennessee campaigns, Spanish Fort; prom. cpl., 1865; p 5/10/65, Meridian, Miss.; returned NO.

RUFFIN, EUGINE. Cpl.
r NO; p 5/10/65, Meridian, Miss.; after war, clerk, Bayset & Glennon (inspectors and gaugers).

RUSSELL, SAMUEL F. (T.?) "SAM." Pvt.
Born *ca.* 1833, Tyler Co., Va.; steamboat man; e 3/6/62, NO; Shiloh, Corinth, Kentucky campaign, Jackson, Chickamauga; prom. cpl.,

7/22/63; Missionary Ridge, Dalton, Crow's Nest, Buzzard's Roost; k Resaca, 5/15/64; buried CSA Cemetery, Resaca.

RYAN, PATRICK "PAT." Pvt.
Joined in Tupelo as substitute for J. A. Blaffer, 7/62; present Sept.–Oct., 1862; missing at Perryville, 10/8/62.

SALTER, RICHARD P. Pvt.
Born N.Y.; clerk in NO; e 3/6/62, NO; commended for Shiloh; discharged 7/16/62, disability from sickness; reenlisted in 2nd La. Cav. and served two years as company commander; in 1863 commended by Gov. Moore for successfully protecting and delivering a valuable boatload of arms; active on Red River and took part in battles of Sabine Cross Roads, Mansfield, and Pleasant Hill; p Alexandria, La. After war, partner in Harrel & Salter, commission merchants, NO; r N.Y. in 1875 where listed as a "capitalist." d N.Y.

SAMBOLA, ANTHONY. Pvt.
Born 2/29/36 in NO; son of Francisco Sambola of Catalonia, Spain, and Dorothea Aramburo, a descendant of settlers in La. during Spanish occupancy; educated at Spring Hill College, near Mobile; graduated from Centenary College, Jackson, La., 1857; read law in office of Christian Roselius; in 1859 graduated in law at Univ. of La.; began practice in NO. Brown eyes, dark hair and complexion, 5'10"; member of old BWA; e 3/6/62, NO; Shiloh, Corinth, Perryville and Murfreesboro; detached at Tullahoma, 3/31/63 by Gen. Bragg; served with rank of capt. of cav. as clerk of military court attached to Gen. Hardee's and Gen. Hood's corps; p Washington, Ga., 5/16/65; returned NO, 5/29/65. After war, lawyer (Sambola & Ducros), NO, 1873; 1874 commissioned capt. in state national guard; organized and commanded 5th Co., Orleans arty., 1874; elected to La. lower house and served 2 yrs.; elected to senate but refused seat; district representative on Seymour and Blair pres. ticket, 1868; delegate to Demo. nat'l conv., 1872; city school director, 1866–70, and aided in estab. of first separate colored school; for 11 yrs served as judge of 2nd recorder's court; Mason; volunteer fireman; introduced Knights of Pythias in La. and served two terms as grand chancellor; supreme archon of the Heptasophs; first deputy supreme chief of Knights of Golden Eagle; d 6/12/03; buried in St. Vincent de Paul Cemetery, NO. Married Gertrude Meyer.

SCHILLEN (SCHILLAN, SCHILLIN), DANIEL "DAN." Driver.
Born ca. 1834 in Prussia; laborer in NO; gray eyes, light hair. e 3/6/62,

NO. Shiloh, Corinth; c Kentucky campaign, 10/62; exchanged 11/1/62; sent to the rear sick, 11/12/63; deserted during evacuation of Mobile, 4/11/65; appears to have been present at Jonesboro.

SCHMIDT, E. F. Commissary sgt., 12/61.

SCOTT, J. WINFIELD. Cpl.
Born *ca.* 1827 in Copiah Co., Miss.; merchant in NO; light complexion, blue eyes, brown hair, 6'1"; e 3/6/62, NO; commended for Shiloh; Corinth, Kentucky campaign, Murfreesboro, Jackson, Glass's Mill, Missionary Ridge; prom. cpl., 1864; w Kennesaw Ridge, 6/22/64; returned for Battle of Atlanta, Tennessee campaign, Spanish Fort. w Overall's Creek; p 5/10/65, Meridian, Miss.; returned to NO, listing occupation in 1873 as "oils"; by 1885 r Miss.; r Grand Lake, Ark., 1899.

SCRUGGS, D. H. (E.?). Pvt.
e 3/9/62, NO in Crescent Regt.; transf. to 5WA, Tupelo, 7/16/62; immediately detailed as clerk to Gen. Sam Jones and never returned.

SEAVEY (SEAVY, SEEVEY, SEVEY), WILLIAM S. E. Pvt.
Born *ca.* 1834, NO; clerk; member of old BWA and 2nd lt. of reserve 6th Co., WA; e 8/1/63, Morton, Miss.; Glass's Mill, Chickamauga; hospitalized 11/4/63; detached, 3/4/64, to Capt. Macon, Asst. Q.M. p 5/10/65, Meridian, Miss.; returned to NO; r NO, 1899.

SEBASTIAN, JOHN B. Pvt.
Born 1827 in Meade Co., Ky.; clerk in NO; blue eyes, light hair and complexion, 5'8"; e 6/1/63, Mobile (refugee from NO); Jackson, Glass's Mill, Chickamauga, Missionary Ridge; sent to hospital from Dalton, 1/4/64; detached, 9/64, with post Q.M., Selma, Ala.; until end of war; 1873 was "porter" in NO.

SEIBRECHT (SIEBRECHT), LOUIS P. Pvt.
Born *ca.* 1846 in NO; clerk; gray eyes, dark hair, light complexion, 5'4"; e 3/6/62, NO; Shiloh, Corinth, Perryville, Murfreesboro, Jackson, Glass's Mill, Missionary Ridge, Atlanta and Tenn. campaigns; k Overall's Creek, 12/4/64; buried in mass grave, Evergreen Cemetery, Murfreesboro, Tenn.

SEIXAS, JAMES MADISON. 2nd Lt.
Born *ca.* 1839 in Charleston, S.C., moved to NO in 1853; associated with one of leading cotton houses of NO and law partner of Gen. A. H. Glad-

den; e 3/6/62, NO; cited for gallant service at Shiloh; discharged 4/12/62; reenlisted; appt. 2nd lt. of 5WA by Gen. Bragg, 6/18/62; Kentucky campaign; prom. to capt. 4/63; served as commercial agent, Bureau of Foreign Supplies, Wilmington; had extensive authority and responsibility; in close contact with Secretary of War Seddon, Governor Vance, and Secretary of Treasury Trenholm.[28] After war, returned to NO; listed 1873 as commission merchant; d 6/27/89; buried in Army of Tenn. tomb, Metairie Cemetery. Married Julia Deslonde, sister of Mrs. John Slidell and Mrs. Pierre G. T. Beauregard.[29]

SEWELL, WILLIAM WASHINGTON "BILLY." Cpl.
Born *ca.* 1842 in NO; clerk; son of Teresa J. and Edward W. Sewell; e 3/6/62, NO; Shiloh, Corinth; prom. cpl., 8/26/62; Kentucky campaign, Murfreesboro, Jackson, Missionary Ridge; k Dallas, 5/28/64; and buried in Lafayette Cemetery #1, NO.

SHERIDAN, MICHAEL. Pvt.
Born *ca.* 1837 in Athlone, Ireland; plasterer; hazel eyes, dark hair, fair complexion, 5'8"; e 3/9/62, NO, in Confederate Guards Response Battery; transf. to 5WA, 7/62; Kentucky campaign, Murfreesboro, Jackson, Chickamauga; c Missionary Ridge, 11/25/63; imprisoned at Rock Island Barracks; took USA oath and e in U.S. Army, 10/13/64, for frontier service. After war, "steward" in NO; d NSH, 7/11/84; buried in Army of Tenn. tomb, Metairie Cemetery.

SHOTWELL, GEORGE H. Sgt.
Born *ca.* 1832 in Rahway, N.J.; brown eyes, dark hair and complexion, 5'1"; e 3/6/62, NO; prom. sergeant of drivers, 4/6/62; commended for Shiloh; resigned appt. as sgt., 6/21/62; Kentucky campaign, Murfreesboro, Jackson; deserted 9/7/63, Covington, La. After war, stock broker at John Klein & Co., NO.

SIMMONS, J. H. Pvt.
Born *ca.* 1838 in Augusta, Ky.; clerk; blue eyes, light hair and complexion, 5'9"; e 3/16/62, Grand Junction, Tenn.; Shiloh, Corinth, Perryville, Mur-

28. D. W. Adams to S. Cooper, November 22, 1862, Confederate Personnel Documents, HTT; *OR,* Vol. XXVIII, Pt. 2, p. 288; Vol. XXIX, Pt. 2, p. 763; Ser. 4, Vol. III, pp. 153, 184, 498, 588.

29. See Shackelford, *George Wythe Randolph,* 127; *OR,* Vol. XXIX, Pt. 2, p. 763; Ser. 4, Vol. III, pp. 153, 184, 498, 588; New Orleans *Times-Democrat,* June 28, 1889; D. W. Adams to S. Cooper, November 22, 1862, Confederate Personnel Documents, HTT; *SHSP,* XII (1884), 80.

freesboro; detached 1/15/63 with Capt. Gayle for Q.M. duty; returned to battery for Atlanta campaign; k Resaca, 5/15/64.

SIMMONS, ROBERT WINSTON. Pvt.
Born 1830 in Shepherdsville, Ky.; educated in Ky., attended Augusta College; r NO, 1846; cotton press business; e 5WA 3/6/62, NO; Shiloh, Corinth; transf. to Orleans Light Horse, 7/5/62; joined command of Gen. Wirt Adams as captain, commissary; prom. to inspector general of Adams' staff. After war, returned to cotton press business in NO until retirement in 1885.

SINGIN, JOHN. Driver.
e 3/6/62, NO; Shiloh, Corinth; discharged, 7/16/62, over age.

SKALAGHAN (SKAYHAN, SKEEHAN), JAMES. Driver.
e 3/6/62, NO; Shiloh, Corinth; discharged 7/16/62, over age.

SKIDMORE, GEORGE W. Pvt.
Born ca. 1842, NO; clerk; e 5WA 4/17/62; Corinth; detached as clerk in Academy Hospital, near Chattanooga, 11/62–11/63.

SKILLMAN, JOSEPH T. Pvt.
Born ca. 1837 in N.J.; e 3/6/62, NO; discharged 6/16/62, disability. After war, collector for Wheelock, Finlay & Co., Importers.

SLAYMAKER, JOHN. Pvt.
e 3/6/62, NO; discharged 5/18/62, disability.

SLOCOMB, CUTHBERT HARRISON. Capt.
Born NO, 8/16/31.[30] Son of Samuel B. and Cora A. Slocomb; wholesale hardware merchant and senior partner in Slocomb, Baldwin & Co.; "always promoting [NO] interests."[31] e 5/26/61, NO; Asst. Q.M. to 1st Lt. in 2WA; at Bull Run, Munson's Hill, Hall's Hill, Lewinsville; resigned 11/7/61; reenlisted 3/6/62, NO, 5WA; prom. 1st lt.; seriously w Shiloh;

30. Cora A. Slocomb to JAC, July 20, 1875, Chalaron Papers, HTT.
31. CHS appears in the 1860 New Orleans census in the household of his mother, Cora. He is shown with real property valued at $200,000 and personal property at $130,000. His mother is listed with $200,000 in real property and $100,000 in personal property. His sisters Ida and Augusta each are shown with $150,000 in real property. In 1861 CHS was a director, Bank of Louisiana and NO Water Works, and 1st Vice Pres. of Mechanical and Agricultural Assoc. of La. See 1860 Census, Louisiana, City of New Orleans, 60; Stuart O. Landry, *History of the Boston Club* (New Orleans, 1938), 327.

prom. capt., 6/13/62; w Jonesboro, 9/1/64; hospitalized Ladies Genl. Hosp., 9/30/64; discharged 11/19/64 and became outpatient; rejoined 5WA on retreat from Nashville; commanded Cobb's battalion, Spanish Fort; p 5/10/65, Meridian, Miss. After war, received pardon and took the oath, 7/28/65; resumed work at Slocomb, Baldwin & Co.; active in Christ Church (Episcopal); delegate to 1866 Democratic Party Convention; officer in Metairie Jockey Club, 1868; Pickwick Club, 1872; leader in Mechanics and Agricultural Fair Association of NO; director of Equitable Life Ins. Co., 1873; d 1/30/73;[32] buried first in Girod Cemetery then removed to Metairie Cemetery. Married Abby Hannah Day (1836–1917), daughter of James A. Day.

SMITH, DAVID WALTER "HAWKEYE." Sgt.
Born ca. 1839, Morristown, N.J.; clerk; dark hair and complexion, 5'8"; sgt. of drivers, 12/61; e 3/6/62, NO; elected 1st cpl. 2/62; commended for Shiloh; prom. to fifth corporal, 6/4/62; commended for Murfreesboro; prom. sixth sergeant, 7/22/63; w Atlanta, 7/22/64; missed Chickamauga—sick in Mobile; c on retreat from Nashville, but escaped in Cincinnati en route to Camp Chase; this "remarkable shot" saw himself as kind of "dreamy" fellow; also known as "Cockeye."[33] d 1/02 in Atlantic City, N.J.

SMITH, JOHN HENRY "BULLY." Sgt.
Born 1837 in Sussex Co., N.J.: clerk in NO; gray eyes, red hair, fair complexion, 5'9"; elected sgt. of drivers, 2/62; e 3/6/62, NO; color sgt. at Murfreesboro; in all battles and campaigns; w Kennesaw Ridge, 6/21/64; p 5/10/65, Meridian, Miss.; with John T. Adams & Co. (location unknown); d 3/1/03 and buried Sussex, N.J.; son was Seymour B. Smith.

SMITH, JOHN M. Pvt.
Born Tallapoosa Co., Ala., 9/30/43; e Co. D, 1st. Ala. Bn. Heavy Arty.; c in attack on Mobile and escaped 4/9/65 by swimming three miles; joined 5WA and p with them at Meridian, Miss. d Choctaw Co., Ala., 1/7/26.

SPEARING, JOHN FARMER. Artificer.
Born in NO, 7/4/28, son of Henry Spearing and Mary Farmer.[34] Student

32. See Obituary, New Orleans *Daily Picayune,* February 1, 1873.

33. PDS refers to him as "Cockeye." Stephenson, *Civil War Memoir,* 166.

34. Spearing's younger brother, Robert McKown, was a member of the First Washington Artillery and was killed at Fredericksburg.

in Doylestown, Pa.; on death of father in 1840, returned to NO to work in father's sailmaking firm, becoming a partner in 1850; e 5WA, 3/6/62, NO; second artificer; commended for Shiloh; returned to ranks from artificer, 5/31/62; discharged, 7/16/62, over age; apparently reenlisted and was c and exchanged; p 7/4/65, NO; after war, partner in Wakeman & Spearing, sailmakers; d 6/17/93. Married Margaretta Jane Sanders.

STAKEMAN (STACKMAN), BENJAMIN "BEN." Pvt.
e 6/1/63, Mobile; Jackson, Glass's Mill; k Chickamauga, 9/20/63; buried in field one-half mile from Anderson's bridge.

STAUB, CHARLES, JR. Pvt.
Born 1843, NO; clerk; blue eyes, dark hair and complexion, 5'10"; e 6/1/63, Mobile (refugee from NO); Jackson, Glass's Mill, Missionary Ridge, Atlanta campaign; w in head at Kennesaw Ridge, 6/22/64; d in Mobile within four months of injury.[35] Buried Magnolia Cemetery, Mobile.

STEPHENSON, PHILIP DAINGERFIELD. Pvt.
Born 9/7/45, St. Louis, Mo.; e 3/9/64, Dalton, Ga.; transf. from 13th Ark. Inf.; p 5/10/65, Meridian, Miss.; d Richmond, Va., 3/12/16; buried Blandford churchyard, Petersburg.

STEVEN, WILLIAM M. "WILL." Pvt.
Born 1836; member of old BWA; e 3/6/62, NO; r Alexandria, La.; seriously w, Shiloh (minié ball through right thigh); returned to NO in company of CHS; carried on rolls until June, 1863, as absent, sick in Alexandria, La.; about two months later escaped and reported at Chattanooga; detained three weeks and pronounced unfit for marching; given sick orders for Mobile; reentered service as captain, Q.M., commissary and ordnance, Dept. of West Louisiana, staff of Gen. Richard Taylor; received favorable reports for action at Pleasant Hill and Mansfield; c on scout in rear of enemy lines, having crossed Mississippi; exchanged and returned to Taylor's staff; helped crossing of troops to reinforce Hood; arranged to have 5WA transported from Meridian to Mobile to NO. After war, became partner in Garrard & Steven, cotton factors and commission merchants, NO. d 1883 in NO; buried in Metairie Cemetery.

---

35. Three death dates are given: July 27, August 29, and October 18, 1864.

STONE, WARREN, JR. Pvt.
Born 1843, East Feliciana, Parish, La.; son of Dr. Warren Stone, Confederate surgeon general of La.; student at the Jesuit College, NO; gray eyes, light hair and complexion, 6'; e 3/6/62, NO; Shiloh, Corinth, Kentucky campaign, Murfreesboro; prom. to cpl. of caissons, 6/1/63; Jackson, Glass's Mill, Chickamauga; relieved of rank at own request; detached, 10/7/63, to medical service; rejoined 5WA at New Hope Church; sick after Jonesboro, Hood's Tennessee campaign; transf. to medical dept., 1/7/65; p 5/3/65, Richmond, Va. After war, studied at Univ. of La., graduating in 1867; appt. to chair of surgical anatomy at NO Charity Hospital, 1874; volunteered for yellow fever assistance in Brunswick, Ga., 1878; d 1/3/83 in NO; buried in Army of Tenn. tomb, Metairie Cemetery. Married Malvina Dunreith Johnson; first cousin of S. B. Newman, Jr.

STONE, WILLIAM. Pvt.
Member of Co. B, 1st. Ala. Bn. of Arty.; temp. assigned to 5WA.

STRONG, ROBERT. Pvt.
Born *ca.* 1839; e 3/6/62, NO; severely w Shiloh, 4/6/62; discharged 4/23/62, disability; either operated or worked in a NO saloon in 1873; was manager of the St. Charles Theater; became general agent for Texas and Pacific Railroad and vice president of NO Pacific; d 1/24/07, NO.

STUART (STEWART, STURART), WILLIAM B. Pvt.
Born *ca.* 1836, Annapolis, Md.; accountant; blue eyes, dark hair and complexion, 5'9"; e 3/6/62, NO; Shiloh, Corinth, Kentucky campaign, Murfreesboro, Jackson, Glass's Mill, Missionary Ridge; mortally w Resaca, 5/15/64; d 6/10/64 at Empire House Hospital; buried Oakland Cemetery, Atlanta.

SWAIN, ANDREW GARDNER "ANDY." Pvt. Bugler.
Born 1837 in Cincinnati, Ohio; reared from infancy in NO; educated at Dayton, Ohio; at time of secession, steamboat pilot on Red River; hazel eyes, dark hair and complexion, 5'8"; member of old BWA; e 5WA, 3/21/62, Grand Junction, Tenn.; Shiloh, Corinth, Perryville, Murfreesboro, Jackson, Chickamauga, Missionary Ridge, Atlanta and Tennessee campaigns; furloughed sick at Spanish Fort; detailed by order of Gen. Rich Taylor, taking steamer *St. Charles,* laden with ordnance, from Demopolis to Gainesville, Ala.; p 5/14/65, Mobile; returned NO and engaged in steamboating; about 1890, captain of Texas & Pacific transfer

steamer, living in NO; d 2/18/15, Rosedale, La.; buried Oakland Cemetery, Shreveport, La.

TAYLOR, ARCHIE.
"Not enlisted, served with the Battery during some of its engagements; at Missionary Ridge on the field & brought up ammunition."

THAYER, FRED NASH. Cpl.
Born 4/8/25 in Augusta, Me.[36] Member of old BWA; elected corporal of drivers, 2/62; light hair, blue eyes, 5'11"; e 3/6/62, NO; furloughed for 25 days to recruit drivers, 4/14/62; apparently sent to hospital at Okolona, Miss., after recruiting mission; dropped from roll in Tullahoma. Went with family to Texas, where served as chief clerk of the chief commissary of Trans-Mississippi Dept.; p Alexandria, La. After war, went into business with John C. Barelli and Gen. J. B. Hood as cotton factors and commission merchants, NO, 1866; r NO in Sept., 1875, as "arranger"; wrote and directed play, "Wounded Soldier," at Varieties Theater.

THOMPSON, F. M. Artificer.
Born *ca.* 1830 in Hudson, N.Y.; carpenter in NO; hazel eyes, dark hair and complexion, 5'6"; e 5/15/62, Corinth; Corinth, Kentucky campaign, Murfreesboro, Jackson, Chickamauga, Missionary Ridge, Atlanta and Tennessee campaigns; w Spanish Fort, 4/3/65; p 5/10/65, Meridian, Miss. After war, river pilot in NO.

TISDALE, EDWARD KING. Pvt.
Born *ca.* 1837 in Mobile; clerk; r Mobile; brown eyes, dark hair and complexion, 5'8"; e 3/6/62, NO; Shiloh, Corinth, Kentucky campaign, Murfreesboro; hospitalized Tullahoma and at Jackson, Miss.; medical discharge 8/7/63; d in NO.

TOMLIN, HIRAM. Cpl.
e 3/6/62, NO; commended for Shiloh; prom. to cpl., 4/11/62; Corinth; discharged 7/16/62, over age.

TURNER, GEORGE A. Driver.
Born 1843 in Van Buren Co., Ark.; steamboat man who r in Shreveport; blue eyes, light hair and complexion, 5'9"; e 3/6/62, NO; Shiloh, Corinth, Kentucky campaign, Murfreesboro, Jackson, Glass's Mill, Missionary Ridge, Atlanta and Tennessee campaigns; p 5/10/65, Meridian, Miss. Af-

36. Another source gives his birthplace as West Indies.

ter war, foreman for Ellis & Co.; d 10/6/15 in Shreveport; buried in Oakland Cemetery, Shreveport.

TURNER, T. A. Pvt.
Member of Culpepper S.C. Battery, Semple's Arty. Bn.; temp. assigned to 5WA; p. 5/10/65, Meridian, Miss.

TURPIN, EDWARD S. Pvt.
Born *ca.* 1844 in NO; clerk in NO; gray eyes, light hair and complexion, 5'11"; e 9/11/63, Mobile and joined at Tullahoma; Glass's Mill, Missionary Ridge, Atlanta and Tennessee campaigns; w Spanish Fort, 4/5/65; absent at surrender, wounded; p 5/10/65, Meridian, Miss. After war, bookkeeper in NO.

TUTT, WILLIAM F. "WILL." Pvt.
Born *ca.* 1844 in Lexington, Ky.; clerk in Clinton, La.; gray eyes, dark hair, fair complexion, 5'10"; e 1/16/63, Tullahoma; Murfreesboro, Jackson, Glass's Mill, Missionary Ridge, Atlanta campaign; absent sick 9/64 until end of war. After war, partner in Stone & Tutt, commission merchants; d 8/31/84 in NO; buried in Army of Tenn. tomb, Metairie Cemetery.

TYNEN (TYNER), WILLIAM. Driver.
Born 1/1/36 in Kilkenny Co., Ireland; laborer in NO; gray eyes, light hair and complexion, 5'11"; e 3/6/62, NO; Shiloh, Corinth, Kentucky campaign, Murfreesboro, Jackson, Glass's Mill, Missionary Ridge, Atlanta and Tennessee campaigns, Spanish Fort; p 5/10/65, Meridian, Miss. Admitted NSH 1892; d Charity Hospital, NO, 8/3/97; buried Greenwood Cemetery, NSH vault #4.

VALCONI, CARL. Bugler.
In original roster of men leaving for Tenn., but not mentioned by JAC.

VANDRELL, B. Pvt. 12/61.

VAUGHT, WILLIAM CRUMM DARRAH "BILLY." 1st Lt.
Born in Tenn.; clerk in NO; member of old BWA; elected 2nd Lt., 2/62; Shiloh, Corinth, Farmington; in command at Cedar Creek, 6/4/62; relieved of command 6/8 on return of CHS; prom. to senior 1st lt., 6/13/62; Perryville, Ky.; commanded 5WA at Murfreesboro; hospitalized with neuralgia and deafness, 8/64; on rolls 5/64–2/65 as absent, sick; present on rolls March–April, 1865; p 5/10/65, Meridian, Miss. After war, clerk for

state auditor; d from drowning, 8/21/70, Natchez; buried in Lafayette Cemetery #1, NO. Married Isadore L. Walker (d 8/8/05, in Birmingham, Ala.); grandson, William N. Bennett, Covington, Ky.; brother, Albert; sister, Mary; daughter, Mrs. Lawrence V. Elder of Tex.

VEGUE, J. Pvt.
Resident of NO; p 5/10/65, Meridian, Miss.; returned with company to NO.

VINCENT, LOUIS (LOUIE). Pvt.
Born *ca.* 1844 in Philadelphia, Pa.; e 3/6/62, NO in Crescent Regiment; apparently c Shiloh and exchanged 11/1/62; joined 5WA and participated in Murfreesboro, Jackson, Glass's Mill, Missionary Ridge, Atlanta campaign; k Jonesboro, 9/1/64.

VINSON, RICHARD TUCKER. Pvt.
Born *ca.* 1842 in Nashville, Tenn.; student; black eyes, dark hair and complexion, 5'12"[*sic*]; e 7/4/62, Tupelo; Kentucky campaign, Murfreesboro, Jackson; appt. cpl., 8/6/63; Glass's Mill; w Chickamauga; on rolls 9/63–10/63; furloughed 40 days, 11/15/63; transferred to Trans-Mississippi, where appt. lt. of arty., 1863. After war, mayor of Shreveport, La.; d 2/22/04, Shreveport; buried Oakland Cemetery, Shreveport.

VIRTUE, EDWARD J., JR. Pvt.
e 3/12/61, Baton Rouge in 1st La.; transf. to 5WA short time before deserting, 6/14/64, Pine Mountain, Ga.; imprisoned Rock Island Barracks; joined USA Army for frontier service, 10/17/64.

WALDON, CHARLES H. 1st Artificer, 12/61.
3/8/62 appt, cpl., second in command, 5WA reserve corps in NO.

WALKER, GARRETT "GARRY." Pvt.
Born *ca.* 1845, NO; student; black eyes, dark hair and complexion, 5'11"; e Crescent Regiment; joined 5WA 8/15/63, Morton, Miss.; Chickamauga, Missionary Ridge; detached about 3 months when in winter quarters at Dalton to assist in making oil for arty. harness; Atlanta and Tennessee campaigns, Spanish Fort. p 5/10/65, Meridian, Miss.; law student in NO, 1873; became associate of former CSA Gen. Harry Hays.

WALSH, JOHN AUSTIN. Pvt.
Born *ca.* 1842 in NO; clerk; black eyes, dark hair and complexion, 5'10"; e 3/6/62, NO; w in hip at Shiloh, 4/7/62; returned to NO to recuperate;

discharged, disability, 4/23/62; reenlisted 10/28/62; commended for Murfreesboro; present at Jackson and retreat to Morton; w Chickamauga, 9/20/63 (bullet through thigh), and sent to Mobile; paymaster's department, CSN, Mobile; commissioned 1st lt. of arty. and transf. to Trans-Mississippi Department; p Vicksburg; 1873 was either distiller or grocer in NO; d 12/86, Dresden, Germany.

WALSH, W. F. Pvt. 12/61.

WATSON, JOHN W. Pvt.
Born in Boston, Mass., 10/14/39; r NO, 1850; clerk; gray eyes, light hair and complexion, 5'11"; e 3/6/62, NO; slightly w in leg at Shiloh, 4/62; rejoined for Kentucky campaign, Murfreesboro, Jackson, Chickamauga, Missionary Ridge; detailed 3/4/64 to Gen. Shoup's hdq. After war, bookkeeper, NO *Daily Picayune;* lived for time at NSH; d 4/24/93; buried in Army of Tenn. tomb, Metairie Cemetery.

WATSON, ROBERT J. Teamster.
Born *ca.* 1837, NO; river pilot; brown eyes, dark hair and complexion, 5'7"; joined 5WA at Tupelo; Kentucky campaign, Murfreesboro, Jackson, Chickamauga, Missionary Ridge; deserted at Dalton, 12/22/63; took USA oath in Nashville, 1/4/65.

WATT, CHARLES BRICE "CHARLIE." Pvt.
Born *ca.* 1844 in Natchez, Miss., son of Harriet L. and John Watt of Woodville, Miss.; student in NO; gray eyes, dark hair, light complexion, 5'8"; e 3/6/62, NO; cited for gallantry and conspicuous action at Shiloh; Corinth, Kentucky campaign, Murfreesboro; commended for Chickamauga by corps commander; Missionary Ridge, Atlanta campaign; w in thigh at Kennesaw Ridge, 6/23/64; hospitalized in Atlanta; transf. to headquarters, Dept. of La and Miss.; with 5WA at Spanish Fort; p 5/19/65, Jackson, Miss. 1873 r NO, no occupation listed; d 1/17/86; married Lucie B., who d 10/1/97.

WEBBER (WEBRE), JULES. Pvt.
Born *ca.* 1838 in St. James Parish; clerk; r Jefferson City, La.; gray eyes, light hair and complexion, 5'10"; e 6/1/63, Mobile; Jackson, Glass's Mill, w Chickamauga, Missionary Ridge, Atlanta and Tennessee campaigns, Spanish Fort. p 5/10/65, Meridian, Miss.; returned with company to NO.

WEINGART, CHARLES. Pvt.
Born *ca.* 1840 in NO; merchant; gray eyes, light hair and complexion,

5'10"; e 3/6/62, NO; Shiloh, Corinth, Kentucky campaign, Murfreesboro, Jackson; w Chickamauga, 9/20/63 ("struck on back by a splinter. Severe"); c Missionary Ridge, 11/25/63; imprisoned at Rock Island barracks; released from prison 3/25/65 after taking USA oath. After war, partner in toy store of C. & G. W. Weingart, NO.

WHEATLEY, ROBERT L. Pvt.
Born *ca.* 1841 in Caldwell Co., Ky.; r Union City, Tenn.; e 8/13/61, Union City, in Cobb's battery; prom. to 2nd lt. and transf. to Hedden's battery; court-martialed for drunkenness, 12/63, and suspended; transf. to 5WA at Palmetto Station, Ga., 9/22/64; Tennessee campaign, Spanish Fort; p 5/10/65, Meridian, Miss.; returned to Union City.

WHITE, F. H. Pvt.
Transf. to 5WA from Orleans Light Horse, 7/5/62, Tupelo.

WHITE, JAMES. Pvt.
Born *ca.* 1842 in Washington, D.C.; medical student; gray eyes, dark hair and complexion, 5'6"; e 3/6/62, NO; Shiloh, Corinth, Kentucky campaign, Jackson; transf. to CSN, 1/15/64, as master's mate; r NO, 1899.

WHITE, JOHN G. Artificer.
Born *ca.* 1831 in Wexford Co., Ireland; harness maker; gray eyes, dark hair, light complexion, 5'6½"; e 3/10/62, NO, in Fla. bn.; transf. to 5WA, 7/18/62, Tupelo; Kentucky campaign, Murfreesboro, Jackson; deserted on retreat from Jackson, 7/16/63.

WHITE, TIMOTHY J. Cpl.
Born *ca.* 1842, NO; clerk; e Orleans Light Horse and transf. to 5WA, 7/1/62, Tupelo, in exchange for R. W. Simmons; Perryville, Murfreesboro, Jackson, Glass's Mill, Missionary Ridge, Atlanta campaign; w Dallas, 5/27/64; hospitalized; w Golgotha Church, 6/15/64, while attempting to rejoin 5WA; hospitalized; rejoined for Peachtree Creek, remainder of Atlanta campaign, Tennessee campaign; prom. to cpl. at Spanish Fort, 4/65; p 5/10/65, Meridian, Miss.

WHITE, WILLIAM. Driver.
e 3/6/62, NO; Shiloh, Corinth; reported missing at Perryville, 10/8/62; listed on rolls as prisoner, 9/63–10/63.

WILD, CHRISTOPHER "CHRIS." Pvt.
Born *ca.* 1828 in Germany; moved to NO, 1842; clerk; e 11/21/63, Mo-

bile, and joined 5WA on retreat from Missionary Ridge; Atlanta and Tennessee campaigns, Spanish Fort; w Overall's Creek; p 5/10/65, Meridian, Miss.; returned with 5WA to NO. After war, engaged in saloon business, general contracting work, employment at the U.S. mint; became invalid in 1901; d 6/11/06; buried in Army of Tenn. tomb, Metairie Cemetery.

WILLARD, E. O. Pvt. 12/61.

WILLIAMS, JAMES. Farrier.
r Bayou Sara; e 4/16/62, Camp Moore, 25th La.; transf. to 5WA, 4/1/63; with 5WA for all campaigns; p Meridian, Miss.; returned with company to NO.

WILLIAMS, MORRIS. Blacksmith.
Born *ca.* 1838 in Wales; blacksmith in NO; gray eyes, light hair and complexion, 5'8"; e 4/5/62, NO; joined 5WA at Corinth; appt. artificer; with 5WA for all campaigns; p Meridian, Miss.; returned with company to NO.

WILLIAMS, THOMAS E. Driver.
Born *ca.* 1841 in Shropshire, England; farmer; blue eyes, light hair and complexion, 5'8"; e 3/6/62, NO; r NO; Shiloh, Corinth, Kentucky campaign, Murfreesboro; discharged 1/19/63 as a British subject; remained with 5WA as Capt. Slocomb's "private attendant"; p 5/10/65, Meridian, Miss.

WILLIAMS, WILLIS P. Pvt.
e 3/6/62, NO; member of family that purchased L. Polk's Leighton Plantation; brother-in-law of Richard L. Pugh; student; Shiloh, Corinth; present on May–June, 1862, rolls; discharged 7/16/62, under age. After war, r Pine Bluff, Ark.; listed 1873 as cotton and sugar factor with John Williams & Sons.

WILLIS, D. H. Pvt.
Born *ca.* 1840 in Rapides Parish; farmer; gray eyes, light hair and complexion, 6'; e 9/29/61, Camp Moore; transf. from 16th La., 12/12/62; Murfreesboro, Jackson, Glass's Mills, Missionary Ridge; transf. back to 16th La., 3/16/64.

WILLOZ, H. Pvt. 12/61.

WILSON, J. L. Ordnance Sgt.
On roll of A. I. Leverich, 12/61.

Wimberly, William B. Pvt.
Member of Co. D, 1st. Ala. Bn. of Arty.; temp. assigned to 5WA.

Wing, C. S. Pvt.
e 3/6/62, NO; commended for Shiloh; at Corinth; discharged 6/11/62, disability. After war, salesman, A. B. Griswold & Co., jewelers; d in NO.

Wingate, E. Charles. Pvt.
Brother of E. H. Wingate; r 1892 in Alexandria, La.

Wingate, E. H. Pvt.
Born 1833 in Wilmington, N.C.; moved to NO as child; member of company before its departure from NO; e 6/4/62, Tupelo; Kentucky campaign, Murfreesboro, Jackson, Glass's Mill; w Missionary Ridge (explosion of limber chest), 11/25/63; Atlanta and Tennessee campaigns; w Overall's Creek, 12/4/64; shot through lungs, but walked off "in the snow rather than be captured"; Spanish Fort; p 5/10/65, Meridian, Miss.; d 3/11/03 Ganadarque, Shelby Co., Ala.

Winston, Avery S. Cpl.
Born 1842 in NO; son of Thos. B. Winston; brother of Thomas B. Winston, Jr.; early education in NO and private schools near NYC; to Europe in 1859 to continue studies until outbreak of war; e 5WA, 3/6/62, NO; elected fourth caisson cpl.; returned to the ranks at own request; participated in all battles and campaigns through Chickamauga; transf. to CSN, 1/15/64, by order of secretary. of war; assigned as master's mate; served as acting lt. in charge of 2nd div. of gunboat *Huntsville;* on *CSS Morgan* in Mobile Bay; after sinking of *Huntsville,* served on *Nashville;* while in navy under fire at Mobile and Blakely; surrendered 5/11/65. After war, engaged in mfg. of hemp, Lexington, Ky., 1867–1887; long-time pres. of Lexington Ice & Storage Co.; director of gas co.; 1902 pres. of 1st Nat'l Bank in Lexington; active in public affairs of city; buried in City Cemetery, Lexington, Ky.

Winston, Thomas B. Pvt.
Born *ca.* 1844 in NO; brother of A. S. Winston; student; e 3/6/62, NO; Shiloh, Corinth, Kentucky campaign, Murfreesboro, Jackson, Glass's Mill, Missionary Ridge, Atlanta campaign; k Dallas, 5/28/64.

Winterhalter, C. Pvt. 12/61.

Witham (Withan), Charles W. Cpl.
Born Mason Co., Ky. *ca.* 1845; clerk; blue eyes, light hair and complex-

ion, 5'7"; e 3/6/62, NO; Corinth, c Kentucky campaign; exchanged 11/1/62; Murfreesboro; prom. to cpl., 1/21/63; Jackson, Glass's Mill; detached to serve with Maj. Dixbury, ordnance officer, by Gen. Hindman until end of war. After war, partner in Witham & Rovira, lumber dealers, NO.

WOLFE, JOSEPH B. Q.M. Sgt.
Member of old BWA; elected Q.M. sgt., 2/14/62; e 3/6/62, NO; detached as Q.M.; transf. to medical dept., 7/16/62, by order Gen. Beauregard, as "unfit for field service." After war, head of Jos. B. Wolfe & Co., cotton factors and commission merchants for Daniel Pratt's improved cotton gins and "Eureka" cotton gins, NO.

WOOD, F. W. "FRANKIE." Pvt.
Born in 1847; r NO; e 9/3/64, Salisbury; Tennessee campaign and Spanish Fort; p 5/10/65, Meridian, Miss. After war, clerk at Page & Moran, boots and shoes.

WOOD, JOHN. Pvt. 12/61.
Became "Treasurer of the Battalion," 3/8/62, when 5WA left NO.

WOOD (WOODS), WILLIAM ASA. Pvt.
Born ca. 1838 in Hamilton Co., Ohio; steamboat man; e 6/1/63, Mobile (refugee from NO); served at Jackson, where he was hospitalized, 7/8/63; rejoined for Chickamauga, where mortally w, 9/20/63; leg amputated below knee; d 10/3/63; buried in Georgia Confederate Cemetery, Marietta.

WORTHINGTON, JOHN L. Pvt.
r Choctaw, Ala.; member of Co. D, 1 Ala. Bn. of Arty.; temp. assigned to 5WA; p 5/10/65, Meridian, Miss.

YOUNG, JOHN. Pvt.
e 6/1/62 in NO; Shiloh, Corinth; discharged at Tupelo, 7/16/62, over age.

YOUNG, JOHN H. Driver.
Born ca. 1843 in NO; carpenter; blue eyes, light hair and complexion, 5'8"; e 6/1/63 at Mobile; Jackson, Chickamauga, Missionary Ridge; deserted at Mobile, 4/11/65.[37]

37. Confusion exists about Pvt. John Young and John H. Young. Chalaron and the compiled service records seem to pick up pieces of the service of one and place it in the record of the other. One of them, apparently still serving with the battery, died July 12, 1863 (*Daily Picayune* states January 12, 1864). A John H. Young died in New Orleans on October 13, 1867.

Appendix B

Songs of the Fifth Company

Song of the "Fifth"

1.

The cannoniers are slumbring on the hill-side,
   The Eastern sky is bright with dawning day,
When, springing gaily from his clover pillow,
   The Bugler sounds the stirring *reveille.*
Awake! awake! The "God of Day" is rising
   The trembling dew drops sparkle in each ray
The distant picket's rifle gives a warning!
   The "Fifth" must strike for liberty today!

Chorus:
   Hurrah! hurrah! We struggle for the right
   From hill to hill resounding, the battle cry is sounding.
   Hurrah! hurrah! We're ready for the fight!
   A grave or Victory!   (repeat)

2.

Now where the deadly struggle rages wildest
  Where shell and shrapnel burst amid the roar,
Our good Napoleons bellow forth in anger,
  And drop the fierce invaders by the score
Again! again! for God and Louisiana!
  Ram home the charge with energy of hate;
Now give them one swift canister for Murnford [Munford?]
  And every gun for Order Twenty-eight!

Repeat chorus.

C. E. McC.
5th Co. W.A.

THE SONG OF THE BUGLE

When the first ray of dawn begins to peep,
And I'm wrapped in my blanket, in sweet sound sleep
Dreaming of home and the loved ones there
Kindred, and friends, and my sweetheart so fair,
'Tis then, the bugle's unwelcome sound
Is heard in echoing notes all around,
Awake! Awake! No more sleep for thee
For this is the call of morn, "Reveille."
Roll Call

And when the breakfast is nearly done
The corn bread baking and the kettle on,
With a hungry air I take my seat,
And just preparing my meal to eat
When, hark! the Bugle begins to play,
The "water your horses," so up and away
The breakfast must go to devil knows where,
For the soldiers you know, live on fighting and air.
Water Call

And alas! if perchance in some quiet work,
I am smoking my pipe, or reading a Book,
Or writing a letter to my lady love fair
With raven blue eyes and bright Golden hair
Or wrapt in deep reverie, my thoughts all astray,

On the home of my boyhood, so far far away,
That confounded bugle with note loud & shrill
Recalls me from dreamland to "fall in for drill."
                    Assembly Call

And thus it is ever, at morn, noon and night
Whatever be my pleasure, my Joy or delight,
Like some evil spirit that hovers in air
That Bugle will haunt me and fill me with care.
So I long for the time, in my home far away,
To be where no Bugle can e'er around me play.
And with the war over there to drill peacefully
Till the last trump shall sound the last "Reveille."
                    Tattoo

        George E. Brown
        5th Co. W.A.

.

BIBLIOGRAPHY

A wealth of material exists for the reconstruction of the life of the Fifth Company. The major manuscript sources are at Tulane University, and one should not be misled by their one-line subject headings. The J. A. Chalaron Papers represent a gold mine, and the Battalion Washington Artillery Collection of the Louisiana Historical Association Collection contains minute books, order books, muster rolls, correspondence, ordnance reports, drawings, and reminiscences.

Unfortunately, I was unable to locate two documents utilized by Chalaron: "Fahrenback's Diary [which] begins August 28th 1862 at Corinth and continues through to August 26 at Morton, 362 days . . . [and] Sgt. John Bartley's memorandum book of Spanish Fort & up to surrender." In addition to these items mentioned by Chalaron, only a fragment of the Edwin Mussina Journal has surfaced, although I believe the entire document still exists. Alex Allain also kept a diary that survived the war, but its location remains unknown.

Manuscripts

Atlanta, Ga.
  Emory University, Robert W. Woodruff Library
    E. Mussina Diary Fragment.
    Frank L. Richardson Letters.
    Bell I. Wiley Papers.
Austin, Tex.
  Center for American History, University of Texas at Austin
    Pugh Family Papers.
Baton Rouge, La.
  Louisiana State University Libraries, Louisiana and Lower Mississippi Valley
      Collections
    Richard L. Pugh Letters.
    Phillip D. Stephenson Papers.
Chapel Hill, N.C.
  Southern Historical Collection, University of North Carolina
    Thomas L. Bayne Autobiography.
    Bayne-Gale Papers.
    John F. H. Claiborne Papers.
    Josiah Gorgas Journal, 1857–1878. Microfilm copy.
    Frank L. Richardson Papers.
Chattanooga, Tenn.
  Chattanooga-Hamilton County Bicentennial Library
    William C. Brown Diary.
    Milo W. Scott Diary.
Chicago, Ill.
  Chicago Historical Society
    Louisiana Relief Association of Mobile Account Book.
Cincinnati, Ohio
  American Jewish Archives
    Lionel C. Levy. "Memoirs of Army Life in Fenner's Louisiana Battery."
Cleveland, Ohio
  Western Reserve Historical Society
    Braxton Bragg Papers.
    Confederate Miscellany.
    William P. Palmer Collection.
Durham, N.C.
  Duke University, William R. Perkins Library
    Confederate States of America Papers.
    John Euclid Magee Diary.

Fort Oglethorpe, Ga.
    Chickamauga and Chattanooga National Military Park
        John Thompson Brown Diary. Typescript.
        Samuel Pasco Diary. Typescript.
        William R. Talley Autobiography. Typescript.
Little Rock, Ark.
    Arkansas History Commission
        Joseph H. Haney Diary.
Montgomery, Ala.
    Alabama Department of Archives
        Jones, Edgar. "History of the 18th Alabama Infantry."
        Henry C. Semple Papers.
New Orleans, La.
    Bayne, Charles. "Tom Bayne is Wounded at the Battle of Shiloh." Manuscript
        in possession of George Denègre, New Orleans.
    Confederate Memorial Hall
        Washington Artillery Papers.
    Historic New Orleans Collection
        James F. Giffen Letter.
        Moses Greenwood Papers.
        Francis Dunbar Ruggles Papers.
        William C. D. Vaught Letters.
        Washington Artillery Letter.
    Jackson Barracks Military History Library
        Powell A. Casey, "Washington Artillery Streamer Study."
        Powell A. Casey Papers.
        J. A. Chalaron, "Slocomb's Battery in the Tennessee Army, 5th Company,
            Washington Artillery."
        Extract from a Soldier's Story of the War, 1861–1865.
        Minute Book, Washington Artillery, Camp #15, United Confederate
            Veterans.
        Register of Admissions, Camp Nicholls Soldiers' Home.
        Register of Discipline and Dismissals, Camp Nicholls Soldiers' Home.
        Washington Artillery Historical Military Data, Louisiana Militia, 1861–
            1865.
    Stoddard, Mary Francis Baldwin. "The Baldwins." Manuscript in possession
        of George Denègre, New Orleans.
    Tulane University, Howard-Tilton Memorial Library
        Association of the Army of Tennessee Papers
            J. A. Chalaron Papers.
            Civil War Papers.

Powell A. Casey Papers
Confederate Personnel Documents
    B. Hildreth Green Letters.
    W. I. Hodgson. "History of the 5th Company Battalion Washington
        Artillery from April, 1861 to June 6, 1862."
Louisiana Historical Association Collection
    Felix Arroyo Journal.
Washington Artillery Battalion Papers.
New York, N.Y.
New-York Historical Society
    John C. Breckinridge Papers.
Richmond, Va.
Museum of the Confederacy
    P. D. Stephenson Letters.
Union Theological Seminary Library
    Diaries and Clippings of Philip D. Stephenson.
Virginia Historical Society
    Blanton Family Papers.
Savannah, Ga.
Georgia Historical Society
    Confederate States of America Army Papers.
Washington, D.C.
National Archives and Record Service
    Record Group 109.
        Compiled Service Records of Confederate Soldiers Who Served in
            Organizations from the State of Louisiana.
        Inspection Records and Related Reports Received, Adjutant General's
            Office.
        Letters Received, Adjutant and Inspector General's Office.
        Letters Received, Secretary of War.
        Letters Sent, Ordnance Officer, Army of Tennessee.
        Letters Sent, Secretary of War.
        Miscellaneous Papers filed with Muster Rolls, 5th Company, Washington
            Artillery.
        Muster Rolls, 5th Company, Washington Artillery.
        Unfiled Papers and Slips Belonging in Confederate Compiled Service
            Records.

New Orleans Newspapers

Bee
Commercial Bulletin
Daily City Item
Daily Crescent
Daily Delta
Daily Picayune
States
Tägliche Deutsche Zeitung
Times
Times Delta
Times-Democrat
Times Picayune

Government Documents

Census of Hamilton County, Tenn., 1860.

Censuses of Orleans Parish, La., 1860, 1870.

Censuses of Pointe Coupée Parish, La., 1900, 1910, 1920.

Senate Documents. 59th Cong., 2d Sess., No. 403.

The War of the Rebellion: A Compilation of the Official Records of the Union and Confederate Armies, 128 vols., Washington, D.C., 1880–1901.

Works Progress Administration, Federal Writers Project. *New Orleans City Guide.* Boston, 1938.

Collected Works, Memoirs, Letters, Diaries, and Reminiscences

"Alex P. Allain." *Confederate Veteran,* XVIII (1910), 392.

Ashkenazi, Elliott, ed. *The Civil War Diary of Clara Solomon: Growing Up in New Orleans, 1861–1862.* Baton Rouge, 1995.

Bakewell, A. Gordon. "The Luck of the War Game Sometimes Makes Heroes. . . ." *Illinois Central Magazine,* IV (1915), 18–20.

———. "Reminiscences of an Orderly Sergeant of the Fifth Company of the Washington Artillery, C. S. Army. . . ." *Illinois Central Magazine,* III (1914), 22–25.

Battalion Washington Artillery. *Washington Artillery Souvenir.* New Orleans, 1894.

Bayne, Thomas L. "Life in Richmond, 1863–1865." *Confederate Veteran,* XXX (1922), 100–101.

Beatty, John. *Citizen Soldier.* Cincinnati, 1879.

———. *Memoirs of a Volunteer.* Edited by Harvey S. Ford. New York, 1946.

Beers, Fannie A. *Memories: A Record of Personal Experience and Adventure During Four Years of War.* Philadelphia, 1888.

Buck, Irving A. *Cleburne and His Command.* Edited by Thomas R. Hay. Jackson, Tenn., 1959.

Butler, Benjamin F. *Autobiography and Personal Reminiscences of Major General Benjamin F. Butler.* Boston, 1892.

Cameron, William L. "The Battles Opposite Mobile." *Confederate Veteran,* XXIII (1915), 305–307.

Carlin, William P. "Military Memoirs," *National Tribune,* July 5, 1885.

Cater, Douglas. *As It Was: Reminiscences of a Soldier of the Third Texas Cavalry & the Nineteenth Louisiana.* Austin, Tex., 1990.

Chalaron, J. Adolphe. "At Missionary Ridge." *Nation Tribune,* May 4, 1899.

———. "Battle Echoes from Shiloh." *Southern Historical Society Papers,* XXI (1898), 215–24.

———. "Hood's Campaign at Murfreesboro." *Confederate Veteran,* XI (1903), 438–40.

———. "How Flag Captured." New Orleans *Times-Democrat,* July 6, 1885.

———. "Memories of Major Rice E. Graves, C.S.A." *Daviess County* [Ky.] *Historical Quarterly,* III (1985), 3–13.

———. "Vivid Experiences at Chickamauga," *Confederate Veteran,* III (1895), 278–79.

———. "The Washington Artillery in the Army of Tennessee." *Southern Historical Society Papers,* XI (1883), 217–22.

Constitution and Bylaws of the Battalion of Washington Artillery, Organized, February 22, 1840. Revised, February 11, 1861. New Orleans, 1861.

Cox, Jacob D. *The March to the Sea.* New York, 1906.

Davis, William C., ed. *Diary of a Confederate Soldier: John S. Jackman of the Orphan Brigade.* Columbia, S.C., 1990.

Fay, Edwin H. *This Infernal War: The Confederate Letters of Sgt. Edwin H. Fay.* Edited by Bell I. Wiley. Austin, Tex., 1958.

Hafendorfer, Kenneth A., ed. "The Kentucky Campaign Revisited: Major General Simon B. Buckner's Unpublished After-Action Report on the Battle of Perryville." *Civil War Regiments,* IV (1995), 50–64.

Haney, Joseph Hancock. "Bragg's Kentucky Campaign: A Confederate Soldier's Account." Edited by Frank Steely and Orville W. Taylor. *Kentucky State Historical Society Register,* LVII (1959), 49–55.

Hazen, William B. *A Narrative of Military Service.* Boston, 1885.

Headley, John W. *Confederate Operations in Canada and New York.* New York, 1906.

Hood, John B. *Advance and Retreat: Personal Experiences in the United States and Confederate States Armies.* Bloomington, Ind., 1959.

Ives, Washington. *Civil War Journal and Letters*. Edited by Jim R. Cabaniss. Tallahassee, 1987.

Jackman, John S. "From Dalton to Atlanta." *Southern Bivouac*, I (1881–82), 319a–28a, 414–28.

Jamison, Henry D., ed. *Letters and Recollections of a Confederate Soldier 1860–1865*. Nashville, 1964.

Johnston, Joseph E. *Narrative of Military Operations Directed During the Late War Between the States by Joseph E. Johnston, General, C.S.A.* New York, 1874.

Jordan, Thomas, and J. P. Pryor. *Campaigns of Lieut. Gen. N. B. Forrest and of Forrest's Cavalry*. New Orleans, 1868.

La Bree, Benjamin, ed. *Camp Fires of the Confederacy*. Louisville, 1898.

Lane, Mills, ed. *Times That Prove People's Principles*. Savannah, 1993.

Liddell, St. John R. *Liddell's Record*. Edited by Nathaniel C. Hughes, Jr. Dayton, Ohio, 1985.

Marshall, Jesse A., ed. *Private and Official Correspondence of General Benjamin F. Butler During the Period of the the Civil War*. 5 vols. Norwood, Mass., 1917.

Maury, Dabney, H. "Defense of Spanish Fort." *Southern Historical Society Papers*, XXXIX (1914), 130–36.

———. *Recollections of a Virginian*. New York, 1894.

McMurray, W. J. *History of the Twentieth Tennessee*. Nashville, 1904.

New Orleans *City Directory*. 1851, 1860, 1873, 1891.

Owen, Edward. "Reminiscences of Washington Artillery of New Orleans." *Blue and Gray* (Philadelphia), II (1893), 43–44.

Patterson, William E. *Campaigns of the 38th Regiment of Illinois Volunteer Infantry, 1861–1863*. Edited by Lowell P. Patterson. Bowie, Md., 1992.

Richardson, Frank Liddell. "War as I Saw It." *Louisiana Historical Quarterly*, VI (1923), 89–106, 223–54.

Ridley, Bromfield L. *Battles and Sketches of the Army of Tennessee*. Mexico, Mo., 1906.

Sanders, David W. "Hood's Tennessee Campaign." *Southern Bivouac* III, IV (1885–86), 97–104 +.

Sandidge, L. D. "Battle of Shiloh." *Southern Historical Society Papers*, VIII (1880), 173–77.

Smith, Jacob H. "Personal Reminiscences—Battle of Shiloh." War Papers, Michigan Commandery, *MOLLUS* (1894), 8–15.

Stephenson, Philip D. *Civil War Memoir*. Edited by Nathaniel C. Hughes, Jr. Conway, Ark., 1995.

———. "Defense of Spanish Fort." Philadelphia *Weekly Times*, July 26, 1894.

Taylor, Richard. *Destruction and Reconstruction*. New York, 1879.

Thompson, Edwin P. *History of the First Kentucky Brigade*. Cincinnati, 1868.

Waterman, George S. "Afloat—Afield—Afloat." *Confederate Veteran,* VIII (1900), 21–24, 53–55.

Waters, Zack C. "The Atlanta Campaign: Reports of William Brimage Bate." In *The Campaign for Atlanta & Sherman's March to the Sea,* edited by Theodore P. Savas and David A. Woodbury. Campbell, Calif., 1994.

Wiggins, Sarah W., ed. *The Journals of Josiah Gorgas, 1857–1878.* Tuscaloosa, Ala., 1995.

Williams, James M. *From that Terrible Field: Civil War Letters of James M. Williams, Twenty-First Alabama Infantry Volunteers.* Edited by John K. Folmar. University, Ala., 1981.

Woodward, C. Vann, ed. *Mary Chesnut's Civil War.* London, 1981.

Worsham, W. J. *The Old Nineteenth Tennessee Regiment.* Knoxville, 1902.

Books

Allardice, Bruce S. *More Generals in Gray.* Baton Rouge, 1995.

Andrews, Charles C. *History of the Campaign of Mobile.* New York, 1867.

Bartlett, Napier. *Military Record of Louisiana, Including Biographical and Historical Papers Relating to the Military Organization of the States.* 1964; rpr. Baton Rouge, 1996.

———. *A Soldier's Story of the War: Including the Marches and Battles of the Washington Artillery, and of Other Louisiana Troops.* New Orleans, 1874.

Bearss, Edwin C. *The Siege of Jackson, July 10–17, 1863.* Baltimore, 1981.

Bergeron, Arthur W., Jr. *Confederate Mobile.* Jackson, Miss., 1991.

———. *Guide to Louisiana Confederate Military Units, 1861–1865.* Baton Rouge, 1989.

Biographical and Historical Memoirs of Louisiana. Chicago, 1892.

Booth, Andrew B., comp. *Records of Louisiana Confederate Soldiers and Louisiana Confederate Commands.* 3 vols. Spartanburg, S.C. 1984.

Casey, Powell A. *An Outline of the Civil War Campaigns and Engagements of the Washington Artillery of New Orleans.* Baton Rouge, 1986.

Castel, Albert. *Decision in the West: The Atlanta Campaign of 1864.* Lawrence, Kans., 1992.

Chandler, J. A. C., ed. *The South in the Building of the Nation.* 12 vols. Richmond, Va. 1909–12.

Coe, David, ed. *Mine Eyes Have Seen the Glory: Combat Diaries of Union Sergeant Hamlin Alexander Coe.* Cranbury, N.J., 1975.

Connelly, Thomas Lawrence. *Army of the Heartland: The Army of Tennessee, 1861–1862.* Baton Rouge, 1967.

———. *Autumn of Glory: The Army of Tennessee, 1862–1865.* Baton Rouge, 1971.

Conrad, Glenn R., ed. *Dictionary of Louisiana Biography*. 2 vols. New Orleans, 1988.

Cozzens, Peter. *No Better Place to Die: The Battle of Stone's River*. Chicago, 1990.

———. *Shipwreck of Their Hopes: The Battles for Chattanooga*. Urbana, Ill., 1994.

———. *This Terrible Sound: The Battle of Chickamauga*. Urbana, Ill., 1992.

Cummings, Charles M. *Yankee Quaker Confederate General: The Curious Career of Bushrod Rust Johnson*. Rutherford, N.J., 1971.

Daniel, Larry J. *Cannoneers in Gray: The Field Artillery of the Army of Tennessee, 1861–1865*. University, Ala., 1984.

———. *Soldiering in the Army of Tennessee*. Chapel Hill, N.C., 1991.

Davis, Edwin A. *The Story of Louisiana*. 3 vols. New Orleans, 1960.

Davis, William C. *Breckinridge: Statesman, Soldier, Symbol*. Baton Rouge, 1974.

Davis, William C., ed. *Diary of a Confederate Soldier: John S. Jackson of the Orphan Brigade*. Columbia, S.C., 1990.

Derby, George, comp. *National Cyclopedia of American Biography*. 63 vols. New York, 1897–1926.

Dickey, Thomas S. and Peter C. George. *Field Artillery Projectiles of the American Civil War*. Edited by Floyd W. McRae. Atlanta, 1980.

Evans, Clement A., ed. *Confederate Military History*. 12 vols. Atlanta, 1899.

Floyd, William B. *The Barrow Family of Old Louisiana*. Lexington, Ky., 1963.

Fontenot, Kevin S. *Serving You Since 1869: A History of Lafayette Insurance Company*. New Orleans, 1994.

Fortier, James I. A., ed. *Carpet-bag Misrule in Louisiana*. New Orleans, 1938.

Gleeson, Ed. *Rebel Sons of Erin*. Indianapolis, 1993.

Goff, Richard D. *Confederate Supply*. Durham, N.C., 1969.

Griffith, Paddy. *Battle Tactics of the Civil War*. New Haven, Conn., 1987.

Hafendorfer, Kenneth A. *Perryville: Battle for Kentucky*. Louisville, 1981.

Hallock, Judith L. *Braxton Bragg and Confederate Defeat*. Tuscaloosa, Ala., 1991.

Hay, Thomas Robson. *Hood's Tennessee Campaign*. Dayton, Ohio, 1976.

Hearn, Chester G. *The Capture of New Orleans, 1862*. Baton Rouge, 1995.

———. *Mobile Bay and the Mobile Campaign: The Last Great Battles of the Civil War*. Jefferson, N.C., 1993.

Hoffman, John. *The Confederate Collapse at the Battle of Missionary Ridge: The Reports of James Patton Anderson and His Brigade Commanders*. Dayton, Ohio, 1985.

Horn, Stanley F. *The Army of Tennessee: A Military History*. Indianapolis, 1940.

———. *The Decisive Battle of Nashville*. 1956; rpr. Baton Rouge, 1991.

Hughes, Buckner L. and Nathaniel C. Hughes. *Quiet Places: The Burial Sites of Civil War Generals in Tennessee*. Knoxville, 1992.

Hughes, Nathaniel Cheairs, Jr. *Bentonville: The Final Battle of Sherman and Johnston.* Chapel Hill, N.C., 1996.

————. *General William J. Hardee: Old Reliable.* Baton Rouge, 1965.

Jewell, Edwin L., ed. *Jewell's Crescent City Illustrated.* New Orleans, 1873.

Kendall, John S. *History of New Orleans.* 2 vols. Chicago, 1922.

Land, John E. *Pen Illustrations of New Orleans, 1881–1882.* New Orleans, 1882.

Landry, Stuart O. *The Battle of Liberty Place.* New Orleans, 1955.

————. *History of the Boston Club.* New Orleans, 1938.

Lestage, H. Oscar, Jr. *The White League.* Baton Rouge, 1935.

Lindsley, John B. *The Military Annals of Tennessee.* Nashville, 1896.

Lonn, Ella. *Foreigners in the Confederacy.* Chapel Hill, N.C., 1940.

Lytle, Andrew N. *Bedford Forrest and His Critter Company.* New York, 1960.

McDonough, James Lee. *Shiloh: In Hell Before Night.* Knoxville, 1977.

————. *Stone's River: Bloody Winter in Tennessee.* Knoxville, 1980.

————. *War in Kentucky, from Shiloh to Perryville.* Knoxville, 1994.

McMurry, Richard M. *John Bell Hood and the War for Southern Independence.* Lexington, Ky., 1982.

McWhiney, Grady. *Braxton Bragg and Confederate Defeat.* New York, 1969.

Marshall, Park. *A Life of William B. Bate.* Nashville, 1908.

Melton, Jack W., Jr., and Lawrence E. Paul. *Introduction to Field Artillery Ordnance.* Kennesaw, Ga., 1994.

Miceli, Augusto P. *The Pickwick Club of New Orleans.* New Orleans, 1964.

Miller, Francis T., ed. *Photographic History of the Civil War.* 10 vols. New York, 1911–12.

Neff, Robert O. *Tennessee's Battered Brigadier.* Nashville, 1988.

O'Conner, Thomas. *History of the Fire Department of New Orleans.* New Orleans, 1895.

Owen, William M. *In Camp and Battle with the Washington Artillery.* Boston, 1885.

Parrish, T. Michael. *Richard Taylor: Soldier Prince of Dixie.* Chapel Hill, N.C., 1992.

Purdue, Howell, and Elizabeth Purdue. *Pat Cleburne: Confederate General.* Hillsboro, Tex., 1973.

Reed, D. W. *The Battle of Shiloh and the Organizations Engaged.* Washington, D.C., 1902.

Ripley, Warren. *Artillery and Ammunition in the Civil War.* New York, 1970.

Roman, Alfred. *The Military Operations of General Beauregard.* 2 vols. New York, 1884.

Scaife, William R. *Campaign for Atlanta.* Atlanta, 1985.

Seitz, Don Carlos. *Braxton Bragg: General of the Confederacy.* Columbia, S.C., 1924.

Shackelford, George G. *George Wythe Randolph and the Confederate Elite*. Athens, Ga., 1988.

Southwood, Marion. *"Beauty and Booty": The Watchword of New Orleans*. New York, 1867.

Stockdale, Paul H. *The Death of an Army: The Battle of Nashville and Hood's Retreat*. Murfreesboro, Tenn., 1992.

Sword, Wiley. *Embrace an Angry Wind*. New York, 1992.

———. *Mountains Touched with Fire: Chattanooga Beseiged, 1863*. New York, 1995.

———. *Shiloh: Bloody April*. Dayton, Ohio, 1983.

Symonds, Craig L. *Joseph E. Johnston: A Civil War Biography*. New York, 1992.

Thomas, Dean S. *Cannons: An Introduction to Civil War Artillery*. Gettysburg, Pa., 1985.

Thompson, Ed Porter. *History of the Orphan Brigade*. Louisville, Ky., 1898.

Tower, R. Lockwood. *A Carolinian Goes to War: The Civil War Narrative of Arthur Middleton Manigault, Brigadier General, C.S.A.* Columbia, S.C., 1983.

Tucker, Glenn. *Chickamauga: Bloody Battle of the West*. Indianapolis, 1961.

Turner, William Bruce. *History of Maury County, Tennessee*. Nashville, 1955.

Urquhart, Kenneth T. *Lineage of the Fourth Regiment and the Washington Artillery*. New Orleans, 1955.

Voss, Louis. *Presbyterianism in New Orleans*. New Orleans, 1931.

Warner, Ezra J. *Generals in Gray: Lives of the Confederate Commanders*. Baton Rouge, 1959.

Wilson, James G., ed. *Appleton's Cyclopedia of American Biography*. 7 vols. New York, 1888.

Winters, John D. *The Civil War in Louisiana*. 1963; rpr. Baton Rouge, 1979.

Wise, Jennings C. *The Long Arm of Lee: The History of the Artillery Corps of the Army of Northern Virginia*. New York, 1959.

Witham, George F. *Shiloh Shells and Artillery Units*. Memphis, 1980.

Wyeth, John A. *Life of General N. B. Forrest*. New York, 1899.

Articles

Anderson, William T., ed. "The Civil War Diary of Captain James Litton Cooper, September 30, 1861, to January, 1865." *Tennessee Historical Quarterly*, XV (1956), 141–74.

Bergeron, Arthur W., Jr. "Fighting Erupts at Jackson, Mississippi." *Civil War*, XII (1995), 26–27.

Casey, Powell A. "The Early History of the Washington Artillery of New Orleans." *Louisiana Historical Quarterly*, XXIII (1940), 471–84.

Cotner, James R. "Horsepower Moves the Guns." *America's Civil War,* IX (1996), 34–40.

Cortright, Vincent. "Last-Ditch Defenders at Mobile." *America's Civil War* X (1997), 58–64.

Dyer, Thomas G. "Georgia History in Fiction—Atlanta's Other Civil War Novel: Fictional Unionists in a Confederate City." *Georgia Historical Quarterly,* LXXIX (1995), 147–68.

Hodges, Glenn. "An Officer and a Gentleman." Owensboro (Ky.) *Messenger-Inquirer,* May 14, 1996.

Huber, Leonard V. "Epitaphs: Brief Postscripts of Louisiana History." *Louisiana History,* XXV (1984), 255–76.

Jones, Joseph. "Roster of the Medical Officers of the Army of Tennessee." *Southern Historical Society Papers,* XXII (1894), 165–280.

Larter, Harry. "Fifth Company, Washington Artillery of New Orleans, CSA, 1862." *Military Collector and Historian,* V (1953), 101–102.

Lathrop, Barnes F. "A Confederate Artilleryman at Shiloh." *Civil War History,* VIII (1962), 373–85.

McIntosh, David G. "The Confederate Artillery—Its Organization and Development." In *Photographic History of the Civil War,* edited by F. T. Miller. New York, 1911. Vol. V of 10 vols.

Owen, Allison. "History of the Washington Artillery." *Louisiana Historical Society Publications,* X (1918), 46–59, 64–67.

———. "Record of an Old Artillery Organization." *Field Artillery Journal,* IV (1914), 5–18.

Reilly, Timothy F. "Benjamin M. Palmer: Secessionist Becomes Nationalist." *Louisiana History,* XVIII (1977), 287–301.

Reinders, Robert C. "Militia in New Orleans, 1853–1861." *Louisiana History,* III (1962), 33–42.

Robbins, Peggy. "New Orleans' Finest." *Civil War Times,* XXXV (1996), 42–49.

Tapp, Hambleton. "The Battle of Perryville, 1862." *Filson Club History Quarterly,* IX (1935), 158–81.

Taylor, Orville W. "Joseph H. Haney, an Arkansas Engineer in the Civil War: The First Phase." *Arkansas Historical Quarterly,* XIV (1955), 62–71.

Walton, J. B. "Sketches of the History of the Washington Artillery." *Southern Historical Society Publications,* XI (1883), 210–17.

Waters, Zack C. "The Atlanta Campaign: Reports of William Brimage Bate." In *The Campaign for Atlanta and Sherman's March to the Sea,* edited by Theodore P. Savas and David A. Woodbury. Campbell, Calif., 1994.

Wooster, Ralph A. "Confederate Success at Perryville." *Kentucky State Historical Register,* LIX (1961), 318–23.

Unpublished Studies

Bearss, Edwin C. "Artillery at Shiloh." Shiloh National Military Park Library, Shiloh, Tenn.
Lathrop, Barnes F. "The Pugh Plantations, 1860–1865: A Study of Life in Lower Louisiana." Ph.D. dissertation, University of Texas, Austin, 1945.
Roberson, Bill L. "Valor on the Eastern Shore: The Mobile Campaign of 1865." Mobile Public Library, Mobile, Ala.

Interment Records

Girod Street Cemetery, New Orleans, La.
Greenwood Cemetery, Metairie, La.
Lafayette Cemeteries, New Orleans, La.
Metairie Cemetery, Metairie, La.

INDEX

168n, 259; battalion of, 95, 108, 115, 120, 141. *See also* Louisiana troops: 14th Battalion Sharpshooters

Averasboro, Battle of, 157n

Bailey, C. P., 125, 127
Bailey Hill, 112
Bainbridge, Ala., 258, 259n, 260n
Baird, Absalom, 135n, 144n, 180
Bakewell, A. Gordon, 9, 26, 28, 35, 40, 41, 43, 50, 50n, 53–55, 280
Baldwin, Albert, 172n, 279n
Baldwin, Harry, 171, 172, 172n
Banfil, Joe, 118
Bankhead, Smith P., 27, 32; battery of, 27
Bannister, Rinaldo J., 5
Bardstown, Ky., 62
Barnes, Mrs. J. E., 112
Barrail, A., 189
Barrow, Cordelius J. "Tony," 182, 199, 280
Barry, Robert L., 271
Bartlett, Thomas C., 173
Bartley, John, 55, 77, 268, 273, 274
Bate, William B., 38, 148, 157–59, 162, 165, 168, 168n, 176, 177, 179, 180, 186, 186n, 187, 191, 196, 197, 200, 202, 205, 205n, 222, 224, 225, 229, 229n, 230, 233, 236n, 237–40, 240n, 241, 243, 243n, 245–47, 249, 249n, 250–52, 257, 282; brigade of, 150, 152, 155n; division of, 154–56, 176, 179, 182, 196, 199, 200, 202, 204, 216, 217, 222–25, 227–29, 237, 238, 240–45, 248, 250–52
Baton Rouge, La., 4, 6
Battalion Washington Artillery, 1, 4, 6, 7, 11, 266n, 278n, 283; monument of, 279
Battery Huger, 270n, 274
Battery Tracy, 270n
Bayle, James, 143
Bayne, Charles, 279n
Bayne, Thomas L., 18, 26, 35, 76, 77n, 279n, 280

Beatty, John, 65, 125, 130n, 133–35, 135n; brigade of, 123, 133
Beauregard, Pierre G. T., 11, 11n, 13, 15, 17, 19, 21, 21n, 32, 33, 39, 41, 52, 58, 225, 264
Beauregard, René, 154n, 223, 248, 250; battery of, 154n, 188, 223, 225, 250, 251, 264; battalion of, 251
Beckham, Robert F., 227
Beers, Fannie A., 75, 182–83, 198
Beggs, John T., 188
Bell Buckle, Tenn., 97
Bellanger, "Alf," 35
Belmont, Battle of, 8, 173n
Belsom, Joseph, Jr., 127
Benjamin, Judah P., 50n, 76
Bennett, Archie, 241, 246, 246n
Bentonville, Battle of, 47
Berry, John, 237
Betts, Edward E., 124n, 128, 164
Big Shanty, Ga., 223
Bingham, John H., 281
Bishop, William, 140n
Black Horse Battery, 270
Bladensburg, Battle of, 6
Blair, Thomas McMillan, 55, 69, 70, 72, 77, 85, 94, 123–25, 127, 151, 151n, 177n
Bledsoe, Hiram M., 256; battery of, 256
Blieml, Emmeran, 220, 293n
Boardman, John, 189, 190
Boatner, Hudson J., 92, 185
Boone's Battery, 325
Boudreaux, John J., 160, 170
Bradford Battery, 304
Bragg, Braxton, 17n, 19, 19n, 21, 23, 33, 33n, 43, 45, 50, 52, 54, 55, 58, 60n, 62–64, 69, 71, 73, 74, 77, 80, 84, 89, 95, 97, 97n, 98, 120, 121, 122, 126, 131, 132, 145, 147, 148, 151–58, 163, 164, 168, 176, 195, 275, 281, 282; corps of, 21, 23
Brannan, John M., 135n, 144n
Brazza Savorgnan, Conte di, 279n
Breckinridge, John C., 33, 39n, 42, 79, 80, 81, 84, 85, 86n, 88, 90, 91n, 92, 96n,